Learn Blackberry Games Development

T0225056

Carol Hamer

Andrew Davison

Apress®

Learn Blackberry Games Development

Copyright © 2010 by Carol Hamer and Andrew Davison

ISBN-13 (pbk): 978-1-4302-2718-2

ISBN-13 (electronic): 978-1-4302-2719-9

Publisher and President: Paul Manning
Lead Editor: Steve Anglin
Developmental Editor: Tom Welsh
Technical Reviewer: Bruce Hopkins and Christophe Droeder
Editorial Board: Clay Andres, Steve Anglin, Mark Beckner, Ewan Buckingham, Gary Cornell, Jonathan Gennick, Jonathan Hassell, Michelle Lowman, Matthew Moodie, Duncan Parkes, Jeffrey Pepper, Frank Pohlmann, Ben Renow-Clarke, Dominic Shakeshaft, Matt Wade, Tom Welsh
Coordinating Editor: Kelly Moritz
Copy Editor: Damon Larson
Compositor: Dan Britt
Indexer: BIM Indexing & Proofreading Services
Artist: April Milne
Cover Designer: Anna Ishchenko

Distributed to the book trade worldwide by Springer-Verlag New York, Inc., 233 Spring Street, 6th Floor, New York, NY 10013. Phone 1-800-SPRINGER, fax 201-348-4505, e-mail orders-ny@springer-sbm.com, or visit www.springeronline.com.

For information on translations, please e-mail rights@apress.com, or visit www.apress.com.

Apress and friends of ED books may be purchased in bulk for academic, corporate, or promotional use. eBook versions and licenses are also available for most titles. For more information, reference our Special Bulk Sales–eBook Licensing web page at www.apress.com/info/bulksales.

The source code for this book is available to readers at www.apress.com. You will need to answer questions pertaining to this book in order to successfully download the code. Source code and other information about the book is also available on the book's website http://frogparrot.net/blackberry/.

To Léo, Nicolas, and Emmanuel
— Carol Hamer

To Supatra and John
— Andrew Davison

Contents at a Glance

Contents

About the Authors

■**Carol Hamer** received her Ph.D. In Number Theory from Rutgers, the State University of New Jersey. Since then, she has worked as a software engineer for ten years in the U.S., France, and Switzerland, including three years working for In-Fusio Mobile Games.

Carol has written two previous books on mobile game programming: *J2ME Games with MIDP2* and *Creating Mobile Games*, both from Apress. She writes a blog called "A Little Bitty Java" (http://bittyjava.wordpress.com/) with programming ideas, troubleshooting tips, and code samples and maintains a website of information about this book at http://frogparrot.net/blackberry/.

■**Andrew Davison** received his Ph.D. from Imperial College in London, was a lecturer at the University of Melbourne for six years, before moving to Prince of Songkla University in Thailand. He has also taught in Bangkok, Khon Kaen, and Hanoi.

His research interests include scripting languages, logic programming, visualization, and teaching methodologies. This led to an interest in teaching games programming.

He is the author of two previous games programming books: *Killer Game Programming in Java* from O'Reilly and *Pro Java 6 3D Game Development* from Apress. Online material from those books can be found at http://fivedots.coe.psu.ac.th/~ad/jg

About the Technical Reviewers

After nine years of being an employee, first of all, of Logica, an IT company, and then of Mobilescope (In-Fusio), a start-up acting in the mobile phone market, **Christophe Droëder** has become his own employer: He's settled as a freelance, seeking for different jobs: project management support, software development, training, website design.

As banks prefer regular fixed income, current 2009, he's been hired again by an IT company, dealing with standalone projects. While this is a full-time job, Christophe has kept his freelance status, reviewing books like this one, for instance!

Bruce Hopkins is the author of Bluetooth for Java, and is an enthusiast for mobile, embedded, and wireless application development. He's currently working for the startup, BlogRadio www.podblogr.com, which converts any RSS feed into a streaming podcast. He also is lead writer for mobile content on Oracle's http://java.sun.com site.

Acknowledgments

I'd like to thank my husband Emmanuel Kowalski for taking the photos of the games running on BlackBerry smartphones throughout this book and also for his support and encouragement. I'd like to thank my parents, Bill and Ginger Hamer, for providing child care during the early stages of this project. I'd like to thank my sons, Nicolas and Léo Kowalski, for providing game ideas and for enthusiastically playing my games to make sure that they're fun.

I'd also like to thank the Institute for Advanced Study in Princeton, New Jersey for providing me with the pleasant and stimulating work environment where I did most of the research and writing for my chapters of this book.

Carol Hamer

I must thank my department (Computer Engineering), faculty (Engineering), and university (Prince of Songkla University) for being so supportive once again. They've always been understanding, and offered every encouragement. Of course, I recommend Thailand as a great place to live and work. None of this would have been possible without my family, Supatra and John, who I love very dearly.

Andrew Davison

We would both like to thank the technical reviewers and the Apress team for their helpful suggestions and ideas, as well as for all their hard work putting this book together.

Chapter 1

Gaming on BlackBerry

Gaming on BlackBerry? Why games on BlackBerry? Aren't BlackBerry smartphones built for business, not pleasure?

The BlackBerry smartphone series—produced by the Canadian firm Research In Motion (RIM)—has enjoyed a decade of success. It's the second most popular smartphone line in the world (after Nokia). Despite the arrival of the iPhone, BlackBerry's market share is still growing. So far, more than 50 million BlackBerry handsets have been sold worldwide. And even if much of Blackberry's popularity has been driven by business applications, that still makes quite a lot of smart BlackBerry gadgets in the hands of users who can't help but want to play with them.

What's in This Book?

This book will give you the information you need—from the basic concepts to the pro-level tips—to create professional games for BlackBerry smartphones. Rather than doing a survey of the BlackBerry API and listing the features, Andrew and I have started from game ideas. We explain the theory and practice of BlackBerry development as you encounter it in real projects and applications. All you need is a basic knowledge of Java programming, and this book will show you how to turn your ideas into games and sell them on BlackBerry App World (Figure 1-1) and beyond!

If your ultimate goal is to get into mobile game development in general, BlackBerry is a great starting platform. BlackBerry smartphones support the Java Micro Edition (ME) *Mobile Information Device Profile* (MIDP), which is found on more than 2 billion handsets. Throughout this book, we provide explanations for how BlackBerry-specific game development compares to other mobile platforms so that you can easily pick up general)Java ME development based on what you learn here. Plus, we cover a range of game-programming techniques (such as graphics, timing, and coordinate systems) that you can apply to mobile game development on any platform.

Figure 1-1. *You can browse BlackBerry App World from a PC as well as from a smartphone.*

If, on the other hand, your ultimate goal is to learn general BlackBerry application programming, these games provide a fun entry point. BlackBerry has its own)Java ME paradigm (full of unexpected, ill-documented quirks) that is quite unlike anything else in mobile development. This book can offer you a painless introduction.

Of course, if your ultimate goal is just to have fun with your BlackBerry, then you've definitely picked up the right book!

This book covers Java development on all BlackBerry models. From the early trackwheel models (which sold for many years and are still common in the wild) to the cool, new touchscreen BlackBerry Storm smartphones, you'll see how to program for them. Plus, we'll show you how to harness the fantastic rich gaming potential of the latest BlackBerry operating system: version 5.

Mastering the Basics

The first half of this book builds the foundation of what you need to know to create and sell a complete, professional game:

Chapter 2: BlackBerry Application Basics: Why are there two types of BlackBerry Java applications? What are all those crazy files the compiler generated? And—most importantly—how do I get an application complied and running on my BlackBerry smartphone? Chapter 2 will answer all of these questions and help you set up a professional build with Ant.

Chapter 3: Game Graphics and Events with MIDP and RIM Classes: Using the classic Maze game as an example, you'll see exactly how the two types of BlackBerry Java applications differ. You get an in-depth look at how the life cycle, events, and graphics work in both cases so you'll be ready to develop whichever kind is best suited to your game's needs.

Chapter 4: Adding a Professional Look and Feel. Gorgeous graphics are critical for the game experience. To get your game's visual theme pixel-perfect on every model, BlackBerry gives you the tools, and Chapter 4 explains how to use them.

Chapter 5: Security and Selling Your Game. As much as you love games for their own sake, at the end of the day it's nice to get paid. In Chapter 5 you'll see how to sell your game on BlackBerry App World (or on your own site)—plus how to apply the cryptography APIs to implement licensing and digital rights management.

Chapter 6: Swingin' Light Saber. With action, music, sound effects, colliding game sprites, and even touchscreen input, Andrew shows you how to put it all together and develop a real game. Plus, BlackBerry's accelerometer lets you wield your saber like a true RIM-i knight!

Exploring Further

The second half of this book takes you beyond the basic games. See how exciting games can be when you add a little imagination to advanced features like 2D and 3D graphics, network communications with other players, GPS, and more.

Chapter 7: Play a Live Opponent with SMS: That classic, tiny packet of data sent by the Short Message Service (SMS) is still a favorite with users and operators alike. And it's all you need to play a game of checkers with a friend on the other side of the world—chosen from your BlackBerry contact list! This chapter will also help you if you have an existing MIDP game and you'd like to make sure it runs well on BlackBerry.

Chapter 8: Using Scalable Vector Graphics: 2D graphics are easy to master and allow you to create surprisingly impressive effects. Check out Chapter 8's spinning spaceship video and learn the tricks to create it.

Chapter 9: Creating Role-Playing Games on the Internet. Since Internet everywhere is BlackBerry's strong point, it was practically born for massively multiplayer online role-playing games (MMORPGs). Chapter 9 uses Twitter to create a virtual asteroid belt that you can explore and find real people in their own virtual ships.

Chapter 10: Remotely Drive a (Toy) Sports Car. What's more fun than driving a remote-controlled car? Driving one from your BlackBerry! Andrew illustrates Bluetooth programming in style.

Chapter 11: Fox and Hounds. Here's something your stationary game console can't do: a real live game of hot pursuit—based on GPS!

Chapter 12: Introducing 3D with JSR 239: Have a look at what the latest-and-greatest version 5 BlackBerry smartphones can do. Andrew explains 3D graphics with OpenGL.

Why Mobile Games?

As soon as people started creating cell phones with enough computing power to run simple applications, games were an obvious choice, starting with the Snake game that came preinstalled on Nokia handsets back in 1998. Handsets have always had a number of limitations that PCs and dedicated game consoles don't have (screen size, computing power, battery life), but their portability makes for an interesting trade-off.

Since people play mobile games in their spare time on the go, the most popular games are usually quick and easy to learn. Mobile games ensure that there will always be a market for simple puzzles and new versions of familiar classic arcade games from the 1980s. For example, my husband isn't much of a gamer, but he'll play Sudoku on his MP3 player, and he'll try to top his BlackBerry BrickBreaker high score every now and then (see Figure 1-2). So, while modern computer and console games practically require the equivalent of a movie studio to produce something that will sell, mobile games have created a space where one engineer working with a simple (but brilliant) idea can still invent a hit.

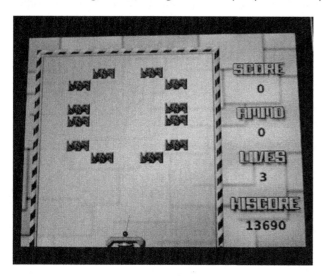

Figure 1-2. *BlackBerry's BrickBreaker is a remake of a classic game.*

Connectivity adds another dimension to what you can do with mobile games. The Internet has sparked craze after craze in social networking. One can hardly guess which service will go viral next, and many of them (e.g., Twitter) are simple enough to be accessed from a handset as well as from a PC. Games are a natural application of online socializing. And when up-to-the-minute news reports affect a social game—as in fantasy football, for instance—a handset-based game actually has the advantage over a PC- or console-based game. Ditto for a GPS-based live chase game (like the one you'll see in Chapter 11)—it wouldn't even be possible to program that one for a fixed console.

Why Java Micro Edition?

With more than 6 billion Java-enabled devices worldwide—including 2.5 billion Java-enabled phones, most of which support MIDP—Java is the most widely supported higher-level programming language ever.

Java's write-once, run-anywhere philosophy makes it the ideal choice for cell phones because they vary so widely. Java smoothes over the differences among native platforms by specifying a *Java Virtual Machine* (JVM) that runs the Java application code. Sun and the *Java Community Process* (http://jcp.org) have defined a series of configurations, profiles, and optional APIs to standardize the way to program for typical cell phone features.

Unfortunately, Java ME has had a bumpy road toward the write-once, run-anywhere dream. Fragmentation—the difference between one device and the next—is still a huge problem, and it's not just a question of different device capabilities. Despite the specifications and the *Technology Compatibility Kits* (TCKs) that handset manufacturers are required to follow, the behavior of the Java platform can vary in unexpected ways. Part of the problem is that once a series of handsets is flashed with its software and sold, platform bugs typically can't be corrected, so applications have to work around them for as long as the handset is still in use.

Another persistent problem that has plagued Java ME is the business model for application developers. There may be 2 billion potential customers out there for MIDP apps, but it's frustratingly difficult to reach any sizable portion of that market. Some of the most successful application distribution platforms have been run by (and for) a single operator or a single device manufacturer, such as BlackBerry App World.

Why BlackBerry?

BlackBerry isn't just another flavor of Java ME. It's got a whole philosophy of network connectivity and input ease that has made RIM a market leader in smartphones.

What Makes BlackBerry So Special?

The BlackBerry experience isn't just about the handsets themselves—there's also the communications network with the tools to create BlackBerry-specific server-side applications. RIM offers the *BlackBerry Enterprise Server* (BES) so that corporations can give their employees secure access to company intranets—inside the company firewall—on their smartphones. RIM also provides the same type of e-mail and Internet service on an individual basis through the *BlackBerry Internet Service* (BIS).

BlackBerry's server-side infrastructure seems to be all business, but it can have game applications too. For example, a multiplayer game server can push game updates to the players' smartphones (rather than requiring the client side of the game to regularly poll the server). Plus, it provides users with cheap, reliable Internet service that is useful for online gaming in general.

RIM also provides the BlackBerry Theme Studio, which makes it easy to create *themes* (also known as *skins*), so you can tie in the user's complete BlackBerry experience with your game or game service.

And don't forget BlackBerry's thumb-friendly QWERTY keyboard, which makes it a natural choice for games that require complex input.

The Berry vs. the Apple

The iPhone may be the media darling of the moment, but there are still plenty of reasons to stick with BlackBerry.

For a developer, there's a question of competition. There are more than 50 million BlackBerry smartphones out there in the wild—a lot more than there are iPhones—but the iPhone's App Store already has more than 30 times as many applications on it than there are on BlackBerry App World. Be warned, however, that this is one point where BlackBerry's business focus can work against game developers: RIM allows businesses to lock an *IT policy* onto all of their company handsets, restricting functionality. In particular, the *IT policy can be set to prevent users from installing any third-party applications*—and it's difficult to estimate precisely how many BlackBerry smartphones have been set with this restriction.

Looking at the big picture, though, the skills (and games) you build programming for BlackBerry are more portable than those you'll create if you get locked into Apple's Objective-C track (along with all of the other developers who created the iPhone's 100,000-plus applications).

RIM also offers the touchscreen Storm series for those who like most of BlackBerry's features but prefer an iPhone-style interface. That's not necessarily good news for developers, since it introduces fragmentation within the BlackBerry platform (increasing the amount of work to create a game that runs on all models). But it also opens up whole new fields of opportunity for game designers with imagination.

And—last but not least—BlackBerry game development gives you the unique opportunity to subversively find ways for people to have fun on their work tools.

So, welcome, and get set for some fun with your BlackBerry smartphone!

Summary

BlackBerry isn't just a great platform for business, it's a great platform for fun. BlackBerry's popularity gives you the opportunity to sell your games to a wide market. This book will show you how to do it.

Chapter 2

BlackBerry Application Basics

A BlackBerry smartphone can run the same Java applications—called *MIDlets*—that an ordinary Java ME handset can run. However, to create applications that are better integrated with the BlackBerry platform's philosophy, RIM has defined an alternate type of application, often called a *RIMlet*. In this chapter you'll see how to develop, build, and install both MIDlets and RIMlets. You'll also learn some of the differences between the two to help you decide which type of application is best for your game.

BlackBerry and MIDP

Variety is the norm for small devices, so Java ME was designed to be flexible enough to accommodate a range of devices. Each device has a *configuration* and a *profile* to define its precise Java capabilities. The configuration is at the base level, specifying the Java Virtual Machine (JVM) and the most basic Java libraries—essentially the java.* *application programming interfaces* (APIs). The profile is built on top of the configuration, specifying the application life cycle and the bulk of the Java libraries (most of the javax.* APIs). Most devices also support additional APIs, both standard APIs defined in *Java Specification Requests* (JSRs) through the Java Community Process (JCP) and proprietary APIs such as RIM's net.rim.* APIs.

The BlackBerry smartphone platform is built on the *Connected Limited Device Configuration* (CLDC) and the Mobile Information Device Profile (MIDP). This is the standard configuration/profile combination for cellular phones, used by the overwhelming majority of Java-enabled handsets. So a typical cell phone Java application (a MIDlet) will run on a BlackBerry. However, the MIDlet life cycle isn't a perfect fit for the BlackBerry platform, and, really, there are some design flaws in the)MIDP screen-handling and user interface libraries. So RIM defined an alternate type of application (sometimes called a "RIMlet") with its own life cycle and user interface. When writing an application for BlackBerry smartphones, regardless of whether you write a MIDlet or a RIMlet, you will typically use both the MIDP APIs and the RIM APIs. Figure 2-1 illustrates how the different Java components fit together.

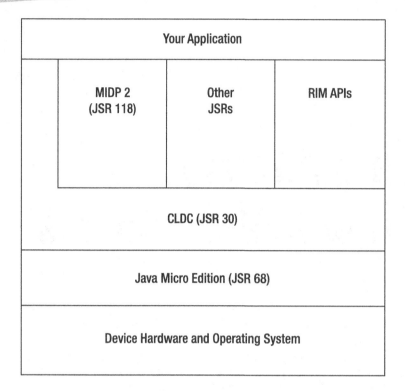

Figure 2-1. *The components of the BlackBerry Java platform*

Most BlackBerry smartphones implement MIDP 2.0 on top of CLDC 1.1, which are the most common versions found on)MIDP handsets. Some early BlackBerry devices implemented MIDP 1.0, but they are rare and aren't compatible with RIM's Java development tools. There's also a third version of MIDP that has been in the)JCP for years, and finally passed its final approval ballot in November of 2009. The BlackBerry platform may eventually support MIDP 3 version 3 (JSR 271). But since MIDP 3 is largely concerned with things like application concurrency and shared libraries (which the RIM platform already handles in its own proprietary fashion), and since RIM participated on the JSR 271 specification team, the shift to MIDP 3 should be relatively painless if and when it arrives. BlackBerry smartphones also typically have some of the standard optional APIs available, such as the Wireless Messaging API (JSR 120) and the Personal Information Management API (JSR 75).

Actually, MIDP, CLDC, and even Java ME itself are all defined in JSRs that are available for download on the JCP web site (http://jcp.org). It's a good idea for Java ME developers to be familiar with the JCP web site because the JSR specifications define what your game is able do on a given handset. Unlike Standard and Enterprise Edition Java programming, in Java ME you have to deal with the fact that different devices have different sets of APIs available for you to use; and for most devices, the set of available APIs cannot be changed. Either the device manufacturer implemented a given JSR or the corresponding functionality is simply not available on that device. In the case of

BlackBerry, you can see exactly which JSRs are implemented on which models in this handy video on the BlackBerry developers site:

www.blackberry.com/DevMediaLibrary/view.do?name=JSRSupport

(The pages of the developer site seem to move around with some frequency, so if the video is not currently at the above URL, you can probably find it by looking around.)

The situation with BlackBerry is slightly different because it's possible to upgrade the operating system (and consequently the Java APIs) on a BlackBerry. However, most BlackBerry users won't upgrade the operating system, so in practice you have to deal with supporting a range of different Java APIs—even if BlackBerry smartphones are your only target platforms.

How a BlackBerry Java Application Works

The software that is responsible for installing and running Java applications is called the *application management system* (AMS). The AMS launches the application and passes user input along to the application by calling the appropriate functions. For a MIDlet, that means calling the startApp() method of the javax.microedition.midlet.MIDlet class, and for a RIMlet, that means calling the main() method of the net.rim.device.api.system.Application class.

Hello MIDP!

In this section, you'll see the basics of how MIDlets work by creating a "Hello World" MIDlet.

At its simplest, a MIDlet consists of a MIDlet class, which is the launch point that handles the MIDlet's life cycle events, and a Displayable that the MIDlet can place on the Display. (Display is the MIDP class corresponding to the device's screen, and Displayable is the MIDP class for objects that can fill the whole screen.) In the "Hello MIDP" example, the MIDlet class is given in Listing 2-1, and the Displayable is given in Listing 2-2.

Listing 2-1. *Hello.java*

```java
package net.frogparrot.hello;

import javax.microedition.midlet.*;
import javax.microedition.lcdui.*;

/**
 * This is the life cycle and event-handling class of the
 * "Hello World" MIDlet.
 */
public class Hello extends MIDlet implements CommandListener {

  /**
   * The canvas is the region of the screen that has been allotted
   * to the game.
   */
  HelloCanvas myCanvas;
```

```
/**
 * On BlackBerry, the Command objects appear as menu items.
 */
private Command myExitCommand = new Command("Exit", Command.EXIT, 99);

/**
 * On BlackBerry, the Command objects appear as menu items.
 */
private Command myToggleCommand = new Command("Toggle Msg", Command.SCREEN, 1);

/**
 * Initialize the canvas and the commands.
 */
public Hello() {
  myCanvas = new HelloCanvas();
  myCanvas.addCommand(myExitCommand);
  myCanvas.addCommand(myToggleCommand);
  // we set one command listener to listen to all
  // of the commands on the canvas:
  myCanvas.setCommandListener(this);
}

//-------------------------------------------------------------------
//   implementation of MIDlet

/**
 * The AMS calls this method to start the application.
 */
public void startApp() throws MIDletStateChangeException {
  // display my canvas on the screen:
  Display.getDisplay(this).setCurrent(myCanvas);
  myCanvas.repaint();
}

/**
 * If the MIDlet was using resources, it should release
 * them in this method.
 */
public void destroyApp(boolean unconditional)
    throws MIDletStateChangeException {
}

/**
 * The AMS calls this method to notify the MIDlet to enter a paused
 * state. The MIDlet should use this opportunity to release
 * shared resources.
 */
public void pauseApp() {
}

//-------------------------------------------------------------------
//   implementation of CommandListener

/*
```

```
 * The AMS calls this method to notify the CommandListener of user
 * command input (either reset or exit).
 */
public void commandAction(Command c, Displayable s) {
  if(c == myToggleCommand) {
    myCanvas.toggleHello();
  } else if(c == myExitCommand) {
    try {
      // The MIDlet calls these two methods to exit:
      destroyApp(false);
      notifyDestroyed();
    } catch (MIDletStateChangeException ex) {
    }
  }
}
```

}

Listing 2-1 shows how a MIDlet receives events from the AMS. The MIDlet class receives life cycle events such as launch, pause, and cleanup by implementing the notification methods.

A MIDlet receives user input primarily through *commands*, which are instances of javax.microedition.lcdui.Command. A command usually corresponds to a *softkey* (a label that is drawn on the screen right above or beside an actual physical button on the device) or to a menu item. Most MIDP handsets have a left softkey and a right softkey at the base of the screen, and if you add exactly two commands to a Displayable, they'll appear as two softkeys. Adding more than two commands typically causes the device to group the commands (except for the one created as type Command.EXIT) in a soft menu, which pops up when the user selects the menu softkey, as shown in Figure 2-2.

Figure 2-2. *Commands usually appear as softkeys (left) or in a soft menu (right) on a typical MIDP device.*

BlackBerry is a little different in that commands are always placed in the soft menu that is accessed through the navigation input (trackwheel or trackball), as you can see in Figure 2-3.

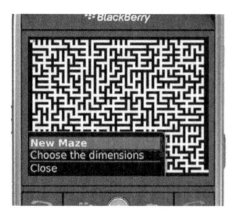

Figure 2-3. *On BlackBerry, commands are placed in a menu.*

Naturally, that's the reason the MIDP API abstracts user input choices as Commands rather than having the MIDlet specify that the Command is a softkey or a menu item: the platform can present the options to the user in whichever manner fits the platform best.

In order for the Commands to be active, they need to be added to a Displayable, and that Displayable must be the one that is currently set on the Display (see the constructor and startApp() method in Listing 2-1). Instead of allowing each Command to receive its own events or having a separate listener for each Command, one CommandListener receives commandAction() notifications for all of the Commands on the Displayable. In the Hello MIDP example, the Displayable is a subclass of javax.microedition.lcdui.Canvas, given in Listing 2-2.

Listing 2-2. *HelloCanvas.java*

```java
package net.frogparrot.hello;

import javax.microedition.lcdui.*;

/**
 * This class represents the region of the screen that has been allotted
 * to the game.
 */
public class HelloCanvas extends Canvas {

  //-----------------------------------------------------------
  //   fields

  /**
   * Whether or not the screen should currently display the
   * "hello world" message.
   */
  boolean mySayHello = true;

  //-----------------------------------------------------------
  //    initialization and game state changes

  /**
```

```
 * toggle the hello message.
 */
void toggleHello() {
  mySayHello = !mySayHello;
  repaint();
}

//---------------------------------------------------------
//  graphics methods

/**
 * clear the screen and display the hello world message if appropriate.
 */
public void paint(Graphics g) {
  // get the dimensions of the screen:
  int width = getWidth();
  int height = getHeight();
  // clear the screen (paint it white):
  g.setColor(0xffffff);
  // The first two args give the coordinates of the top-
  // left corner of the rectangle. (0,0) corresponds
  // to the top-left corner of the screen.
  g.fillRect(0, 0, width, height);
  // display the hello world message if appropriate:
  if(mySayHello) {
    Font font = g.getFont();
    int fontHeight = font.getHeight();
    int fontWidth = font.stringWidth("Hello World!");
    // set the text color to red:
    g.setColor(255, 0, 0);
    g.setFont(font);
    // write the string in the center of the screen
    g.drawString("Hello World!", (width - fontWidth)/2,
                 (height - fontHeight)/2,
                 g.TOP|g.LEFT);
  }
 }

}
```

The HelloCanvas class illustrates the technique for drawing on the screen that you'll use regardless of whether your application is a MIDlet or a RIMlet. You have a method that you use to tell the platform that you're ready to update the display (repaint() in this case), and then when the AMS is ready, it calls paint() with a Graphics object that can be used for drawing. You'll see some variations—you might paint into a bitmap image instead of directly onto the device's screen, for example, and the RIM APIs use a different implementation of the Graphics class (net.rim.device.api.ui.Graphics instead of javax.microedition.lcdui.Graphics)—but the basic idea doesn't change.

Hello BlackBerry!

In this section, you'll see the basics of how RIMlets work by creating a "Hello World" RIMlet.

> **Note** The term "RIMlet" is an informal name that you'll see in discussions on the Internet, but it doesn't appear in RIM's official documentation. As you'll see in the sections on compiling and building your application, RIM uses the term "CLDC application" for BlackBerry applications that aren't MIDlets. This choice of terminology is confusing because a MIDlet is also a type of CLDC application. Since RIM's proprietary APIs define the application life cycle, they act like an alternate profile, so the name "RIMlet" emphasizes the parallel and makes a lot more sense. I assume that the term "RIMlet" is a casualty of one of the usual hazards of making up names: alternate meanings (e.g., RIM looked up "RIMlet" in Urban Dictionary and decided it wasn't appropriate). Nonetheless, since the term "CLDC application" is ambiguous, in this book I'll use the term "RIMlet" for BlackBerry CLDC applications that are not MIDlets.

A RIMlet has the same two basic building blocks as a MIDlet, namely a main life cycle class (Listing 2-3) and a class that defines what appears on the screen (Listing 2-4). However, there are a couple of interesting differences, essentially due to the fact that a BlackBerry smartphone can run multiple applications simultaneously.

Running multiple applications concurrently isn't forbidden in MIDP, but since MIDP devices typically aren't capable of doing it, the precise behavior isn't specified prior to MIDP 3. On BlackBerry, you can specify that your application is to run in the background, and you can even specify that it is to be launched when the device is turned on and should run in the background the whole time. So the display screen component is not technically required. Since games typically don't run in the background, we're not going to spend much time on applications that don't use the screen.

The other big difference is that the BlackBerry platform has a screen stack built in, allowing the user to go to the previous screen just by pressing the back key. The RIM APIs are set up so that you can follow this same design pattern, pushing and popping your screens on the stack. This is one of the points where the RIM APIs improve on the design of MIDP. A user interface typically involves a stack of screens, but since MIDP doesn't have built-in support for stacking the screens, (outside of BlackBerry), your ad hoc implementation of a screen stack won't be well integrated with the device's standard navigation style.

Listing 2-3. *HelloBlackBerry.java*

```java
package net.frogparrot.hello;

import net.rim.device.api.ui.UiApplication;

/**
 * A simple Hello World example for BlackBerry.
 */
public class HelloBlackBerry extends UiApplication {

  /**
   * The RIMlet starts with main, just like an
   * ordinary Java app!
   */
```

```
   public static void main(String[] args) {
     HelloBlackBerry helloBB = new HelloBlackBerry();
     // Create a screen to write on and push it
     // to the top of the screen stack.
     helloBB.pushScreen(new HelloWorldScreen());
     // Set the current thread to notify this application
     // of events such as user input.
     helloBB.enterEventDispatcher();
     // don't put any code here - it won't be reached because
     // enterEventDispatcher() does not return.
   }

}
```

After reading Listing 2-3, two questions should jump out at you: "What's the event dispatcher?" and "How does the application end?"

The event dispatcher is the thread that the platform uses to notify the application of user input events and update the screen. Even though a BlackBerry smartphone can run multiple applications at the same time, only one screen is at the top of the screen stack, and that's the screen that receives input events. Calling enterEventDispatcher() sets the event dispatcher thread to begin sending events to the screen that this application has pushed to the top of the stack.

If you have experience programming in Java, threading should be familiar to you. But if not, the metaphor of a "thread" (or string) works well. Just picture a thread passing through the code, making the different calls in the method. When one method calls another, the thread of command passes into the new method and returns when it's done. You can see that two threads can potentially be working their way through the same method simultaneously, for example.

Any sequence of commands that was launched by the platform calling a method, such as keyChar(), is running on the event thread (whereas methods called from within the run() method of a thread you started yourself won't be). If you're not sure, you can always call Application.isEventThread().

> **Note** The enterEventDispatcher() method normally does not return because the thread that calls this method becomes the event-dispatching thread. Since the application ends with a call to System.exit()—which terminates the program completely—the enterEventDispatcher() method never returns to complete the method that called it. So any last-minute cleanup should be performed before calling System.exit().

The RIM user interface APIs follow the Java Swing philosophy of performing all user interface updates on the event thread instead of designing the user interface components to be thread safe. MIDP components work in essentially the same way—you may be able to access MIDP GUI components from multiple threads simultaneously, but you shouldn't. In either case, the platform uses the event thread when launching the application and when calling the methods that notify the application of user input. So, as long as you don't create any new threads yourself, all of your screen-update code (all of your code, in fact) will run on the event thread.

You can't just always use the event thread for everything, though—if a call on the event thread doesn't return quickly, the device can freeze up and crash. So you need to create a new thread when performing calculations that take a long time, for repeated events that are scheduled by a timer (as you'll see in Chapter 9), and for methods that block, such as communication code (as you'll see in Chapters 7 and 9). When using your own thread (not the event thread), the Java ME platform is designed to make it easy to delegate display updates to the event thread. You just call `invalidate()` on RIM components or `repaint()` on MIDP components to queue a request to update the screen, and the platform will call the `paint()` method from the event thread to carry it out.

If that's not sufficient, and you've created a method that needs to run on the event thread (to be synchronized with screen updates), then you can use `Display.callSerially()` (from a MIDlet) or `Application.invokeLater()` (from a RIMlet). You'll see how to use `Application.invokeLater()` in Chapter 5, as well as a more detailed example of how to use threads with `Application.invokeAndWait()` to update the game animation in Andrew's Swinging Saber game of Chapter 6.

The "Hello BlackBerry" application ends with a call to `System.exit()`, as shown in Listing 2-4. Typically you do this as soon as the last application screen has been popped off the stack. Since the Hello BlackBerry example program has only one screen, we have the program end itself as soon as the event dispatcher notifies the screen that it has been closed (i.e., popped off the screen stack). In more complex applications, I like to place the `System.exit()` call in a method in the `UiApplication` class, in order to keep the life cycle logic grouped, but as you can see from this example, it can be placed anywhere.

Actually, it's not even technically necessary to call `System.exit()` yourself since the platform's default behavior when closing the last screen on the screen stack is to call `System.exit()`. So, if the call to `super()` in Listing 2-4 were replaced by the call `super(DEFAULT_CLOSE)`, then the `onClose()` method can be deleted from this class without affecting the behavior. But I think it's instructive to keep track of the application's life cycle explicitly so that there's no confusion about what it's doing behind the scenes.

> **Caution** The BlackBerry platform doesn't launch your application in a separate virtual machine, which means that you have to be very careful about cleanup. The remains of an earlier run (such as static variables and other data still in memory) can potentially affect later runs of the application. It also means that there's a global namespace, so if two classes have the same name, errors can arise.

Of course, you still need to know how the screen got popped off the screen stack. The BlackBerry platform automatically places a **Close** option on the menu and handles its implementation (to close the screen and pop it off the screen stack). Listing 2-4 shows how you can add your own items to the menu as well, by overriding the screen's menu creation method, `makeMenu()`. Unlike the `javax.microedition.lcdui.Command` objects in Listing 2-1, `net.rim.device.api.ui.MenuItem` is an implementation of `Runnable` that handles its own command action in its run() method (which the platform calls when the user selects the MenuItem). That means that you have to implement a separate subclass for every MenuItem to specify its action. You can do this simply with an anonymous inner class, as you can see in the implementation of myToggleHelloItem in Listing 2-4.

Listing 2-4. *HelloWorldScreen.java*

```java
package net.frogparrot.hello;

import net.rim.device.api.ui.MenuItem;
import net.rim.device.api.ui.component.BitmapField;
import net.rim.device.api.ui.component.RichTextField;
import net.rim.device.api.ui.component.Menu;
import net.rim.device.api.ui.container.MainScreen;
import net.rim.device.api.i18n.ResourceBundle;

/**
 * The screen to draw the message on.
 */
public class HelloWorldScreen extends MainScreen implements HelloBBResResource {

//-------------------------------------------------------------
//    instance fields

  /**
   * This bundle contains all of the texts, translated by locale.
   */
  ResourceBundle myLabels = ResourceBundle.getBundle(BUNDLE_ID, BUNDLE_NAME);

  /**
   * Whether or not the screen should currently display the
   * "hello world" message.
   */
  boolean mySayHello = false;

  /**
   * The user interface component to write hello on.
   */
  RichTextField myTextField;

  /**
   * The "toggle hello" menu item.
   */
  MenuItem myToggleHelloItem
          = new.MenuItem(this.myLabels.getString(HELLOBB_TOGGLE), 0, 0) {
      public void run() {
         toggleHello();
      }
    };

//-------------------------------------------------------------
//    initialization and state changes

  /**
   * Write "Hello World!" on the screen.
```

```
  */
HelloWorldScreen() {
  super();
  myTextField = new RichTextField(myLabels.getString(HELLOBB_SAYHELLO),
      RichTextField.NON_FOCUSABLE | RichTextField.READONLY);
  add(myTextField);
}

/**
 * Override the screen's menu creation method
 * to add the custom commands.
 */
protected void makeMenu(Menu menu, int instance) {
  menu.add(myToggleHelloItem);
  // separate the custom menu items from
  // the default menu items:
  menu.addSeparator();
  super.makeMenu(menu, instance);
}

/**
 * Remove or replace the "Hello World!" message.
 */
void toggleHello() {
  if(mySayHello) {
    myTextField.setText(myLabels.getString(HELLOBB_SAYHELLO));
    mySayHello = false;
  } else {
    myTextField.setText("");
    mySayHello = true;
  }
}

/**
 * This is called by the BlackBerry platform when
 * the screen is popped off the screen stack.
 */
public boolean onClose() {
  // end the program.
  System.exit(0);
  // confirm that the screen is closing.
  return true;
}

}
```

The ResourceBundle class and the HelloBBResResource interface (which HelloWorldScreen
implements) are part of RIM's built-in internationalization functionality. This is another
point where RIM improves on MIDP. It makes sense to internationalize your application
right from the beginning, but it's not built into MIDP. So, in MIDP you have to either
reinvent the wheel—implementing your own way of mapping bundles of text data to the
device language options—or use JSR 238, which was a bit of an afterthought and hence
is not available on many platforms. For BlackBerry, the RIM Java platform defines a
format for the resource files you include in your build, and it automatically generates a

corresponding interface that your application can use to access the resources, as explained in the following section. Then the BlackBerry device transparently selects the right language resource bundle at runtime.

Compiling and Building Your Game

Now that you've seen the code, let's see how to build an application out of it.

Using the BlackBerry JDE

You can download the build tools you'll need from the BlackBerry developers site:

`http://na.blackberry.com/eng/developers/javaappdev/devtools.jsp`

Start by downloading a BlackBerry *Java Development Environment* (JDE). You'll see a choice of different versions of the JDE, which correspond to the different versions of the BlackBerry operating system. I would start with whichever version corresponds to the device you have on hand for development testing. While you're at it, you can also download additional simulators so you can see what your application looks like on different device models.

If you don't know which operating system version is installed on your BlackBerry device, it's easy to find out. Just select **Options ↗ About** from the main menu. It will give you a screen showing the operating system version, as well as a bunch of other interesting information about the Java platform installed on the device, as shown in Figure 2-4.

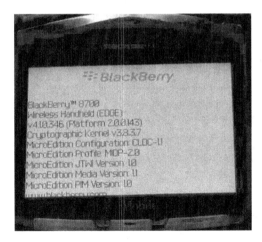

Figure 2-4. *The About screen gives information about the operating system and Java platform installed on the device.*

The BlackBerry)JDE comes with a number of useful tools, including a device simulator (with skins representing different BlackBerry models), a debugger, a Java loader program that allows you to install Java applications on a device via serial port or USB cable, and naturally compile and build tools. All of these tools are designed to run on Windows only, so even if you prefer another operating system for your development environment (like I do), you'll need to use a Windows system for your BlackBerry project. You'll also need to have a recent Java Standard Edition SDK installed on your machine, which you can download from http://java.sun.com.

The BlackBerry JDE comes with an installer, so installation is a snap. Once it's installed, you can launch the JDE from the Windows Start menu. For a typical installation of, say, JDE 4.1.0, the launch command is found under Start ␫ All Programs ␫ Research In Motion ␫ BlackBerry JDE 4.1.0 ␫ JDE. In the JDE, you can build and run the sample programs that come with the JDE by selecting File ␫ Open Workspace, and then browsing to select the sample workspace, which would typically be found at C:\Program Files\Research In Motion\BlackBerry JDE 4.1.0\samples\samples.jdw. Then you can select **Build** ␫ **Build All and Run** to build all of the sample programs and try them out on the simulator. Similarly, you can build and run the two Hello World applications from this chapter by downloading the source code from the Apress web site (www.apress.com) and then opening the chapter02.jdw workspace file in the chapter02/jde folder. Figure 2-5 shows what it looks like.

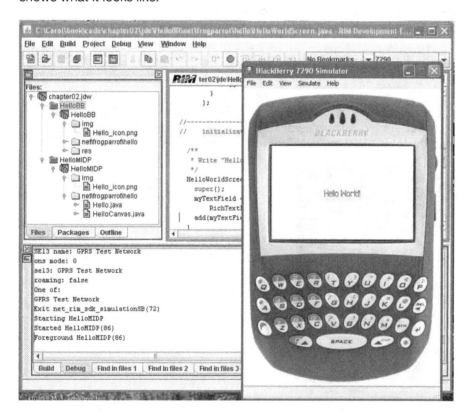

Figure 2-5. *Hello BlackBerry running in the BlackBerry JDE and simulator*

It's easy to create a complete project from scratch from within the BlackBerry JDE. Just close the open workspace (if there is one), and then select **File** ␫ **New Workspace**. Then create a project within the workspace by selecting **Project** ␫ **Create New Project**. The JDE defines the workspace and project configuration by creating a JDW file for each workspace and a JDP file for each project within the workspace. Both of these are short, simple text files, so you can open them up and see exactly what information the JDE needs to have in order to build your project.

The JDW and JDP files store the properties that are defined for a given workspace or project. To edit the workspace properties within the JDE, right-click the workspace file in the explorer tree on the left side and then select **Properties** from the workspace file's context menu. Similarly, each project has its own set of properties that can be edited in the same way. For example, you can set a project to be compiled as a MIDlet by selecting MIDlet as the Project Type on the Application tab of the project's Properties window.

Since the BlackBerry JDE behaves like a typical IDE, creating (or adding) Java source code files is intuitive: just select **Project ↗ Create New File in Project**, and then make sure that your new file's extension is .java. Adding the application's icon (which will appear in the BlackBerry's menu) is almost as simple. Just choose **Project ↗ Add File to Project** and browse to select the icon image file. Once the image has been added to the project, right-click the image file in the JDE explorer tree to edit the image properties. There you'll have the option of setting the image to be the application icon. (See the "Creating Icon Image Files" sidebar for more details on creating the icon.) Creating the resource files is the step that requires a little extra information, as explained in the next section.

CREATING ICON IMAGE FILES

The gateway to your game is the icon that appears on the BlackBerry menu (see Figure 2-6), so it's important for this image to be attractive and enticing. Ideally, this image (and all of your game graphics) will be created by a professional graphic designer. But you'll still need to understand what types of image files need to be created—if you're not living in an ideal world, or to explain to your graphic designer exactly what files you need if you are.

Figure 2-6. *The main menu of the BlackBerry 7290 simulator with the Hello BB icon*

BlackBerry supports GIF- and JPEG-encoded images in addition to PNG-encoded images. Throughout this book we'll stick with PNG-encoded images because PNG is the standard format for MIDP devices. Any decent graphics program (e.g., not the Paint accessory that comes with Windows) will give you the option of saving your drawings in PNG format, usually just by naming the file with the .png file extension. If you don't have a decent graphics program, you can download GIMP from www.gimp.org for free. It's a full-featured graphics program that has all you'll need to create the graphics files for a typical game.

Different BlackBerry devices display different-size icons on the application menu. Most BlackBerry models will resize the icon for you if it's the wrong size, but it will look best if you build the game with the right-size icon. That means making a series of icons in different sizes, corresponding to the different device models (see the following "Building for Multiple Devices with Ant" section for size and build information).

If you're creating the icons yourself with GIMP, you start by creating a new image file with the desired dimensions (in pixels). Then, in the Create a New Image window under Advanced Options, be sure to change the "fill with" option from "Background color" to Transparency. Since the BlackBerry menu places the image icons over a background image (as shown in Figure 2-7), you definitely want to draw your icon onto a transparent background, not onto an ugly opaque square.

Figure 2-7. *The icons are painted over an image on the menu of the BlackBerry Curve 8320.*

For more ideas on how to draw your icon, see the "Simple 3D Image Tricks" section in Chapter 4.

Creating Resource Files

In order to be sure that your game's labels and texts are presented to the user in the correct language, you need to create a set of localized data files that map a set of key constants to the sets of strings to display. To create the resource bundle and generate the corresponding resource interface, the BlackBerry build tool needs a resource header file (with the extension .rrh) and a set of resource files (with the extension .rrc), one for each of the locales that your application supports. These are all simple text files, which you can create for yourself in a text editor if you know the syntax and file name conventions.

In a nutshell, the header file gives the following information:

1. The package for the interface that is generated to access the resource bundle

2. The default locale

3. The list of access keys

The *locale* specifies the user's desired language and optionally also the user's country. It is defined according to the usual Java locale-naming convention used by the java.util.Locale class from Java Standard Edition, and by the microedition.locale system property that is returned by the System.getProperty() method in MIDP. The locale name format is ll_CC, where ll is a pair of lowercase letters identifying the language, and CC is a pair of uppercase letters identifying the country. For example, en_CA indicates English as spoken in Canada, and en indicates generic English resources that will be used for any English-speaking locale for which you haven't created a country-specific resource bundle.

The Hello BlackBerry resource header file is given in Listing 2-5.

Listing 2-5. *HelloBBRes.rrh*

```
package net.frogparrot.hello;

originalLocale en;

HELLOBB_SAYHELLO#0=1;
HELLOBB_TOGGLE#0=2;
```

In this example, you can see how the two resource keys are mapped to numbers. If you look back at Listing 2-4, you can see how the resource file fits together with the rest of the code. Since I named the file HelloBBRes.rrh, the BlackBerry build tool generated an interface named HelloBBResResource, which has the key string HELLOBB_SAYHELLO defined as the name of a constant. The interface also defines the constants BUNDLE_ID and BUNDLE_NAME, where BUNDLE_ID is a long assigned by the build tool and BUNDLE_NAME is the fully qualified name (net.frogparrot.hello.HelloBBRes in this case). The exact values of the two constants aren't important, though—just keep in mind that they're the arguments to pass to ResourceBundle.getBundle() to get the bundle of localized strings.

The resource data files are even simpler than the resource header files. They merely contain a list of the key constants mapped to the corresponding display strings, as shown in Listing 2-6.

Listing 2-6. *HelloBBRes_en.rrc*

```
HELLOBB_SAYHELLO#0="Hello World!";
HELLOBB_TOGGLE#0="toggle";
```

For each locale you support, you create a corresponding resource data file. The file name tells the platform which data file corresponds to which locale. For example, the BlackBerry build tool will automatically identify `HelloBBRes_fr.rrc` as the French data file corresponding to `HelloBBRes.rrh`. Each localized data file should contain the list of key strings mapped to the corresponding translated strings, using the following syntax:

```
KEY#0="translated text to display";
```

When you create the resource files, you need to be careful about the character encoding. Since BlackBerry handsets are MIDP devices—and MIDP devices are required to support the UTF-8 character encoding—you should use UTF-8 for encoding the texts of all languages that have special characters. And be sure to test the localized labels on an actual device, because apparently there have been some issues with foreign character sets not displaying correctly, even when the data files are saved in UTF-8 format.

You can also create the resource files in the JDE just by selecting Project ↗ Create New File in Project, and then using the correct file name conventions when creating the files. In the Hello BlackBerry example program, I started by creating a resource header file called `HelloBBRes.rrh`. The JDE simplifies the resource creation process because the file editor is set up to allow you to add new keys, and the keys added to the resource header files are automatically propagated to the resource data files, so all you have to do is fill in the translations. The JDE then creates the underlying text files in the correct format and character encoding behind the scenes.

Understanding BlackBerry Application Files

Once you build your project (using one of the build options under the project menu), the BlackBerry build tools will create a series of files. Some of these files are standard MIDP files, and some are BlackBerry specific.

> The *JAR* file (extension `.jar`) is the main application file for MIDP. It's the file containing the resources and compiled class files to run on the device. It's a standard *Java Archive* file with the added requirement that the *manifest* file (META-INF/MANIFEST.MF in the JAR file) has some special MIDP-specific properties.

> The *JAD* file (extension `.jad`) is the *Java Application Descriptor* file, which is used by MIDP's *Over-the-Air* (OTA) provisioning protocol. It's a Java properties file that contains information about the application to help the device (and user) decide whether to proceed with the download and installation before downloading the JAR file. It gives security-related information such as the permissions the MIDlet requires, and it gives download and installation information such as the size of the JAR file and its location. It also gives information about the application, such as the name, icon, and version as well as the fully qualified name of the `MIDlet` subclass that the AMS must call to launch the MIDlet. The application properties in the JAD file must match the corresponding properties in the manifest file (in the JAR) exactly; otherwise, the application won't install (for security reasons).

> The *RAPC* file (extension `.rapc`) is a helper file used by the BlackBerry JDE and the BlackBerry compile-and-build tool (`rapc.exe`). It contains many of the same

properties that go in the JAD and manifest files. The BlackBerry JDE creates this file (with your application's properties) and then uses it as input for the rapc.exe build tool, which then writes the properties to the JAD and manifest files. This file is not needed if you're building with Ant (see the "Building with Multiple Devices for Ant" section, which follows).

The *debug* file (extension .debug) and the *CSO* file (extension .cso) are additional helper files for running the application in the debugger and for digitally signing the application, respectively. You'll use the debug file when optimizing the game and graphics in Chapter 6, and you'll use the CSO file when signing and selling the game in Chapter 5.

The *ALX* file (extension .alx) is an XML format descriptor file to help users install your game locally using RIM's desktop management software. The JDE doesn't create this file automatically with every build, but it's one of the menu options you can select. You don't need this file if you're planning to distribute your game entirely over the air (having your customers install your game directly from the Internet to their BlackBerry devices). You only need to create this file if you're planning on using a distribution model where your customers download the application files from your site onto a PC and then load the game from the PC onto the BlackBerry.

The *COD* file (extension .cod) is the main application file for BlackBerry. This is the file you use when you're installing the application onto the device directly from your PC, and it can also be used when installing the application over the air. It's a proprietary binary format, so you can't just inspect and extract its contents the way you can with a JAR file. You can install your game by loading this file onto your BlackBerry device with the JavaLoader tool (as you'll see in the "Installing and Distributing Your Game" section of this chapter), or by creating a corresponding ALX file to use with the desktop management software. COD files have a size limit (64KB maximum in order to install the application over the air), so they're often grouped in a ZIP file, which (confusingly enough) has its extension changed to .cod. (Zipping "sibling" COD files together is explained in more detail in Chapter 5.)

Building for Multiple Devices with Ant

Once you understand the basic steps for creating a BlackBerry application, you can put away the BlackBerry JDE and use your favorite build tools. Both Eclipse and NetBeans have plug-ins available for building for BlackBerry. My personal favorite is Ant.

For a professional Java ME project, Ant is the way to go. It's a command-line build tool that allows you to define (and combine) build tasks in XML. Ant makes it simple to automate your build, and in particular makes it easier to build different versions of the same application for different device models. Building individual binaries for each target device model is a good idea in general, and it's especially critical for games since you need to optimize your graphics to fit the screen exactly. In this section you'll see how to use Ant (and the BlackBerry preprocessing directives) to build different versions of an application from the same code—even if they have different operating systems and support different APIs.

And there's another advantage to using Ant that you'll see in this section: when creating an Ant build file, you'll learn exactly how all of the build steps work and how to execute them from the command line. Having the IDE handle all of the build steps behind the scenes seems like less work, but it's a false savings because troubleshooting problems is a lot easier if you understand all of the build steps and how all of the intermediate build files are used.

If you don't already have Ant installed on your machine, you can download it from http://ant.apache.org and follow the installation instructions on the site. You'll also need to download the BlackBerry Ant tools from http://bb-ant-tools.sourceforge.net. The only installation step is to copy the bb-ant-tools.jar file to your Ant installation's lib directory. If you're planning to build your game for non-BlackBerry MIDP devices as well, then you'll want to download and install Antenna (see the "Building for other MIDP devices with Antenna" sidebar).

BUILDING FOR OTHER MIDP DEVICES WITH ANTENNA

Antenna is the standard package of Ant tools for building MIDP applications. Antenna includes tasks to perform all of the MIDP build steps, such as creating the JAR and JAD files, preprocessing, signing the JAR, and so on.

The BlackBerry JDE's build tools will create valid JAR and JAD files that can be installed and run on non-BlackBerry devices. But when building a professional project, you want to choose the right tools for the job. Naturally, BlackBerry's tools are optimized for BlackBerry's special needs and are not optimized to create the simplest, best application files for other manufacturers' devices.

If you want to design a cross-platform game, you should probably choose to write a MIDlet (not a RIMlet, aka CLDC application), and then look at the Antenna documentation to see how to write an Ant build file for all of your non-BlackBerry target devices. Some of the general ideas in this section—such as defining a properties file for each target device—will also work when using Antenna Ant tasks in the place of the BlackBerry Ant Tools tasks. Then you can write a build file (like the one in Listing 2-10) that will call the BlackBerry Ant build file to build for the BlackBerry devices, and call the Antenna build file to build for the other devices.

It is also possible to write a cross-platform game using the RIMlet application type for the BlackBerry target platforms while creating a corresponding MIDlet for other MIDP target platforms. It's merely a question of isolating the life cycle and user interface code in a few classes and then selecting the correct set of source code files for each device (using Ant). See Chapter 3 for an example game that can be compiled as either one.

Listing 2-7 shows the Ant build file for building the Hello BlackBerry example.

Listing 2-7. *build.xml*

```
<project default="deliver">

    <!-- set the project and platform properties to defaults -->
    <property name="project.name" value="HelloBB"/>
    <property file="models\7290.properties"/>
    <!-- the app.type property is used by the build task to indicate -->
    <!-- whether the application is a MIDlet or a RIMlet. -->
    <!-- The value "cldc" indicates a RIMlet. -->
    <property name="app.type" value="cldc"/>
```

```xml
<!-- set the configuration -->
<!-- these values should be changed to match your local dev environment -->
<property name="jde.home"
    value="C:\Program Files\Research In Motion\BlackBerry JDE ${rim.version}"
/>
<property name="build.root" value="C:\Carol\book\code\chapter02\antbuild" />
<property name="project.root" value="${build.root}\${project.name}" />
<property name="build.output" value="${project.root}\build_${model}" />

<!-- tell ant where to find the bb-ant-tools.jar -->
<taskdef resource="bb-ant-defs.xml"
    classpath="C:\Carol\apache-ant-1.7.1\lib\bb-ant-tools.jar"/>

<target name="clean">
    <!-- delete all files created by the build process -->
    <delete dir="${build.output}"/>
    <delete file="${jde.home}\simulator\${project.name}_${model}.cod"/>
</target>

<target name="clean-simulator">
    <!-- run the cleaning script provided with the simulator -->
    <!-- sets the simulator back to its initial state -->
    <exec executable="${jde.home}\simulator\clean.bat"
            dir="${jde.home}\simulator"
    />
    <!-- delete the application and its data from the simulator's memory -->
    <exec executable="${jde.home}\simulator\fledge.exe"
            dir="${build.root}\simulator-data">
        <arg value="/app=${jde.home}\simulator\Jvm.dll"/>
        <arg value="/handheld=${model}"/>
        <arg value="/clear-flash"/>
        <arg value="/shutdown-after-startup"/>
    </exec>
</target>

<target name="setup">
    <!-- create a build directory to hold exactly the source -->
    <!-- and resource files for the selected device model -->
    <echo message="creating ${build.output}\res"/>
    <mkdir dir="${build.output}\img"/>
    <mkdir dir="${build.output}\res"/>
    <mkdir dir="${build.output}\src"/>
    <mkdir dir="${build.output}\${project.name}"/>
    <copy todir="${build.output}\src">
        <fileset dir="${project.root}\src"/>
    </copy>
    <copy file="${project.root}\icon\${project.name}_icon_${size.icon}.png"
            tofile="${build.output}\img\${project.name}_icon.png"
    />
    <copy todir="${build.output}\img">
        <fileset dir="${project.root}\img\${size.screen}"/>
    </copy>
    <copy todir="${build.output}\res">
        <fileset dir="${project.root}\res"/>
```

```xml
        </copy>
    </target>

    <target name="build" depends="setup">
        <rapc destdir="${build.output}\${project.name}"
              output="${project.name}_${model}"
              srcdir="${build.output}">
            <jdp type="${app.type}"
                 vendor="frog-parrot"
                 version="1.0"
                 description="a maze game"
                 title="${project.name}"
                 icon="../img/${project.name}_icon.png"
            />
            <define tag="RIM_${rim.version}"/>
            <define tag="SCREEN_${size.screen}"/>
        </rapc>
    </target>

    <target name="deliver" depends="clean, build">
        <!-- install the application on the simulator by -->
        <!-- placing the .cod file in the simulator's directory -->
        <mkdir dir="${build.root}\release\${project.name}_${model}_${rim.version}"/>
        <copy file="${build.output}\${project.name}\${project.name}_${model}.cod"
              tofile="${build.root}\release\${project.name}_${model}_${rim.version}•
\${project.name}_${model}.cod"
        />
        <copy file="${build.output}\${project.name}\${project.name}_${model}.cod"
              tofile="${jde.home}\simulator\${project.name}_${model}.cod"
        />
    </target>

    <target name="run">
        <!-- run the application on the simulator -->
        <mkdir dir="${build.root}\simulator-data"/>
        <exec executable="${jde.home}\simulator\fledge.exe"
              dir="${build.root}\simulator-data"
              output="${build.root}\simulator-data\${project.name}-log.txt">
            <arg value="/app=${jde.home}\simulator\Jvm.dll"/>
            <arg value="/handheld=${model}"/>
            <arg value="/app-param=DisableRegistration"/>
            <arg value="/app-param=JvmAlxConfigFile:${model}.xml"/>
            <arg value="/pin=0x2100000A"/>
            <!-- without this line the app is saved in the simulator's flash -->
            <!-- <arg value="/no-save-flash"/> -->
        </exec>
    </target>

    <target name="load">
        <!-- install the application onto a BlackBerry device via USB -->
        <exec executable="${jde.home}\bin\JavaLoader.exe">
            <arg value="-u"/>
            <arg value="load"/>
            <arg value="${build.root}\release\${project.name}_${model}_•
${rim.version}\${project.name}_${model}.cod"/>
```

```
        </exec>
    </target>
```

```
</project>
```

An Ant build file is made of a set of procedures called targets. To run a particular target, open a command prompt, navigate to the directory containing the build.xml file, and type ant <targetname>. Or, if you'd like to run the default target (defined in the default attribute of the project node), just type ant. Naturally this assumes that your PATH environment variable contains the path to the Ant bin directory. If not, you can edit your PATH variable from the Windows Start menu: **Start ↗ Control Panel ↗ System ↗ Advanced ↗ Environment Variables.**

Ant uses properties for project-specific data, such as the device model and version number in this example. An Ant property is not a variable—once its value has been set, it can't be updated during the build. The property's value can be accessed during the build by enclosing the property name in curly braces preceded by a dollar sign: ${like.this}. In any quoted string, the property name indicator will be replaced by the corresponding value.

Ant property values can be set using a property element or read from a properties file. Either way, you can override the properties in the build file by using the -D or -propertyfile option on the command line when you call Ant. In this example, each target device has a corresponding properties file containing the operating system, the screen size, and the icon size values. For example, the properties file describing the BlackBerry 8900 is shown in Listing 2-8. (The devices property in Listing 2-8 is used when preparing the game for sale on BlackBerry App World, as explained in Chapter 5.)

Listing 2-8. *8900.properties*

```
model=8900
size.screen=480x360
size.icon=80x80
devices=8900,9000
rim.version=4.6.1
```

Each time the build.xml file is run, the properties from this file are loaded by the <property file="models\8900.properties"/> element near the top of Listing 2-7. As you can probably guess from the file attribute, the file should be placed in a subdirectory called models, along with the corresponding data files for any other devices that you might want to build for. You'll need to do some research to find the data for all of your target devices in order to create the properties files. Most of the information is on the RIM developers' site (http://na.blackberry.com/eng/developers). You can also get precise information about each device's screen and graphics capabilities from the BlackBerry Theme Studio. (Like the JDE, it's a free download on the BlackBerry developers' site, and it has a built-in library of device model information.)

The key step in Listing 2-7 is the build target. This is the point where Ant calls BlackBerry build tools that came with the JDE you downloaded (as described earlier in the "Using the BlackBerry JDE" section). The build executable is the rapc.exe application found in the JDE's `bin` directory, which calls the build tools in the `rapc.jar` file, also found in the JDE's `bin` directory.

You can actually build your entire project from the command line using `rapc.exe`. The JDE tells you the exact command to use—it appears in the JDE's output console when you build your project. For the Hello BlackBerry example, the JDE used the following command:

```
"C:\Program Files\Research In Motion\BlackBerry JDE 4.1.0\bin\rapc.exe"  -quiet •
import="..\..\..\..\..\Program Files\Research In Motion\BlackBerry JDE 4.1.0\lib•
\net_rim_api.jar" codename=HelloBB\HelloBB HelloBB\HelloBB.rapc •
warnkey=0x52424200;0x52525400;0x52435200;0x52434300 •
C:\Carol\book\code\chapter02\jde\HelloBB\img\Hello_icon.png •
C:\Carol\book\code\chapter02\jde\HelloBB\net\frogparrot\hello\HelloBlack•
Berry.java C:\Carol\book\code\chapter02\jde\HelloBB\net\frogparrot\hello\•
HelloWorldScreen.java C:\Carol\book\code\chapter02\jde\HelloBB\res\•
HelloBBRes.rrc C:\Carol\book\code\chapter02\jde\HelloBB\res\HelloBBRes.rrh •
C:\Carol\book\code\chapter02\jde\HelloBB\res\HelloBBRes_de.rrc •
C:\Carol\book\code\chapter02\jde\HelloBB\res\HelloBBRes_en.rrc •
C:\Carol\book\code\chapter02\jde\HelloBB\res\HelloBBRes_es.rrc •
C:\Carol\book\code\chapter02\jde\HelloBB\res\HelloBBRes_fr.rrc •
C:\Carol\book\code\chapter02\jde\HelloBB\res\HelloBBRes_it.rrc
```

It's not too hard to interpret what this command is doing. It's calling the `rapc.exe` build tool, importing the RIM Java API libraries (see Figure 2-1), reading the JAD/manifest properties from the `HelloBB.rapc` file (see the "Understanding the BlackBerry Application Files" section), setting some preferences on warning output, and then specifying all of the code and resource files.

You can launch this build command directly from within Ant since the Ant `exec` task will allow you to call a command-line executable with your desired parameter list. That's how the `run` and `load` targets work in Listing 2-7. But since the command arguments include every single code file and every single resource file individually, the `exec` task would be a huge mess to maintain. That's where the BlackBerry Ant tools come in. The `bb-ant-tools.jar` contains an Ant task called `rapc`, which essentially just constructs the correct calling parameters for your project, and then uses them to execute the build procedure in `rapc.jar`.

The `rapc` Ant task uses the `jde.home` property to find `rapc.jar` and `net_rim_api.jar` (containing the RIM Java API libraries). For a professional project, you should download a number of different BlackBerry JDEs—one for each RIM operating system version you're planning to support. If you look near the top of Listing 2-7, you can see that the `jde.home` property is set based on the `rim.version` property that is set in the target device's property file (Listing 2-8).

The `rapc` task is fairly straightforward (and well documented on the BlackBerry Ant Tools site: `http://bb-ant-tools.sourceforge.net`), but there are a couple of points that require further explanation. First, the `jdp` child element is the place where the game's JAD/manifest properties are specified (see the preceding "Understanding BlackBerry Application Files" section). So, instead of using the RAPC file, application properties like the name and icon are specified as attributes in the `jdp` element. The other interesting feature is the `define` element, which allows you to preprocess the code based on C-style `define` statements.

Preprocessing makes it very simple to build your game for a range of devices using the same code. To see how it works, let's build a "Hello Plus" example. It's the same as the Hello BlackBerry example except that you replace the HelloWorldScreen.java class in Listing 2-4 with the more interesting HelloWorldScreen.java given in Listing 2-9, and you change the project.name property (in Listing 2-7) from HelloBB to HelloPlus.

Listing 2-9. *HelloWorldScreen.java*

```java
//#preprocess
package net.frogparrot.hello;

import net.rim.device.api.ui.component.RichTextField;
import net.rim.device.api.ui.component.BitmapField;
import net.rim.device.api.ui.container.MainScreen;
import net.rim.device.api.system.Bitmap;
import net.rim.device.api.i18n.ResourceBundle;

/**
 * The screen to draw the message on.
 */
public class HelloWorldScreen extends MainScreen implements HelloBBResResource {

  /**
   * This bundle contains all of the texts, translated by locale.
   */
  ResourceBundle myLabels = ResourceBundle.getBundle(BUNDLE_ID, BUNDLE_NAME);

  /**
   * Write "Hello World!" on the screen.
   */
  HelloWorldScreen() {
    super();
    add(new RichTextField(myLabels.getString(HELLOBB_SAYHELLO),
        RichTextField.NON_FOCUSABLE | RichTextField.READONLY));
    //#ifdef RIM_4.1.0
    add(new RichTextField("version 4.1.0",
        RichTextField.NON_FOCUSABLE | RichTextField.READONLY));
    //#else
    add(new RichTextField("not version 4.1.0",
        RichTextField.NON_FOCUSABLE | RichTextField.READONLY));
    //#endif
    //#ifdef RIM_4.6.1
    add(new RichTextField("version 4.6.1",
        RichTextField.NON_FOCUSABLE | RichTextField.READONLY));
    //#else
    add(new RichTextField("not version 4.6.1",
        RichTextField.NON_FOCUSABLE | RichTextField.READONLY));
    //#endif
    // Let's try adding an image!
    Bitmap imgBitmap = Bitmap.getBitmapResource("HelloPlus_icon.png");
    add(new BitmapField(imgBitmap));
  }

  /**
   * This is called by the BlackBerry platform when
```

```
 * the screen is popped off the screen stack.
 */
public boolean onClose() {
  // end the program.
  System.exit(0);
  return true;
}

}
```

The //#preprocess line at the top of the file tells the rapc compiler to preprocess this file based on the define statements. Then the code between the //#ifdef, //#else, and //#endif lines is either included or removed, based on the define elements in the rapc task (in Listing 2-7). You can see that the Hello Plus example will display which JDE version was used when it was built, as shown in Figure 2-8. (Note that this JDE version may not be the same as the actual operating system version on the device—for example, if the user installed the wrong version of Hello Plus for the device model or if the user upgraded the device's operating system.) For clarity, the toggle command (myToggleCommand) is omitted.

Figure 2-8. *Hello Plus running on the BlackBerry 8900 simulator*

The Hello Plus example also shows how to access and display an image. To get a handle to the image resource, you just call Bitmap.getBitmapResource() with the name of the image file. Unlike a MIDP JAR file, the RIM COD file format doesn't have an internal file structure, so you don't have to worry about the path to the image file inside of the COD file—there isn't one. Any PNG files that were included in the build will be accessible within the application, using just the file name that identified the image when the .cod file was built.

Unfortunately, the RIM APIs aren't consistent about using the file name alone when loading resources. Depending on the resource-loading method you use, you sometimes have to prepend some path-like elements (as you'll see in Chapter 4).

Now you're ready to create a wrapper build file that will build a series of COD application files—one for each of your target devices—in a single command. The build file is given in Listing 2-10.

Listing 2-10. *build-all.xml*

```xml
<project default="build-all">

    <!-- set the project and platform properties to defaults -->
    <property name="build.root" value="C:\Carol\BlackBerry\antbuild" />
    <property name="project.name" value="HelloPlus"/>
    <property name="app.type" value="cldc"/>

    <target name="clean">
        <delete dir="${build.root}\delivery"/>
        <ant antfile="build.xml" target="clean">
            <property file="models\7290.properties"/>
        </ant>
        <ant antfile="build.xml" target="clean">
            <property file="models\8900.properties"/>
        </ant>
        <ant antfile="build.xml" target="clean-simulator">
            <property name="rim.version" value="4.1.0"/>
        </ant>
        <ant antfile="build.xml" target="clean-simulator">
            <property name="rim.version" value="4.6.1"/>
        </ant>
    </target>

    <target name="build-all">
        <mkdir dir="${build.root}\delivery"/>
        <ant antfile="build.xml" target="deliver">
            <property file="models\7290.properties"/>
        </ant>
        <ant antfile="build.xml" target="deliver">
            <property file="models\8900.properties"/>
        </ant>
    </target>

</project>
```

The build file in Listing 2-10 only builds two versions of Hello Plus—one for the BlackBerry 7290 and one for the BlackBerry 8900—but you can easily see how to extend it to add builds for more device models. In the `build-all` target, the ant task calls the original `build.xml` file with the properties defined in each device model's properties files. It doesn't matter that the `build.xml` file in Listing 2-7 has other values defined for the model properties, because (as explained) once you set a property value inside your Ant build file, later attempts to change the property's value are ignored. The reason the `build-all.xml` file in Listing 2-10 is able to change the property values from one version build to the next is because it's only setting the properties for the individual calls to `build.xml`—it's not setting the property values for the `build-all.xml` file itself.

The one point I've kind of glossed over in this section concerns the file structure that you need to create in order to run the Ant build. You can probably see from Listing 2-7 that you need to create a working directory that contains your Ant build files and has two subdirectories: a models directory containing the device model property files, and a project directory that has the same name as the project. Under the project directory, you create subdirectories for the source code, the text resource files, the images (grouped in subdirectories by screen size), and the icons (where the icon files are named according to size). You don't have to worry about the details, though, because you can just download the complete build directory for this project from www.apress.com.

> **Caution** The Ant build files in Listings 2-7 and 2-10 use the rim-version property in the model properties files (see Listing 2-8) when selecting a JDE installation for the build task. Thus, you should be sure that the model properties files contain only rim-version values that correspond to JDEs that you have installed on your machine; otherwise, the build will fail.

Now that you know all about how to build a BlackBerry application, let's see it running on a real BlackBerry smartphone.

Installing and Distributing Your Game

The simplest way to install your game on a device for testing is by connecting the device to your PC with a USB cable and using the JavaLoader.exe tool. The simplest way to distribute your game to users is to allow them to download the game directly onto their BlackBerry devices. Let's talk about both.

Local Installation

In the bin directory of the BlackBerry JDE, you'll find the JavaLoader.exe tool. If you open a command prompt and type JavaLoader in the bin directory, it will print out a list of all of the available options, including listing the applications that are on the device, installing an application, removing an application, and much more.

> **Note** In order for the JavaLoader application to connect to your device, you must have the BlackBerry Desktop Manager application installed and running on your PC. This application comes with the device, but if you somehow got a device without it, you can download it from the BlackBerry web site (www.blackberry.com). When you plug your device into the PC using a USB cable, BlackBerry Desktop Manager will detect it and display the device's PIN number at the base of the application window. The JavaLoader tool will be able to connect to your device if and only if BlackBerry Desktop Manager is connected to the device.

Assuming that the COD file is in the same directory with the JavaLoader executable, installing an application is as simple as typing the following command:

```
JavaLoader.exe -u load HelloBB.cod
```

If you're building with multiple versions of the JDE, then it's better not to put any one JDE's bin directory in your PATH environment variable. Instead, just create a load target in your Ant build file, as shown in Listing 2-7. That way you can automatically load the correct version just by specifying the correct model property. For example, if you've connected a BlackBerry 8900 to your USB port and you'd like to load the current application onto it, just go to the directory containing the build.xml file and type the following:

```
ant -propertyfile models\8900.properties load
```

Similarly, you can launch the current application on different versions of the simulator using the run task in the build.xml file in Listing 2-7. The command to run the simulator is trickier to figure out than the load command since the JDE console doesn't tell you what command it uses to launch the simulator, and the help screens of the simulator executable (fledge.exe) could stand to be a little more helpful. I eventually figured it out by creating a shortcut to the simulator launch option from the Windows **Start** menu, and then looking at the shortcut's properties to see the precise command to execute.

The run target first creates a simulator-data folder where the simulator is executed because the executable creates a number of files in its execution directory, including a run log and some binary files representing the simulator's flash memory.

Remote Installation

Installing a BlackBerry game over the Internet couldn't be easier. All you have to do is open the BlackBerry's browser to a page that contains a link to the JAR or JAD file, and then click the link. The BlackBerry device does the rest.

Uploading the file to the Internet is pretty trivial as well. Any web page–hosting service that allows you to upload files to a publicly accessible directory will do. If you can download the JAR or JAD file with your PC's browser, then your BlackBerry device can download and install it.

There are a few extra steps, however, if you're planning to sell your game over the Internet. If you're distributing the game from your own web site, then you'll probably want to have the web server automatically detect the BlackBerry's model and transparently select the right JAD file. If you don't want the extra work of distributing the game yourself, you can sell it through BlackBerry App World. Both of these options are explained in Chapter 5. But first you'll need to create a game that's worth selling. For that, go to Chapters 3 and 4.

Summary

Setting up your development environment isn't the most entertaining step in a project, but it's a critical one. When developing for BlackBerry—even if you plan to set up an automated build with Ant—you need to start by familiarizing yourself with the BlackBerry JDE, because the JDE includes the build executable (rapc.exe) that generates BlackBerry's proprietary binaries.

The next step is to build a Hello World application and get it running on both a simulator and an actual smartphone. BlackBerry offers you two possible application types. MIDlets are designed to run on much less powerful handsets and have the advantage that they run on any MIDP handset, whereas RIMlets—designed for BlackBerry by RIM—allow you to exploit the BlackBerry smartphone's full potential, as you'll see throughout this book.

Chapter **3**

Game Graphics and Events with MIDP and RIM Classes

The graphics and user interface (UI) classes are the place where you'll have to choose between using the MIDP libraries and the RIM libraries. For most other types of functionality, RIM has made the choice for you by implementing either a standard JSR or a proprietary RIM library. In this chapter, you'll learn how the philosophies of the two types of applications differ, and you'll see how, when, and why to use either the RIM graphics/UI classes, the MIDP graphics/UI classes, or both.

The Maze Game

For small devices, don't underestimate the value of basic games. Particularly on a BlackBerry—which people use at work, and have handy while waiting in line or commuting by train—a little diversion like solitaire or mahjong is often just what the user is looking for.

We'll start with a game where the user solves a randomly generated maze. Not only is Maze a complete game by itself, but it can serve as a building block for more complex platform- and arcade-style games. It also illustrates the basic principles of handling user navigation input and drawing the game on the screen for both types of BlackBerry applications.

Drawing with the Graphics Class

You'll notice—right at the top of Listing 3-1—that we're importing a proprietary RIM class (`net.rim.device.api.ui.Graphics`) when we might have chosen the corresponding MIDP class (`javax.microedition.lcdui.Graphics`). In fact, RIM's version of the `Graphics` class is so close in functionality to the MIDP version that the `import` statement is the only thing you need to change in order to use this game class in a MIDlet instead of in a RIMlet. In the "MIDP vs. RIM" section of this chapter, you'll use this same game logic to make two versions of the maze game example: MIDP Maze and BB Maze. And if you wrap that import statement in an #ifdef preprocessing directive like we did in Listing 2-9, you can build both examples from the same code.

Listing 3-1. *MazeGame.java*

```java
package net.frogparrot.maze;

import net.rim.device.api.ui.Graphics;

/**
 * This class controls the game logic.
 */
public class MazeGame {

//------------------------------------------------------------
//   static fields

  /**
   * color constants.
   */
  public static final int BLACK = 0;
  public static final int WHITE = 0xffffff;
  public static final int GRAY = 0x888888;

  /**
   * The single instance of this class.
   */
  private static MazeGame theInstance;

//------------------------------------------------------------
//   instance fields

  /**
   * The data object that describes the maze configuration.
   */
  private Grid myGrid;

  /**
   * Whether or not the currently displayed maze has
   * been completed.
   */
  private boolean myGameOver = false;

  /**
   * The dimensions of the screen in pixels.
   */
  private int myScreenWidth;
  private int myScreenHeight;

  /**
   * The maze wall width dimensions in pixels.
   */
```

```java
int mySquareSize;
private int myMaxSquareSize;
private int myMinSquareSize;

/**
 * The top-corner coordinates in pixels
 * according to the screen/grid coordinate system.
 */
private int myStartX = 0;
private int myStartY = 0;

/**
 * The dimensions of the maze grid.
 * In terms of grid squares. Each grid square
 * has length and width (in pixels) given by mySquareSize.
 */
private int myGridHeight;
private int myGridWidth;
private int myMaxGridWidth;
private int myMinGridWidth;

/**
 * The current location of the player in the maze
 * (in terms of the coordinates of the maze grid, NOT in terms
 * of the pixel coordinate system of the Canvas/Screen).
 */
private int myPlayerX = 1;
private int myPlayerY = 1;

//-------------------------------------------------------
//    gets / sets

/**
 * @return the single instance of this class.
 */
public static MazeGame getInstance() {
  return theInstance;
}

/**
 * Set the single instance of this class.
 */
static void setInstance(MazeGame mazeGame) {
  theInstance = mazeGame;
}

/**
 * Changes the width of the maze walls and calculates how
 * this change affects the number of rows and columns
 * the maze can have.
 * @return the number of columns now that the the
 *         width of the columns has been updated.
 */
public int setColWidth(int colWidth) {
  if(mySquareSize != colWidth) {
```

```
        clearGrid();
        mySquareSize = colWidth;
        PrefsStorage.setSquareSize(mySquareSize);
        myGridWidth = myScreenWidth / mySquareSize;
        // only odd values are valid for the
        // number of rows and columns:
        if((myGridWidth & 0x1) == 0) {
          myGridWidth -= 1;
        }
        myGridHeight = myScreenHeight / mySquareSize;
        if((myGridHeight & 0x1) == 0) {
          myGridHeight -= 1;
        }
        // Center the maze in the screen:
        myStartX = (myScreenWidth - (myGridWidth*mySquareSize))/2;
        myStartY = (myScreenHeight - (myGridHeight*mySquareSize))/2;
      }
    return(myGridWidth);
  }

  /**
   * @return the minimum width possible for the maze walls.
   */
  public int getMinColWidth() {
    return(myMinSquareSize);
  }

  /**
   * @return the maximum width possible for the maze walls.
   */
  public int getMaxColWidth() {
    return(myMaxSquareSize);
  }

  /**
   * @return the minimum number of columns the display can be divided into.
   */
  public int getMinNumCols() {
    return(myMinGridWidth);
  }

  /**
   * @return the maximum number of columns the display can be divided into.
   */
  public int getMaxNumCols() {
    return(myMaxGridWidth);
  }

  /**
   * @return the width of the maze walls.
   */
  public int getColWidth() {
    return(mySquareSize);
  }
```

```
/**
 * @return the number of maze columns the display is divided into.
 */
public int getNumCols() {
  return(myGridWidth);
}


//-------------------------------------------------------
//    initialization and game state changes

/**
 * Constructor initializes the maze dimension data.
 * @param screenWidth the width of the play area in pixels
 * @param screenHeight the height of the play area in pixels
 */
MazeGame(int screenWidth, int screenHeight) {
  myScreenWidth = screenWidth;
  myScreenHeight = screenHeight;

  // Calculate how many rows and columns of maze
  // can (and should) be placed on the screen.
  mySquareSize = PrefsStorage.getSquareSize();
  myMinSquareSize = 5;
  myMaxGridWidth = myScreenWidth / myMinSquareSize;
  if((myMaxGridWidth & 0x1) == 0) {
    myMaxGridWidth -= 1;
  }
  myGridWidth = myScreenWidth / mySquareSize;
  if((myGridWidth & 0x1) == 0) {
    myGridWidth -= 1;
  }
  myGridHeight = myScreenHeight / mySquareSize;
  if((myGridHeight & 0x1) == 0) {
    myGridHeight -= 1;
  }
  myMinGridWidth = 15;
  myMaxSquareSize = myScreenWidth / myMinGridWidth;
  if(myMaxSquareSize > myScreenHeight / myMinGridWidth) {
    myMaxSquareSize = myScreenHeight / myMinGridWidth;
  }
  // Center the maze in the screen:
  myStartX = (myScreenWidth - (myGridWidth*mySquareSize))/2;
  myStartY = (myScreenHeight - (myGridHeight*mySquareSize))/2;
}

/**
 * discard the current maze.
 */
void clearGrid() {
  myGameOver = false;
  // throw away the current maze.
  myGrid = null;
  // set the player back to the beginning of the maze.
  myPlayerX = 1;
  myPlayerY = 1;
```

```java
}

/**
 * discard the current maze and draw a new one.
 */
void newMaze() {
  clearGrid();
  // paint the new maze
  MazeScreen.getInstance().paintMaze();
}

/**
 * Draw a new maze when the size is changed.
 * This is used only in the RIMlet version
 * of the game (not the MIDlet version),
 * to initialize new maze data when the BB platform
 * notifies the MazeScreen that it has been exposed,
 * after the SelectScreen is popped off the screen stack.
 */
void doneResize() {
  if(myGrid == null) {
    MazeScreen.getInstance().paintMaze();
  }
}

//----------------------------------------------------------
//   graphics and game actions

/**
 * Create and display a maze if necessary, otherwise just
 * move the player. For simplicity we repaint the whole
 * maze each time, but this could be optimized by painting
 * just the player and erasing the square that the player
 * just left.
 */
void drawMaze(Graphics g) {
  // If there is no current maze, create one and draw it.
  if(myGrid == null) {
    // create the underlying data of the maze.
    myGrid = new Grid(myGridWidth, myGridHeight);
  }
  // draw the maze:
  // loop through the grid data and color each square the
  // right color
  for(int i = 0; i < myGridWidth; i++) {
      for(int j = 0; j < myGridHeight; j++) {
        if(myGrid.isWall(i, j)) {
          g.setColor(BLACK);
        } else {
          g.setColor(WHITE);
        }
        // fill the square with the appropriate color
        g.fillRect(myStartX + (i*mySquareSize),
                   myStartY + (j*mySquareSize),
                   mySquareSize, mySquareSize);
```

```
        }
      }
      // fill the extra space outside of the maze
      g.setColor(BLACK);
      g.fillRect(myStartX + ((myGridWidth) * mySquareSize),
                 myStartY, myScreenWidth, myScreenHeight);
      g.fillRect(myStartX,
                 myStartY + ((myGridHeight) * mySquareSize),
                 myScreenWidth, myScreenHeight);
      g.fillRect(0, 0, myStartX, myScreenHeight);
      g.fillRect(0, 0, myScreenWidth, myStartY);
      // erase the exit path:
      g.setColor(WHITE);
      g.fillRect(myStartX + ((myGridWidth) * mySquareSize),
                 myStartY + ((myGridHeight-2) * mySquareSize),
                 mySquareSize + myStartX, mySquareSize);

      // draw the player in gray:
      g.setColor(GRAY);
      g.fillRoundRect(myStartX + (mySquareSize)*myPlayerX,
                      myStartY + (mySquareSize)*myPlayerY,
                      mySquareSize, mySquareSize,
                      mySquareSize, mySquareSize);
    }

    /**
     * Handle user input.
     * @param direction the code to tell which direction the user selected.
     * @return whether the user exits the maze on this move.
     */
    boolean move(int direction) {
      MazeScreen screen = MazeScreen.getInstance();
      if(! myGameOver) {
        switch(direction) {
          case MazeScreen.LEFT:
            if(!myGrid.isWall(myPlayerX-1, myPlayerY) &&
               (myPlayerX != 1)) {
              myPlayerX -= 2;
              screen.paintMaze();
            }
            break;
          case MazeScreen.RIGHT:
            if(!myGrid.isWall(myPlayerX+1, myPlayerY)) {
              myPlayerX += 2;
              if(myPlayerX == myGridWidth) {
                myGameOver = true;
              }
              screen.paintMaze();
            }
            break;
          case MazeScreen.UP:
            if(!myGrid.isWall(myPlayerX, myPlayerY-1)) {
              myPlayerY -= 2;
              screen.paintMaze();
            }
```

```
            break;
        case MazeScreen.DOWN:
            if(!myGrid.isWall(myPlayerX, myPlayerY+1)) {
                myPlayerY += 2;
                screen.paintMaze();
            }
            break;
        default:
            break;
    }
}
return myGameOver;
}

}
```

The Graphics object is always associated with a virtual drawing surface. It's like a drawing pen that can be used draw things like lines, shapes, text, or images onto its underlying drawing surface. The surface can be a region of the screen itself, or it can be an image buffer in memory. The drawMaze() method in Listing 3-1 is designed to draw the maze without regard for what type of surface it's drawing on.

The coordinates of the drawing surface are given in pixels, with (0, 0) representing the top-left corner. Drawing with the Graphics class is a little like graphing a function in mathematics, except that the value of the y coordinate increases as you go down instead of up.

In the Maze example, the drawing surface will cover the entire screen, so the MazeGame object is initialized with the actual length and width of the device's display. Then, in the constructor, you do some calculations to decide how large a grid of squares will fit on the screen, given the square size that the user selected (as you'll see in Listing 3-3). You draw the maze itself in the drawMaze() method by coloring some of the grid squares black (to represent the maze walls) and others white (to represent the path that the player can follow). Figure 3-1 shows what the finished maze looks like.

Figure 3-1. *The BB Maze example running on the 7290 simulator*

> **Note** Centering objects on the screen often involves dividing values by 2. For readability, I usually just use the division operator in code examples. But you should be aware that when dividing by powers of 2, the shift operator does the same thing and is more efficient. In other words, x / 2 is the same as x >> 1. Some compilers may perform this optimization for you behind the scenes.

Now all you need is the data to decide which squares are walls and which are paths. That's computed in Listing 3-2.

Listing 3-2. *Grid.java*

```java
package net.frogparrot.maze;

import java.util.Random;
import java.util.Vector;

/**
 * This class contains the data necessary to draw the maze.
 */
public class Grid {

  /**
   * Random number generator to create a random maze.
   */
  private Random myRandom = new Random();

  /**
   * data for which squares are filled and which are blank.
   * 0 = black
   * 1 = white
   * values higher than 1 are used during the maze creation
   * algorithm.
   * 2 = the square could possibly be appended to the maze this round.
   * 3 = the square will be white but is
   * not close enough to be appended to the maze this round.
   */
  private int[][] mySquares;

//----------------------------------------------------------
// accessors

  /**
   * @return whether the current square is filled
   * (part of the wall).
   * @param x the X-coordinate in the grid's coordinate
   *          system (not screen graphics coordinates).
   * @param y the Y-coordinate in the grid's coordinate
   *          system (not screen graphics coordinates).
   */
  public boolean isWall(int x, int y) {
    // anything outside the maze is not a wall:
    if((x < 0)
       || (y < 0)
```

```
          || (x >= mySquares.length)
          || (y >= mySquares[0].length)) {
        return false;
      }
      return mySquares[x][y] == 0;
    }

//----------------------------------------------------------
//   maze generation methods

  /**
   * Create a new maze.
   */
  Grid(int width, int height) {
    mySquares = new int[width][height];
    // initialize all of the squares to white except a lattice
    // framework of black squares.
    for(int i = 1; i < width - 1; i++) {
      for(int j = 1; j < height - 1; j++) {
        if(((i & 0x1) != 0) || ((j & 0x1) !=0)) {
          mySquares[i][j] = 1;
        }
      }
    }
    // the entrance to the maze is at (0,1).
    mySquares[0][1] = 1;
    // the exit is at (width - 1, height - 2)
    mySquares[width-1][height-2] = 1;
    createMaze();
  }

  /**
   * This method randomly generates the maze.
   */
  private void createMaze() {
    // create an initial framework of black squares.
    for(int i = 1; i < mySquares.length - 1; i++) {
      for(int j = 1; j < mySquares[i].length - 1; j++) {
        if(((i + j) & 0x1) != 0) {
          mySquares[i][j] = 0;
        }
      }
    }
    // initialize the squares that will be white and act
    // as vertices: set the value to 3, which means the
    // square has not been connected to the maze tree.
    for(int i = 1; i < mySquares.length - 1; i+=2) {
      for(int j = 1; j < mySquares[i].length - 1; j+=2) {
        mySquares[i][j] = 3;
      }
    }
    // Then those squares that can be selected to be open
    // (white) paths are given the value of 2.
    // We randomly select the square where the tree of maze
    // paths will begin. The maze is generated starting from
```

```java
        // this initial square and branches out from here in all
        // directions to fill the maze grid.
        Vector possibleSquares = new Vector(mySquares.length
                                    * mySquares[0].length);
        int[] startSquare = new int[2];
        startSquare[0] = getRandomInt(mySquares.length / 2)*2 + 1;
        startSquare[1] = getRandomInt(mySquares[0].length / 2)*2 + 1;
        mySquares[startSquare[0]][startSquare[1]] = 2;
        possibleSquares.addElement(startSquare);
        // Here we loop to select squares one by one to append to
        // the maze pathway tree.
        while(possibleSquares.size() > 0) {
            // the next square to be joined on is selected randomly.
            int chosenIndex = getRandomInt(possibleSquares.size());
            int[] chosenSquare = (int[])possibleSquares.elementAt(chosenIndex);
            // we set the chosen square to white and then
            // remove it from the list of possibleSquares (i.e. squares
            // that can possibly be added to the maze), and we link
            // the new square to the maze.
            mySquares[chosenSquare[0]][chosenSquare[1]] = 1;
            possibleSquares.removeElementAt(chosenIndex);
            link(chosenSquare, possibleSquares);
        }
        // now that the maze has been completely generated, we
        // throw away the objects that were created during the
        // maze creation algorithm and reclaim the memory.
        possibleSquares = null;
        System.gc();
    }

    /**
     * internal to createMaze. Checks the four squares surrounding
     * the chosen square. Of those that are already connected to
     * the maze, one is randomly selected to be joined to the
     * current square (to attach the current square to the
     * growing maze). Those squares that were not previously in
     * a position to be joined to the maze are added to the list
     * of "possible" squares (that could be chosen to be attached
     * to the maze in the next round).
     */
    private void link(int[] chosenSquare, Vector possibleSquares) {
        int linkCount = 0;
        int i = chosenSquare[0];
        int j = chosenSquare[1];
        int[] links = new int[8];
        if(i >= 3) {
            if(mySquares[i - 2][j] == 1) {
                links[2*linkCount] = i - 1;
                links[2*linkCount + 1] = j;
                linkCount++;
            } else if(mySquares[i - 2][j] == 3) {
                mySquares[i - 2][j] = 2;
                int[] newSquare = new int[2];
                newSquare[0] = i - 2;
                newSquare[1] = j;
```

```
          possibleSquares.addElement(newSquare);
        }
      }
      if(j + 3 <= mySquares[i].length) {
        if(mySquares[i][j + 2] == 3) {
          mySquares[i][j + 2] = 2;
          int[] newSquare = new int[2];
          newSquare[0] = i;
          newSquare[1] = j + 2;
          possibleSquares.addElement(newSquare);
        } else if(mySquares[i][j + 2] == 1) {
          links[2*linkCount] = i;
          links[2*linkCount + 1] = j + 1;
          linkCount++;
        }
      }
      if(j >= 3) {
        if(mySquares[i][j - 2] == 3) {
          mySquares[i][j - 2] = 2;
          int[] newSquare = new int[2];
          newSquare[0] = i;
          newSquare[1] = j - 2;
          possibleSquares.addElement(newSquare);
        } else if(mySquares[i][j - 2] == 1) {
          links[2*linkCount] = i;
          links[2*linkCount + 1] = j - 1;
          linkCount++;
        }
      }
      if(i + 3 <= mySquares.length) {
        if(mySquares[i + 2][j] == 3) {
          mySquares[i + 2][j] = 2;
          int[] newSquare = new int[2];
          newSquare[0] = i + 2;
          newSquare[1] = j;
          possibleSquares.addElement(newSquare);
        } else if(mySquares[i + 2][j] == 1) {
          links[2*linkCount] = i + 1;
          links[2*linkCount + 1] = j;
          linkCount++;
        }
      }
      if(linkCount > 0) {
        int linkChoice = getRandomInt(linkCount);
        int linkX = links[2*linkChoice];
        int linkY = links[2*linkChoice + 1];
        mySquares[linkX][linkY] = 1;
        int[] removeSquare = new int[2];
        removeSquare[0] = linkX;
        removeSquare[1] = linkY;
        possibleSquares.removeElement(removeSquare);
      }
    }

  /**
```

```
 * a randomization utility.
 * @param upper the upper bound for the random int.
 * @return a random nonnegative int less than the bound upper.
 */
int getRandomInt(int upper) {
  int retVal = myRandom.nextInt() % upper;
  if(retVal < 0) {
    retVal += upper;
  }
  return(retVal);
}

}
```

As you can see, the logic of how to create the random maze is completely isolated in this class. See the "Understanding the Maze Algorithm" sidebar for how it works. All that the other classes need to do to create a new maze is create an instance of Grid with valid grid dimensions, and then use the isWall() accessor to decide which squares are empty path squares and which squares are filled wall squares.

UNDERSTANDING THE MAZE ALGORITHM

Like a lot of game algorithms, creating a random maze just takes a little bit of mathematical reasoning. Think of the pathways through the maze as being a graph. The vertices are the points where two pathways join or where you might turn, and the pathways connecting the vertices are the edges. It's clear that for a maze, you want your graph to be one connected tree—in other words, a graph with no cycles. As long as the entry point and the exit point are part of one connected tree, there will be exactly one path from the beginning to the end.

To apply this idea and create the maze, the first step is to use the screen and graphics dimensions to determine the size of your grid of vertices (how many squares across and how many down). Start by dividing the entire playing field into equal-size squares, which form part of the maze pathways if colored white and part of the maze wall if colored black. You can see in Figure 3-2 that there's a lattice of squares that you know should be black and a lattice that you know should be white. The trick is to figure out which colors to give to the wildcard squares.

In Figure 3-2, all of the squares whose color should be decided by the algorithm are colored gray (note that this screen never appears in the final game). In graph terms, the white squares are the vertices and the gray squares are the squares that might potentially be edges by being added to the maze pathway and turned white. You can see from this that the number of rows and number of columns both need to be odd numbers.

The algorithm works by picking one of the white squares at random from the middle of the grid and growing the tree from there by picking undecided (gray) squares and turning them white. Throughout the algorithm, you maintain a list of all of the white squares (vertices) that are not yet connected to the maze, but are only one gray square away from being linked in. At each round of the algorithm, you use the java.util.Random class to pick one square from the list and attach it to the maze (by turning a gray square white, hence adding an edge to the graph). Then just keep going until there are no white squares left that aren't connected to the maze pathway graph, and color the remaining gray squares black.

Figure 3-2. *The starting point for the maze algorithm*

By only adding edges to connect vertices that weren't already connected to the graph, you can see that you'll never get a cycle. And by growing the graph from one central point, you can be sure that all of the vertices will be connected to the same component. So in the end, for every two white squares in the maze, there's exactly one path that leads from one to the other; notably, there's a unique path from the entry square to the exit square.

When creating the Grid class, there's one optimization point that needs to be taken into consideration for BlackBerry: memory.

Using Memory

BlackBerry devices have limitations on how many Java objects they can hold in memory. For example, a BlackBerry smartphone with 16MB of flash memory can hold 56,000 objects. That's a lot of objects, but keep in mind that that's the count of all of the objects in the entire system, including objects created by the AMS and those created by other applications running in the background.

In general, you should beware of creating lots of complex objects (objects with fields that are other objects), and especially of filling Vectors and Hashtables with complex objects. In Listing 3-2, the maze algorithm uses a Vector when constructing the maze data, but, as you can see in the constructor, the Vector is freed for garbage collection as soon as it is no longer needed. Another possible optimization might be to clear and reuse the Grid object when creating a new maze rather than creating a new instance of

Grid each time. Ultimately, the number of objects remains the same, but releasing one Grid instance to create another adds some extra work for the garbage collector. That's why many of the classes in this chapter are singletons (which are released for garbage collection when the game ends) if only one instance of the class is necessary.

BlackBerry devices also have limitations on the use of persistent storage. The RIM device platform has built-in functionality for serializing objects in persistent memory, using net.rim.device.api.system.PersistentStore and net.rim.device.api.system.PersistentObject. Like the number of live objects, the number of persistent objects is also limited, and in this case you have more to worry about from competition with other applications since the other applications' data remains in storage whether the application is running or not.

The Maze game uses a tiny amount of persistent storage—just enough to store the user's preferred square size. The maze walls can vary in width, which affects the complexity of the maze. The user can change the square size, and if he does, the application saves the chosen square size. Then that's the size the maze grid squares will be the next time the user plays the game, even if the device is powered down and the battery is removed between plays.

Since we're optimizing the BB Maze and MIDP Maze examples for cross-platform compatibility, the PrefsStorage class (Listing 3-3) uses the MIDP Record Management System (RMS), which is available on every MIDP device. For applications that require a more complex file structure, the File Connection API (of JSR 75) would be a better choice.

The MIDP RMS on BlackBerry doesn't have the same size restrictions as the RIM persistent object store. From BlackBerry version 4.1 and up, the size of an individual RecordStore is limited at either 64KB or 512KB, but the total amount of memory that can be assigned for use by the MIDP RMS is only limited by how much free memory remains in the device. There can still be optimization issues, however, because a device typically sets aside a fixed-size block of memory when a RecordStore is created (and when a Record is created in the RecordStore), and the default block size can vary from one device to another.

Listing 3-3. *PrefsStorage.java*

```java
package net.frogparrot.maze;

import javax.microedition.rms.*;

/**
 * This class helps to store and retrieve the data about
 * the maze size preferences.
 *
 * This is a utility class that does not contain instance data,
 * so to simplify access, all of the methods are static.
 */
public class PrefsStorage {

//-----------------------------------------------------------
//    static fields

  /**
   * The name of the datastore.
```

```
    */
    private static final String STORE = "SizePrefs";

//-------------------------------------------------------------
//   business methods

  /**
   * This gets the preferred square size from the stored data.
   */
  public static int getSquareSize() {
    // if data retrieval fails, the default value is 7
    int retVal = 7;
    RecordStore store = null;
    try {
      // if the record store does not yet exist, we
      // send "false" so it won't bother to create it.
      store = RecordStore.openRecordStore(STORE, false);
      if((store != null) && (store.getNumRecords() > 0)) {
        // the first record has id number 1
        // (In fact this program stores only one record)
        byte[] rec = store.getRecord(1);
        retVal = rec[0];
      }
    } catch(Exception e) {
      // data storage is not critical for this game and we're
      // not creating a log, so if data retrieval fails, we
      // just skip it and move on.
    } finally {
      try {
        store.closeRecordStore();
      } catch(Exception e) {
        // if the record store is open this shouldn't throw.
      }
    }
    return(retVal);
  }

  /**
   * This saves the preferred square size.
   */
  public static void setSquareSize(int size) {
    RecordStore store = null;
    try {
      // since we are storing the int as a single byte,
      // it is very important that its value be less than 128.
      // This could be changed to serialize and store a whole int.
      if(size > 127) {
        size = 127;
      }
      // if the record store does not yet exist, the second
      // arg "true" tells it to create.
      store = RecordStore.openRecordStore(STORE, true);
      byte[] record = new byte[1];
      record[0] = (new Integer(size)).byteValue();
      int numRecords = store.getNumRecords();
```

```
     if(numRecords > 0) {
       store.setRecord(1, record, 0, 1);
     } else {
       store.addRecord(record, 0, 1);
     }
   } catch(Exception e) {
     // data storage is not critical for this game, and we're
     // not creating a log, so if data storage fails, we
     // just skip it and move on.
   } finally {
     try {
       store.closeRecordStore();
     } catch(Exception e) {
       // if the record store is open, this shouldn't throw.
     }
   }
 }

}
```

A MIDP `RecordStore` is a numbered collection of `byte` arrays. If the data to store is more complex than a `byte` array, the MIDlet is responsible for serializing or unserializing its own data into `byte` array format. Each `RecordStore` is associated with a MIDlet suite (the collection of MIDlets within a single JAR file), and it's deleted if the MIDlet suite is deleted.

> **Note** Although a game's MIDP record stores are deleted when the game is deleted, the same is not true for BlackBerry persistent objects or files created with JSR 75's File Connection API. You should take this into account when deciding which type of persistence is best for your application.

Each MIDlet can create multiple `RecordStores`. It gives the `RecordStore` a name (`String`) when creating it in order to identify it when opening it again later. The MIDlets within a single MIDlet suite can access each other's `RecordStores` but can't normally access the `RecordStores` of other MIDlet suites—unless the MIDlet specifies `AUTHMODE_ANY` when creating the `RecordStore`, in which case any MIDlet on the device can access it.

Even though the MIDP RMS specification only covers MIDlets, RIMlets can create and use `RecordStores` as well, as the BB Maze example shows. In general, the MIDP APIs on a BlackBerry device are available to RIMlets just as the RIM APIs on the device are available to MIDlets running on a BlackBerry device. The exceptions—the places where you're forced to choose one or the other—are the life cycle classes (as you saw in Chapter 2), and the graphics, input event handling, and UI classes you'll see in the next section.

Handling Platform Events with MIDP vs. RIM

The maze game logic you've seen so far in the chapter can be applied to either a MIDlet or a RIMlet. In this section you'll create the rest of the game in two versions: a MIDlet version called MIDP Maze and a RIMlet version called BB Maze. You can use this technique to create an automated build that will build a RIMlet version of the game for

BlackBerry and a MIDP version for other devices by having your Ant build file select the right set of classes before building for each device. You don't technically need to create a RIMlet version for the BlackBerry devices (since the MIDlet will run on them), but when you see how much more you can do with a RIMlet—in the Maze Deluxe example in Chapter 4—you may want to.

Even if you don't need to program for MIDlet/RIMlet interoperability in your own games, this side-by-side comparison—the MIDP Maze and BB Maze examples—will show you the differences so you'll know how to choose and use whichever one is best for a given project. After this chapter, we'll just stick with RIMlets for most of the rest of the book (except the checkers game of Chapter 7, which is another example that relies on cross-platform compatibility).

Getting a Handle on the Drawing Surface

Now let's have a look at how to get the right `Graphics` object to draw on the screen.

Listing 3-4 shows how you paint a RIMlet's screen. The `net.rim.device.api.ui.Screen` is designed to allow you to add a set of UI components to it. On the main game screen, all you want is to cover the entire display with a blank canvas to draw on, so—like in Listing 2-4 of the Hello BlackBerry example—you add only one component to the screen. In this case, the component is a `BitmapField` holding a `Bitmap` that is constructed to be the same size as the device's screen.

The `Bitmap` itself is just an image data buffer. In the BB Maze example, you create two `Bitmaps` so that you can draw on one in the background while the other is displayed on the screen. Once you're done drawing on the one in the background, you place it in the `BitmapField` frame, moving it to the foreground of the device's display. This technique is called *double-buffering*. Most MIDP devices double-buffer the screen graphics automatically by having the `paint()` method draw into a back buffer and having the platform move it to the foreground when `paint()` is done. But some MIDP devices may have the `paint()` method write directly onto the current display, so potentially the user could see intermediate drawing steps. Explicitly double-buffering by controlling the two `Bitmap` buffers yourself takes the guesswork out of it.

Listing 3-4. *MazeScreen.java*

```
//#preprocess
package net.frogparrot.maze;

import net.rim.device.api.system.Bitmap;
import net.rim.device.api.ui.Graphics;
import net.rim.device.api.ui.MenuItem;
import net.rim.device.api.ui.XYRect;
import net.rim.device.api.ui.component.BitmapField;
import net.rim.device.api.ui.component.Dialog;
import net.rim.device.api.ui.component.Menu;
import net.rim.device.api.ui.container.MainScreen;
import net.rim.device.api.i18n.ResourceBundle;

/**
```

```java
 * This class represents the main display screen/canvas of the game.
 */
public class MazeScreen extends MainScreen implements MazeResource {

//-----------------------------------------------------------
//   static fields

  /**
   * The input code constants are chosen to match the MIDP GameAction codes.
   */
  public static final int UP = 1;
  public static final int DOWN = 6;
  public static final int LEFT = 2;
  public static final int RIGHT = 5;

  /**
   * This bundle contains all of the texts, translated by locale.
   */
  private static ResourceBundle myLabels =
      ResourceBundle.getBundle(BUNDLE_ID, BUNDLE_NAME);

  /**
   * The single instance of this class.
   */
  private static MazeScreen theInstance;

//-----------------------------------------------------------
//   instance fields

  /**
   * a graphics area.
   */
  private Bitmap myBitmap0;

  /**
   * alternate graphics area.
   */
  private Bitmap myBitmap1;

  /**
   * Which bitmap is currently displayed.
   */
  private Bitmap myCurrentBitmap;

  /**
   * The playing field.
   */
  private BitmapField myBitmapField;

  /**
   * The "new maze" menu item.
   */
  private MenuItem myNewMazeItem = new MenuItem(getLabel(MAZE_NEWMAZE), 0, 0) {
        public void run() {
            MazeGame.getInstance().newMaze();
```

```
        }
      };

  /**
   * The "size selection" menu item.
   */
  private MenuItem mySelectSizeItem
         = new MenuItem(getLabel(MAZE_SELECTSIZE), 0, 0) {
      public void run() {
          Main.getInstance().pushScreen(new SelectScreen());
      }
    };

//-----------------------------------------------------
//    gets / sets

  /**
   * @return the singleton instance of this class.
   */
  public static MazeScreen getInstance() {
    if(theInstance == null) {
      theInstance = new MazeScreen();
    }
    return theInstance;
  }

  /**
   * Delete the singleton instance of this class.
   * (For end-of-game cleanup only)
   */
  static void clearInstance() {
    theInstance = null;
  }

  /**
   * @return a label from the resource bundle resources.
   */
  public static String getLabel(int key){
    return myLabels.getString(key);
  }

//-----------------------------------------------------
//    initialization and game state changes

  /**
   * Create the game and graphics data.
   */
  private MazeScreen() {
    super();

    // prepare the game logic for this screen size:
    // (the nondeprecated versions of these methods require permission)
    int screenWidth = Graphics.getScreenWidth();
    int screenHeight = Graphics.getScreenHeight();
    MazeGame.setInstance(new MazeGame(screenWidth, screenHeight));
```

```java
    // Create two buffers to draw the graphics into:
    // While one is displayed, the other is painted in
    // the background before being flushed to the screen
    myBitmap0 = new Bitmap(screenWidth, screenHeight);
    myBitmap1 = new Bitmap(screenWidth, screenHeight);
    // Wrap the data buffer in a Field object that
    // can be added to this Screen:
    myBitmapField = new BitmapField(myBitmap0);
    add(myBitmapField);
    // paint the initial maze onto the screen:
    paintMaze();
    // One more time to be sure that the second
    // bitmap is initialized:
    paintMaze();
  }

  /**
   * Override the screen's menu creation method
   * to add the custom commands.
   */
  protected void makeMenu(Menu menu, int instance) {
    menu.add(myNewMazeItem);
    menu.add(mySelectSizeItem);
    // separate the custom menu items from
    // the default menu items:
    menu.addSeparator();
    super.makeMenu(menu, instance);
  }

  /**
   * The platform calls this when the screen is popped
   * off the screen stack (triggered by commands that
   * are added by default).
   */
  public boolean onClose() {
    Dialog.alert(getLabel(MAZE_GOODBYE));
    Main.getInstance().terminate();
    return true;
  }

  /**
   * Draw a new maze when the size is changed.
   */
  protected void onExposed() {
    MazeGame.getInstance().doneResize();
  }

//-----------------------------------------------------------
// graphics and game actions

  /**
   * Paint the screen with the current playing board.
   */
  void paintMaze() {
```

```
      Bitmap boardBitmap = getNextBitmap();
      Graphics g = new Graphics(boardBitmap);
      // Here you could optimize by just pushing the region
      // around the player:
      g.pushRegion(new XYRect(0, 0, g.getScreenWidth(), g.getScreenHeight()));
      g.clear();
      // The game logic takes over deciding precisely what to paint:
      MazeGame.getInstance().drawMaze(g);

      // since the region was pushed onto the context stack,
      // it must be popped off:
      g.popContext();
      // set the newly painted bitmap to be visible:
      myBitmapField.setBitmap(boardBitmap);
    }

  /**
   * This method keeps track of which buffer is visible
   * and which is being painted.
   * @return the data buffer to paint into
   */
  private Bitmap getNextBitmap() {
    if(myCurrentBitmap == myBitmap1) {
      myCurrentBitmap = myBitmap0;
    } else {
      myCurrentBitmap = myBitmap1;
    }
    return myCurrentBitmap;
  }

public boolean keyChar(char key, int status, int time) {
    boolean gameOver = false;
    MazeGame game = MazeGame.getInstance();
    // Map the characters to the MIDP game action codes
    // for compatibility. The first character (e.g., 's')
    // corresponds to a QWERTY keyboard, the second (e.g., 'd')
    // is for the models with just a number pad.
    if((key == 's') || (key == 'd')) { //left
      gameOver = game.move(LEFT);
    } else if((key == 'f') || (key == 'j')) { // right
      gameOver = game.move(RIGHT);
    } else if((key == 'e') || (key == 't')) { // up
      gameOver = game.move(UP);
    } else if((key == 'x') || (key == 'b')) { // down
      gameOver = game.move(DOWN);
    } else {
      // the keystroke was not relevant to this game
      return false;
    }
    // congratulate the player for winning:
    if(gameOver) {
      Dialog.alert(getLabel(MAZE_CONGRATS));
      game.newMaze();
    }
    // the keystroke was used by this game
```

```
      return true;
    }

//#ifndef RIM_4.1.0
  /**
    * The BB platform calls this method to notify
    * the screen of user keyboard input.
    * @return true if the application used the input
    *          false to pass it along
    */
  public boolean navigationMovement(int dx,
                                    int dy,
                                    int status,
                                    int time) {
    boolean gameOver = false;
    MazeGame game = MazeGame.getInstance();
    // Map the movement to the MIDP game action codes
    // for compatibility:
    if(dx < 0) { //left
      gameOver = game.move(LEFT);
    } else if(dx > 0) { // right
      gameOver = game.move(RIGHT);
    } else if(dy > 0) { // down
        gameOver = game.move(DOWN);
    } else if(dy < 0) { // up
        gameOver = game.move(UP);
    } else {
      // the motion was not relevant to this game
      return false;
    }
    // congratulate the player for winning:
    if(gameOver) {
      Dialog.alert(getLabel(MAZE_CONGRATS));
      game.newMaze();
    }
    // the motion was used by this game
    return true;
  }
//#endif

}
```

Looking in the paintMaze() method, you can see that you create the Graphics object for drawing on the Bitmap drawing surface. Contrast this with the corresponding class for the MIDP Maze version of this class in Listing 3-5. The Graphics object for drawing on the MIDP Canvas is provided by the platform when the AMS calls paint() to paint the screen.

In either case, the MazeGame class (Listing 3-1) calls paintMaze() to update the screen after the player moves, but the control flow that comes next is a little different in the two examples. In the MIDP Maze version (Listing 3-5), paintMaze() merely calls repaint() in order to prompt the platform to queue a paint request. When the platform is ready, it calls MazeScreen's paint(), providing the Graphics object to paint on the Canvas, and then MazeScreen passes the Graphics along to MazeGame by calling the drawMaze() method to draw the maze. In the BB Maze version (Listing 3-4), the paintMaze() method (called by MazeGame after the player moves) creates the Graphics object for the Bitfield and then passes it along to call MazeGame's drawMaze() method. It is only after the maze drawing is done and the new Bitmap is placed in the BitmapField that the platform gets into the act and updates the display.

Listing 3-5. *MazeScreen.java*

```java
package net.frogparrot.maze;

import javax.microedition.lcdui.*;

/**
 * This class represents the main display screen/canvas of the game.
 */
public class MazeScreen extends javax.microedition.lcdui.Canvas {

//-------------------------------------------------------------
//   static fields

  /**
   * The single instance of this class.
   */
  private static MazeScreen theInstance;

//-------------------------------------------------------------
//   instance fields

  /**
   * a handle to the display.
   */
  private Display myDisplay;

//-------------------------------------------------------------
//    gets / sets

  /**
   * @return the singleton instance of this class.
   */
  public static MazeScreen getInstance() {
    return theInstance;
  }

  /**
   * Delete the singleton instance of this class.
   * (For end-of-game cleanup only)
   */
  static void clearInstance() {
    theInstance = null;
  }

//-------------------------------------------------------------
//    initialization and game state changes

  /**
   * Create the game and graphics data.
```

```java
    */
  public MazeScreen(Display d) throws Exception {
    myDisplay = d;
    // prepare the game logic for this screen size:
    int width = getWidth();
    int height = getHeight();

    MazeGame.setInstance(new MazeGame(width, height));
    theInstance = this;
  }

  /**
   * discard the current maze and draw a new one.
   */
  void newMaze() {
    MazeGame.getInstance().newMaze();
    paintMaze();
  }
//----------------------------------------------------------
//  graphics and game actions

  /**
   * Set the canvas to be visible and paint it.
   */
  public void paintMaze() {
    myDisplay.setCurrent(this);
    repaint();
  }

  /**
   * This overrides Canvas#paint, and is called by
   * the platform after a repaint() request.
   */
  protected void paint(Graphics g) {
    MazeGame.getInstance().drawMaze(g);
  }

  /**
   * This is called by the platform when the user presses a key.
   */
  public void keyPressed(int keyCode) {
    int action = getGameAction(keyCode);
    boolean gameOver = MazeGame.getInstance().move(action);
    if(gameOver) {
      // create a new maze that will
      // appear once the alert is dismissed:
      MazeGame.getInstance().newMaze();
      // create the alert with the default
      // alert behavior: a default dismiss
      // command with a displayable to display
      // after the alert is dismissed
      myDisplay.setCurrent(new Alert("Done", "Great Job!",
          null, AlertType.INFO), this);
    }
  }
```

```
}
```

Handling User Input Events

The code in Listings 3-4 and 3-5 also shows how to handle user input from the keypad and from the trackball or optical trackpad. In each case, all you have to do is override the methods that the platform calls in response to user input. (Handling input from the touchscreen and from the accelerometer is covered in Chapter 6.)

In the MIDP Maze case (Listing 3-5), the platform calls the keyPressed() method of the javax.microedition.lcdui.Canvas class with a code indicating which key was pressed. Since MIDP devices can have all sorts of different types of keyboards, the keyCode values are not standardized—the mapping between the keyCode value and the corresponding key varies from one device to the next. That's why you have to interpret the value with the getGameAction() method, which tells you whether the key press action logically corresponds to a navigation action. The getGameAction() method maps the action to the constants UP, DOWN, LEFT, and RIGHT, which can be used to move the player in the MazeGame.move() method (see Listing 3-1).

The keyChar() and navigationMovement() methods in the BB Maze example (Listing 3-4) are even more intuitive than the MIDP Maze version because the platform gives you the actual character that was typed into the keypad (or the delta distance navigated by the trackball movement) instead of mapping the input to cryptic key code values. In this example, you map the character or delta value to the MIDP game action codes before passing the action along to MazeGame.move() so that the two versions of MazeScreen are both compatible with the same MazeGame class.

The navigationMovement() method in Listing 3-4 only gives four-way movement events for BlackBerry devices that have a trackball. That's why the method is surrounded in preprocessing directives to eliminate it when the class is compiled for trackwheel devices; otherwise, it would cause linking errors at runtime. Since it's confusing to accept one-dimensional trackwheel input for two-dimensional maze navigation, the trackwheel input is merely ignored.

The menu command implementation in Listings 3-4 and 3-5 shouldn't offer any surprises since it's the same as the implementation in the Hello World examples in Listings 2-2 and 2-4. The missing piece is the implementation of the MIDP Maze commands, which (like in the Hello MIDP example) takes place in the MIDlet class given in Listing 3-6.

Listing 3-6. *Maze.java*

```java
package net.frogparrot.maze;

import javax.microedition.midlet.*;
import javax.microedition.lcdui.*;

/**
 * This is the main class of the maze game.
 */
public class Maze extends MIDlet implements CommandListener {
```

```java
//------------------------------------------------------------------
//   command fields

  /**
   * The command to exit the game. On BlackBerry, it's placed in a menu.
   */
  private Command myExitCommand = new Command("Exit", Command.EXIT, 99);

  /**
   * The command to create a new maze. On BlackBerry, it's placed in a menu.
   */
  private Command myNewCommand = new Command("New Maze", Command.SCREEN, 1);

  /**
   * The command to go to the screen that allows the user
   * to alter the size parameters. On BlackBerry, it's placed in a menu.
   */
  private Command myPrefsCommand
    = new Command("Size Preferences", Command.SCREEN, 1);

//------------------------------------------------------------------
//   implementation of MIDlet

  /**
   * Start the application.
   */
  public void startApp() throws MIDletStateChangeException {
    try {
      MazeScreen screen = new MazeScreen(Display.getDisplay(this));
      screen.addCommand(myExitCommand);
      screen.addCommand(myNewCommand);
      screen.addCommand(myPrefsCommand);
      screen.setCommandListener(this);
      screen.paintMaze();
    } catch(Exception e) {
      System.out.println("startApp caught: " + e);
      e.printStackTrace();
    }
  }

  /**
   * Clean up.
   */
  public void destroyApp(boolean unconditional)
      throws MIDletStateChangeException {
    MazeGame.setInstance(null);
    MazeScreen.clearInstance();
    SelectScreen.clearInstance();
    System.gc();
  }

  /**
   * Does nothing since this program occupies no shared resources
   * and little memory.
```

```
    */
    public void pauseApp() {
    }


//-----------------------------------------------------------------
//  implementation of CommandListener

  /*
   * Respond to a command issued on the Canvas.
   * (reset, exit, or change size prefs).
   */
  public void commandAction(Command c, Displayable s) {
    MazeScreen screen = MazeScreen.getInstance();
    if(c == myNewCommand) {
      screen.newMaze();
    } else if(c == myPrefsCommand) {
      Display.getDisplay(this).setCurrent(SelectScreen.getInstance());
    } else if(c == myExitCommand) {
      try {
        destroyApp(false);
        notifyDestroyed();
      } catch (MIDletStateChangeException ex) {
      }
    }
  }

}
```

As in the Hello BB example, the life cycle class for BB Maze (Listing 3-7) doesn't handle the command input.

Listing 3-7. *Main.java*

```
package net.frogparrot.maze;

import net.rim.device.api.ui.UiApplication;

/**
 * The life cycle class.
 *
 * @author Carol Hamer
 */
public class Main extends UiApplication {

//-----------------------------------------------------------
//   static fields

  /**
   * The single instance of this application.
   */
  static Main theInstance;


//-----------------------------------------------------------
//   accessors

  /**
```

```
   * @return the single instance of this application.
   */
  public static Main getInstance() {
    return theInstance;
  }

//-----------------------------------------------------------
//    life cycle methods

  /**
   * The BlackBerry platform calls this when it launches
   * the application.
   */
  public static void main(String[] args) {
    try {
      theInstance = new Main();
      // create the application's main screen and
      // push it onto the top of the screen stack:
      theInstance.pushScreen(MazeScreen.getInstance());
      // Set this thread to notify this application for
      // events such as user input.
      theInstance.enterEventDispatcher();
    } catch(Exception e) {
      System.out.println("main caught: " + e);
      e.printStackTrace();
    }
  }

  /**
   * Exit the game.
   */
  void terminate() {
    // cleanup:
    MazeGame.setInstance(null);
    MazeScreen.clearInstance();
    System.gc();
    // You must actively end the program,
    // just popping the base screen off the
    // stack isn't sufficient.
    System.exit(0);
  }

}
```

Now you have almost all of the pieces you need to build the two versions of the maze game. Listings 3-1, 3-2, 3-3, 3-5, and 3-7 combine to form MIDP Maze, and Listings 3-1, 3-2, 3-3, 3-4, and 3-6 combine to form BB Maze. In each case there's just one piece missing: the graphical user interface (GUI) screen that allows the user to select the dimensions of the maze.

Using GUI Components

In addition to the play area, a game typically also has some UI screens for actions like entering your name when you get a high score or selecting an opponent to play against. Naturally, you can implement the UI functionality yourself, just by drawing all of the widgets onto a blank canvas and then interpreting the keystroke and navigation data, in the same way that you implement the main part of the game. But since a UI is usually composed of standard components—a set of input widgets on a stack of screens—you can take advantage of the platform's built-in UI functionality to create widgets that match the device's standard navigation style.

Both MIDP and RIM offer a set of built-in classes for standard widgets such as text input fields and choice lists. Unfortunately, the MIDP user interface package—called LCDUI (Limited Capability Device User Interface)—is a lot more limited than you want for a professional game. The philosophy is that the device knows better than you do how to lay out the UI, so it takes care of the look and feel completely. Unfortunately, you don't have the option to override the default look and feel even when you do know what you're doing. And the MIDP widgets are so ugly—on every device I've ever seen—that they're not appropriate for use in a professional game. Just look at the size selection screen for the maze game (using default widgets) in Figure 3-3.

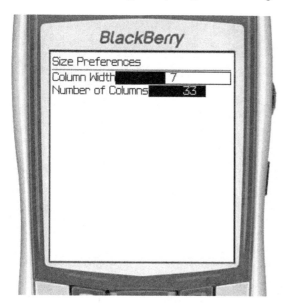

Figure 3-3. *The size selection screen of the MIDP Maze example running on the 7100r simulator*

Inability to customize the UI is one of the biggest design flaws in MIDP. In MIDP, you have three choices:

- Create an ugly, generic UI that doesn't have any of your game's colors or images.

- Reinvent the wheel by drawing your widgets on a blank canvas and interpreting the different key codes for all of your target devices to implement all of the widget navigation and functionality for the UI.

- Use a third-party solution such as J2ME Polish.

One third-party solution to be aware of is Sun's open source Lightweight UI Toolkit (LWUIT). The LWUIT is based on Swing—just like the RIM UI classes—so a lot of the classes in these two APIs are nearly identical. To create a cross-platform application from a single code base, you can use preprocessing to import the RIM classes when building for BlackBerry, and import the corresponding LWUIT classes when building for another platform (just as the MazeGame class from Listing 3-1 was written to be compatible with either version of the Graphics class). It's also possible to use the LWUIT classes on BlackBerry, but there's no particular reason to do that when you have access to a native optimized-for-BlackBerry-by-RIM version of the same API. For simplicity, however, in the MIDP Maze example, we'll go with the first choice (in Listing 3-8) and create a javax.microedition.lcdui.Screen with two javax.microedition.lcudui.Gauge objects on it. The first one will allow the user to select the size of the squares that make up the maze walls, and the second will show the user the corresponding number of columns that will fit on the screen.

Listing 3-8. *SelectScreen.java*

```java
package net.frogparrot.maze;

import javax.microedition.midlet.*;
import javax.microedition.lcdui.*;

/**
 * This is the screen that allows the user to modify the
 * width of the maze walls.
 */
public class SelectScreen extends Form
  implements ItemStateListener, CommandListener  {

//------------------------------------------------------------
//   static fields

  /**
   * The single instance of this class.
   */
  private static SelectScreen theInstance;

//------------------------------------------------------------
//   instance fields

  /**
   * The "Done" button to exit this screen and return to the maze.
   */
  private Command myExitCommand = new Command("Done", Command.EXIT, 1);

  /**
   * The gauge that modifies the width of the maze walls.
   */
```

```
    private Gauge myWidthGauge;

  /**
   * The gauge that displays the number of columns of the maze.
   */
  private Gauge myColumnsGauge;

//--------------------------------------------------------
//    gets / sets

  public static SelectScreen getInstance() {
    if(theInstance == null) {
      theInstance = new SelectScreen();
    }
    return theInstance;
  }

  static void clearInstance() {
    theInstance = null;
  }

//---------------------------------------------------------
//   initialization

  /**
   * Create the gauges and place them on the screen.
   */
  public SelectScreen() {
    super("Size Preferences");
    addCommand(myExitCommand);
    setCommandListener(this);
    setItemStateListener(this);
    //myCanvas = canvas;
    MazeGame game = MazeGame.getInstance();
    myWidthGauge = new Gauge("Column Width", true,
                             game.getMaxColWidth(),
                             game.getColWidth());
    myColumnsGauge = new Gauge("Number of Columns", false,
                               game.getMaxNumCols(),
                               game.getNumCols());
    myWidthGauge.setLayout(Item.LAYOUT_CENTER);
    myColumnsGauge.setLayout(Item.LAYOUT_CENTER);
    append(myWidthGauge);
    append(myColumnsGauge);
  }

//---------------------------------------------------------
//   implementation of ItemStateListener

  /**
   * Respond to the user changing the width.
   */
  public void itemStateChanged(Item item) {
    if(item == myWidthGauge) {
      MazeGame game = MazeGame.getInstance();
```

```
      int val = myWidthGauge.getValue();
      if(val < game.getMinColWidth()) {
        myWidthGauge.setValue(game.getMinColWidth());
      } else {
        int numCols = game.setColWidth(val);
        myColumnsGauge.setValue(numCols);
      }
    }
  }
}

//----------------------------------------------------------
//  implementation of CommandListener

  /*
   * Respond to the exit command.
   */
  public void commandAction(Command c, Displayable s) {
    if(c == myExitCommand) {
      PrefsStorage.setSquareSize(myWidthGauge.getValue());
      MazeScreen.getInstance().paintMaze();
    }
  }

}
```

You can see that the widgets themselves receive input through the ItemStateListener
interface, which receives events for all of the Items (widgets) in the screen in much the
same way that MIDP LCDUI command events are all grouped by screen and sent to a
single listener interface. As you might expect, the RIM Fields (widgets) receive their
own events in the same way as the RIM MenuItems from Listings 2-4 and 3-4, so you
have to provide your own subclass implementations. As with the earlier MenuItems, the
command functionality of myWidthGauge in Listing 3-9 is implemented with an
anonymous inner class.

Listing 3-9. *SelectScreen.java*

```
package net.frogparrot.maze;

import net.rim.device.api.ui.*;
import net.rim.device.api.ui.component.*;
import net.rim.device.api.ui.container.*;

/**
 * This is the screen that allows the user to modify the
 * width of the maze walls.
 */
public class SelectScreen extends MainScreen {

//----------------------------------------------------------
//  fields

  /**
   * The gauge that modifies the width of the maze walls.
   */
  private GaugeField myWidthGauge;
```

```
    /**
     * The gauge that displays the number of columns of the maze.
     */
    private GaugeField myColumnsGauge;

//----------------------------------------------------------
//  initialization

    /**
     * Create the gauges and place them on the screen.
     */
    SelectScreen() {
      MazeGame game = MazeGame.getInstance();

      LabelField title
            = new LabelField(MazeScreen.getLabel(MazeScreen.MAZE_SELECTSIZE),
          LabelField.HCENTER );
      setTitle(title);
      // create the gauge that allows the user to modify the width of the columns
      myWidthGauge = new GaugeField(MazeScreen.getLabel(MazeScreen.MAZE_COLWIDTH),
                            game.getMinColWidth(),
                            game.getMaxColWidth(),
                            game.getColWidth(),
                            Field.FOCUSABLE | Field.EDITABLE
                                         | Field.HIGHLIGHT_SELECT){
        protected void fieldChangeNotify(int context) {
          int val = getValue();
          int numCols = MazeGame.getInstance().setColWidth(val);
          myColumnsGauge.setValue(numCols);
        }
      };

      // Since the number of columns depends on the cloumn width, the user
      // isn't allowed to modify the column number value:
      myColumnsGauge = new GaugeField(MazeScreen.getLabel(MazeScreen.MAZE_NUMCOLS),
                            game.getMinNumCols(),
                            game.getMaxNumCols(),
                            game.getNumCols(),
                            Field.NON_FOCUSABLE);

      // Let the platform decide how to place the gauges on the screen:
      FlowFieldManager ffm = new FlowFieldManager(Field.FIELD_HCENTER);
      ffm.add(myWidthGauge);
      ffm.add(myColumnsGauge);
      add(ffm);
    }

}
```

Sadly, even though the implementation of the RIM widgets is different than the implementation of the MIDP LCDUI widgets, the result is just as ugly, as you can see in Figure 3-4.

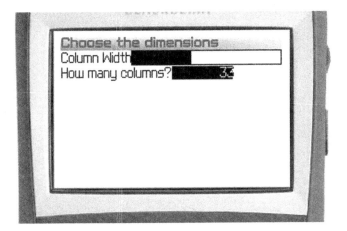

Figure 3-4. *The size selection screen of the BB Maze example running on the 7290 simulator*

The RIM widgets, however, have one *huge* advantage over the MIDP widgets: you can repaint them. That's what you'll do in Chapter 4.

Summary

A BlackBerry smartphone supports two different types of Java ME applications. Logically, they're like two different profiles (MID Profile and RIM Profile)—with separate life cycle and UI classes—built on top of CLDC. The two sets of life cycle and interface classes have a lot of superficial similarities, but for a given application you must pick one set or the other (no mix-and-match). It's a good idea to understand how to use both profiles, because the MID Profile is useful when programming for cross-platform compatibility, whereas the RIM Profile allows you to optimize for BlackBerry.

Chapter 4

Adding a Professional Look and Feel

The most obvious element that separates a professional game from an amateur garage project isn't the complexity of the game—it's the use of graphics. The BB Maze example from Chapter 3 is already a complete game, but it suffers from one fatal flaw: it doesn't look any better than the maze game people were playing on the Atari 2600 back in 1981. Nowadays, even on small devices, we can do a lot better than that.

In this chapter, you'll see some simple techniques to improve the look and feel of the BB Maze example from the previous chapter. Figure 4-1 shows what it will look like when it's done.

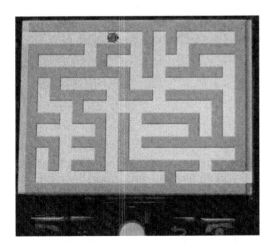

Figure 4-1. *The Maze Deluxe example running on the BlackBerry Curve 8320*

Simple 3D Image Tricks

First, let's replace the player's bland gray circle with a cute ladybug image.

The fact that the image has to be small simplifies the procedure. All of the 3D effects have to be done in the space of a few pixels, and you can take existing images made for small devices and blow them up to see how they're done. These days, the "glossy shine" look is all the rage (as opposed to a metallic shine or a pearly shine), probably due to the fact that the iPhone has a glossy surface. Fortunately, a glossy shine is a simple effect to create.

As you can see from Figure 4-2, the key is in the way the light reflects on the surface. You get a glossy surface by starting with a rich color and then placing a reflection on it that has a sharp edge. On a nonshiny (matte) surface, by contrast, the edge of the reflection fades out.

Figure 4-2. *A glossy button and a matte button*

To draw a shiny surface, you just start with a solid shape and add the shine. For the shine, you start with a transparent background and then select the gradient tool with the "foreground to transparent" option to create a colored region that fades from opaque white to transparent. Then you cut out a patch of the white/transparent shine and paste it onto your solid-colored shape.

For the ladybug image, I started by looking at photos of ladybugs on the Internet. Since it has to be small, it was easy to draw it freehand by copying what I saw in the photos. Then I added a white-to-transparent reflection to make the shell look shiny (see Figure 4-3).

Figure 4-3. *The ladybug image for the Maze Deluxe game*

You can see that I've created one image file with the ladybug facing all four directions so that it can turn as it navigates through the maze. If you've already developed Java ME games, you're probably thinking that this rotation can be done more easily with the `javax.microedition.lcdui.game.Sprite` class, which can perform this same rotation on the fly. Unfortunately, the `Sprite` class is one of the classes you give up when you choose to use the RIM UI classes instead of the MIDP UI classes. But anyway, there's another good reason not to use it. In the Maze Deluxe game, the light is always shining on the maze from the top-left corner, so the shine on the ladybug's shell needs to keep the same orientation, regardless of which way the ladybug is facing. The easiest way to do that is to create four copies of the image, rotating the base ladybug image but not the shine. (You'll see more BlackBerry sprite strategies in Chapters 6 and 9.)

> **Caution** When loading image resources, the file name format depends on which function you use. If you're writing a MIDlet that uses `Image.createImage()`, then the file name argument should be the image's full path within your project directory. In other words, if your image `spriteimage.png` is in the folder `img` under your project directory, then the string argument to use would be `/img/spriteimage.png`. When you're not writing a MIDlet, the path information should be omitted, but there's still a name-formatting quirk to be aware of: when loading a resource from the JAR using `Class.getResourceAsStream()`, you need to add a leading forward slash (/) to the file name, whereas the method `Bitmap.getBitmapResource()` takes the image's file name alone (with no leading forward slash).

Before you can add the player image to the game, though, you have to decide which sizes are appropriate on different-size screens. A little experimentation shows that you can create a nice maze on smaller screens (such as 240×160, 240×260, and 320×240 pixels) with an 8×8, 12×12, or 16×16 player; and on larger screens (like 480×360 pixels), all of those player sizes work, as well as 24×24-pixel players. So, in addition to the 24×24-pixel ladybug shown in Figure 4-3, I also had to draw three smaller ladybugs (which, naturally, are even easier to draw than the largest one). In general, it's a good idea to use simple scratch images during the development phase to determine exactly which image sizes you'll need before starting on the real game graphics. That way you'll avoid wasting your time (or your graphic designer's) drawing beautiful images that ultimately can't be used in the game.

To use the ladybug image, the `MazeGame` class from Listing 3-1 needs a bit of an overhaul. The biggest change is that instead of having a spectrum of possible sizes of the squares that make up the maze grid, you now have only three or four fixed sizes, corresponding to the four possible player image sizes. So, as you can see in Listing 4-1, `mySquareSize` is replaced throughout with `mySquareSizeIndex`, which is an index into an array of possible square sizes. The array itself depends on the screen size, and the correct array is chosen at build time using preprocessing directives, as explained in the "Building for Multiple Devices with Ant" section from Chapter 2.

Listing 4-1. *MazeGame.java*

```
//#preprocess
package net.frogparrot.maze;

import net.rim.device.api.ui.Graphics;
import net.rim.device.api.system.Bitmap;

/**
 * This class controls the game logic.
 */
public class MazeGame {

//----------------------------------------------------------
//   static fields

  /**
```

```
   * color constants.
   */
  public static final int BLACK = 0;
  public static final int WHITE = 0xffffff;
  public static final int WALL_GRAY = 0x00808080;
  public static final int HIGHLIGHT_GRAY = 0x00cccccc;
  public static final int SHADOW_GRAY = 0x00303030;
  public static final int WALL_BACKGROUND = 0x00efcc8a;
  public static final int HIGHLIGHT_BACKGROUND = 0x00efcc8a;
  public static final int SHADOW_BACKGROUND = 0x006f4d0b;

  /**
   * Image orientation constants.
   */
  public static final int IMAGE_RIGHT = 0;
  public static final int IMAGE_DOWN = 1;
  public static final int IMAGE_LEFT = 2;
  public static final int IMAGE_UP = 3;

  /**
   * maze dimension: the possible width values of the maze walls.
   */
//#ifdef SCREEN_240x160
  static int[] mySquareSizes = { 8, 12, 16 };
  public static final int NUM_SIZES = 3;
//#endif
//#ifdef SCREEN_240x260
  static int[] mySquareSizes = { 8, 12, 16 };
  public static final int NUM_SIZES = 3;
//#endif
//#ifdef SCREEN_320x240
  static int[] mySquareSizes = { 8, 12, 16 };
  public static final int NUM_SIZES = 3;
//#endif
//#ifdef SCREEN_480x360
  static int[] mySquareSizes = { 8, 12, 16, 24 };
  public static final int NUM_SIZES = 4;
//#endif

  /**
   * The single instance of this class.
   */
  private static MazeGame theInstance;

//-----------------------------------------------------------
//    instance fields

  /**
   * The data object that describes the maze configuration.
   */
  private Grid myGrid;

  /**
   * Whether or not the currently displayed maze has
   * been completed.
   */
```

```
    */
    private boolean myGameOver = false;

    /**
     * maze dimension: the width of the screen.
     */
    private int myScreenWidth;

    /**
     * maze dimension: the height of the screen.
     */
    private int myScreenHeight;

    /**
     * top corner of the playing area: x-coordinate
     */
    private int myStartX = 0;

    /**
     * top corner of the playing area: y-coordinate
     */
    private int myStartY = 0;

    /**
     * maze dimension: the index to the current width of the maze walls.
     */
    int mySquareSizeIndex;

    /**
     * the possible numbers of columns the display can be divided into.
     */
    private int[] myGridWidths = new int[NUM_SIZES];

    /**
     * the possible numbers of rows the display can be divided into.
     */
    private int[] myGridHeights = new int[NUM_SIZES];

    /**
     * current location of the player in the maze: x-coordinate
     * (in terms of the coordinates of the maze grid, NOT in terms
     * of the coordinate system of the Canvas/Screen.)
     */
    private int myPlayerX = 1;

    /**
     * current location of the player in the maze: y-coordinate
     * (in terms of the coordinates of the maze grid, NOT in terms
     * of the coordinate system of the Canvas/Screen.)
     */
    private int myPlayerY = 1;

    /**
     * The most recently selected direction (for orienting the image).
     */
```

```java
  private int myPlayerDirection;

  /**
   * The bitmap image to use for the player.
   */
  private Bitmap myPlayerBitmap;

//-------------------------------------------------------
//    gets / sets

  /**
   * @return the single instance of this class.
   */
  public static MazeGame getInstance() {
    return theInstance;
  }

  /**
   * Set the single instance of this class.
   */
  static void setInstance(MazeGame mazeGame) {
    theInstance = mazeGame;
  }

  /**
   * Changes the width of the maze walls and calculates how
   * this change affects the number of rows and columns
   * the maze can have.
   * @return the number of columns now that the the
   *         width of the columns has been updated.
   */
  public int setColWidthIndex(int colWidthIndex) {
    if(mySquareSizeIndex != colWidthIndex) {
      clearGrid();
      mySquareSizeIndex = colWidthIndex;
      PrefsStorage.setSquareSizeIndex(mySquareSizeIndex);
      // get the new player image:
      myPlayerBitmap = getPlayerBitmap();
      // Center the maze in the screen:
      myStartX = (myScreenWidth
          - (myGridWidths[mySquareSizeIndex]*mySquareSizes[mySquareSizeIndex]))/2;
      myStartY = (myScreenHeight
          - (myGridHeights[mySquareSizeIndex]*mySquareSizes[mySquareSizeIndex]))/2;
    }
    return(myGridWidths[mySquareSizeIndex]);
  }

  /**
   * @return the minimum square size index.
   */
  public int getMinColWidthIndex() {
    return(0);
  }

  /**
```

```
   * @return the maximum square size index.
   */
  public int getMaxColWidthIndex() {
    return(mySquareSizes.length - 1);
  }

  /**
   * @return the current square size index.
   */
  public int getColWidthIndex() {
    return(mySquareSizeIndex);
  }

  /**
   * @return the actual square size in pixels corresponding to the index.
   */
  public int getColWidth(int index) {
    return(mySquareSizes[index]);
  }

  /**
   * @return the minimum number of columns the display can be divided into.
   */
  public int getMinNumCols() {
    return(myGridWidths[myGridWidths.length - 1]);
  }

  /**
   * @return the maximum number of columns the display can be divided into.
   */
  public int getMaxNumCols() {
    return(myGridWidths[0]);
  }

  /**
   * @return the current number of maze columns the display is divided into.
   */
  public int getNumCols() {
    return(myGridWidths[mySquareSizeIndex]);
  }

  /**
   * @return the current player bitmap image.
   */
  public Bitmap getPlayerBitmap() {
    return Bitmap.getBitmapResource("player_" +
        mySquareSizes[mySquareSizeIndex] + ".png");
  }

//-------------------------------------------------------
//    initialization and game state changes

  /**
   * Constructor initializes the maze dimension data.
   * @param screenWidth the width of the play area in pixels
```

```
 * @param screenHeight the height of the play area in pixels
 */
MazeGame(int screenWidth, int screenHeight) {
  myScreenWidth = screenWidth;
  myScreenHeight = screenHeight;
  // Calculate how many rows and columns of maze
  // can (and should) be placed on the screen.
  mySquareSizeIndex = PrefsStorage.getSquareSizeIndex();
  if((mySquareSizeIndex < 0) || (mySquareSizeIndex >= mySquareSizes.length)) {
    mySquareSizeIndex = 1;
  }

  myPlayerBitmap = getPlayerBitmap();

  // initialize the grid dimensions corresponding
  // to the possible square sizes:
  for(int i = 0; i < mySquareSizes.length; i++) {
    myGridWidths[i] = myScreenWidth / mySquareSizes[i];
      if((myGridWidths[i] & 0x1) == 0) {
      myGridWidths[i] -= 1;
    }
    myGridHeights[i] = myScreenHeight / mySquareSizes[i];
      if((myGridHeights[i] & 0x1) == 0) {
      myGridHeights[i] -= 1;
    }
  }
  // Center the maze in the screen:
  myStartX = (myScreenWidth
      - (myGridWidths[mySquareSizeIndex]*mySquareSizes[mySquareSizeIndex]))/2;
  myStartY = (myScreenHeight
      - (myGridHeights[mySquareSizeIndex]*mySquareSizes[mySquareSizeIndex]))/2;
}

/**
 * discard the current maze.
 */
void clearGrid() {
  myGameOver = false;
  // throw away the current maze.
  myGrid = null;
  // set the player back to the beginning of the maze.
  myPlayerX = 1;
  myPlayerY = 1;
  myPlayerDirection = IMAGE_RIGHT;
}

/**
 * discard the current maze and draw a new one.
 */
void newMaze() {
  clearGrid();
  // paint the new maze
  MazeScreen.getInstance().paintMaze();
}
```

```java
/**
 * Draw a new maze when the size is changed.
 * This is used only in the RIMlet version
 * of the game (not the MIDlet version),
 * to initialize new maze data when the BB platform
 * notifies the MazeScreen that it has been exposed,
 * after the SelectScreen is popped off the screen stack.
 */
void doneResize() {
  if(myGrid == null) {
    MazeScreen.getInstance().paintMaze();
  }
}


//--------------------------------------------------------
//  graphics and game actions

/**
 * Create and display a maze if necessary, otherwise just
 * move the player. For simplicity we repaint the whole
 * maze each time, but this could be optimized by painting
 * just the player and erasing the square that the player
 * just left.
 */
void drawMaze(Graphics g) {
  // If there is no current maze, create one and draw it.
  int gridWidth = myGridWidths[mySquareSizeIndex];
  int gridHeight = myGridHeights[mySquareSizeIndex];
  int squareSize = mySquareSizes[mySquareSizeIndex];
  if(myGrid == null) {
    // create the underlying data of the maze.
    myGrid = new Grid(gridWidth, gridHeight);
  }
  // draw the maze:
  // loop through the grid data and color each square the
  // right color, checking the surrounding squares in
  // order to determine where to draw highlights and shadows
  for(int i = 0; i < gridWidth; i++) {
    for(int j = 0; j < gridHeight; j++) {
      if(myGrid.isWall(i, j)) {
        // draw the wall block with shadows and highlights:
        g.setColor(WALL_GRAY);
        g.fillRect(myStartX + (i*squareSize),
                myStartY + (j*squareSize),
                squareSize, squareSize);
        // start with the shadow:
        g.setColor(SHADOW_GRAY);
        if(!myGrid.isWall(i+1, j)) {
          g.drawLine(myStartX + ((i+1)*squareSize) - 1,
                myStartY + (j*squareSize),
                myStartX + ((i+1)*squareSize) - 1,
                squareSize + ((j+1)*squareSize));
        }
        if(!myGrid.isWall(i, j+1)) {
          g.drawLine(myStartX + (i*squareSize),
```

```
                    myStartY + ((j+1)*squareSize - 1),
                    myStartX + ((i+1)*squareSize),
                    myStartY + ((j+1)*squareSize - 1));
          }
          if(!myGrid.isWall(i+1, j+1)) {
            g.drawPoint(myStartX + ((i+1)*squareSize) - 1,
                    myStartY + ((j+1)*squareSize - 1));
          }
          // then do the highlight:
          g.setColor(HIGHLIGHT_GRAY);
          if(!myGrid.isWall(i-1, j)) {
            g.drawLine(myStartX + (i*squareSize),
                    myStartY + (j*squareSize),
                    myStartX + (i*squareSize),
                    squareSize + ((j+1)*squareSize));
          }
          if(!myGrid.isWall(i, j-1)) {
            g.drawLine(myStartX + (i*squareSize),
                    myStartY + (j*squareSize),
                    myStartX + ((i+1)*squareSize),
                    myStartY + (j*squareSize));
          }
          if(!myGrid.isWall(i-1, j-1)) {
            g.drawPoint(myStartX + (i*squareSize),
                      myStartY + (j*squareSize));
          }
        } else {
          g.setColor(WHITE);
          // clear the square as white:
          g.fillRect(myStartX + (i*squareSize),
                    myStartY + (j*squareSize),
                    squareSize, squareSize);
        }
      }
    }
    drawBorder(g);
    // erase the exit path:
    g.setColor(WHITE);
    g.fillRect(myStartX + (gridWidth * squareSize),
              myStartY + ((gridHeight-2) * squareSize),
              squareSize + myStartX, squareSize);

    // draw the player as an image bitmap:
    g.drawBitmap(myStartX + (squareSize)*myPlayerX,
              myStartY + (squareSize)*myPlayerY,
              squareSize, squareSize,
              myPlayerBitmap, myPlayerDirection*squareSize, 0);
  }

/**
 * Draw the border area around the maze.
 */
void drawBorder(Graphics g) {
  int gridHeight = myGridHeights[mySquareSizeIndex];
  int squareSize = mySquareSizes[mySquareSizeIndex];
```

```java
        // shade in the extra space outside of the maze
        int[] xPts = { 0,
                       myScreenWidth,
                       myScreenWidth,
                       myScreenWidth - myStartX,
                       myScreenWidth - myStartX,
                       myStartX,
                       myStartX,
                       0 };
        int[] yPts = { 0,
                       0,
                       myStartY + ((gridHeight-2) * squareSize),
                       myStartY + ((gridHeight-2) * squareSize),
                       myStartY,
                       myStartY,
                       myStartY + squareSize,
                       myStartY + squareSize };
        int[] colors = { HIGHLIGHT_BACKGROUND,
                         WALL_BACKGROUND,
                         WALL_BACKGROUND,
                         SHADOW_BACKGROUND,
                         SHADOW_BACKGROUND,
                         HIGHLIGHT_BACKGROUND,
                         HIGHLIGHT_BACKGROUND,
                         HIGHLIGHT_BACKGROUND };
        g.drawShadedFilledPath(xPts, yPts, null, colors, null);
        int[] xPts2 = { 0,
                        myScreenWidth,
                        myScreenWidth,
                        myScreenWidth - myStartX,
                        myScreenWidth - myStartX,
                        myStartX,
                        myStartX,
                        0 };
        int[] yPts2 = { myScreenHeight,
                        myScreenHeight,
                        myScreenHeight - (myStartY + squareSize),
                        myScreenHeight - (myStartY + squareSize),
                        myScreenHeight - myStartY,
                        myScreenHeight - myStartY,
                        myStartY + 2*squareSize,
                        myStartY + 2*squareSize };
        int[] colors2 = { WALL_BACKGROUND,
                          WALL_BACKGROUND,
                          SHADOW_BACKGROUND,
                          SHADOW_BACKGROUND,
                          SHADOW_BACKGROUND,
                          WALL_BACKGROUND,
                          HIGHLIGHT_BACKGROUND,
                          HIGHLIGHT_BACKGROUND };
        g.drawShadedFilledPath(xPts2, yPts2, null, colors2, null);
    }

    /**
     * Handle user input.
```

```
     * @param direction the code to tell which direction the user selected.
     * @return whether the user exits the maze on this move.
     */
    boolean move(int direction) {
      MazeScreen screen = MazeScreen.getInstance();
      if(! myGameOver) {
        switch(direction) {
          case MazeScreen.LEFT:
            myPlayerDirection = IMAGE_LEFT;
            if(!myGrid.isWall(myPlayerX-1, myPlayerY)
               && (myPlayerX != 1)) {
              myPlayerX -= 2;
            }
            screen.paintMaze();
            break;
          case MazeScreen.RIGHT:
            myPlayerDirection = IMAGE_RIGHT;
            if(!myGrid.isWall(myPlayerX+1, myPlayerY)) {
              myPlayerX += 2;
              // handle the player exiting the maze:
              if(myPlayerX == myGridWidths[mySquareSizeIndex]) {
                myGameOver = true;
              }
            }
            screen.paintMaze();
            break;
          case MazeScreen.UP:
            myPlayerDirection = IMAGE_UP;
            if(!myGrid.isWall(myPlayerX, myPlayerY-1)) {
              myPlayerY -= 2;
            }
            screen.paintMaze();
            break;
          case MazeScreen.DOWN:
            myPlayerDirection = IMAGE_DOWN;
            if(!myGrid.isWall(myPlayerX, myPlayerY+1)) {
              myPlayerY += 2;
            }
            screen.paintMaze();
            break;
          default:
            break;
        }
      }
      return myGameOver;
    }

}
```

Note that this class modification also requires modifying the PrefsStorage class from
Listing 3-3: it needs to store and return a size index with default value equal to 1 instead
of storing an absolute size in pixels with default value 7. This change is trivial enough
that I won't clutter up the page by reprinting it, but you can see the change in the source
code, which you can download from www.apress.com.

The other big change in this class is the additional drawing code to improve the appearance of the maze itself.

Simple 3D Drawing Tricks

Image files are great for graphical elements that have a fixed set of sizes per screen size and don't change during the game. For very simple graphical elements that have a range of minor variations within the game, however, you'll probably want to use the Graphics class to draw them.

As with image icons, you can get ideas of how to create simple effects just by looking closely at existing programs. The BlackBerry JDE itself has 3D effects that are created with very simple tricks that you can do with the Graphics class, as you can see in Figure 4-4.

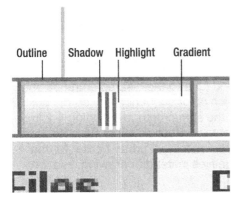

Figure 4-4. *Simple 3D tricks used in the GUI of the BlackBerry JDE*

Similarly, the maze in this example looks a lot more professional with just a little bit of perspective to give the illusion that the maze is raised a bit, with a light shining on it from the top-left corner. All you have to do is add a highlight color to the top and left sides of the maze walls and a shadow color to the right and bottom sides.

There's one catch, though: if you add the same highlight and shadow to every block, it will look ugly because it will emphasize the fact that the maze is built of squares (as opposed to being made of continuous walls). It looks better if you add highlight and shadow only on the sides where a wall meets a path, not on the sides where two wall blocks meet. That means that the appearance of each wall block depends on the status of each of the eight blocks around it. There are 2^8 (256) possible combinations of eight surrounding blocks, 81 of which are valid configurations in the Maze Deluxe game. So if you're thinking of building the maze walls out of image files, that's a lot of image files to store and keep track of, especially when you consider the fact that—given the different possible square sizes— you have to multiply that number by three or four. In this case, it's simpler to draw on the highlight and shadow, as you can see in the drawMaze() method in Listing 4-1.

Of course, if the maze is raised and there's a light shining on it from the top-left corner, then the whole board should also have a shadow on the bottom and right sides. Since the `net.rim.device.api.ui.Graphics` class is capable of doing a gradient fill, you can actually draw a shadow that fades out rather than drawing a hard-edged shadow, as you can see in Figure 4-5. If you look at the `drawBorder()` method of Listing 4-1, you can see that you can create a gradient effect by sending an array of different colors to the `Graphics` class's `drawShadedFilledPath()` method.

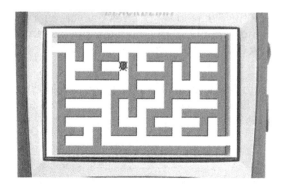

Figure 4-5. *The Maze Deluxe game running on the 7290 simulator*

Since the region around the maze is irregularly shaped (due to the cleared entrance and exit paths), I used a little trial and error to decide which color sequence looked the best. You'll see a little more logical and systematic use of the same method in Listing 4-2 in the next section. Also note that since there are only three or four possible sizes for the maze border (per screen size), you might also consider building a pretty border for the maze from image files. For tips on when to use image files instead of drawing, see the "Using Image Files vs. Drawing with Graphics" sidebar.

USING IMAGE FILES VS. DRAWING WITH GRAPHICS

You can create a number of graphic effects with the `Graphics` class, as you've seen throughout this chapter. But just because you can do something, it doesn't mean you always should.

If you have a complex image—even if it can easily be broken down into simple components like gradients and transparent layers—it's usually better to construct it with image files rather than drawing it in the code. Each option has its costs: you either have to spend computing time (to construct the image) or memory (to store and load it). Then there's also the question of optimizing for maintainability. If the artwork isn't quite right (or if you just want to change it), it's obviously a lot easier for the artist to fix it if it's just a question of replacing a few image files than if you have to update a drawing algorithm that's hard-coded into game.

User interface components present a special challenge. You have to consider the file sizes as well as internationalization when deciding whether to draw your button text as part of the button image file or whether to construct your buttons using text strings. Chapter 6 illustrates how to use the `Font` class to customize the text style.

A good rule of thumb is to draw with the `Graphics` class when you have a drawing effect that is very simple and may need to be drawn in several sizes or configurations within a single run on a single device.

For example, the maze itself and its border in the Maze Deluxe example (Listing 4-1) are very simple and change size depending on the size of the player, so it makes sense to draw them in the code. By contrast, the border of the SelectSizeManager (Listing 4-2) never changes size for a given device, so it might be more efficient to draw it with image files.

Painting a Custom User Interface

Any special features your game offers will probably require user interface screens. It's hard to improve on the time-tested design pattern of placing widgets (lists, buttons, text fields, etc.) on the screen and letting the user navigate from one to the next to fill them in. Not only is this design familiar (hence simple) for the user, but it also has the advantage that RIM has already implemented the underlying widget navigation and interaction functionality for you. The biggest remaining task is to design the look of the user interface screens with your game's colors, images, and animations.

Most user interface libraries (including both the MIDP LCDUI library and the RIM Device UI library) have built-in drawing and layout functionality so that you can just select the widgets you like and let the platform worry about what they'll look like and where they'll go on the screen. However, dynamic layout is far less useful on small devices (where the application has a small, fixed screen size) than it is on a PC (where the user is constantly resizing the application's window). When you're writing a game on a BlackBerry, there are only a few standard screen sizes, you know exactly how big the screen will be for the duration of the game (because the user can't resize it), and it's so small that every pixel counts. So if you want your BlackBerry game to look good, you'll typically want to have your graphic designer specify all of your game's user interface screens—in all of the standard screen sizes—down to the pixel. And (unlike the MIDP LCDUI library), the RIM Device UI library will allow you to code it that way.

In this section, you'll see how to rewrite the SelectSize screen from Listing 3-9 to give it a customized look and feel. Figure 4-6 shows what the size selection screen will look like when it's done.

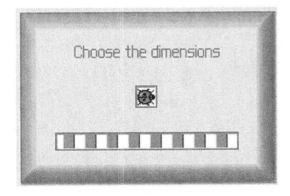

Figure 4-6. *The size selection screen of the Maze Deluxe game running on the 7290 simulator*

Laying Out the Screen with a Manager

The first step is to create a custom Manager (Listing 4-2), designed specifically to draw the user interface screen.

Listing 4-2. *SelectSizeManager.java*

```java
//#preprocess
package net.frogparrot.maze;

import net.rim.device.api.ui.*;

/**
 * This is a custom layout manager to draw the look and feel
 * exactly as desired.
 */
class SelectSizeManager extends Manager {

//-----------------------------------------------------------
//  static fields

  /**
   * Dimension constants depend on the screen size:
   */
//#ifdef SCREEN_240x160
  public static final int SCREEN_WIDTH = 240;
  public static final int SCREEN_HEIGHT = 160;
  public static final int BORDER_WIDTH = 4;
  public static final int INNER_BORDER_WIDTH = 16;
  public static final int H_GAUGE_BUFFER_WIDTH = 16;
  public static final int V_GAUGE_BUFFER_WIDTH = 12;
  public static final int WIDGET_WIDTH = 200;
  public static final int WIDGET_HEIGHT = 40;
  public static final int WIDGET_X = 20;
  public static final int WIDGET_Y = 20;
//#endif
//#ifdef SCREEN_240x260
  public static final int SCREEN_WIDTH = 240;
  public static final int SCREEN_HEIGHT = 260;
  public static final int BORDER_WIDTH = 4;
  public static final int INNER_BORDER_WIDTH = 16;
  public static final int H_GAUGE_BUFFER_WIDTH = 16;
  public static final int V_GAUGE_BUFFER_WIDTH = 12;
  public static final int WIDGET_WIDTH = 200;
  public static final int WIDGET_HEIGHT = 40;
  public static final int WIDGET_X = 20;
  public static final int WIDGET_Y = 70;
//#endif
//#ifdef SCREEN_320x240
  public static final int SCREEN_WIDTH = 320;
  public static final int SCREEN_HEIGHT = 240;
  public static final int BORDER_WIDTH = 6;
  public static final int INNER_BORDER_WIDTH = 24;
  public static final int H_GAUGE_BUFFER_WIDTH = 24;
  public static final int V_GAUGE_BUFFER_WIDTH = 18;
```

```java
  public static final int WIDGET_WIDTH = 260;
  public static final int WIDGET_HEIGHT = 60;
  public static final int WIDGET_X = 30;
  public static final int WIDGET_Y = 30;
//#endif
//#ifdef SCREEN_480x360
  public static final int SCREEN_WIDTH = 480;
  public static final int SCREEN_HEIGHT = 360;
  public static final int BORDER_WIDTH = 8;
  public static final int INNER_BORDER_WIDTH = 32;
  public static final int H_GAUGE_BUFFER_WIDTH = 32;
  public static final int V_GAUGE_BUFFER_WIDTH = 24;
  public static final int WIDGET_WIDTH = 400;
  public static final int WIDGET_HEIGHT = 80;
  public static final int WIDGET_X = 40;
  public static final int WIDGET_Y = 40;
//#endif

  /**
   * color constants.
   */
  public static final int OUTLINE = 0x00025cb8;
  public static final int DK_BLUE = 0x00037ffd;
  public static final int MED_BLUE = 0x0066b0fb;
  public static final int LT_BLUE = 0x00c7e2fd;
  public static final int BLACK = 0x00000000;

  /**
   * The screen title.
   */
  public static String myLabel;

//-----------------------------------------------------------
// initialization and life cycle

  /**
   * Constructor initializes the data.
   */
  SelectSizeManager() {
    super(USE_ALL_HEIGHT | USE_ALL_WIDTH);
    myLabel = MazeScreen.getLabel(MazeScreen.MAZE_SELECTSIZE);
  }

//-----------------------------------------------------------
// graphics

  /**
   * This layout covers the entire screen.
   */
  public int getPreferredHeight() {
    return SCREEN_HEIGHT;
  }

  /**
   * This layout covers the entire screen.
```

```
    */
    public int getPreferredWidth() {
      return SCREEN_WIDTH;
    }

    /**
     * This is called by the platform to prompt the
     * manager to lay out its contents.
     * @param width The width of the area allotted to the manager
     * @param height The height of the area allotted to the manager
     */
    protected void sublayout(int width, int height) {
      // set the positions and sizes of the gauges using
      // screen-specific constants:
      Field widthField = getField(0);
      setPositionChild(widthField, WIDGET_X, WIDGET_Y + WIDGET_HEIGHT);
      layoutChild(widthField, WIDGET_WIDTH, WIDGET_HEIGHT);
      Field columnsField = getField(1);
      setPositionChild(columnsField, WIDGET_X, WIDGET_Y + WIDGET_HEIGHT*2);
      layoutChild(columnsField, WIDGET_WIDTH, WIDGET_HEIGHT);
      // Tell the platform how much space this manager is taking:
      setExtent(SCREEN_WIDTH, SCREEN_HEIGHT);
    }

    /**
     * This is called by the platform to prompt the manager to
     * paint its contents. It is not necessary to override this method.
     * @param g The Graphics instance to use to paint the region.
     */
    protected void subpaint(Graphics g) {
      g.setColor(LT_BLUE);
      // clear the screen to background color
      g.fillRect(0, 0, SCREEN_WIDTH, SCREEN_HEIGHT);
      // draw the border frame, made of four trapezoids
      // (like a picture frame), with gradient shading
      // to make the central area appear raised.
      // first the top:
      int[] xPts = { BORDER_WIDTH,
                     WIDGET_X,
                     SCREEN_WIDTH - WIDGET_X,
                     SCREEN_WIDTH - BORDER_WIDTH };
      int[] yPts = { BORDER_WIDTH,
                     WIDGET_Y,
                     WIDGET_Y,
                     BORDER_WIDTH };
      // set the colors to create a gradient,
      // darker on the outside edge, lighter on the inside
      int[] colors = { MED_BLUE,
                       LT_BLUE,
                       LT_BLUE,
                       MED_BLUE };
      g.drawShadedFilledPath(xPts, yPts, null, colors, null);
      // now draw the left side:
      xPts[0] = BORDER_WIDTH;
      xPts[1] = WIDGET_X;
```

```
xPts[2] = WIDGET_X;
xPts[3] = BORDER_WIDTH;
yPts[0] = BORDER_WIDTH;
yPts[1] = WIDGET_Y;
yPts[2] = SCREEN_HEIGHT - WIDGET_Y;
yPts[3] = SCREEN_HEIGHT - BORDER_WIDTH;
g.drawShadedFilledPath(xPts, yPts, null, colors, null);
// now the bottom:
// change the colors to give more shading to the
// bottom/right sides for a 3D effect:
colors[0] = DK_BLUE;
colors[3] = DK_BLUE;
xPts[0] = BORDER_WIDTH;
xPts[1] = WIDGET_X;
xPts[2] = SCREEN_WIDTH - WIDGET_X;
xPts[3] = SCREEN_WIDTH - BORDER_WIDTH;
yPts[0] = SCREEN_HEIGHT - BORDER_WIDTH;
yPts[1] = SCREEN_HEIGHT - WIDGET_Y;
yPts[2] = SCREEN_HEIGHT - WIDGET_Y;
yPts[3] = SCREEN_HEIGHT - BORDER_WIDTH;
g.drawShadedFilledPath(xPts, yPts, null, colors, null);
// now the right side:
xPts[0] = SCREEN_WIDTH - BORDER_WIDTH;
xPts[1] = SCREEN_WIDTH - WIDGET_X;
xPts[2] = SCREEN_WIDTH - WIDGET_X;
xPts[3] = SCREEN_WIDTH - BORDER_WIDTH;
yPts[0] = BORDER_WIDTH;
yPts[1] = WIDGET_Y;
yPts[2] = SCREEN_HEIGHT - WIDGET_Y;
yPts[3] = SCREEN_HEIGHT - BORDER_WIDTH;
g.drawShadedFilledPath(xPts, yPts, null, colors, null);
// put a shadow along the right side of the
// raised area:
xPts[0] = SCREEN_WIDTH - BORDER_WIDTH;
xPts[1] = SCREEN_WIDTH;
xPts[2] = SCREEN_WIDTH;
xPts[3] = SCREEN_WIDTH - BORDER_WIDTH;
yPts[0] = BORDER_WIDTH;
yPts[1] = BORDER_WIDTH;
yPts[2] = SCREEN_HEIGHT;
yPts[3] = SCREEN_HEIGHT - BORDER_WIDTH;
g.drawShadedFilledPath(xPts, yPts, null, colors, null);
// Then put a shadow below the raised area:
xPts[0] = BORDER_WIDTH;
xPts[1] = BORDER_WIDTH;
xPts[2] = SCREEN_WIDTH;
xPts[3] = SCREEN_WIDTH - BORDER_WIDTH;
yPts[0] = SCREEN_HEIGHT - BORDER_WIDTH;
yPts[1] = SCREEN_HEIGHT;
yPts[2] = SCREEN_HEIGHT;
yPts[3] = SCREEN_HEIGHT - BORDER_WIDTH;
g.drawShadedFilledPath(xPts, yPts, null, colors, null);
// Draw a dark outline around the raised area to
// separate it from its shadow:
g.setColor(OUTLINE);
```

```
    g.drawRect(BORDER_WIDTH, BORDER_WIDTH,
            SCREEN_WIDTH - 2*BORDER_WIDTH,
            SCREEN_HEIGHT - 2*BORDER_WIDTH);

    // draw the title
    g.setColor(DK_BLUE);
    Font font = g.getFont();
    int textWidth = font.getAdvance(myLabel);
    int textHeight = font.getHeight();
    g.drawText(myLabel, WIDGET_X + (WIDGET_WIDTH - textWidth)/2,
        WIDGET_Y + (WIDGET_HEIGHT - textHeight)/2);

    // paint the fields
    Field widthField = getField(0);
    paintChild(g, widthField);
    Field columnsField = getField(1);
    paintChild(g, columnsField);
  }

}
```

Looking at Figure 4-6, you can see that the border is made of four trapezoids that fit together like a picture frame, getting lighter as you move toward the center of the frame. This border (drawn in the subpaint() method in Listing 4-2) is built out of four gradient-shaded regions created with the drawShadedFilledPath() method, just like the maze's shadow from Listing 4-1.

> **Note** The colors are defined in standard RGB format, which means that if you write the color value in hexadecimal format, you can read the RGB values right off of it: 0x00RRGGBB. In some contexts, the first two digits give the "alpha" (transparency), but it's ignored by the Graphics.setColor() function. You can set the transparency used for drawing by calling Graphics.setGlobalAlpha()—with 0 indicating fully transparent and 255 indicating fully opaque. Since this operation is *global*, be sure to change it back when you're done!

You can see that the drawShadedFilledPath() method takes a set of arrays describing the set of points of the path. The first argument gives the x-coordinates of the list of points, the second gives the list of corresponding y-coordinates, and the fourth gives the colors of the points in the list. (The other two arguments allow you to specify curvature and split the path into a set of connected subpaths.) You define the gradient shading by setting the colors for the list of points and letting the Graphics object interpolate. For a simple linear gradient like the one you see on the four trapezoids, you just color the inner corner points lighter and the outer corner points darker.

Continuing in the theme of adding perspective with lighting from the top-left corner, you make the top and left trapezoids of the frame a little lighter than the bottom and right ones. Then you add two more gradient trapezoids just outside the frame on the bottom and right sides to create a shadow. As a finishing touch, you draw an outline around the frame to separate it from its shadow.

If you define your widgets to cover the entire screen, then you don't actually have to override the Manager's subpaint() method—you can just let the default implementation call the widgets' paint() methods. But since border and background elements don't require user interaction, there's no reason to implement them as widgets. It's simpler to override subpaint() to paint the background when the Manager is painted, and from there call paintChild() for each widget to paint it on top.

Since the widget navigation functionality is handled by the BlackBerry platform, the platform naturally has a default way of indicating which widget has the focus: it draws an ugly rectangle around the focused widget. You can override this behavior by implementing the drawFocus() method. In this case, there's only one widget that can be focused, so the functionality to indicate the focus is irrelevant. As you can see in Listing 4-3, it's overridden by the instruction to do nothing.

In practice, the focus is often indicated by a change in the color of the widget, which doesn't really lend itself to the model where you paint the widget and then paint the focus indicator on top using a drawFocus() method. Chapter 9 gives a more detailed example of using graphics to show which field currently has the focus.

The critical method for a Manager implementation to override is sublayout(). That's the method where you specify where each widget goes and how much room it is allowed to occupy. In Listing 4-2, you specify the exact sizes and positions of the two widgets using screen size–specific constants that are selected in the preprocessing phase (as explained in the "Building for Multiple Devices with Ant" section of Chapter 2). Don't forget to call the setExtent() method with the dimensions of the area you're using—that's the method that defines the size of the area that the Manager can paint on with its Graphics object.

Note that the platform calls both sublayout() and subpaint() from the event thread, as discussed in the "Hello BlackBerry!" section in Chapter 2. When a Screen with a Manager added to it is placed on the top of the screen stack, the event thread calls the Manager's layout() method, which calls the sublayout() method. You should override sublayout()—instead of layout()—to avoid overwriting any additional functionality that RIM has placed in the layout() method. The paint() and subpaint() methods work the same way when it's time to repaint the Screen.

In the Maze Deluxe example, you add the SelectSizeManager in Listing 4-2 to the SelectScreen from Listing 3-9 with some minor modifications. Naturally, you replace the FlowFieldManager in the constructor with this SelectSizeManager and replace the two GaugeFields with the two custom gauge classes you'll see in Listings 4-3 and 4-4.

Painting Custom Widgets

Now you have almost all of the pieces to build the Maze Deluxe example game, with the code in this chapter plus slightly modified versions of the classes in Listings 3-3 and 3-9. The last step is to create the two custom widgets.

As you can see in Figure 4-6, the WidthGauge and the ColumnsGauge are both little indented display screens that show the user exactly what value she's selecting. The

WidthGauge (Listing 4-3) shows the ladybug character in its currently selected actual size, and the ColumnsGauge (Listing 4-4) shows the corresponding number of maze columns.

Listing 4-3. *WidthGauge.java*

```java
package net.frogparrot.maze;

import net.rim.device.api.ui.Graphics;
import net.rim.device.api.ui.component.*;

/**
 * The gauge to display how many columns wide the maze is.
 */
class WidthGauge extends GaugeField {

//-----------------------------------------------------------
//   instance fields

  /**
   * The Columns gauge to inform when the square size changes.
   */
  private ColumnsGauge myColumnsGauge;

  /**
   * The size of this gauge's view window.
   */
  private int myMaxSquareSize;

//-----------------------------------------------------------
//   initialization and state changes

  /**
   * Constructor initializes the data.
   */
  WidthGauge(ColumnsGauge cg, String label, int min, int max,
      int start, long style) {
    super(label, min, max, start, style);
    myMaxSquareSize = MazeGame.getInstance().getColWidth(
        MazeGame.getInstance().getMaxColWidthIndex());
    myColumnsGauge = cg;
  }

  /**
   * This is called by the platform (prompted by the
   * layer manager) to tell this field to lay out its
   * own contents. This gauge has nothing to lay out,
   * but we do need to inform the platform of how much
   * of the allotted space this widget will take.
   * @param width The width (in pixels) allotted to this gauge.
   * @param height The height (in pixels) allotted to this gauge.
   */
  protected void layout(int width, int height) {
    // tell the platform that this gauge uses all of its
    // allotted space:
    setExtent(width, height);
  }
```

```
/**
 * This is called by the platform to inform the gauge
 * that the user has edited its contents.
 * @param context Information specifying the origin
 *                of the change (not relevant here).
 */
protected void fieldChangeNotify(int context) {
  // get the gauge's new value and pass it along
  // to the underlying game logic.
  int val = getValue();
  int numCols = MazeGame.getInstance().setColWidthIndex(val);
  // inform the columns gauge that its value has
  // changed accordingly:
  myColumnsGauge.setValue(numCols);
}

//------------------------------------------------------------
//    graphics methods

/**
 * This is called by the platform to tell the Field to
 * draw itself in its focused (or unfocused) state.
 * Since only one field on this screen can be focused,
 * it is always focused, hence there's no need to draw
 * a focused and unfocused version. We override the
 * method to prevent the superclass from drawing its
 * (ugly) default focus indicator.
 */
protected void drawFocus(Graphics g, boolean on) {}

/**
 * Paint the gauge. It appears as an indented window
 * showing the player at its current size.
 * @param g The Graphics instance to use for painting.
 */
protected void paint(Graphics g) {
  // color the background:
  g.setColor(SelectSizeManager.LT_BLUE);
  g.fillRect(0, 0, getWidth(), getHeight());
  // calculate where to place the window:
  int x = (getWidth() - myMaxSquareSize)/2;
  int y = (getHeight() - myMaxSquareSize)/2;
  // clear the window:
  g.setColor(MazeGame.WHITE);
  g.fillRect(x, y, myMaxSquareSize, myMaxSquareSize);
  // draw a border around the window to make it appear indented:
  g.setColor(SelectSizeManager.OUTLINE);
  g.drawRect(x - 2, y - 2, myMaxSquareSize + 4, myMaxSquareSize + 4);
  g.setColor(SelectSizeManager.MED_BLUE);
  g.drawLine(x - 1, y - 1, x + myMaxSquareSize - 1, y - 1);
  g.drawLine(x - 1, y - 1, x - 1, y + myMaxSquareSize - 1);
  // draw the player as an image bitmap:
  MazeGame game = MazeGame.getInstance();
  int squareSize = game.getColWidth(game.getColWidthIndex());
```

```
    if(squareSize == myMaxSquareSize) {
      g.drawBitmap(x, y,
                 squareSize, squareSize,
                 game.getPlayerBitmap(), 0, 0);
    } else {
      // if the player size is smaller than the window size,
      // then center the small image in the window and draw
      // a light-gray border around it:
      int innerX = x + (myMaxSquareSize - squareSize)/2;
      int innerY = y + (myMaxSquareSize - squareSize)/2;
      g.drawBitmap(innerX, innerY,
                 squareSize, squareSize,
                 game.getPlayerBitmap(), 0, 0);
      g.setColor(MazeGame.HIGHLIGHT_GRAY);
      g.drawRect(innerX, innerY, squareSize, squareSize);
    }
  }

}
```

Unlike the Manager class, the widgets (classes in the package
net.rim.device.api.ui.component) don't have a sublayout() or subpaint() method. So to
create a widget with a custom look, you override layout() (to call setExtent() to declare
your custom size), and you override paint() to implement your custom paint job.

In both cases, you use the usual shading tricks to create a slight 3D illusion, only this
time—since the screens are indented instead of raised—you put the highlight color on
the right and bottom sides and the shadow on the top and left sides.

Listing 4-4. *ColumnsGauge.java*

```
package net.frogparrot.maze;

import net.rim.device.api.ui.component.*;
import net.rim.device.api.ui.*;

/**
 * The gauge to display how many columns wide the maze is.
 */
class ColumnsGauge extends GaugeField {

//-----------------------------------------------------------
//   initialization and state changes

  /**
   * Constructor does nothing.
   */
  ColumnsGauge(String label, int min, int max,
      int start, long style) {
    super(label, min, max, start, style);
  }

  /**
   * This is called by the platform (prompted by the
   * layer manager) to tell this field to lay out its
   * own contents. This gauge has nothing to lay out,
```

```
 * but we do need to inform the platform of how much
 * of the allotted space this widget will take.
 * @param width The width (in pixels) allotted to this gauge.
 * @param height The height (in pixels) allotted to this gauge.
 */
protected void layout(int width, int height) {
  // tell the platform that this gauge uses all of its
  // allotted space:
  setExtent(width, height);
}


//----------------------------------------------------------
//    graphics methods

/**
 * Paint the gauge. It appears as an indented window
 * showing how many columns the maze is divided into.
 * @param g The Graphics instance to use for painting.
 */
protected void paint(Graphics g) {
  // color the background:
  g.setColor(SelectSizeManager.LT_BLUE);
  g.fillRect(0, 0, getWidth(), getHeight());
  // get the data on where to place the window
  // and how big to make it:
  int x = SelectSizeManager.H_GAUGE_BUFFER_WIDTH;
  int y = SelectSizeManager.V_GAUGE_BUFFER_WIDTH;
  int width = getWidth() - 2*SelectSizeManager.H_GAUGE_BUFFER_WIDTH;
  int height = getHeight() - 2*SelectSizeManager.V_GAUGE_BUFFER_WIDTH;
  // color the window white:
  g.setColor(MazeGame.WHITE);
  g.fillRect(x + 2, y + 2, width - 4, height - 4);
  // draw a border around the window to make it look indented:
  g.setColor(SelectSizeManager.OUTLINE);
  g.drawRect(x, y, width, height);
  g.setColor(SelectSizeManager.MED_BLUE);
  g.drawLine(x + 1, y + 1, x + width - 2, y + 1);
  g.drawLine(x + 1, y + 1, x + 1, y + height - 2);
  // now draw in the columns in the window:
  int columns = getValue();
  int colWidth = (width-4)/columns;
  int innerX = x + ((width-4) % columns)/2;
  boolean colored = true;
  for(int i = 0; i < columns; i++) {
    if(colored) {
      g.setColor(MazeGame.WALL_GRAY);
      int startX = innerX + i*colWidth;
      g.fillRect(startX, y + 2, colWidth, height - 4);
      g.setColor(MazeGame.HIGHLIGHT_GRAY);
      g.drawLine(startX, y + 2, startX, y + height - 3);
      g.setColor(MazeGame.SHADOW_GRAY);
      g.drawLine(startX + colWidth, y + 2, startX + colWidth, y + height - 3);
    }
    colored = !colored;
  }
```

```
    }
}
```

That's it for the Maze Deluxe example game. Now it's ready to sell on BlackBerry App World, as you'll see in the next chapter.

Summary

Beautiful graphics are a critical part of a professional game. The user interface screens should be attractive, fun, and well-integrated with the look of the game's main playing screen(s). RIM's proprietary user interface API gives you the tools to do just that. It's not hard to create impressive effects using simple tricks with image files and accents drawn in the code.

Chapter 5

Security and Selling Your Game

Security is one of BlackBerry's biggest selling points. Corporations can use BlackBerry Enterprise Solution to keep their confidential business data safe even when it's on smartphones that employees are carrying out of the office. But even if you're in the business of fun (instead of the business of business), the BlackBerry security model can help you when you're selling your game.

A platform's security model works in two directions: it protects customers from malicious applications that may harm their device or data, and it can also protect the application developer's intellectual property—that is, it can help ensure that users pay for the applications they use. Both directions are useful when selling your game, since a user will be more willing to download and install an application if he knows it can't harm his device or data.

Understanding BlackBerry Java Security

The Java Virtual Machine (JVM) naturally provides a layer of protection against malicious code. The JVM itself is the executable that is interacting with the device hardware. Thus it can ensure that it doesn't execute any commands that perform restricted actions such as reading from sensitive areas of memory or sending messages across the network without the user's permission.

Java security is based on a sandbox model. The JVM runs each application in a sandbox, which is essentially a place where it has enough room to run around and have fun but can't get out and make trouble. The JVM can place more toys in the sandbox (like access to network communications) if the application can be positively identified and is given permission (by the user) to play with a given toy. Identification is generally based on digital signatures and certificates.

Using Digital Signatures and Certificates

A digital signature ensures that a given block of data (e.g., a JAR file) has not been modified since the signer signed it. It's based on a standard asymmetric-key encryption technique in which a private key is used to encrypt data and a public key is used to decrypt it. The signer creates a hash of the data block (using a standard algorithm) and then encrypts the hash using the private key. The resulting encrypted hash is the *signature*.

If you have the public key, you can decrypt the signature and confirm that the decrypted result is the correct hash for the data block. And since the correct signature can't be created without access to the private key, you know that the data block is identical to the data block that the signer signed. (This assumes that the hashing algorithm is not easily reversible; i.e., there's no simple way of creating or modifying a data block to yield a desired hash.)

The remaining problem is to ensure that you have the public key that corresponds to the private key of someone you can positively identify. This is normally done using digital certificates.

A digital certificate is essentially a block of data giving the public key of someone you'd like to identify, signed with the private key of someone you already know. The device comes with root certificates installed that identify well-known trusted organizations (such as VeriSign) authorized to act as a *certificate authority* (CA). You can view and configure the root certificates on your BlackBerry smartphone by looking under **Options** ↗ **Options - Security** ↗ **Certificates**, as shown in Figure 5-1.

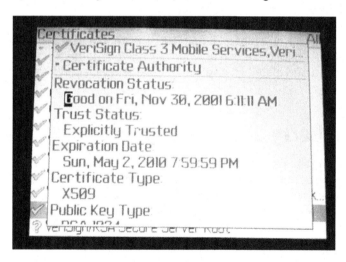

Figure 5-1. *Viewing the root certificates on the BlackBerry 8700*

If you have a digital certificate confirming that a CA can identify you, and you use it to sign your application, then the user knows that the application can be traced to its source (you), making the application a little more trustworthy than an application whose source can't be positively identified. To get a digital certificate, you need to contact the CA and follow the CA's procedure. Usually this entails generating your own key pair (using standard utilities such as the key tools bundled with the Sun WTK) and then sending a certificate signing request along with whatever real-world evidence the CA requires in order to confirm your identity, plus a fee.

The MIDP specification requires that a MIDlet declare all of the restricted actions it needs to perform. Most of these restricted actions have to do with making network communications (which may cost the user money). The desired actions are listed as permissions in the `MIDlet-Permissions` attribute of the JAD file and the manifest file (or in the `MIDlet-Permissions-Opt` attribute if the MIDlet can function without performing the restricted action). The AMS uses this information to warn the user about the MIDlet's intentions before proceeding with the download and installation of the MIDlet.

The device places the MIDlets into different *protection domains* based on the signatures and X509 digital certificates (or lack thereof) in the JAD file. Each protection domain corresponds to a set of permissions and a set of certificates. The permissions identify what the MIDlets in the domain are allowed to do. If the protection domain doesn't contain a given permission (permission to send an SMS message, for example), then when a MIDlet in that domain attempts to perform the action, the AMS will pop up a warning screen to ask the user whether it's OK for the MIDlet to proceed. If the user says no, then the MIDlet's attempted action fails with a `SecurityException`. If the MIDlet's protection domain contains the given permission, the MIDlet can perform the action without the AMS first displaying a warning screen. The certificates indicate which MIDlets should be placed in which domain.

Generally a device will have four protection domains: the manufacturer domain, the operator domain, the identified third-party domain, and the unidentified third-party domain (though it is possible for the manufacturer to define other protection domains as well). The manufacturer domain and the operator domain are for MIDlets signed by the manufacturer's certificate or the operator's certificate, embedded in the device or in the SIM card. (The SIM card is a removable smart card containing secure data that links the user to her account with a mobile phone operator.) Such MIDlets are automatically granted a wide range of freedom. The identified third-party domain is for MIDlets that are signed by a well-known CA. These usually have more permissions than unsigned MIDlets (which are banished to the "unidentified third-party domain"). Unsigned MIDlets require the user's permission before performing any restricted actions.

Signing with Credentials from RIM

When developing applications for BlackBerry, the most important digital credentials you'll need come from RIM. RIM's proprietary APIs contain a number of specially protected methods that can't be called on a BlackBerry smartphone unless the calling application has been signed with credentials provided by RIM. These methods are marked with a padlock symbol in the JavaDoc, and include lots of outside-the-sandbox activities, such as accessing the device's home screen or the user's call log.

The signing credentials provided by RIM are not exactly the same as the X509 digital certificates required by the MIDP security model, but they operate on the same principle.

Getting signing credentials from RIM is a very simple procedure. It's explained on the BlackBerry developers' web site, which at the time of this writing is on the following page:

```
http://na.blackberry.com/eng/developers/javaappdev/codekeys.jsp
```

In a nutshell, you fill out a form online (linked from the preceding page), which includes paying a fee (currently $20) by credit card.

> **Note** The set of functions from the MIDP API that require MIDP permissions are completely separate from the set of BlackBerry-specific APIs that require a signature from RIM. So signing your application with your RIM credentials will not automatically grant your application access to sensitive MIDP operations like reading the user's address book or sending an SMS (illustrated in Chapter 7).

Once RIM has processed your request, you'll receive three CSI files via e-mail containing the signing credentials. The e-mail will tell you just to click the attached CSI files, but there are a few things to be aware of before you do it. When you execute the files, they will look for an installation of the BlackBerry JDE on your computer, and they will modify it. Naturally, this means that you should be sure to execute the files on your development machine, not on some other computer. The executable contacts RIM (via the Internet) during this procedure, so your development machine needs to have an active Internet connection. Also, you'll be prompted for a password (that you'll later need to enter every time you sign an application), so be sure to have a strong standard-length password ready before you begin.

Once the CSI files have successfully done their job of updating your JDE, they are of no further use since they cannot be used again. Notably, you can't reuse the CSI files to add signing credentials to another BlackBerry JDE installation. The files that you need to guard carefully are the files created by the CSI files: sigtool.csk, sigtool.db, and sigtool.set, which you'll find in the BlackBerry JDE's bin directory. For example, if you've installed JDE 4.6.1, you'll find the three files in the following directory:

```
C:\Program Files\Research In Motion\BlackBerry JDE 4.6.1\bin
```

To add the same signing credentials to another JDE installation (on the same machine or on another), you just copy the sigtool files to the bin of the other JDE. Keep in mind, however, that the format of the sigtool files changed with version 4.3.0 of the JDE. So if you're copying signing credentials from a more recent JDE to an older (pre-4.3.0) JDE, you also need to copy the SignatureTool.jar executable (which is found in the bin folder with the sigtool files).

To sign your application, just click the SignatureTool.jar executable to launch it, browse to the directory containing your application's COD file, and select it. (In theory you can also launch the SignatureTool executable from within the JDE, but in practice I've gotten weird errors such as having the **Request Signatures** menu item grayed out and inaccessible even for projects that require signatures.) Once you've selected the COD file, SignatureTool will automatically detect exactly which restricted RIM APIs your application is using, and it will display the required signature requests, as shown in Figure 5-2.

Once you click Request Signatures, the signature tool will prompt you for your password and will contact RIM (via the Internet) as part of the signing procedure, so again you need to be on a computer with a live Internet connection for this step. If the signing process succeeds (or if the COD file you selected is already signed), the signature requests in the spreadsheet will turn green, and you'll be notified of the successful signing by a pop-up dialog box and via e-mail. If it fails, the requests will turn red (and you'll be notified of the failure by a pop-up dialog box and via e-mail).

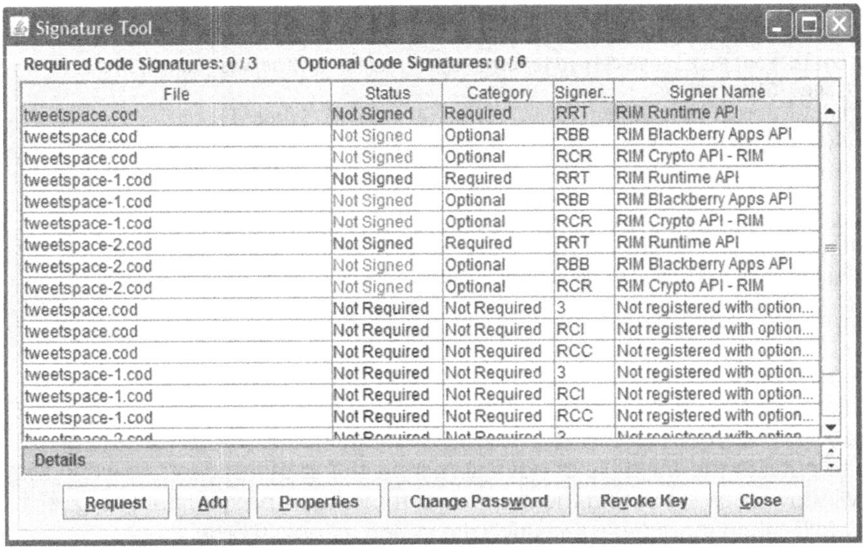

Figure 5-2. *SignatureTool preparing to sign an application*

One nice thing about this system is that if someone else is using your credentials to sign applications, you'll know about it as soon as you look in your inbox. The annoying aspect is that it clutters up your inbox with junk pretty fast if you're doing a lot of development or debug work. If you're using RIM's restricted APIs, then you have to sign each intermediate development version before you can install and test it on the device. And since a given application may require multiple signatures (which translates to multiple e-mails per signed version), you might want to set up a separate professional e-mail address just for communicating with RIM and BlackBerry App World.

> **Tip** If a signing request fails, there are several possible culprits in addition to the obvious one (you fat-fingered your password). The two other signing errors I've encountered were caused by a `SignatureTool` version mismatch (explained previously) and by attempting to sign a COD file that has been renamed or moved out of the directory where it was built. `SignatureTool` expects to find exactly the files generated by the JDE, hence any modification to the generated file set can cause signing errors.

Like the rest of the build procedure, the signing step can be automated with Ant. All you need to do is add the signature request to the `deliver` target in the `build.xml` file from Chapter 2 (Listing 2-7), as shown in Listing 5-1.

Listing 5-1. *The Modified deliver Target for the build.xml File from Listing 2-7*

```
<target name="deliver" depends="clean, build">
  <sigtool jdehome="C:\Program Files\Research In Motion\BlackBerry JDE 4.6.1"
           codfile="${build.output}\${project.name}\${project.name}_${model}.cod"
           password="***your*password***" />
  <!-- copy the signed file to the appropriate release folder -->
  <mkdir dir="${build.root}\release\${project.name}_${model}_${rim.version}"/>
  <echo file="${build.root}\release\${project.name}_${model}_${rim.version}\~CCC
devices.txt" message="${devices}" />
  <copy file="${build.output}\${project.name}\${project.name}_${model}.cod"
        tofile="${build.root}\release\${project.name}_${model}_${rim.version}\~CCC
${project.name}_${model}.cod"
  />
  <!-- install the signed application on the appropriate simulator -->
  <copy file="${build.output}\${project.name}\${project.name}_${model}.cod"
        tofile="${jde.home}\simulator\${project.name}_${model}.cod"
  />
</target>
```

Looking at Listing 5-1, you probably immediately noticed that the password you use to sign the COD files is right there in clear text. (Obviously you need to replace ***your*password*** with your password.) The sigtool task needs the password, so you either need to put it in the build file or have someone sitting there type it in when the SignatureTool window pops up during the build. Just remember that you have to guard the build file carefully when it contains sensitive data such as passwords.

You've probably also noticed that the sigtool task's jdehome attribute is set to one specific JDE installation, which may not be the same as the installation in the ${jde.home} property. By default, the sigtool task will use the SignatureTool executable found in the installation given by the ${jde.home} property. This example illustrates what to do if you'd like to always use SignatureTool in one particular JDE installation rather than maintaining the sigtool data files in all of the different JDE installations used by your build process.

Selling Your Game on BlackBerry App World

Once your game is signed and ready, the simplest way to sell it is on BlackBerry App World. In this section you'll see how to do that, using the Maze Deluxe example from Chapter 4 (after giving it the more marketing-friendly name Ladybug Maze).

Getting Started with BlackBerry App World

Once you have your signing credentials from RIM, you can create a vendor account on BlackBerry App World. The only prerequisite is that you must have a PayPal account. BlackBerry App World does not currently support any means of transferring your customer payments to you except via PayPal.

If you don't have an account with PayPal, you can go to http://paypal.com and set one up. It would be nice if there were other payment options available, but for most independent developers, PayPal is the simplest way to allow your customers to buy your game online anyway. Note that you can use the same PayPal account to sell your game on your own web site in addition to selling it on BlackBerry App World.

To create a vendor account, go to the BlackBerry App World vendor portal (at `http://appworld.blackberry.com/isvportal`). Once you've filled out the online forms there, the BlackBerry App World Store Front Manager will contact you with information about how to provide proof of your identity. If you're applying as a company, you will need to e-mail or fax BlackBerry App World some official documentation to validate your company information (such as your company's name and address). If you're applying as an individual, you'll receive a PDF Notarized Statement of Identification form. All you need to do is print it out, fill it out, and take it to a notary public with some official photo-bearing identification (such as a passport or driver's license). Then the notary public confirms your identity by signing and stamping the form, and then you fax it (or e-mail a scan of it) back to BlackBerry App World.

Finding a notary public is a simple matter in the United States. If you have a bank account, your bank will typically have a notary public on hand who will notarize your form free of charge. Otherwise, you can search online to find a notary public near you. Outside the United States, RIM will provide you with instructions on establishing your identity if the procedure is different.

You will be required to pay a fee up front, which is currently set at $200. This fee allows you to sell ten different applications on BlackBerry App World. In other words, you pay BlackBerry App World $20 per application to do a minimal inspection to ensure that your application doesn't have any egregious problems before they distribute it. Their QA engineers actually install your application on a BlackBerry smartphone and run it at least once to make sure it works reasonably well and doesn't crash the device. Twenty dollars is actually a pretty low price for a professional inspection—even a very minimal one. But it's obviously in their interest to offer a good deal for this service because they want lots of applications available on their portal, and they want end customers to be satisfied (which won't happen if the portal is full of broken, handset-crashing apps). Figure 5-3 shows what the BlackBerry App World client looks like.

When you first sign up as a vendor, it takes BlackBerry App World about a week to process your identity papers. Then, once you submit an application to sell, it takes BlackBerry App World about two weeks to inspect it and validate it so that you can set it to be available to customers on the portal.

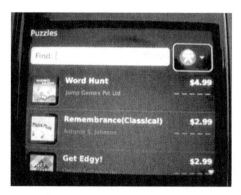

Figure 5-3. *The BlackBerry Curve accessing BlackBerry App World*

Preparing Your Game for Sale on BlackBerry App World

Preparing your game for sale on BlackBerry App World is surprisingly simple. If your game has different versions for use on different models, BlackBerry App World has defined a file structure so you can zip all of the versions into a single release bundle to upload. The BlackBerry App World portal will automatically unzip the bundle and assign each COD file to the correct devices according to the instructions you place in the release bundle.

> **Note** If your game has different COD files corresponding to different device models, these different builds don't count as separate applications against your total of ten apps. Resubmitting a corrected version of a rejected application also doesn't count against your total. Submitting a new release of an accepted application, however, does count against your total number of applications.

You can also define your release manually by uploading the COD files individually and assigning them to different device models, as shown in Figure 5-4. And even if you start by uploading your game in an automatically interpreted release bundle, you can still modify the release parameters manually using the same form you'd use to manually define your release.

To create a release bundle that can be automatically interpreted, you do the following: First, create the root-level release folder. In it, you create a subdirectory for each different version. Place the built (and signed) COD files into their respective subdirectories. (You don't need any of the other files generated by the build.) The name of each subdirectory must end with the lowest BlackBerry operating system version number supported by the COD file in the subdirectory. The only other file that you place in the subdirectory with the COD file is a text file called `devices.txt`, which lists exactly which devices the COD file was built for. If you have any questions about how to identify the different models, you can always open the Manage Applications page for uploading a release (shown in Figure 5-3)—all of the supported model numbers are listed right there. Lastly, you can add a `release.xml` file in the root folder to give the release number and the release notes. Then all you have to do is zip up the root folder, and it's ready to upload.

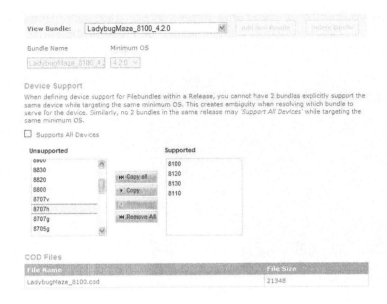

Figure 5-4. *Assigning different COD files to different device models when uploading a release to BlackBerry App World*

If you use the Ant build files from Chapter 2 (with the modification given in Listing 5-1) the correct release folder is created automatically. The devices.txt file is created in the deliver target (from Listing 5-1) by echoing the value of the ${devices} parameter to a file. The value of this parameter comes from the model properties file shown in Listing 2-8.

There are only a couple of steps missing from the Ant build files: I didn't have it generate a release.xml file, and I didn't have Ant zip the release directory. I skipped adding these steps to the automated build because I'd rather manually inspect the release folder and manually add the release number and release notes when the release is finally done. But if you prefer to automate these steps as well, you can easily do it with Ant.

Once your release bundle is ready, there are still a few more items to prepare. You'll need a 480×480-pixel PNG file to serve as an icon for your game in the BlackBerry App World catalog. BlackBerry App World will shrink this icon to various sizes, so be sure to create an image that looks good even when it's small. For Ladybug Maze, I created the 480×480-pixel icon with some fine detail that ultimately didn't look as nice shrunken down as my original 80×80-pixel icon that I'd drawn as the menu icon for the BlackBerry 8900, as you can see in Figure 5-5. The trick is to hire a professional graphic designer to do your game graphics, and then you won't have this problem.

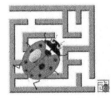

Figure 5-5. *The 480×480-pixel icon and the 80×80-pixel icon for the Ladybug Maze game*

In addition to the icon, you should prepare some screenshots of your game. These will also appear on the game's BlackBerry App World catalog page to show potential customers what they'll be getting. Figure 5-6 shows the catalog page for Ladybug Maze.

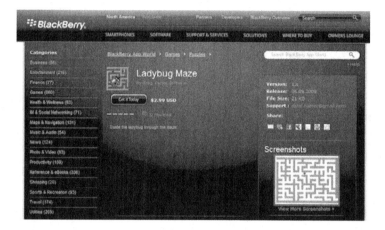

Figure 5-6. *The BlackBerry App World catalog page for Ladybug Maze in a browser on a PC*

Once you have all of your graphics ready, you need to be prepared with some additional information about how to market your game. You need to select exactly one category from the list of categories. For most people reading this book, the category will be Games, but keep in mind that you'll also have to select a subcategory.

You'll also need to have a short description of the game, again for use on the catalog page. The description should be translated into every language that is supported both by your game and by BlackBerry App World. At the time of this writing, BlackBerry App World is only available in English, French, Italian, German, and Spanish (and all applications are required to support English at least).

You should also have a support e-mail address handy for BlackBerry App World to display to customers so that they can contact you about problems in your game. If you have restrictions about which operator networks can support your game, you should have that information ready at submission time as well.

And last—but certainly not least—you need to know exactly what payment model you're planning to use.

Selecting a Billing Model for BlackBerry App World

BlackBerry App World allows you a choice of several different payment models for selling your game. In the simplest model, the user has to pay BlackBerry App World up front to get a download link to download the game. But—even if you've provided enticing screenshots—users often prefer to take the game for a test drive before committing to pay, so BlackBerry App World offers a few different choices for a try-and-buy system.

The first try-and-buy option is the *static model*. You simply create two versions of your game—the free teaser and the complete game—and you upload them both. BlackBerry

App World takes care of distributing the teaser for free and charging for download of the complete game.

The second try-and-buy model is the *license key model*. In this model, the game's default mode is the trial version, and after a certain amount of play, the game prompts the user to enter a license key that unlocks the complete game. You have to implement your own unlocking functionality in your game (as shown in the Access Control example in this chapter, for example). BlackBerry App World takes care of selling the license keys to the users (for the price you've chosen), and supports three types of license key models: single, pool, and dynamic.

In the *single-license model*, there's just one key that can be used by any user on any device. I doubt I need to explain the security hole in this model, but it is discussed (along with all the others) in the "Cracking Your Game's Billing System" sidebar. In the *pool model*, you must generate a set of single-use keys and upload them to BlackBerry App World (to sell to your customers). In this scenario, you normally would have your game contact your game server to map the given license key to the user (and ensure that the key is not reused by someone else). The last license key model is the *dynamic model*, in which you generate a user-specific key based on the user's data. For example, you can generate a key based on the unique PIN that identifies the user's device. This model is illustrated in detail in the "Sending Dynamic Keys to BlackBerry App World" and "Decrypting Dynamic License Keys" sections of this chapter.

The other standard try-and-buy model is the *post-download sales* model, in which the game can sell the player different items throughout its lifetime. The classic example would be an adventure game in which the player can pay extra for premium armor or spells for the character. BlackBerry App World allows this model but does not support it. Unlike the dynamic-licensing model, which you'll see in the next section, there's no standard way to build post-download purchases into the BlackBerry App World sales model. Here's what the current BlackBerry App World Vendor Agreement says about it:

> *Vendor shall pay to RIM twenty percent (20%) of Application Revenue (which as defined in this Agreement excludes any fees paid by an End User to an MoR to obtain a copy of an Application through an MoR Kiosk) ("Application Revenue Fee") on a calendar quarterly basis in arrears, payable within thirty (30) days of the end of each calendar quarter. Vendor shall provide to RIM a monthly report outlining calculation of the Application Revenue Fee for the applicable month in accordance with United States generally accepted accounting principles. Vendor shall pay the Application Revenue Fee in United States dollars by electronic funds transfer as directed by RIM to Vendor in writing.*

Translated into plain English, I suspect this means that if your game charges money in any way other than the BlackBerry App World–supported billing models just described, then you have to pay RIM 20 percent of the money it earns you. What's more, you have to do the accounting yourself ("in accordance with United States generally accepted accounting principles") and send the money to RIM. The agreement goes on to say that you're responsible for the taxes and that they may audit you to ensure that your accounting is correct. In a nutshell, if you want to use this billing model, you'll need to contact RIM and work out a payment plan.

Sending Dynamic Keys to BlackBerry App World

If you'd like to generate a user-specific license key, and you want BlackBerry App World to sell it to the user for you, then you'll need to dynamically transfer the keys to BlackBerry App World. Fortunately, RIM has defined a simple protocol for this transaction, found in a document called "Dynamic License Flow," which you can download here:

http://na.blackberry.com/eng/developers/appworld/Dynamic_License_Flow.pdf

All you need to do is set up a web server to accept a simple HTTP POST command from BlackBerry App World (containing the user's data) and then return the corresponding license key. If you're not familiar with HTTP and how to use servlets, they're explained in more detail in Chapters 9 and 11.Here's the exact HTTP request that Blackberry App World will send to your license key server:

```
POST /pathfromdeveloper HTTP/1.1
Content-Type: application/www-url-encoded
Content-Length: 120
Host: hostfromdeveloper
PIN=12341234&email=customeremail@email.com&product=product&version=1.2~CCC
&transactionid=123&test=false
```

Note that you specify the pathfromdeveloper and the hostfromdeveloper (along with the URL of your license key server) when you configure this licensing option.

In the body of the POST, you'll receive two pieces of user-specific data: the user's e-mail address and the PIN that identifies the user's device. In this example, you'll use the PIN number, but note that using the e-mail address may be more convenient for users that upgrade their device frequently. (Your game can find out the user's e-mail address through the ServiceConfiguration class of the net.rim.blackberry.api.mail package.)

The transactionid is the one security measure that you can use to protect against fraudulent access. Since this transaction is a simple HTTP request over the open Internet, anyone who knows the URL of your license server can send you a fake request and get a real license key for your game. But you can monitor the transaction ID numbers and reject requests that have unexpected values. Of course, someone who knows your license server's URL and knows how to send a POST request with the right parameters may also know how to read a few packets of data headed for your server, read the transaction ID off of a real request, and use that information to create a transaction ID that will fool your server. Your only line of defense against that attack is that most people won't go through that much trouble to unlock your game, especially if it's not very expensive. This defense is a key part of the security behind other billing methods as well, as shown in the "Cracking Your Game's Billing System" sidebar.

When your license server receives the POST from BlackBerry App World, it must return the key in a response with the following format:

```
HTTP/1.1 200 OK
Content-Type: application/www-url-encoded
Content-Length: 20
key=ABCDEFGHIJK
```

Listing 5-2 shows a simple servlet that receives the license request from BlackBerry App World and returns a license key based on the PIN. This example servlet was developed for an Apache Tomcat 4.1 server and illustrates the bare bones of what you need to do to implement the BlackBerry App World license protocol. In practice, your license server should include a few additional features such as checking the transaction ID (as explained previously) and recording the transaction data in a database.

Listing 5-2. *GetLicense.java*

```java
import java.io.*;
import javax.servlet.*;
import javax.servlet.http.*;
import javax.crypto.*;
import javax.crypto.spec.*;

/**
 * A minimal servlet that returns the license key for
 * the given PIN.
 */
public class GetLicense extends HttpServlet {

  /**
   * Get the license corresponding to the PIN.
   */
  String getLicense(int pin) {
    String retString = "";
    try {
      ByteArrayOutputStream baos = new ByteArrayOutputStream();
      DataOutputStream dos = new DataOutputStream(baos);
      dos.writeInt(pin);
      baos.close();
      dos.close();
      baos.close();
      byte[] pinData = baos.toByteArray();

      SecretKeyFactory scf = SecretKeyFactory.getInstance("DES");
      // The DES key used to generate the license is hard-coded:
      byte[] keyData = {
          (byte)-29, (byte)14, (byte)-22, (byte)35,
          (byte)-53, (byte)4, (byte)-3, (byte)-48
      };
      DESKeySpec keySpec = new DESKeySpec(keyData);
      SecretKey desKey = scf.generateSecret(keySpec);
      Cipher desCipher;

      // Create the cipher
      desCipher = Cipher.getInstance("DES/ECB/PKCS5Padding");
      // Initialize the cipher for encryption
```

```java
        desCipher.init(Cipher.ENCRYPT_MODE, desKey);

        // Encrypt the pin
        byte[] ciphertext = desCipher.doFinal(pinData);

        // Turn the encrypted byte array into a human-readable string
        DataInputStream stream
            = new DataInputStream(new ByteArrayInputStream(ciphertext));
        int val1 = stream.readInt();
        int val2 = stream.readInt();
        stream.close();
        retString = val1 + "z" + val2;

    } catch (Exception e) {
        e.printStackTrace();
    }
    return retString;
}

/**
 * Use an input stream to convert an array of bytes to an int.
 */
public static int parseInt(byte[] data) throws IOException {
    DataInputStream stream
        = new DataInputStream(new ByteArrayInputStream(data));
    int retVal = stream.readInt();
    stream.close();
    return(retVal);
}

/**
 * Handle the POST request (others are ignored).
 */
public void doPost(HttpServletRequest request, HttpServletResponse response)
        throws IOException, ServletException {

    int length = request.getContentLength();
    byte[] content = new byte[length];
    // get the input stream to read the user data from BlackBerry App World:
    InputStream is = request.getInputStream();
    int read = is.read(content);
    // Many errors are ignored in this minimal example.
    if(read != length) {
        response.sendError(400);
    } else {
        // get the PIN from the data:
        String contentString = new String(content);
        int startIndex = contentString.indexOf("PIN=");
        int endIndex = contentString.indexOf("&", startIndex);
        String pinString = contentString.substring(startIndex+4, endIndex);
        // it is sent as a hexidecimal string, hence the "16"
        // argument when parsing it:
        int pin = Integer.parseInt(pinString, 16);

        // Prepare the response data:
```

```
        String responseString = "key=" + getLicense(pin);
        byte[] responseBytes = responseString.getBytes();
        response.setContentType("application/www-url-encoded");
        response.setContentLength(responseBytes.length);
        OutputStream os = response.getOutputStream();
        // send the message
        os.write(responseBytes);
        os.close();
        response.flushBuffer();
    }
  }
}
```

As you can see, this servlet uses the DES encryption algorithm to encrypt the PIN number, and then returns the encrypted PIN. More precisely, it extracts the PIN string from the request, interprets the string as an int, converts the int to a byte array, encrypts the byte array using the DES encryption algorithm, converts the encrypted byte array into two ints, encodes the pair of ints as a String, and then returns the result in a response that conforms to BlackBerry App World's specified protocol. Now all you need is a game that will accept this string as the license key to unlock it, as you'll see in the next section.

CRACKING YOUR GAME'S BILLING SYSTEM

Choosing a billing model for your game means finding the right balance between simplicity and security. Making your game completely uncrackable requires—in most cases—far more effort than it's worth, especially if the game is inexpensive. If the game isn't too easy to crack, but it's easy to buy (such as through BlackBerry App World) and it's sold at a reasonable price, then the cost/effort to crack it will be greater to than the cost/effort to buy it. If you know how to crack your own game, then you can easily decide what level of security is appropriate.

The most basic type of security on BlackBerry App World is via restricted download. In order to download the game directly from BlackBerry App World onto the device, you have to pay. This model, however, is easy for anyone with a basic knowledge of BlackBerry to go around. Once an application has been downloaded, you can use the Desktop Manager to save it onto your PC. This gives you a COD file that you can distribute and upload onto other devices.

Protecting your game with a license key adds an extra layer of protection, but it's not perfect. If you use a single key, naturally the key itself can get posted on the Internet, leaving your game wide open to anyone who googles it. The key pool method is quite secure if there's no simple way of guessing the valid key values, and if there's no simple way of intercepting (and spoofing) the game's call to your server to validate the key. (Of course, if the game doesn't need to contact your server to validate the key, then the pool method is no different than the single method.) Since the extra effort to have the game contact your server is costly (and potentially annoying to the user), the pool method is most useful for games that ordinarily contact your server anyway in order to play (such as networked games).

Using a dynamic license key gives you the advantage that the game can validate itself without contacting your server. The disadvantage is that it may be possible to crack the algorithm used to generate the key. The Access Control example in this chapter uses a symmetric-key algorithm to encrypt the PIN. Since symmetric-key algorithms use the same encryption key for both encryption and decryption, the encryption data (to generate the license key) is present in the game code (since the game needs it in order to validate the license key). BlackBerry's COD file format is proprietary, but it's not too hard to convert it to a JAR file, and from there decompile it sufficiently to find the encryption key. Note that the Access Control example uses the DES algorithm (which is inherently weak enough to be cracked by computational brute force), but even if you replace it with the less-crackable triple DES, you still have the problem that the encryption key is present in the game file. Only a very advanced user can crack your license code in this way, but one person can crack it once and then set up a web site with a simple applet that returns a valid license key to your game for anyone who types in a PIN.

The next obvious idea is to encrypt some identifying data (such as the PIN, phone number, or e-mail address) using asymmetric-key encryption. You encrypt the data with your private key and then place the public key in the game code to decrypt it. Since the BlackBerry has all sorts of encryption and decryption algorithms built in, you could, for example, sign the user's PIN with a digital signature and then have the game validate the signature using your public key (hard-coded/compiled into the game). The main disadvantage is that the signature returned by the built-in signing API is so long that it's not reasonable to expect the user to type it in. Using digital signatures, however, is feasible if you're selling your license from your own site (where the game itself communicates with your site using your own invented protocol) instead of selling license keys through BlackBerry App World.

Then there's the question of how to securely store your key. You can't insist that the user type in the license key every time, so you have to store the information that the game has been purchased. If you merely store a "purchased" flag somewhere in memory, the user may be able to spoof it by creating a fake file that matches the one the game would normally create. You can gain some additional protection by storing the "purchased" flag in the smart card, or by storing the license key itself (instead of a generic flag), as shown in the Access Control example.

If you're not selling through BlackBerry App World, then you have a bit more leeway to create a very secure handshake between your game and your server, or—if you have an agreement with an operator (carrier)—to sell access to parts of your game using SMS short codes (with security ensured by the operator). It's just a question of optimizing your security solution to fit your particular business model.

Decrypting Dynamic License Keys

If want to use license keys to sell your game, you need to add a little bit of code to read in the key, validate it, and store it. This section will introduce you to the Access Control application, which does exactly that. This example application is designed to be compatible with the servlet in Listing 5-2, so the license key that the servlet generates for a given PIN can be validated by this application (running on a device with the given PIN).

The Access Control example is a complete application, but it's meant to be used as a building block to incorporate into a larger game. When it's launched, it first checks its memory for a license key. If it finds some data in its repository, it attempts to decrypt the data (using its hard-coded DES encryption/decryption key), and if the decrypted data matches the device's PIN, then it displays the message "code valid." Otherwise, it displays a text field where the user can enter a license key. When the user enters a key, the application decrypts it (again using DES and the hard-coded encryption/decryption key), and if the decrypted value equals the device PIN, then it stores the license data in the RMS and displays the message "code valid." The program flow can be seen in the main UIApplication class, shown in Listing 5-3.

Listing 5-3. *AccessControl.java*

```java
package net.frogparrot.crypt;

import net.rim.device.api.ui.UiApplication;
import net.rim.device.api.system.EventLogger;
import net.rim.device.api.system.DeviceInfo;

/**
 * A simple encryption/decryption example for BlackBerry.
 * This application reads in a license key that the user has
 * purchased and checks whether it is a valid key for the
 * current device by checking it against the device PIN.
 */
public class AccessControl extends UiApplication implements Runnable {

//-----------------------------------------------------------------
//   instance fields

  /**
   * The PIN number that uniquely identifies the device.
   */
  int myPin;

  /**
   * Whether a valid license has been provided (either this session
   * or from a previously entered license in memory).
   */
  boolean myIsValid;

  /**
   * The screen to communicate with the user.
   */
  AccessScreen myAccessScreen;

  /**
   * A special inner class that is used to update the display
   * on the event thread (for cases where the update was prompted
   * from another thread).
   */
  Runnable myUpdateScreen = new Thread() {
      public void run() {
        myAccessScreen.setup();
      }
    };

//-----------------------------------------------------------------
//   initialization and accessors

  /**
   * The application entry point
   */
  public static void main(String[] args) {
    // each BlackBerry application that wants to log
    // messages must register with a unique ID:
    EventLogger.register(0x40b0f6f6c6052cdaL, "accesscontrol",
```

```java
        EventLogger.VIEWER_STRING);
    AccessControl ac = new AccessControl();
    // Create a thread to perform memory access and decryption
    // functionality that may take too long to be run on
    // the event thread:
    Thread t = new Thread(ac);
    t.start();
    // Set the current thread to notify this application
    // of events such as user input.
    ac.enterEventDispatcher();
}

/**
 * The constructor initializes the data.
 */
private AccessControl() {
    myAccessScreen = new AccessScreen(this);
    pushScreen(myAccessScreen);
    myPin = DeviceInfo.getDeviceId();
}

/**
 * Tells whether a valid license has been provided
 * (either this session or from a previously entered
 * license in memory).
 */
public boolean isValid() {
    return myIsValid;
}

//----------------------------------------------------------------
// Business methods to check the license key

/**
 * A runnable method to perform time-consuming memory
 * access and decryption functions that should not be performed
 * on the event thread.
 */
public void run() {
    try {
        DesPinEncryptor dpe = DesPinEncryptor.getInstance();
        // check the input field for user text:
        String userText = myAccessScreen.getUserText();
        if((userText == null) || (userText.trim().length() == 0)) {
            // if no text has been entered, try the memory:
            byte[] licenseKey = AccessStorage.getLicenseKey();
            // Check whether the license data in memory is valid:
            if((licenseKey != null) && (dpe.validateLicenseBytes(licenseKey, myPin))) {
                myIsValid = true;
            }
        } else {
            byte[] licenseBytes = dpe.licenseStringToBytes(userText);
            if((licenseBytes != null)
                    && (dpe.validateLicenseBytes(licenseBytes, myPin))) {
                myIsValid = true;
```

```java
      // set the license data in memory:
      AccessStorage.setLicenseKey(licenseBytes);
    }
  }
  // The screen needs to be updated, but can't be updated from
  // this thread. So we call invokeLater to tell the platform
  // to call myUpdateScreen.run() from the event thread at
  // the next opportunity:
  invokeLater(myUpdateScreen);
} catch(Exception e) {
  postException(e);
}
}

//------------------------------------------------------------------
// debug logging utilities

/**
 * A utility to log debug messages.
 */
public static void setMessage(String message) {
  EventLogger.logEvent(0x40b0f6f6c6052cdaL, message.getBytes());
  System.out.println(message);
}

/**
 * A utility to log exceptions.
 */
public static void postException(Exception e) {
  System.out.println(e);
  e.printStackTrace();
  String exceptionName = e.getClass().getName();
  EventLogger.logEvent(0x40b0f6f6c6052cdaL, exceptionName.getBytes());
  if(e.getMessage() != null) {
    EventLogger.logEvent(0x40b0f6f6c6052cdaL, e.getMessage().getBytes());
  }
}

}
```

The debug code using the EventLogger class is explained in the "Logging Messages with the EventLogger" sidebar in Chapter 7.

The main thing to notice in Listing 5-3 is the use of threading. The RMS memory access and the DES decoding algorithm are both probably fast enough that there's no danger in calling them from the event thread. But as soon as you start doing things that are complex (in terms of computation or resource access or both), it's a good idea to run them on another thread, just to be on the safe side. Deadlocking the event thread is the easiest way to crash the handset, creating a critical bug and an unhappy customer. So, since main() is called from the event thread, you have it start up a new thread to call the run() method, instead of just calling the memory and decryption methods directly from main().

Once the run() method has reached its verdict (that there's valid license data or not), it needs to update the display with that information. The problem is that (as discussed in the "Hello BlackBerry!" section of Chapter 2) you can't update the display from any thread other than the event thread if you're using RIM's proprietary UI APIs (i.e., your application is a RIMlet and not a MIDlet). Fortunately, this problem is easy to solve. Just wrap the UI update code in a little Runnable, like the myUpdateScreen field of Listing 5-3. Then, if you pass this Runnable as an argument to the invokeLater() method, its run() method will be called by the event thread at its earliest convenience.

The run() method is not only called at launch time (from main()), but it's also called when the user clicks OK (after entering the license key) to check whether the license is valid (and, if so, to store it in memory). As you can see in Listing 5-4, it's actually launched from the run() method of the MenuItem myOK. It may look like it's redundant to create a new thread and start it from within the run() method of the Runnable MenuItem, but it's not. Keep in mind that the platform calls the MenuItem's run() method from the event thread.

Listing 5-4. *AccessScreen.java*

```java
package net.frogparrot.crypt;

import net.rim.device.api.ui.MenuItem;
import net.rim.device.api.ui.component.*;
import net.rim.device.api.ui.container.MainScreen;

/**
 * The screen to draw the message on, to inform the user whether or
 * not the application has been validated with the key.
 */
public class AccessScreen extends MainScreen {

//------------------------------------------------------------------
//  instance fields

  /**
   * A handle to the main class of the application.
   */
  AccessControl myMain;

  /**
   * The "OK" menu item that checks whether the String that the
   * user entered is a valid license key for this device.
   */
  MenuItem myOK = new MenuItem("OK", 0, 0) {
      // This is called when the user selects the OK menu item:
      public void run() {
        Thread t = new Thread(myMain);
        myMain.run();
      }
    };

  /**
   * The input field where the user types in the license key.
   */
  EditField myEnterLicenseField = new EditField(
          EditField.JUMP_FOCUS_AT_END | EditField.NO_NEWLINE
```

```
                 | RichTextField.NO_LEARNING | RichTextField.NO_COMPLEX_INPUT
                 | RichTextField.FOCUSABLE | RichTextField.EDITABLE);


//------------------------------------------------------------------
//  initialization and life cycle

  /**
   * @return the text the user has entered.
   */
  String getUserText() {
    return myEnterLicenseField.getText();
  }

  /**
   * The constructor initializes the data.
   */
  AccessScreen(AccessControl ac) {
    super();
    myMain = ac;
  }

  /**
   * Once the application has decided whether the user has
   * entered a valid license key, this method fills the screen
   * with the corresponding items: either a message that the
   * key has been validated or an editable field that the
   * user can type the key into.
   */
  public void setup() {
    deleteAll();
    if(myMain.isValid()) {
      add(new RichTextField("code valid",
          RichTextField.NON_FOCUSABLE | RichTextField.READONLY));
    } else {
      add(new RichTextField("enter code",
          RichTextField.NON_FOCUSABLE | RichTextField.READONLY));
      add(myEnterLicenseField);
    }
  }

  /**
   * Override the screen's menu creation method
   * to add the custom command.
   */
  protected void makeMenu(Menu menu, int instance) {
    menu.add(myOK);
    // separate the custom menu items from
    // the default menu items:
    menu.addSeparator();
    super.makeMenu(menu, instance);
  }

  /**
   * This is called by the BlackBerry platform when
```

```
 * the screen is popped off the screen stack.
 */
public boolean onClose() {
  // end the program:
  System.exit(0);
  // confirm that the screen has been removed:
  return true;
}

}
```

Listing 5-4 is a bit of a placeholder. It's the UI component that would normally be replaced with the game's custom UI when the Access Control code is incorporated into a game to validate license keys. In a complete game, once the run() method has checked whether a valid license key is present in memory, it would go ahead and launch the game, either in trial mode or in full mode. Then—if it's in trial mode—after the user has completed a few levels, the game would show a screen prompting the user to enter a license key (which is then validated exactly as in this example).

The encryption code can also be customized to suit your game. As explained in the "Cracking Your Game's Billing System" sidebar, RIM provides a whole array of cryptography options, so you can pick whichever encryption type fits your needs. Listing 5-5 illustrates how to use the very simplest one. If you decide to use this example implementation in a game, be sure to use the DESKey class to generate your own DES key—don't just use the hard-coded key that's published in this book.

Listing 5-5. *DesPinEncryptor.java*

```java
package net.frogparrot.crypt;

import net.rim.device.api.crypto.*;
import java.io.*;

/**
 * A simple decryption example for BlackBerry. This class takes
 * an int and uses a hard-coded DES key to encode it, for use
 * as a license.
 */
public class DesPinEncryptor {

//------------------------------------------------------------------
//  static fields

  /**
   * The singleton instance of this class.
   */
  private static DesPinEncryptor theInstance;

  /**
   * A character to separate the two ints that make up the
   * license string.
   */
  public static String LICENSE_SEPARATOR = "z";

//------------------------------------------------------------------
```

```java
//  instance fields

  /**
   * Hard-coded key data representing the DES key.
   * To create your own, just create a DESKey with the empty
   * constructor, and then call getData() on it to get the
   * key data.
   */
  private byte[] myKeyData = {
          (byte)-29, (byte)14, (byte)-22, (byte)35,
          (byte)-53, (byte)4, (byte)-3, (byte)-48
      };

  /**
   * The object holding the DES key data.
   */
  private DESKey myKey;

//-----------------------------------------------------------------
//  initialization and accessors

  /**
   * get the singleton instance.
   */
  static DesPinEncryptor getInstance() {
    if(theInstance == null) {
      theInstance = new DesPinEncryptor();
    }
    return theInstance;
  }

  /**
   * Constructor initializes data.
   */
  private DesPinEncryptor() {
    myKey = new DESKey(myKeyData);
  }

//-----------------------------------------------------------------
//  decryption and formatting utilities

  /**
   * Uses an input stream to convert an array of bytes to an int.
   */
  public static int parseInt(byte[] data) throws IOException {
    DataInputStream stream
      = new DataInputStream(new ByteArrayInputStream(data));
    int retVal = stream.readInt();
    stream.close();
    return(retVal);
  }

  /**
   * Takes a human-readable string and converts it to
   * a byte array of eight bytes, to be decrypted with
```

```java
 * the DES key.
 */
public byte[] licenseStringToBytes(String license) {
  byte[] retVal = null;
  try {
    // First split the string into two strings,
    // each corresponding to one int:
    int index = license.indexOf(LICENSE_SEPARATOR);
    String sval1 = license.substring(0, index);
    int val1 = Integer.parseInt(sval1);
    String sval2 = license.substring(index + 1, license.length());
    int val2 = Integer.parseInt(sval2);
    // Convert the two ints to an array of eight bytes
    // using output streams:
    ByteArrayOutputStream baos = new ByteArrayOutputStream(8);
    DataOutputStream dos = new DataOutputStream(baos);
    dos.writeInt(val1);
    dos.writeInt(val2);
    baos.close();
    dos.close();
    retVal = baos.toByteArray();
  } catch(Exception e) {
    AccessControl.postException(e);
  }
  return retVal;
}

/**
 * Takes a human-readable string and decrypts it with the
 * DES key to determine whether it corresponds to the given PIN.
 */
public boolean validateLicenseKey(String license, int pin) {
  boolean retVal = false;
  try {
    byte[] licenseBytes = licenseStringToBytes(license);
    retVal = validateLicenseBytes(licenseBytes, pin);
  } catch(Exception e) {
    AccessControl.postException(e);
  }
  return retVal;
}

/**
 * Takes an array of eight bytes and decrypts it with the
 * DES key to determine whether it corresponds to the given PIN.
 */
public boolean validateLicenseBytes(byte[] edata, int pin) {
  boolean retVal = false;
  try {
    // Set up the decryptor engine with the local key:
    DESDecryptorEngine de = new DESDecryptorEngine(myKey);
    PKCS5UnformatterEngine ue = new PKCS5UnformatterEngine(de);
    ByteArrayInputStream bais = new ByteArrayInputStream(edata);
    BlockDecryptor decryptor = new BlockDecryptor(ue, bais);
```

```
      // Decrypt the given byte array into a new byte array
      // of length 4:
      byte[] result = new byte[4];
      int bytesRead = decryptor.read(result);
      // Use input streams to convert the byte array to an int:
      int licenseInt = parseInt(result);
      // Check whether the resulting int equals the given PIN:
      retVal = (pin == licenseInt);
    } catch(Exception e) {
      AccessControl.postException(e);
    }
    return retVal;
  }

//------------------------------------------------------------------
//   encryption utilities
//   These are not used by the access control functionality.
//   They are included only for convenience to illustrate how
//   to do an encryption parallel to the decryption code.

  /**
   * Takes a PIN and returns the corresponding string
   * encrypted with DES and the included key.
   */
  private byte[] byteCryptPin(int pin) {
    byte[] retVal = null;
    try {
      DESEncryptorEngine ee = new DESEncryptorEngine(myKey);
      PKCS5FormatterEngine fe = new PKCS5FormatterEngine(ee);
      ByteArrayOutputStream baos = new ByteArrayOutputStream();
      BlockEncryptor encryptor = new BlockEncryptor(fe, baos);
      encryptor.write(intToFourBytes(pin));
      encryptor.close();
      retVal = baos.toByteArray();
    } catch(Exception e) {
      AccessControl.postException(e);
    }
    return retVal;
  }

  /**
   * Takes a PIN and returns the corresponding string
   * encrypted with DES and the included key.
   */
  private String encryptPin(int pin) {
    String retString = "error";
    try {
      byte[] encryptedData = byteCryptPin(pin);
      DataInputStream stream
          = new DataInputStream(new ByteArrayInputStream(encryptedData));
      int val1 = stream.readInt();
      int val2 = stream.readInt();
      stream.close();
      retString = (val1 + LICENSE_SEPARATOR) + val2;
      boolean same = retString.equals("-717057553X2024320075");
```

```
    } catch(Exception e) {
      AccessControl.postException(e);
    }
    return retString;
  }

  /**
   * Uses an output stream to convert an int to four bytes.
   */
  public static byte[] intToFourBytes(int i) throws IOException {
    ByteArrayOutputStream baos = new ByteArrayOutputStream(4);
    DataOutputStream dos = new DataOutputStream(baos);
    dos.writeInt(i);
    baos.close();
    dos.close();
    byte[] retArray = baos.toByteArray();
    return(retArray);
  }

}
```

The code in Listing 5-5 undoes the work performed by the servlet in Listing 5-2. It decodes the string formatting that is used to make the encrypted PIN human-readable, and then it decrypts the data to confirm that it corresponds to the correct PIN.

I've also included some encryption code in Listing 5-5 as well. These are only for your information, to illustrate how to perform the encryption using the RIM APIs. If you compare Listing 5-5 with Listing 5-2, you'll see that the Java SE encryption APIs are used slightly differently. Yet the resulting values are exactly the same because both the RIM encryption API and the Java SE encryption API are implementations of standard algorithms. In a real game, the unused encryption methods would be removed from this class.

The remaining piece of the Access Control example is the memory access class, given in Listing 5-6.

Listing 5-6. *AccessStorage.java*

```
package net.frogparrot.crypt;

import javax.microedition.rms.*;

/**
 * This class helps to store and retrieve the license key.
 *
 * This is a utility class that does not contain instance data,
 * so to simplify acess all of the methods are static.
 */
public class AccessStorage {

//-------------------------------------------------------------
//    static fields

  /**
   * The name of the datastore.
   */
```

```java
    private static final String STORE = "Validation";

//------------------------------------------------------------
//    business methods

  /**
   * This gets the user's license key, if one has been stored.
   */
  public static byte[] getLicenseKey() {
    // if data retrieval fails, the default value is 7
    byte[] retVal = null;
    RecordStore store = null;
    try {
      // if the record store does not yet exist, we
      // send "false" so it won't bother to create it.
      store = RecordStore.openRecordStore(STORE, false);
      if((store != null) && (store.getNumRecords() > 0)) {
        // the first record has ID number 1
        // (In fact this program stores only one record)
        retVal = store.getRecord(1);
      }
    } catch(Exception e) {
      AccessControl.postException(e);
    } finally {
      try {
        store.closeRecordStore();
      } catch(Exception e) {
        // if the record store is open this shouldn't throw.
      }
    }
    return(retVal);
  }

  /**
   * Sets the user's license key.
   */
  public static void setLicenseKey(byte[] licenseKey) {
    RecordStore store = null;
    try {
      // if the record store does not yet exist, the second
      // arg, "true," tells it to create.
      store = RecordStore.openRecordStore(STORE, true);
      int numRecords = store.getNumRecords();
      if(numRecords > 0) {
        store.setRecord(1, licenseKey, 0, licenseKey.length);
      } else {
        store.addRecord(licenseKey, 0, licenseKey.length);
      }
    } catch(Exception e) {
      AccessControl.postException(e);
    } finally {
      try {
        store.closeRecordStore();
      } catch(Exception e) {
        // if the record store is open, this shouldn't throw.
```

```
        }
      }
    }
  }
```

The AccessStorage class stores the game credentials in the RMS because they're game-specific—this data doesn't need to be left hanging around if the game isn't there. However, for added security, it's possible to store this sort of sensitive data directly onto the user's smart card. The net.rim.device.api.smartcard package implements the ISO 7816-4 interchange protocol, which allows you to send the smart card simple commands to read, write, and update data. By storing your game key on the smart card (and not tying the user credentials to the device PIN), you can create a licensing model that allows the user to change devices without having to buy/unlock your game again.

Selling Your Game on Other Web Portals

BlackBerry App World is probably the simplest distribution system to use since RIM takes care of testing, distribution, and billing for you. There are a few other options to consider, though.

The biggest portal that allows you upload and distribute your games is *GetJar*. GetJar is a portal specializing in free application downloads for all sorts of handsets. They boast 700 million downloads so far.

The GetJar business model is that you (the developer) pay them to list your game on their site and to serve it to the customers (that is, direct the users to the right binary and allow them to download). You pay a few cents per completed download, and you can also buy premium placement and advertising on their site. For the moment, you have to design and implement your own billing model (such as a try-and-buy system with a license key, as illustrated in the Access Control example). However, on the developer site, they promise, "Soon, GetJar will offer the missing ingredient in the mobile app ecosystem: a global payments system that works." You can have a look at their developer site for more details:

http://my.getjar.com/site/Developers

Another popular choice is *Handmark*. Handmark distributes applications and other content for a variety of platforms. In particular, it hosts operator- and manufacturer-specific content portals for Sprint Nextel and Samsung. However, since Handmark is also a content producer (in addition to being just a distributor), it doesn't have a simple, automated system where anyone can make an account and upload applications. It works through partnerships with other firms. For more information, see their web site:

http://www.handmark.com/company/solutions/mobile-stores.php

Selling Your Game on Your Own Site

Whether or not you're planning to sell your games through an existing web portal, you can also sell your game from your own web site. A lot of the same techniques apply. For example, you can use the same dynamic license key implementation from the "Decrypting Dynamic License Keys" section—you just need to implement your own web interface that collects the user's PIN (and money) and returns the license key. Similarly, if your game has different versions for different models, you have to implement the code that returns the correct version of the game, depending on the user's handset model.

Listing 5-7 shows a simple servlet that returns a catalog page with a link to the correct binary, depending on the User-Agent of the calling device. The User-Agent is a standard HTTP header that tells the server exactly what kind of client is calling it so that it can return the appropriate page for that client. On BlackBerry, the User-Agent value starts with BlackBerry, followed by the model number, followed by the operating system version. For example, my 8700g returns the following value:

```
BlackBerry8700/4.1.0 Profile/MIDP-2.0 Configuration/CLDC-1.1
```

As with Listing 5-2, the servlet in Listing 5-7 was developed on an Apache Tomcat 4.1 server and illustrates only the bare bones of the functionality needed. In practice, your web site would return a more elaborate catalog page in addition to supporting multiple device models, monitoring the user's session, and so on.

Listing 5-7. *GamePage.java*

```java
import java.io.*;
import javax.servlet.*;
import javax.servlet.http.*;

/**
 * A minimal servlet that returns the link to the correct
 * version of the game for the BlackBerry handset
 * to download the game OTA.
 */
public class GamePage extends HttpServlet {

  /**
   * Handle the GET request (others are ignored).
   */
  public void doGet(HttpServletRequest request, HttpServletResponse response)
      throws IOException, ServletException {
    // get the User-Agent to identify the device accessing the page:
    String userAgent = request.getHeader("User-Agent");

    // Prepare the response page:
    response.setContentType("text/html");
    PrintWriter out = response.getWriter();

    out.println("<html>");
    out.println("<head>");
    out.println("<title>Ladybug Maze download page</title>");
    out.println("</head>");
    out.println("<body bgcolor=\"white\">");

    // get the context to construct the correct URL
    // for the JAD file, relative to this installation
    String context = request.getContextPath();
    if((userAgent != null) && (userAgent.startsWith("BlackBerry8700"))) {
```

```
        out.println("<a href=\"" + context
            + "/binaries/8700/LadybugMaze.jad\">Ladybug Maze</a> ");
    } else {
        out.println("Sorry, but this game is not available for your handset.");
    }
    out.println("</body>");
    out.println("</html>");
    }
}
```

Note that this servlet requires you to place the JAD and the JAR or COD files in a set of web-accessible directories—organized by model number—under a directory called binaries. If your game needs to be signed with RIM credentials in order to function, then you should use the COD files instead of the JAR files for web-based installation.

> **Note** Your game's COD file may be made up of multiple sibling COD files zipped together into a compound COD file. This structure is generated automatically by the RAPC tool. A compound COD file is merely a ZIP file that has been given the .cod extension, so you can unzip it with any standard unzipping application (after first renaming it to change the extension to .zip).

To distribute a compound COD file on the Internet, you must first unzip it and deploy (upload) the component COD files individually to your site. The JAD file contains the correct information to identify the individual sibling COD files because the simple COD files zipped inside the compound COD file follow a standard naming format (with -1, -2, etc. appended to the file name just before the .cod extension). The SignatureTool application shows you the number of COD files present when you sign the application (see Figure 5-2). Selling your game on your own site (or through free downloads on GetJar) gives you a lot of flexibility. For one thing, you can support any device model you like. BlackBerry App World has some limitations on which devices can access it, and notably my ancient BlackBerry 8700g *can't* because the BlackBerry App World client requires an operating system version of at least 4.2.0. But the Ladybug Maze game from Chapter 4 runs just fine on the 4.1.0 operating system, so there's nothing to stop me from supporting this model on my own catalog page.

Another thing you can do when distributing your game from your own site is distribute it in the form of COD and ALX files. As explained in the "Understanding BlackBerry Application Files" section of Chapter 2, an ALX file is a very simple XML-format descriptor file that allows Desktop Manager to install an application from a PC via a USB cable. Just put the two files in the same directory, and (from Desktop Manager's Application Loader option) navigate to the ALX file on the PC.

If you have a number of customers who have Internet access from their desktop—but not from their BlackBerry smartphones—it may be convenient to allow them to download a zipped bundle containing the COD file and the ALX file. The ALX file can be easily generated from the JDE or with an Ant task. Actually, the format is so simple and obvious, you can write your own script to generate it—just open one and have a look.

Unfortunately, if you allow the user to download the game as a COD/ALX bundle, then you don't have the convenience of reading the User-Agent to determine the correct handset model. So if your game has multiple versions, you'll need to make the user select the right handset model from the catalog. This is not terribly difficult (since the model is given on the About screen, as shown in Figure 2-4), yet it would be considered an annoying step for the average user.

The biggest advantage of distributing the game yourself is that you're not limited to RIM's billing models, so if your business model involves post-download revenue, you don't have to give RIM a cut. Naturally, BlackBerry App World offers a service that is likely to be very helpful to individuals and small companies selling BlackBerry games, but larger, more established game design houses might not need it.

Summary

If you want to make money from your game, you have to think about your business model. One of the most popular business models for games is the try-and-buy system, where the user downloads the game for free and can unlock access to the complete game by buying a license key. BlackBerry's cryptography APIs can help you implement a license key system using the same digital encryption techniques that you use for other security-related applications. To distribute the game binaries to customers, you can create your own web portal or use an existing portal such as BlackBerry App World.

Now that the dry business of business is out of the way, you can get back to the fun part: the games! In Chapter 6 you'll see all the techniques you need to make a complete arcade-style game, including music, sound effects, and moving game pieces that can interact with one another!

Chapter 6

Swingin' Light Saber

When I was a youngling, I vowed to learn the ways of the BlackBerry and become a RIM-i master. I went in search of Yogurt the Wise!, Yogurt the All-Powerful!, Yogurt the Magnificent! Just plain blackberry Yogurt to his friends.

I learned of a young RIM-i named Dark Helmet, who was a pupil of Yoghurt's until he turned bad, and helped the Empire hunt down and destroy the RIM-i Knights. Dark Helmet was seduced by the Dark Side of the BlackBerry, stopped washing, and so became the odious black knight.

Only a fully trained RIM-i Knight with the BlackBerry as his ally will conquer Dark Helmet. But read this chapter first, for if you end your training now, if you choose the quick-and-easy path as Dark Helmet did, you may become an agent of naughtiness.

> If you're interested in the adventures of Dark Helmet, Yogurt, and others, I recommend the Mel Brooks movie *Spaceballs*.

Sadly, I'm not going to make a piercing beam of bluish light shoot out the top of your BlackBerry. Instead, I'll describe the SwingSaber game shown in Figure 6-1.

Figure 6-1. *The SwingSaber game*

The light saber can be swung to the left and right across the screen to destroy laser blasts dropping from above (three can be seen in Figure 6-1, with one of them exploding). The current playing time and score are displayed, and a medley of exciting theme tunes play in the background, often drowned out by explosions (which occur when your saber hits descending blasts). The light saber in Figure 6-1 looks a bit odd because a trail of light follows behind the main blue beam. The trail is made up of three lighter beams, which disappear when your saber stops moving. The saber can be swung by shaking the BlackBerry, touching the screen on the left or right, by moving the trackball, or by pressing the left and right arrow keys. The BlackBerry vibrates a little whenever you destroy a blast.

At the end of the game, the black knight makes a comment on your prowess with a saber. You can quit at any time by press the Esc key, or the green and red keys (the Send and End/Power keys) on either side of the trackball.

The game has an introductory screen, shown in Figure 6-2, which appears when you first select the game icon.

Figure 6-2. *The SwingSaber introductory screen*

An introductory screen like this is a good place to supply game instructions or other information. The game begins when the user selects the New Game menu item, clicks the screen, or presses Enter or the spacebar.

Novel game features include

- Several fonts and colors on the introductory screen, made possible by an `ActiveRichTextField` component

- Game animation employing an update-draw-sleep loop running in its own thread

- Animated explosions read from image strips

- The utilization of reusable `Sprite` and `ExplodingSprite` classes, which aren't based on MIDP 2.0's `Sprite`

- A sound clip–playing class (`ClipsPlayer`). which can handle MIDI, MP3, AU, tone sequences (JTS files), and individual tones

The class diagrams for SwingSaber are shown in Figure 6-3, with only the public and protected methods and data shown.

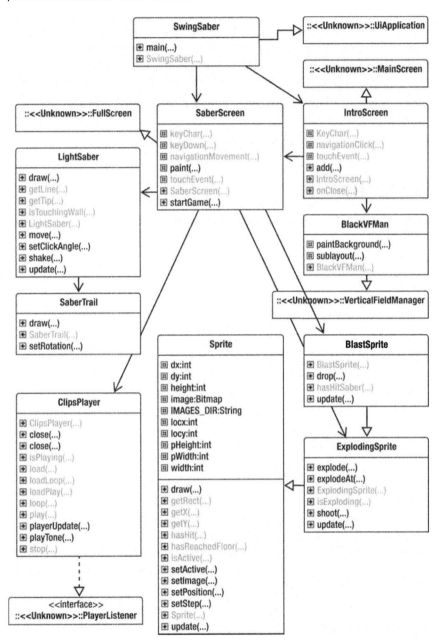

Figure 6-3. *Class diagrams for the SwingSaber game*

The top-level UIApplication is SwingSaber, which does little more than create two screen objects: IntroScreen for the introductory screen (Figure 6-2), and SaberScreen for the game (Figure 6-1). `IntroScreen` employs a specialized `VerticalFieldManager`, called `BlackVFMan`, to make its background black and nonscrollable.

`SaberScreen` creates the light saber (and its trail) by invoking the `LightSaber` class, and the blasts dropping from the top of the game are `BlastSprite` objects. `BlastSprite` is quite small since it inherits most of its functionality from the more general-purpose `ExplodingSprite`, which itself is a subclass of `Sprite`. Remember that this `Sprite` class is not `javax.microedition.lcdui.game.Sprite` even though it has some of the same features.

The game audio: the background music, the black knight's comments, and explosions, are handled by `ClipsPlayer`.

All the code can be found online at http://frogparrot.net/blackberry/ch06/.

Starting the Application

`SwingSaber` initializes the `SaberScreen` and `IntroScreen` objects, and pushes `IntroScreen` onto the stack.

```
public class SwingSaber extends UiApplication
{
  public SwingSaber()
  {
    Ui.getUiEngineInstance().setAcceptableDirections(
                                  Display.DIRECTION_PORTRAIT);
    // create the game-play and introduction screens
    SaberScreen gameScreen = new SaberScreen();
    IntroScreen introScreen = new IntroScreen(gameScreen);
    pushScreen(introScreen);   // start with introduction screen
  } // end of SwingSaber()


  public static void main(String args[])
  { SwingSaber theApp = new SwingSaber();
    theApp.enterEventDispatcher();
  }

} // end of SwingSaber
```

The call to `UiEngineInstance.setAcceptableDirections()` ensures that the screen orientation isn't affected by tilting, which simplifies two aspects of the game: I can assume that the screen dimensions (width and height) don't change while the program is running, and also that the accelerometer settings for the x-, y-, and z-axes don't need to take account of changing screen orientation.

Introducing the Game

The `IntroScreen` class foreground contains an image and text employing various fonts and colors in an `ActiveRichTextField` instance. The components are positioned inside a nonscrollable black background vertical field manager.

The game can be started by selecting the New Game menu item, touching the screen, clicking with the trackball, pressing Enter of the spacebar.

The `IntroScreen()` constructor sets up the manager, image, and `ActiveRichTextField` component:

```
// globals
private static final String SPLASH_FNM = "images/title.png";
private BlackVFMan manager = new BlackVFMan();
private SaberScreen gameScreen;    // ref to game-playing screen


public IntroScreen(SaberScreen gScreen)
{
  super.add(manager);

  gameScreen = gScreen;
  setMenu();
  positionSplash(SPLASH_FNM);
  positionInfo();
}  // end of IntroScreen()
```

The `BlackVFMan` class is a subclass of `VerticalFieldManager` to ensure that scrolling is disabled and the background is black.

```
class BlackVFMan extends VerticalFieldManager
{
  public BlackVFMan()
  {  super( Manager.NO_VERTICAL_SCROLL |
          Manager.NO_VERTICAL_SCROLLBAR ); }

  protected void paintBackground(Graphics g)
  { g.setBackgroundColor(Color.BLACK);
    g.clear();    // clear graphics area so background redrawn
  }

  protected void sublayout(int width, int height)
  { super.sublayout(width, height);
    setExtent(width, height);
  }

}  // end of BlackVFMan class
```

`paintBackground()` could be used to used to paint more interesting things, such as a bitmap of stars.

Back in `IntroScreen`, `setMenu()` adds a **New Game** menu item to the screen:

```
private void setMenu()
{
  MenuItem startGame = new MenuItem("New Game", 10, 10) {
    public void run()
    { startGame(); }
  };
  addMenuItem(startGame);
}  // end of setMenu()
```

IntroScreen's startGame() uses the reference to the game-playing screen, gameScreen, to invoke its startGame() method:

```
private void startGame()
{ UiApplication.getUiApplication().pushScreen(gameScreen);
  gameScreen.startGame();
}
```

positionSplash() places an image near the top of the screen, centered on the x-axis:

```
private void positionSplash(String fnm)
{
  BitmapField splash = new BitmapField(Bitmap.getBitmapResource(fnm));

  HorizontalFieldManager hfm = new HorizontalFieldManager();
  hfm.add(splash);

  // calculate left and top empty spaces
  int leftEmptySpace = (Display.getWidth() - hfm.getPreferredWidth())/2;
  int topEmptySpace = (Display.getHeight() - hfm.getPreferredHeight())/8;

  // make sure the picture fits on the screen
  if ((topEmptySpace >= 0) && (leftEmptySpace >= 0))
    hfm.setMargin(topEmptySpace, 0, 0, leftEmptySpace);

  add(hfm);
}  // end of positionSplash()
```

One issue with a splash screen image is to test that it is small enough to fit on the device's screen. Another is whether the remaining space after the placement of the image is sufficient for the text, remembering that the screen manager disables scrolling.

Figure 6-2 shows how positionInfo() displays text using several fonts and colors. This is fairly easily done with an ActiveRichTextField component, but requires text offsets, font names, and foreground and background colors to be specified. The resulting code is quite lengthy since the font attributes are changed three times in my introductory screen.

```
private void positionInfo()
{
  String info = "\nSwing your Light Saber\n" +
                "to destroy laser blasts.\n" +
                "Or use the arrow keys\n" +
                "or click on the screen.\n" +
                "\nMay the Force be with You...\n";

  // positions where the font changes: changes occur three time
  int orOffset = info.indexOf("Or use");
  int mayOffset = info.indexOf("May the");

  // all the change positions, and the total text length
  int offsets[] = new int[]{0, orOffset, mayOffset, info.length()};

  // load the casual font (an italic font), or use the default font
  Font casFont;
  try {
    FontFamily ff = FontFamily.forName("BBCasual");
```

```
      casFont = ff.getFont(FontFamily.SCALABLE_FONT, 24);
    }
    catch (ClassNotFoundException ex) {
      casFont = Font.getDefault();
    }

    // list of font changes
    Font[] fonts = new Font[]{Font.getDefault().derive(Font.BOLD),
                              Font.getDefault(),
                              casFont.derive(Font.BOLD)};

    // lists of the background and foreground colors of the text
    int bg[] = new int[]{Color.BLACK, Color.BLACK, Color.BLACK};  //black
    int fg[] = new int[]{Color.YELLOW, Color.WHITE, Color.LIGHTBLUE};
    byte attributes[] = new byte[]{0, 1, 2};

    // add the user's text, varying the font and color,
    add( new ActiveRichTextField(info, offsets, attributes,
                      fonts, fg, bg, RichTextField.TEXT_ALIGN_HCENTER));
}  // end of positionInfo()
```

I use String.indexOf() to calculate the text positions where the font attributes change rather than use fixed integer values. This makes the code a bit more resilient if I change the text string in the future.

I use the BlackBerry BBCasual font for the "May the Force be with You" quote, with the default device font as a fallback. A list of BlackBerry fonts can be found at http://docs.blackberry.com/en/developers/deliverables/6625/Fonts_2_0_514368_11. jsp, but the list will vary slightly between devices.

Moving On to the Game

It's important that the user can quickly move past the introductory screen into the game (players probably won't want to look at an introduction more than once). A **New Game** menu item is a fine, time-honored mechanism, but there should be a range of other possibilities, such as touching the screen, moving the trackball, and pressing keys. These can be easily added by implementing the touch, navigation click, and key listeners inherited from MainScreen:

```
protected boolean touchEvent(TouchEvent message)
{ if (message.getEvent() == TouchEvent.CLICK) {
    startGame();
    return true;
  }
  return super.touchEvent(message);
}  // end of touchEvent()

protected boolean navigationClick(int status, int time)
{ startGame();
  return true;
}

protected boolean keyChar(char key, int status, int time)
```

```
{ if (key == Characters.ENTER || key == Characters.SPACE) {
    startGame();
    return true;
  }
  return false;
}
```

The Game Screen

SaberScreen starts by loading the required images and sound clips, and creating fonts and game sprites.

```
// globals
private static int FPS = 20;    // frames/sec
private static final String BG_IM = "knight.png";  // background image
private static final int NUM_BLAST_SPRITES = 7;

private long period;        // period between drawing in ms

private Bitmap backIm;      // background image
private int bgWidth, bgHeight;

private Font msgFont, endFont;    // fonts for messages

private Channel accelChannel = null;

private ClipsPlayer clipsPlayer;

// sprites
private LightSaber saber;
private BlastSprite[] blasts;
private ExplodingSprite wallExplSprite;


public SaberScreen()
{
  super();
  period = (int) 1000.0/FPS;

  // load images, sounds, accelerometer channel, message fonts
  backIm = loadImage(BG_IM);
  bgWidth = backIm.getWidth();
  bgHeight = backIm.getHeight();

  clipsPlayer = new ClipsPlayer();
  loadSounds();

  if (AccelerometerSensor.isSupported())
    accelChannel = AccelerometerSensor.openRawDataChannel(
                             Application.getApplication() );

  msgFont = Font.getDefault().derive(Font.BOLD, 24);
  endFont = Font.getDefault().derive(Font.BOLD, 48);    // bigger
```

```
  // create sprites
  saber = new LightSaber();
  blasts = new BlastSprite[NUM_BLAST_SPRITES];
  for (int i=0; i < NUM_BLAST_SPRITES; i++)
    blasts[i] = new BlastSprite();
  wallExplSprite = new ExplodingSprite("wallBlast.png", "wallBlasts.png", 7);

  invalidate();    // draw the screen in its initial state
}  // end of SaberScreen()
```

The speed of the game's animation loop is determined by the FPS constant (the number of frames rendered per second), which by being set to 20 means that each animation cycle will have a period of 1000 / 20 = 50ms. An average BlackBerry is capable of about 30 FPS, but 20 is sufficient for this game. Nevertheless, a game should be tested on its intended devices to make sure that the FPS assumption is valid.

It's quite likely that the game won't be running on a device with an accelerometer, so an acceleration input channel (accelChannel) is only opened if AccelerometerSensor.isSupported() returns true.

Two fonts appear in the game: msgFont for the status line and timing information at the bottom of the screen (see Figure 6-1), and a larger font, called endFont, to report the outcome of the game.

SwingSaber utilizes three sprites, of which the most complicated is the light saber, consisting of a rotating light beam, handle, and three beam trails. Fortunately, the complexity is hidden away inside the LightSaber class.

A BlastSprite object represents a blast that drops from the top of the screen, either exploding on the saber or disappearing through the floor. Seven BlastSprite objects are created and reused repeatedly until the game finishes. As Figure 6-3 indicates, BlastSprite is a subclass of ExplodingSprite, which is itself a subclass of Sprite.

The wallExplSprite object displays an animated explosion when the saber hits the left or right sides of the screen (see Figure 6-4 for an example).

Figure 6-4. *The saber hits the left side of the screen.*

Loading Sounds

ClipsPlayer loads and plays sound files, but SaberScreen supplies the file names, and specifies when they are played.

```
// globals
private static final int NUM_HIT_SOUNDS = 3;
private void loadSounds()
{
  // start looping through the background music
  clipsPlayer.loadLoop("starWars.mid");

  if (System.getProperty("supports.mixing").equals("false"))
    System.out.println("mixing not supported on this device");
  else {    // load others sounds
    // load hit clips
    for (int i=0; i < NUM_HIT_SOUNDS; i++)
      clipsPlayer.load("hit" + i + ".wav");
  }
} // end of loadSounds()
```

As I'll explain later, ClipsPlayer uses the Mobile Media API (MMAPI) to load and play audio, such as MIDI and WAV files, and tone sequences (JTS files).

Unfortunately, there's quite a bit of variation between MMAPI implementations across different devices, most notably in the range of media controls offered and URI types supported. Of particular concern for gaming is whether audio mixing is available. If System.getProperty("supports.mixing") returns "true", then the device should have the following features:

- The ability to play at least two tones simultaneously

- The ability to call Manager.playTone() while another Player instance is playing audio

- The playback of at least two audio Player instances at once

In practice, not all MMAPI implementations follow these guidelines, and the best thing is to test the game on the devices in question. It's also necessary to take into account the operating system version; for instance, version 4.7.0.75 is well known for having audio playback problems (see http://supportforums.blackberry.com/rim/board/message?board.id=java_dev&thread.id=11963).

A reasonable worst-case scenario is to assume that audio mixing support only means that the device will be able to play one piece of sampled audio (e.g., a WAV, AU, or MP3 file) and one piece of synthesized audio (e.g., a MIDI file, a tone, or tone sequence) at the same time.

This limitation is just about bearable for a game, by using MIDI for the background music and WAV files for sound effects. Even so, some thought (and testing) must be put into investigating what will happen when the game attempts to play two sound clips at the same time. In SwingSaber, this can happen if two blasts hit the saber simultaneously. Most likely, one of the sounds will not be played, which isn't too bad for this game. I also found that the simulator would occasionally raise an exception if it tried to play two instances of the *same* clip at the same time. This is one reason why SwingSaber cycles through three different "hit" sound clips as blasts explodes on the saber.

Another concern is the number of Player instances created by the application. In the original version of this game, whooshing sounds were heard as the saber moved to and fro, and there were explosion sounds when the saber hit a wall. Each of these used it's own Player instance, which seriously reduced the game's speed.

When a Player instance is in a REALIZED state, it becomes a memory liability if kept around for a long time, especially if the players request exclusive access to system audio resources. So, even if your device's MMAPI implementation allows more than two active Player instances at a time, it might still be better to limit the number.

SwingSaber creates a total of four realized Players, which doesn't impact playing speed noticeably.

Interestingly, the BlackBerry simulator returns false for "supports.mixing", but can play one MIDI and WAV file concurrently. If an additional MIDI file is started, or tones are played, then the first MIDI sequence falls silent. Similarly, starting a second WAV file stops the first.

Sampled audio behavior may depend on the encoding scheme for the file; where possible use a simple WAV encoding, such as single-channel (mono), 8000 KHz, 8-bit PCM. Audacity is a good tool for manipulating WAV files (http://audacity.sourceforge.net/).

Starting the Game

The game starts when SaberScreen.gameStart() is invoked from the introductory screen. A thread begins that carries out an update-draw-sleep cycle.

```
// globals
private Thread animator;      // the thread for the animation
private volatile boolean isRunning = false;   // for stopping

private long period;        // period between drawing in ms
private long startTime;     // in ms


public void startGame()
{
  if (animator != null || isRunning)
    return;   // thread already exists

  animator = new Thread (new Runnable() {
    public void run()
    // an update-draw-sleep cycle
    {
      long beforeTime, sleepTime;
      startTime = System.currentTimeMillis();
      isRunning = true;
```

```
while(isRunning) {
  beforeTime = System.currentTimeMillis();

  processShakes();    // poll for accelerometer input
  update();

  // wait for the screen to be drawn
  UiApplication.getUiApplication().invokeAndWait( new Runnable() {
    public void run()
    { invalidate(); }   // force a repaint
  });

  sleepTime = period - (System.currentTimeMillis() - beforeTime);
  try {
    if (sleepTime > 0)      // animation is running too fast
      Thread.sleep(sleepTime);   // sleep for some ms
  }
  catch(InterruptedException ex){}
}
clipsPlayer.close();
System.exit(0);    // make sure app. disappears
    }
  });
  animator.start();
} // end of startGame()
```

The drawing step of the update-draw-sleep cycle is carried out by a call to `invalidate()` in the event dispatch thread. `UIApplication.invokeAndWait()` blocks until the painting has been completed, so allowing the combined updating and drawing time to be calculated (`System.currentTimeMillis()-beforeTime`). If this is less than the required period for the cycle, then the sleep step pauses for the surplus time.

This animation loop doesn't deal with the case when the processing time exceeds the period (i.e., updating and drawing take too long). There are techniques for dealing with this problem, but they're arguably too complicated for such a simple game. Interested readers can consult Chapter 2 of my *Killer Game Programming in Java* book (O'Reilly, 2005), or visit its web page at `http://fivedots.coe.psu.ac.th/~ad/jg/`.

`invokeAndWait()` blocks the event queue, which makes the application unresponsive to user input. and may let the event queue overflow. Therefore, it's important that the drawing is done as quickly as possible. One way of achieving this is to make sure that all data manipulation, reading of input, and lengthy computations are performed in the update step.

This approach introduces the potential for race conditions between event listeners that change game data, and the processing of that data in the update step of the animation thread. I'll discuss this point when I describe the listener code.

When the animation loop stops (after `isRunning` is set to `false`), the only clean-up operation is to stop the `ClipsPlayer`, by calling `close()`.

Processing Shakes

Accelerometer input is obtained through *polling* rather than by event listeners. processShakes() reads the accelerometer channel and passes its current x-axis acceleration to the light saber object.

```
// globals accelerometer info
private Channel accelChannel = null;
private short[] xyzAccels = new short[3];

private boolean gameOver = false;


private void processShakes()
{
  if (accelChannel == null)
    return;
  if (gameOver)
    return;
  accelChannel.getLastAccelerationData( xyzAccels );
  saber.shake(xyzAccels[0]);   // pass x-axis accel to saber
} // end of processShakes()
```

Since this input is initiated by the animation thread, not by event listeners, there's no chance of race conditions.

Updating the Game

update() performs regular updates while the game is in progress (in gameUpdate()), and special updates at the end of the game (in finalUpdates()). This separation of tasks requires update() to test for game termination, which is recorded in a gameOver global.

```
// global
private boolean gameOver = false;

private void update()
{
  if (!gameOver) {
    gameOver = isGameFinished();
    if (gameOver)
      finalUpdates();
    else
      gameUpdate();
  }
}
```

The game ends when the score reaches one of two possible value. A score of 0 means that the black knight has won, while MAX_SCORE or higher means the player has won.

```
// globals
private static final int MAX_SCORE = 30;

private int score = MAX_SCORE/2;       // current score
private String gameOverMessage;
```

```
private boolean playerHasWon = true;


private boolean isGameFinished()
{
  if (score <= 0) {
    gameOverMessage = "You lose";
    playerHasWon = false;
    return true;      // game is over
  }
  else if (score >= MAX_SCORE) {
    gameOverMessage = "Victory!";
    return true;
  }
  return false;    // game not over yet
}  // end of isGameFinished()
```

Several globals are set, which are used by finalUpdates() to finish the game.

In a more full-featured game, finalUpdates()would be the place to update and display a high scores table, or to save player data to external files. In SwingSaber, most of finalUpdates() is concerned with playing a suitable MIDI file.

```
private void finalUpdates()
// things to update when the game finishes
{
  clipsPlayer.close("starWars.mid");
        // close background music, avoiding lack of mixer support
  accelChannel.close();
  if (playerHasWon)
    clipsPlayer.loadPlay("forcestrong.wav");     // player has won
  else
    clipsPlayer.loadPlay("underestimate.wav");  // player has lost
}
```

Since it's unlikely that two MIDI files can play at the same time on a device, the background musical medley is closed, reclaiming its player. There's a slight delay while a new MIDI file is loaded and played, but this brief pause occurs while the screen is busy being repainted, so it's hardly noticeable (at least on the devices I used).

Regular Game Updates

When a regular update starts (i.e., during the update-draw-sleep cycle), the sprites are examined first to see if they need to interact with other sprites or with the screen. For example, the game blast sprites communicate with the saber when they hit it and have to explode. When blasts drop off the bottom of the screen, they must be deactivated. Also, the saber has to set off explosions when it hits the sides of the screen.

After SaberScreen has processed any inter-sprite communication and dealt with sprite/screen conditions, it calls each sprite's update() method to have the sprites update themselves.

```
// global sprites
private LightSaber saber;
```

```
private BlastSprite[] blasts;
private ExplodingSprite wallExplSprite;


private void gameUpdate()
// handle inter-sprite conditions, then have the sprites update
{
  checkBlasts();

  // check for saber hitting a wall
  if (!wallExplSprite.isExploding()) {
    if (saber.isTouchingWall())
      wallExplSprite.explodeAt( saber.getTip() );
  }

  // update sprites
  saber.update();
  for(int i=0; i < blasts.length; i++)
    blasts[i].update();
  wallExplSprite.update();
}  // end of gameUpdate()
```

checkBlasts() examines the blast sprites, performing the following tasks:

- Reactivating inactive blast sprites (by dropping them from the top of the screen)

- Making a blast explode if it's touching the saber

- Deactivating sprites that have descended below floor level

```
// globals
private static final int NUM_HIT_SOUNDS = 3;
private int hitCounter = 0;
private BlastSprite[] blasts;


private void checkBlasts()
{
  BlastSprite blast;
  for(int i=0; i < blasts.length; i++) {
    blast = blasts[i];
    if(!blast.isActive())    // drop inactive blasts
      blast.drop();

    // check for blast contact with saber
    if (!blast.isExploding()) {
      if (blast.hasHitSaber(saber)) {
        blast.explode();      // the blast starts exploding
        clipsPlayer.play("hit" + hitCounter + ".wav");
        Alert.startVibrate(300);    // vibrate for 0.3 secs
        hitCounter = (hitCounter+1)%NUM_HIT_SOUNDS;
        score++;
      }
    }
  }
```

```
      // check if blast has reached the floor
      if (blast.hasReachedFloor()) {
        score--;
        blast.setActive(false);   // can be reused next time
      }
    }
  }
} // end of checkBlasts()
```

The animated visual for an exploding sprite is managed by the sprite, but is started by SaberScreen calling BlastSprite.explode(). SaberScreen also plays an explosion clip and vibrates the device using Alert.startVibrate().

The hitCounter variable is used to cycle through three explosion sounds stored in hit0.wav, hit1.wav, and hit2.wav.

Painting the Game

Two essential features of painting is that it be quick and not try to process events because the event queue is blocked by the UIApplication.invokeAndWait() call in startGame().

paint() delegates most of its duties to the sprites, but draws the background and status information, and some additional visuals when the game finishes.

```
// globals
private Bitmap backIm;
private int bgWidth, bgHeight;


protected void paint(Graphics g)
{
  // clear the background by painting it all black
  g.setColor(Color.BLACK);
  g.fillRect (0, 0, screenWidth, screenHeight);

  // draw background image
  g.drawBitmap((screenWidth-bgWidth)/2, 0, bgWidth, bgHeight, backIm, 0,0);
  // draw the sprites
  saber.draw(g);
  for(int i=0; i < blasts.length; i++)
    blasts[i].draw(g);
  wallExplSprite.draw(g);

  showStatus(g);

  if (gameOver)
    showGameOver(g);
} // end of paint()
```

An important consideration in paint() is the *ordering* of the operations since a later draw to the screen can overwrite earlier ones. For this reason, paint() displays the background first, and then the sprites, followed by status details.

The status information consists of yellow text along the bottom of the screen (see Figure 6-2): the playing time is on the left and the current score is on the right.

```
// globals
private final int screenWidth = Display.getWidth();
private final int screenHeight = Display.getHeight();

private int timeSpent;    // time spent playing the game (in secs)

private String gameOverMessage;
private Font endFont;    // the font for the status messages


private void showStatus(Graphics g)
{
  g.setColor(Color.YELLOW);
  g.setFont(msgFont);

  if (!gameOver)
    timeSpent = (int)(System.currentTimeMillis() -
                                      startTime)/1000;   // in secs

  int y = screenHeight - 10; // near bottom
  g.drawText( timeSpent+"s", 10, y,
              DrawStyle.BOTTOM|DrawStyle.LEFT);     // text on left

  int x = screenWidth - msgFont.getAdvance("Score: XXX");
  g.drawText( "Score: "+score, x, y,
              DrawStyle.BOTTOM|DrawStyle.LEFT);     // text on right
}  // end of showStatus()
```

The positioning of the Score string requires its width, which includes the current score. Since this varies during the game, *XXX* is used instead as an approximate width.

The timeSpent variable is protected by an if test so that the time stops being updated when the game finishes. However, the information is still drawn to the screen.

showGameOver() draws the "game over" message in a large red font near the center of screen, as illustrated by Figure 6-5.

```
// globals
private String gameOverMessage;
private Font endFont;

private void showGameOver(Graphics g)
{
  if (gameOverMessage == null)
    gameOverMessage = "Game Over!!";

  int x = (screenWidth - endFont.getAdvance(gameOverMessage))/2;
  int y = (screenHeight - endFont.getHeight())/2;

  g.setColor(Color.RED);
  g.setFont(endFont);

  g.drawText(gameOverMessage, x, y,
                    DrawStyle.BOTTOM|DrawStyle.LEFT);
}  // end of showGameOver()
```

Figure 6-5. *"Game over" message*

User Input

The game supports four types of user input: device shaking through the accelerometer, clicking the screen, trackball movement, and key presses. They are translated into left and right saber rotations across the screen.

I've already discussed accelerometer processing, which utilizes polling in processShakes(), and calls LightSaber.shake() to rotate the saber. Touch, trackball clicks, and key presses are handled by overriding their relevant listener methods inherited from FullScreen.

```
// globals
private volatile boolean isRunning = false;   // to stopping
private LightSaber saber;


protected boolean touchEvent(TouchEvent message)
// pass touchscreen click info to the saber
{
  if (message.getEvent() == TouchEvent.CLICK) {
    if (!gameOver)    // use the (x,y) touch coordinate
      saber.setClickAngle(message.getX(1), message.getY(1));
  }
  return true;
} // end of touchEvent()



protected boolean navigationMovement(int dx,int dy,
                                      int status, int time)
// pass trackball movement info to the saber
{ if (!gameOver)
    saber.move(dx);  // -ve for a move left, +ve for a move right
  return true;
} // end of navigationMovement()
```

```
protected boolean keyChar(char key, int status, int time)
// left/right movement, and terminate the game by typing <ESC>
{
  if (key == Characters.CONTROL_LEFT && !gameOver) {
    saber.move(-1);   // negative for a move left
    return true;
  }
  else if (key == Characters.CONTROL_RIGHT && !gameOver) {
    saber.move(1);   // positive for a move right
    return true;
  }
  else if (key == Characters.ESCAPE) {
    isRunning = false;
    return true;
  }
  return false;
}  // end of keyChar()
```

Returning true from a listener method means that the event has been consumed and requires no further processing. For example, in touchEvent(), I don't need FullScreen's inherited behavior for the touch event, so true is returned. However, in most applications it's usually better to return super.touchEvent(message) after handling a message so that the screen can provide additional handling, such as scrolling.

The isRunning global is declared volatile because it can be changed by the keyChar() listener method executing in the event thread, and this change should be noticed by the animation thread, which will then finish the animation cycle.

The listeners all update the light saber object (via LightSaber.setClickAngle() and LightSaber.move()). These updates may occur *at the same time* that the animation thread is updating or accessing the saber, leading to race conditions for the shared state in the saber; I'll consider this problem in the next section.

Aside from responding to the Esc key, it's also a good idea to handle the BlackBerry's Send and End/Power keys, informally known as the green and red keys, positioned to the left and right of the trackball. Unfortunately, there aren't any Characters class constants for these keys, so they must be caught using their keycodes in keyDown():

```
// global keycodes for the green and red keys
private static final int GREEN_KEY = 1114112;   // Send key
private static final int RED_KEY = 1179648;      // End/Power key


protected boolean keyDown(int keycode, int time)
// terminate the game if the green or red keys are pressed
{
  if ((keycode == GREEN_KEY) || (keycode == RED_KEY)) {
    isRunning = false;
    return true;
  }
  return false;
}  // end of keyDown()
```

The Light Saber

The light saber consists of five polygons: one for the light beam, one for the handle, and three for the trails (see Figure 6-6).

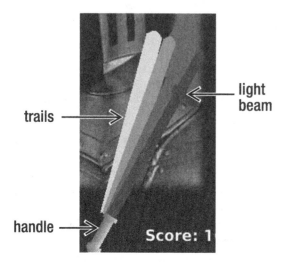

Figure 6-6. *Parts of a light saber*

The trails (which are SaberTrail objects) are copies of the light beam polygon that rotate a little behind the light beam to give the impression of blur and speed. The copies are a lighter color than the beam, and somewhat wider, to enhance the effect.

The light beam, handle, and trails all rotate around a pivot point. The beam also includes a saber tip point that is used to detect collisions with the sides of the screen. An invisible line runs up the light beam, from the pivot to the tip, which is used for detecting blast sprite hits.

The polygons making up the light beam and handle, and the pivot and saber tip points, are illustrated in Figure 6-7.

The saber beam polygon is represented by two arrays of x- and y-coordinates in the LightSaber class:

```
private int[] xsSaber = new int[] {0,   3,   7, 7,   -7, -7, -3};
private int[] ysSaber = new int[] {267, 265, 260, 20, 20,260, 265};
```

The first coordinate is the beam's topmost point, and the other coordinates define the polygon in a clockwise order according to Figure 6-7.

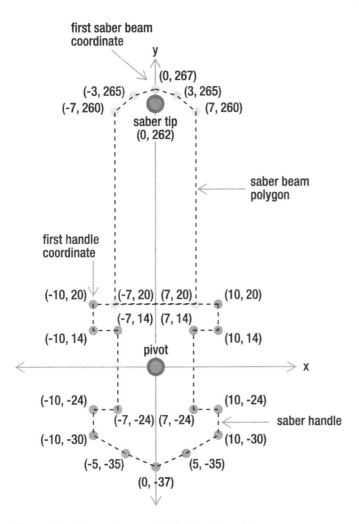

Figure 6-7. *Saber polygons and points (not to scale)*

The handle is specified in a similar manner:

```
private int[] xsHandle = new int[] {-10, 10, 10,  7,   7,
                 10,   10,  5,   0,  -5, -10, -10, -7,  -7, -10};
private int[] ysHandle = new int[] { 20, 20, 14, 14, -24,
                -24, -30, -35, -37, -35, -30, -24, -24, 14,  14};
```

The points start with the top-left coordinate, and then follow in clockwise order according to Figure 6-7. The top of the handle touches the base of the light beam.

The saber tip is an XYPoint object a little below the topmost beam coordinate since it seems to look more convincing if wall explosions originate there.

```
private XYPoint saberTip = new XYPoint( xsSaber[0], ysSaber[0]-5);
```

All the coordinates are defined relative to the pivot location at (0,0) (see Figure 6-7), but the pivot is defined using the screen's coordinate space—where (0,0) is the top-left corner of the screen:

```
// dimensions of the screen
private int pWidth = Display.getWidth();
private int pHeight = Display.getHeight();
private XYPoint pivot = new XYPoint(pWidth/2, pHeight-30);
```

This means that the beam and handle coordinates can be quickly converted to screen coordinates by adding the pivot point to them.

The saber beam, handle, and tip rotate around the pivot point as the game progresses, and it's useful to define a second set of data structures for the beam, handle, and tip that holds their changing coordinates, separate from their original values:

```
// globals
private int[] xs, ys;        // the coords of the rotated saber beam
private int[] xsH, ysH;      // coords of the rotated handle
private XYPoint rotatedTip;


// in the LightSaber() constructor:


// rotated saber beam coords are original beam coords initially
int numPts = xsSaber.length;
xs = new int[numPts];
ys = new int[numPts];
for (int i=0; i < numPts; i++) {
  xs[i] = pivot.x + xsSaber[i];
  ys[i] = pivot.y - ysSaber[i];
}


// rotated handle coords are the original handle coords initially
numPts = xsHandle.length;
xsH = new int[numPts];
ysH = new int[numPts];
for (int i=0; i < numPts; i++) {
  xsH[i] = pivot.x + xsHandle[i];
  ysH[i] = pivot.y - ysHandle[i];
}


rotatedTip = new XYPoint(pivot.x+saberTip.x, pivot.y-saberTip.y);
```

The rotated polygons and tip utilize screen coordinates by adding the pivot's coordinates to their values.

The line between the pivot and saber tip is implemented as an array of two XYPoints:

```
private XYPoint[] saberLine = new XYPoint[2];
saberLine[0] = pivot;
saberLine[1] = rotatedTip;
```

saberLine[1] references the rotatedTip object, so the line will rotate as rotatedTip rotates.

The trails are represented by three SaberTrail objects, which build polygons based on the saber beam coordinates, and use the pivot to map them to screen coordinates:

```
// globals
private static final double[] TRAIL_WIDTH_FACTORS =
                         new double[] {1.1, 1.4, 1.7};
                        // the trails get gradually wider

private static final int[] TRAIL_COLORS =
                         new int[] {0x6363FF, 0xA5A5FF, 0xD8D8FF};
                        // the trails are lighter shades of blue

private SaberTrail[] saberTrails;


// in the LightSaber() constructor:
// initialize the saber trails
saberTrails = new SaberTrail[TRAIL_WIDTH_FACTORS.length];
for (int i=0; i < TRAIL_WIDTH_FACTORS.length; i++)
  saberTrails[i] = new SaberTrail(xsSaber, ysSaber, pivot,
                   TRAIL_WIDTH_FACTORS[i], TRAIL_COLORS[i]);
```

A trail polygon utilizes the saber beam coordinates, but widened and differently colored. The details of the SaberTrail class are explained in the next section.

Rotation information also has to be maintained for the saber beam and handle, and separately for the trails that lag behind the beam as it turns.

```
// global rotation information
private int currRotAngle = 90; // saber starts pointing straight up

private int[] prevRotations = new int[saberTrails.length];
```

The current rotation angle is measured counterclockwise from the pivot's x-axis (see Figure 6-7), so starts at 90 degrees (i.e., vertically up the y-axis). The prevRotations[] array stores the old values of currRotAngle, which are passed to the SaberTrail objects when they need to be rotated.

Responding to User Input

The LightSaber methods for rotating the saber (its beam, handle, and trails) are based on calculating a clickAngle value. clickAngle is the angle that the saber should rotate counterclockwise relative to the positive x-axis in the local coordinate space (where the pivot point is at the origin). This idea is shown in Figure 6-8.

The saber should gradually rotate around the pivot point, over the course of a few animation frames, until it is clickAngle degrees away from the x-axis.

The most direct way of obtaining the clickAngle is by the user clicking the screen. Inside SaberScreen, this results in the touchEvent() method sending the click position (in screen coordinate) to LaserSaber.setClickAngle(). The angle is obtained by converting the click to the local coordinate space, followed by a bit of trigonometry.

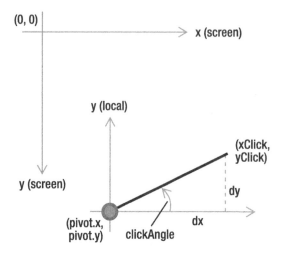

Figure 6-8. *The ClickAngle for rotating the saber*

```
// global
private volatile int clickAngle = 90;    // starts straight up


public void setClickAngle(int xClick, int yClick)
// convert a touch click into an angle relative to the pivot
{
  if (yClick >= pivot.y)  // ignore clicks below the pivot point
    return;

  int dy = pivot.y - yClick;    // get (dx,dy) in local space
  int dx = xClick - pivot.x;
  clickAngle = (int) Math.toDegrees( MathUtilities.atan2(dy, dx));
} // end of setClickAngle()
```

The various variables used in setClickAngle() (e.g., dx and dy) are shown in Figure 6-8.

Note that the screen click is ignored if it occurs below the pivot point.

Another way of obtaining clickAngle is by the user shaking the device from side to side. SaberScreen responds by having processShake() send the x-axis accelerometer value to LightSaber.shake().

```
// global
private static final int ROTATE_STEP = 5;    // in degrees

public void shake(short xAccel)
{
  if (xAccel < 0)        // movement east
    clickAngle -= (2*ROTATE_STEP);   // reduce clickAngle
  else if (xAccel > 0)   // movement west
    clickAngle += (2*ROTATE_STEP);   // increase clickAngle
  limitAngle();
} // end of shake()
```

Relative to the ground, a negative value for xAccel means an eastward movement (i.e., to the right), while positive denotes west (left). Rather arbitrarily, shakes() converts these into a decrease or increase in the current clickAngle by 2*ROTATE_STEP. I chose this value after experimenting with a more complicated mapping based on the magnitude of the movement, which didn't seem any more realistic than this simpler approach.

limitAngle() prevents the clickAngle from moving outside a specified angular range.

```
// globals
private static final int MIN_ROTATE = 30;   // right-most angle
private static final int MAX_ROTATE = 150; // left-most angle

private void limitAngle()
{ if (clickAngle < MIN_ROTATE)
     clickAngle = MIN_ROTATE;
  else if (clickAngle > MAX_ROTATE)
     clickAngle = MAX_ROTATE;
}
```

It might be better to calculate the minimum and maximum angles based on the dimensions of the screen, the length of the light saber, and the location of the pivot.

The other two ways of moving the saber are via trackball clicks and the arrow keys. Both of the SaberScreen listeners call LightSaber.move() with an integer argument, where negative means move left and positive is for going right.

```
public void move(int dx)
{ if (dx < 0)   // move left
     clickAngle += (2*ROTATE_STEP);
  else if (dx > 0)   // move right
     clickAngle -= (2*ROTATE_STEP);
  limitAngle();
}
```

As in shake(), the integer is converted into an arbitrary increase or decrease of the current clickAngle value.

A quick look at the movement methods (setClickAngle(), shake(), and move()) shows that they only modify the clickAngle integer. This is important to note since the methods are called by listeners in SaberScreen, and so are executed in the event thread of the device.

Rotating the Saber

The animation thread in SaberScreen regularly calls LightSaber.update() to rotate the saber (i.e., the beam, the handle, the trails, and saber tip) toward the current clickAngle angle.

```
// global
private volatile int clickAngle = 90;
private int currRotAngle = 90;   // starts by pointing straight up

public void update()
```

```
{
  updateTrails();

  if (!stopRotation()) {    // update the saber's rotation angle
    if (clickAngle < currRotAngle)
      currRotAngle -= ROTATE_STEP;    // move right
    else
      currRotAngle += ROTATE_STEP;    // move left
  }

  // rotate the saber beam and handle
  rotateCoords(xsSaber, ysSaber, xs, ys);
  rotateCoords(xsHandle, ysHandle, xsH, ysH);

  rotateTip();        // rotate the saber tip (and line)
} // end of update()
```

First the trails are updated, utilizing the old rotations of the beam. Then clickAngle is examined to see whether to increment or decrement currRotAngle, the aim being to rotate the saber gradually toward the required clickAngle value, not to make it "jump" to that angle in one step.

clickAngle raises questions about concurrency since it's updated in the event thread by the listener (see the last section), and is also accessed (but not changed) by the animation thread in update(). clickAngle is therefore declared volatile to guarantee that its data is synchronized across all the threads, so that whenever it's updated in one, the others will immediately see the value.

Although volatile has the same visibility features as a synchronized block, it doesn't guarantee atomicity (i.e., the indivisibility of operations applied to the variable). That isn't a major concern here since the data is only read by update() (and stopRotation()), and it doesn't matter (much) when clickAngle changes. The worst that can happen is that the current rotation angle is incremented or decremented too much, but this will be corrected on the next update.

updateTrails() shifts the old beam rotations to the right in the prevRotations[] array, making room for the current beam rotation (which is about to be changed in update()). The array values are used to rotate each of the trails by calling SaberTrail.setRotation().

```
private void updateTrails()
{
  for (int i=saberTrails.length-2; i >= 0; i--)
    prevRotations[i+1] = prevRotations[i];    // shift to right
  prevRotations[0] = currRotAngle;        // add current rotation

  // update saber trails rotations with prevRotations[]
  for (int i=0; i < saberTrails.length; i++)
    saberTrails[i].setRotation(prevRotations[i]);
} // end of updateTrails()
```

stopRotation() tests various conditions that should make the saber stop rotating:

```
// global
```

```
private static final int SABER_WIDTH = 15; //for wall collision tests

private boolean stopRotation()
{
  // don't rotate the saber beyond the left or right sides
  if ((rotatedTip.x <= SABER_WIDTH) &&
      (clickAngle > currRotAngle))
    return true;       // since saber on left and moving left

  if ((rotatedTip.x >= pWidth-SABER_WIDTH) &&
      (clickAngle < currRotAngle))
    return true;       // since saber on right and moving right

  /* stop rotating the saber when its angle is close
     enough to the click angle */
  if ( Math.abs(currRotAngle-clickAngle)< ROTATE_STEP)
    return true;

  return false;    // don't stop rotating
} // end of stopRotation
```

stopRotation() returns true if the saber has hit the left or right sides of the screen, which is a trickier test than it may at first appear. The saber should only stop if it is moving *toward* a side; if it's moving away, then its proximity to the wall should be ignored, and it should be allowed to rotate away. Another concern is that the saber has a width, which must be factored into the test.

rotateCoords() is called twice from update(): once to rotate the saber beam polygon, and once to rotate the handle. The (x,y) coordinates in the polygons are rotated around the pivot's positive x-axis, and their new values are stored in the rotation arrays.

```
private void rotateCoords(int[] xsOrig, int[] ysOrig,
                          int[] xsNew, int[] ysNew)
// rotate original (x,y) coords to get new (x,y) values
{
  int angleFP = Fixed32.toFP(currRotAngle-90);
            // -90 since the saber is vertical at the start

  // calculate x and y change due to the angle change
  int dux = Fixed32.cosd(angleFP);
  int dvx = -Fixed32.sind(angleFP);
  int duy = Fixed32.sind(angleFP);
  int dvy = Fixed32.cosd(angleFP);·

  /* update coordinates, and map them to screen coordinates
     by using the pivot */
  for(int i=0; i < xsOrig.length; i++) {
    xsNew[i] = pivot.x + Fixed32.toInt(
                Fixed32.round( dux*xsOrig[i] + dvx*ysOrig[i]));
    ysNew[i] = pivot.y - Fixed32.toInt(
                Fixed32.round( duy*xsOrig[i] + dvy*ysOrig[i]));
  }
} // end of rotateCoords()
```

rotateCoords() employs the rotation transformation illustrated by Figure 6-9.

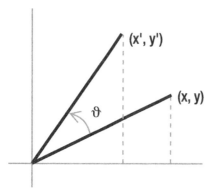

Figure 6-9. *Rotating an (x,y) coordinate*

The math for rotating an (x,y) coordinate through an angle θ about the origin to produce (x',y') can be expressed as the matrix multiplication:

$$\begin{pmatrix} x' \\ y' \end{pmatrix} = \begin{bmatrix} \cos\theta & -\sin\theta \\ \sin\theta & \cos\theta \end{bmatrix} \begin{pmatrix} x \\ y \end{pmatrix}$$

The values inside the rotation matrix are calculated using BlackBerry's Fixed32 class, which represent the fixed-point numbers by the integer variables dux, dvx, duy, and dvy. They are applied to each (x,y) coordinate in the original polygon, producing (x',y') values relative to the origin of the local coordinate system. They are converted to screen coordinates by adding the pivot position to them in a similar way to in Figure 6-8. The resulting coordinates are stored in the rotation arrays.

rotateTip() rotates the tip of the saber around the origin, employing the same rotation and translation operations as in rotateCoords().

```
// globals
private XYPoint pivot, saberTip, rotatedTip;


private void rotateTip()
{
  int angleFP = Fixed32.toFP(currRotAngle-90);
                    // since saber vertical at start
  // calculate x and y change due to the angle change
  int dux = Fixed32.cosd(angleFP);
  int dvx = -Fixed32.sind(angleFP);
  int duy = Fixed32.sind(angleFP);
  int dvy = Fixed32.cosd(angleFP);

  /* update coordinates, and map them to
     screen coordinates by using the pivot */
  int x = pivot.x + Fixed32.toInt(
          Fixed32.round( dux*saberTip.x +dvx*saberTip.y));
```

```
  int y = pivot.y - Fixed32.toInt(
          Fixed32.round( duy*saberTip.x +dvy*saberTip.y));

  rotatedTip.set(x,y);
} // end of rotateTip()
```

The original saber tip is transformed, and the result stored in `rotatedTip`. The saber line references `rotatedTip`, and so is also rotated.

Drawing the Saber

After the hard work of rotating the saber in `update()`, drawing it is quite straightforward:

```
// globals
private static final int SABER_COLOR = 0x0000FF;    // bright blue

private int[] handleColors =
   new int[] { 0x808080, 0xDCDCDC, 0xDCDCDC, 0xDCDCDC, 0xDCDCDC,
               0xDCDCDC, 0xDCDCDC, 0xDCDCDC, 0xDCDCDC, 0x808080,
               0x808080, 0x808080, 0x808080, 0x808080, 0x808080, };
   // dark gray to light gray (going from left to right side)


public void draw(Graphics g)
{
  // draw saber trails
  for (int i = saberTrails.length-1; i >= 0; i--)  // reverse order
    saberTrails[i].draw(g);

  // draw the rotated saber tip (useful when debugging)
  // g.setColor(0xFFFFFF);    // white
  // g.fillArc(rotatedTip.x, rotatedTip.y, 8, 8, 0, 360);

  // draw the rotated saber line
  g.setColor(SABER_COLOR);
  g.drawFilledPath(xs, ys, null, null);

  // draw the rotated shaded handle
  g.drawShadedFilledPath( xsH, ysH, null, handleColors, null);
} // end of draw()
```

As mentioned earlier, ordering is an important aspect of drawing, since later draws can write over earlier ones. In `draw()`, the trails are drawn first, then the beam, and finally the handle. The handle is drawn with a gradient fill, such that points on the left side of the handle are painted dark gray, while those on the right are lighter (see Figure 6-10 for a close-up of the handle).

Figure 6-10. *The gradient-filled handle*

Figure 6-10 seems to show a gradient effect on the beam, but this is caused by the lighter trails being drawn behind the blue beam.

The Saber Trails

A trail's coordinates are based on the beam's, but widened along the x-axis and colored differently.

```
// globals
private int[] xsSaber, ysSaber;    // coords of the saber trail
private int[] xs, ys;       // coords of the rotated saber trail

private XYPoint pivot;    // rotation point
private int color;


public SaberTrail(int[] xsCore, int[] ysCore, XYPoint pvt,
                                  double widthFactor, int col)
{ pivot = pvt;
  color = col;

  // trail's coordinates are based on the beam's coordinates
  int numPts = xsCore.length;
  xsSaber = new int[numPts];
  ysSaber = new int[numPts];
  for (int i=0; i < numPts; i++) {
    xsSaber[i] = (int)(xsCore[i]*widthFactor);
                            // widen x-dimensions
    ysSaber[i] = ysCore[i];    // y-dimensions are unchanged
  }

  // rotated trail coords are the trail coords initially
  xs = new int[numPts];
  ys = new int[numPts];
  for (int i=0; i < numPts; i++) {
    xs[i] = pivot.x + xsSaber[i];   // convert to screen coords
    ys[i] = pivot.y - ysSaber[i];
  }
}  // end of SaberTrail()
```

As in LightSaber, the polygon's coordinates are stored twice: the original coordinates are in xsSaber[] and ysSaber[], while the rotated ones are in xs[] and ys[].

Updating a trail is done by passing it a rotation angle, and calling a variant of rotateCoords() described in the last section. The only difference is that the method accesses the rotation as an input argument rather than via a global.

```
public void setRotation(int angle)
{  rotateCoords(angle, xsSaber, ysSaber, xs, ys);  }
```

Drawing the trail is fast:

```
public void draw(Graphics g)
{ g.setColor(color);
  g.drawFilledPath(xs, ys, null, null);
}
```

Game Sprites

A game's active entities are often encoded as *sprites*: moving graphical objects that can represent the player (and so respond to key presses and other input actions) or be driven by "intelligent" code in the game.

The Game API in MIDP 2.0 offers a Sprite class, but I want something specific to SwingSaber and the BlackBerry. RIM implemented the javax.microedition.lcdui.game package for use with MIDlets, but it's not compatible with RIM's native UI classes such as Field.

A general-purpose Sprite class is surprisingly hard to design, since many of its features depend on the application and the gaming context. For example, a sprite's onscreen movement greatly depends on the type of game. In Tetris, Breakout, and Space Invaders (and many more), the sprite moves within the gaming area while the background scenery remains stationary. In some of these games, the sprite may be unable to move beyond the edges of the panel, while in others it can wrap around to the opposite edge. In side-scrolling games, such as *Super Mario*, the sprite hardly moves at all (perhaps only up and down); instead the background shifts behind it. The Tweet Space game in Chapter 9 works the same way—the background scrolls up and down or side-to-side while the spaceship sprite stays centered on the screen.

A sprite must monitor the game environment, for example, reacting to collisions with different sprites, or stopping when it encounters an obstacle. Collision processing can be split into two basic categories: collision detection and collision response, with the range of responses being very application specific. There are also many varieties of collision detection: a sprite may be represented by a single bounding box, a reduced-size bounding box, or several bounding areas.

Coding a Sprite

My Sprite class is quite simple, storing little more than the sprite's current position, its speed specified as step increments in the x and y directions, and a single image.

A sprite is initialized with the name of its image, and assigned a default position and step increments, as shown in the following code:

```
// globals
// default step sizes (how far to move in each update)
private static final int STEP = 3;

// protected variables
protected int pWidth, pHeight;   // screen dimensions
protected int locx, locy;        // location of sprite
protected int dx, dy;            // step to move in each update


public Sprite(String fnm)
{
  pWidth = Display.getWidth();
  pHeight = Display.getHeight();

  loadImage(fnm);

  // start in center of screen by default
  locx = pWidth/2;
  locy = pHeight/2;

  dx = STEP; dy = STEP;
} // end of Sprite()
```

The sprite's coordinate (locx,locy) and its step values (dx,dy) are stored as integers. This simplifies certain tests and calculations, but restricts positional and speed precision. For instance, a blast sprite can't move 0.5 pixels at a time.

locx, locy, dx, and dy are protected rather than private, due to their widespread use in Sprite subclasses. They also have getter and setter methods, so can be accessed and changed by objects outside of the Sprite hierarchy.

When an image is loaded by loadImage(), its dimensions are recorded:

```
// globals
protected static final String IMAGES_DIR = "images/";

// default step sizes (how far to move in each update)
private static final int STEP = 3;

// protected variables
protected Bitmap image = null;
protected int width, height;     // sprite dimensions


private void loadImage(String fnm)
{
  image = Bitmap.getBitmapResource(IMAGES_DIR + fnm);
  if (image != null) {
    width = image.getWidth();
    height = image.getHeight();
  }
  else {
```

```
      System.out.println("Could not load image from " + fnm);
      width = SIZE;
      height = SIZE;
   }
}  // end of loadImage()
```

There's a setImage() public method that permits the sprite's image to be altered at runtime.

A Sprite's Bounding Box

Specialized collision detection should be implemented in Sprite subclasses, but can make use of Sprite.getRect() to obtain the sprite's bounding box:

```
public XYRect getRect()
{   return  new XYRect(locx, locy, width, height);   }
```

There is a hasHit() method that checks if the bounding boxes of two sprites intersect:

```
// global
private boolean isActive = true;
   // a sprite is updated and drawn only when it is active

public boolean hasHit(Sprite sprite)
{
  if (!isActive)
    return false;
  if (!sprite.isActive())
    return false;

  XYRect thisRect = getRect();
  XYRect spriteRect = sprite.getRect();
  if (thisRect.intersects(spriteRect))
    return true;
  return false;
}  // end of hasHit()
```

Intersection only occurs if both the sprites are *active*, which means they are currently part of the game. Sprite offers public methods for testing and setting the isActive variable. isActive allows a sprite to be (temporarily) removed from the game, since the sprite won't be updated or drawn when isActive is false.

hasReachedFloor() detects if the sprite is touching the floor.

```
public boolean hasReachedFloor()
{ if (isActive() && ((locy + height) >= pHeight) )
    return true;
  return false;
}
```

Many other collision-related methods could be added to Sprite, such as whether the sprite is touching the top of the screen or its sides.

Updating a Sprite

A sprite is updated by adding its step values (dx and dy) to its current location (locx and locy):

```
public void update()
// move the sprite
{ if (isActive()) {
    locx += dx;
    locy += dy;
  }
} // end of update()
```

No attempt is made to test for collisions with other sprites, obstacles, or the edges of the gaming area. These must be added by the subclasses when they override update().

Sprites are utilized in an update-draw-sleep animation cycle that tries to maintain a fixed frame rate. SaberScreen calls update() in all the sprites at a frequency as close to the specified frame rate as possible. For example, if the frame rate is 20 FPS (as it is in SwingSaber), then update() will be called 20 times per second in each sprite.

This allows me to make assumptions about a sprite's update timing. For instance, if the x-axis step value (dx) is 10, then the sprite will be moved 10 pixels in each update. This corresponds to a speed of about 10 * 20 = 200 pixels per second along that axis.

An alternative approach is to call update() with an argument holding the elapsed time since the previous call. This time value can be multiplied to a velocity value to get the step amount for this particular update. This technique is preferable in animation cycles where the frame rate can vary.

Drawing a Sprite

The animation loop will call update() in a sprite, followed by draw() to draw it:

```
public void draw(Graphics g)
{
  if (isActive()) {
    if (image == null) {    // the sprite has no image
      g.setColor(Color.YELLOW);    // draw a yellow circle instead
      g.fillArc(locx, locy, SIZE, SIZE, 0, 360);
      g.setColor(Color.BLACK);
    }
    else
      g.drawBitmap(locx, locy, width, height, image, 0, 0);
  }
} // end of draw()
```

If the image is null, then the sprite's default appearance is a small yellow circle.

Exploding Sprites

A common type of sprite is a bullet or bomb that is shot at the player, and may explode later. ExplodingSprite is a subclass of Sprite that adds this capability: its normal image can be changed to a series of explosion images, which are changed over the space of a few updates. When all the explosion pictures have been displayed, the sprite is made inactive, and so disappears.

ExplodingSprite demonstrates the use of an image strip—a file containing a series of images (e.g., as in Figure 6-11) that are split into multiple individual images at load time.

Figure 6-11. *An image strip containing seven images*

The ExplodingSprite constructor requires two file names: one for the normal sprite image, and the other for the image strip. It also needs to be told how many images are in the strip.

```
// global
private Bitmap normalIm;    // the sprite's normal image

public ExplodingSprite(String fnm, String explFnm, int numImages)
{
  super(fnm);
  normalIm = image;   // backup initial sprite image
  loadImagesStrip(explFnm, numImages);

  setStep(0, 0);
  setActive(false);
} // end of ExplodingSprite()
```

loadImagesStrip() extracts the individual images from the supplied strip, assuming they are stored in a single row and are of equal size, and that there are numImages of them. The images are stored in an array of Bitmaps called explIms[], and each image is assigned an alpha channel so that it can be partially transparent (as in Figure 6-11) or translucent.

```
// global
private Bitmap[] explIms;    // stores the explosion images

private void loadImagesStrip(String fnm, int numImages)
{
  System.out.println("Loading image strip from " + IMAGES_DIR+fnm);
  Bitmap stripIm = Bitmap.getBitmapResource(IMAGES_DIR + fnm);
  if (stripIm == null) {
    System.out.println("Image strip is empty");
    System.exit(1);
  }

  // calculate image dimensions
```

```
    int imWidth = (int) stripIm.getWidth()/numImages;
    int imHeight = stripIm.getHeight();

    explIms = new Bitmap[numImages];
    int[] picData = new int[imWidth * imHeight];
    Bitmap newIm;
    Graphics stripG2D;

    // each Bitmap in the explIms is stored in explIms[]
    for (int i=0; i < numImages; i++) {
      newIm = new Bitmap(imWidth, imHeight);
      newIm.createAlpha(Bitmap.ALPHA_BITDEPTH_8BPP);
                      // allow image to have an alpha channel
      newIm.setARGB(picData, 0, imWidth, 0, 0, imWidth, imHeight);
      stripG2D = Graphics.create(newIm);

      // draw image from explIms into offscreen buffer
      stripG2D.drawBitmap(0, 0, imWidth, imHeight, stripIm, i*imWidth, 0);
      explIms[i] = newIm;
    }
  } // end of loadImagesStrip()
```

A new `Bitmap` object is created for each image in the strip, and its dimensions are set with `Bitmap.setARGB()`. The required part of the image strip is copied into the bitmap by calling `Graphics.drawBitmap()` on a graphics context linked to the bitmap.

Making a Sprite Explode

A sprite is exploded by calling `ExplodingSprite.explode()`:

```
// globals
private boolean isExploding = false;
private int explodingCounter;   // which explosion image to display

public void explode()
{
  isExploding = true;
  explodingCounter = 0;    // start with the first explosion image
  setStep(0, 0);    // the sprite stops moving
}  // end of explode()
```

`explode()` prepares the sprite by setting the `isExploding` boolean to true, and initializing a counter, `explodingCounter`, which will iterate through the explosion images.

Another way to trigger an explosion is with `ExplodingSprite.explodeAt()`, which places the explosion at a given point:

```
public void explodeAt(XYPoint pt)
{
  // calculate the sprite location so that pt is its center
  XYRect rect = getRect();
  setPosition( pt.x-rect.width/2, pt.y-rect.height/2 );
  setActive(true);
  explode();
```

```
}  // end of explodeAt()
```

The sprite can be checked to see if it's currently exploding by calling
ExplodingSprite.isExploding():

```
public boolean isExploding()
{  return isExploding;  }
```

Updating the Sprite

ExplodingSprite extends Sprite.update(), so the sprite draws the current explosion
image based on the current value of explosionCounter. explosionCounter is
incremented each time update() is called until the final explosion image has been
displayed.

```
// globals
private boolean isExploding = false;
private int explodingCounter;   // which explosion image to display
private Bitmap[] explIms;       // stores the explosion images


public void update()
{
  if (isExploding) {
    if (explodingCounter == explIms.length) {    // end of explosion
      isExploding = false;
      setActive(false);    // the sprite disappears
    }
    else {
      setImage(explIms[explodingCounter]);
      explodingCounter++;  // show next explosion image next time
    }
  }
  super.update();
}  // end of update()
```

Using ExplodingSprite in SwingSaber

The Sprite class isn't used directly by SwingSaber, but ExplodingSprite is employed to
create an explosion when the saber touches the sides of the screen (as illustrated in
Figure 6-12).

The sprite is created in the SaberScreen constructor, along with the other game sprites:

```
// global
private ExplodingSprite wallExplSprite;

// in SaberScreen()
wallExplSprite = new ExplodingSprite("wallBlast.png", "wallBlasts.png", 7);
```

It uses the wallBlasts.png image strip shown in Figure 6-11.

Figure 6-12. *Wall explosions using ExplodingSprite*

wallExplSprite is inactive initially, so won't be displayed. This changes when the saber touches the wall:

```
private void gameUpdate()
// check sprite conditions, then update all the sprites
{
  // check interaction conditions
  checkBlasts();

  // check for saber hitting a wall
  if (!wallExplSprite.isExploding()) {
    if (saber.isTouchingWall())
      wallExplSprite.explodeAt( saber.getTip() );
  }

  // update sprites
  saber.update();
  for(int i=0; i < blasts.length; i++)
    blasts[i].update();
  wallExplSprite.update();
}  // end of gameUpdate()
```

ExplodingSprite.explodeAt() is called by SaberScreen to make it display the explosion sequence. The explosion is positioned at the saber's tip.

Each call to ExplodingSprite.update() will cause the next explosion image to become the sprite's visual, which is displayed when wallExplSprite is drawn in SaberScreen.paint():

```
wallExplSprite.draw(g);
```

The Blast Sprite

As Figure 6-3 shows, BlastSprite is a specialization of ExplodingSprite, mainly to add intersection testing between a sprite and the saber, which can't be adequately modeled by the intersection of two bounding boxes.

The constructor specifies the standard blast image (blast.png shown in Figure 6-13) and the explosion image strip (explosion.png in Figure 6-14).

```
public BlastSprite()
{  super("blast.png", "explosion.png", 5);  }
```

Figure 6-13. *The blast sprite image (blast.png)*

Figure 6-14. *The explosion image strip for a BlastSprite (explosion.png)*

BlastSprite.drop() randomly positions the sprite at the top of the screen, and drops it with a random speed.

```
// global
private static final int YSTEP = 14;     // max dropping speed

public void drop()
{ int yStep = YSTEP/2 + rand.nextInt(YSTEP/2);
  super.shoot( rand.nextInt(pWidth), 0, 0, yStep);
}
```

A blast is updated with ExplodingSprite.update(), but adds a test to deactivate itself when it has dropped off the screen. Once deactivated, the blast is eligible to be restarted at a new position at the top of the screen.

```
public void update()
{
  if (!isExploding()) {
    if (locy > pHeight)     // if dropped through floor
      setActive(false);
  }
  super.update();
} // end of update()
```

An unusual part of BlastSprite is how it tests if it has collided with the saber. Employing a bounding box around the blast is fine, but the saber's rotation means that its bounding box would be too large most of the time. Instead, the saber is represented by a line joining its pivot to its tip, as in Figure 6-15.

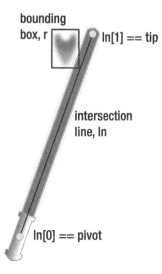

bounding
box, r

ln[1] == tip

intersection
line, ln

ln[0] == pivot

Figure 6-15. *The intersection of a blast and the saber*

The intersection of the blast's bounding box and the saber line is tested by checking if any of the box's edges touch the line.

```
public boolean hasHitSaber(LightSaber saber)
// has the blast hit the light saber?
{
  XYRect r = getRect();               // rectangle for sprite
  XYPoint[] ln = saber.getLine();     // saber line

  /* check intersection of 4 line segments of rectangle against
     saber line segment */
  if (VecMath.intersects(ln[0].x, ln[0].y, ln[1].x, ln[1].y,
                          r.x, r.y, (r.x + r.width), r.y)   ||        // top
        VecMath.intersects(ln[0].x, ln[0].y, ln[1].x, ln[1].y,
                          r.x, r.y, r.x, (r.y + r.height))   ||       // left
        VecMath.intersects(ln[0].x, ln[0].y, ln[1].x, ln[1].y,
                          (r.x + r.width), r.y, (r.x + r.width),
                                          (r.y + r.height)) ||   // right
        VecMath.intersects(ln[0].x, ln[0].y, ln[1].x, ln[1].y,
                          r.x, (r.y + r.height), (r.x + r.width),
                                          (r.y + r.height)))   // bottom
      return true;
    return false;
}  // end of hasHitSaber()
```

Game Music

ClipsPlayer stores a collection of MMAPI Player objects in a Hashtable whose keys are their file names. The clips can be MIDI, MP3, AU, or tone sequences (JTS files). There's also a static method for playing a note for a certain period, with the notes specified using a simple music notation (e.g., C4, B5#, etc.).

Perhaps the most difficult aspect of `ClipsPlayer` is not its implementation, but how it should best be utilized on a particular device. As I outlined in the "Loading Sounds" section earlier, these device-specific concerns include

- The degree of support for audio mixing (which may not be reflected by the value returned by the "`supports.mixing`" property)

- The interplay between sampled and synthesized music (e.g., what happens when two WAV or MIDI files are played at once)

- The drain on resources of having multiple `Players`

The best way of dealing with these issues is by testing the application on the intended device, also bearing in mind the operating system version that most users will have.

`SwingSaber` illustrates a fairly conservative use of `ClipsPlayer`—a single MIDI player for background music, and three WAV players for sound effects.

The MIDI player is closed at game completion, so its resources can be potentially reused for playing a short MIDI speech by the black knight.

The sound effects players are each utilized in turn to vary the audio responses of the game. It's possible to reduce the number of players to save on device resources, perhaps getting by with one WAV player that repeatedly loads and plays different sounds. This approach would need to be tested on the planned application device to compare the trade-off between resource utilization and playing time delay.

Loading a Clip

The `ClipsPlayer` object maintains a `Hashtable` of sound clips that can be played as required.

```
// global
private Hashtable clipsMap;
   // the key is the file name string, the value is a Player object

public ClipsPlayer()
{  clipsMap = new Hashtable();  }
```

When `ClipsPlayer.load()` is called, its `String` argument is used to create a prefetched player for the file in the sounds/ directory.

```
// global
private final static String SOUND_DIR = "/sounds/";

public boolean load(String fnm)
// create a ClipInfo object for name and store it
{
  if (clipsMap.containsKey(fnm)) {
    System.out.println(fnm + "already stored");
    return true;
  }
  Player clip = loadClip(fnm);
  if (clip != null) {
```

```
    clipsMap.put(fnm, clip);
    System.out.println("Loaded " + fnm);
    return true;
  }
  return false;
}  // end of load()


private Player loadClip(String fnm)
{
  String contentType = extractContentType(fnm);
  Player clip = null;
  try {
    clip = Manager.createPlayer(getClass().getResourceAsStream(SOUND_DIR+fnm),
                            contentType);
    clip.addPlayerListener(this);
    clip.realize();
    clip.prefetch();
    useSpeaker(clip);
  }
  catch (Exception e)
  { System.out.println("Could not load " + fnm); }
  return clip;
}  // end of loadClip()
```

extractContentType() utilizes the file name's extension to decide on the audio's content type.

```
private String extractContentType(String fnm)
{
  int lastDot = fnm.lastIndexOf('.');
  if (lastDot == -1)
    return "audio/x-wav";   // default content type
  String extStr = fnm.substring(lastDot+1).toLowerCase();
  if (extStr.endsWith("au"))
    return "audio/basic";
  else if (extStr.endsWith("mp3"))
    return "audio/mpeg";
  else if (extStr.endsWith("mid"))
    return "audio/midi";
  else if (extStr.endsWith("jts"))   // tone sequences
    return "audio/x-tone-seq";

  return "audio/x-wav";          // default content type
}  // end of extractContentType()
```

The call to Player.addPlayerListener(this) in loadClip() allows ClipsPlayer (which implements PlayerListener) to monitor the players and device.

Player.realize() and Player.prefetch() move the player through the REALIZED state into a PREFETCHED state. Prefetching reduces the player's startup latency since it forces the acquisition and initialization of all the necessary audio resources.

useSpeaker() ensures that sound output goes to the device's speakers rather than the headphones or elsewhere.

```
private void useSpeaker(Player clip)
{
  try {
    AudioPathControl apc = null;
    Control[] ctrls = clip.getControls();
    for(int i = ctrls.length-1; i >= 0; i--)
      if(ctrls[i] instanceof AudioPathControl) {
        apc = (AudioPathControl) ctrls[i];
        break;
      }
    if(apc != null)
      apc.setAudioPath(AudioPathControl.AUDIO_PATH_HANDSFREE);
                                            // use the speakers
  }
  catch (Exception e) {
    System.out.println("Could not use speaker");
  }
}  // end of useSpeaker()
```

Playing a Clip

play(), like most of the ClipsPlayer methods, uses its string argument as a key to retrieve a player from the Hashtable. play() calls Player.start(), but precedes it with lots of error checking (always a good idea when programming with MMAPI).

```
// global
private boolean isDeviceAvailable = true;


public boolean play(String fnm)
// play a clip once
{  return play(fnm, false);  }


private boolean play(String fnm, boolean isRepeating)
// play a clip once or multiple times
{
  if (!isDeviceAvailable) {
    System.out.println("Device not available");
    return false;
  }
  Player clip = (Player) clipsMap.get(fnm);
  if (clip == null) {
    System.out.println("No loaded clip for " + fnm);
    return false;
  }
  if (clip.getState() == Player.STARTED){
    System.out.println("Clip for " + fnm + " already playing");
    return true;
  }

  try {
    if (isRepeating)
      clip.setLoopCount(-1);  // play indefinitely
```

```
    clip.start();
    return true;
  }
  catch(Exception e)
  { System.out.println("Could not play " + fnm);
    return false;
  }
} // end of play()
```

The isRepeating boolean in the two-argument play() allows the same method to be used for looping a clip.

loadPlay() combines loading and playing into a single convenience function:

```
public boolean loadPlay(String fnm)
{
  boolean isLoaded = load(fnm);
  if (!isLoaded)
    return false;
  else
    return play(fnm);
} // end of loadPlay()
```

isPlaying() checks if a player is already in use:

```
public boolean isPlaying(String fnm)
{
  if (!isDeviceAvailable) {
    System.out.println("Device not available");
    return false;
  }
  Player clip = (Player) clipsMap.get(fnm);
  if (clip == null) {
    System.out.println("No loaded clip for " + fnm);
    return false;
  }
  return (clip.getState() == Player.STARTED);
} // end of isPlaying()
```

In application code, isPlaying() could be used to avoid trying to invoke an already active player, which might cause problems in some MMAPI implementations.

Looping

The loop() and loadLoop() methods are similar to play() and loadPlay() except that the player's loop count is set to -1 in the two-argument play() to make the audio play indefinitely.

```
public boolean loop(String fnm)
// keep repeating the clip
{  return play(fnm, true);  }


public boolean loadLoop(String fnm)
{
```

```
    boolean isLoaded = load(fnm);
    if (!isLoaded)
      return false;
    else
      return loop(fnm);
}  // end of loadPlay()
```

Closing and Stopping

The difference between closing and stopping a player is a matter of resource deallocation. Closing should release all the resources, including any locks held on audio hardware. An advantage of using stop() instead is that subsequent playing of the same clip should have a smaller startup cost since its resources are still available.

The choice between using closing or stopping needs to be based on device testing, considering the trade-offs between resource usage and player latency.

```
public void close()
// close all the players
{
  Enumeration keys = clipsMap.keys();
  while (keys.hasMoreElements())
    close( (String) keys.nextElement() );
}


public void close(String fnm)
// close a player
{
  Player clip = (Player) clipsMap.get(fnm);
  if (clip != null) {
    try {
      clip.stop();
      clip.deallocate();
      clip.close();
      clip = null;
    }
    catch(Exception e){}
  }
}  // end of close()


public boolean stop(String fnm)
{
  Player clip = (Player) clipsMap.get(fnm);
  if (clip == null) {
    System.out.println("No loaded clip for " + fnm);
    return false;
  }
  try {
    clip.stop();
    return true;
  }
  catch(Exception e)
```

```
  { System.out.println("Could not stop " + fnm);
    return false;
  }
}  // end of stop()
```

Monitoring Players

As each clip is loaded and allocated to a player in loadClip(), ClipsPlayer becomes its listener (by calling clip.addPlayerListener(this)). This lets ClipsPlayer receive asynchronous events related to the players' states, and device details such as hardware availability.

playerUpdate() in ClipsPlayer watches for DEVICE_AVAILABLE and DEVICE_UNAVAILABLE events, and changes the global isDeviceAvailable boolean accordingly.

```
// global
private boolean isDeviceAvailable = true;


public void playerUpdate(Player clip, String event, Object eventData)
{
  try {
    if (event.equals(PlayerListener.DEVICE_UNAVAILABLE))
      isDeviceAvailable = false;          // incoming phone call
    else if (event.equals(PlayerListener.DEVICE_AVAILABLE))
      isDeviceAvailable = true;           // finished phone call.

    // System.out.println("playerUpdate() event: " + event);
  }
  catch (Exception e)
  { System.out.println(e); }
}  // end of playerUpdate()
```

Player events are another MMAPI feature that may be less-than-fully implemented, so their use must be checked on the intended device. On BlackBerry, DEVICE_UNAVAILABLE typically means that the speaker has been grabbed back by the device to handle a phone call, but this may not occur if the phone output has been redirected through the headphones.

Another possibility is that a particular MMAPI implementation may support additional device-specific events. For this reason, make sure to study the MMAPI documentation for that device (and operating system version).

Playing Tones

MMAPI's Manager class can play tones through the device's speaker with

```
static void playTone(int tone, int duration, int volume)
```

The sound duration is in milliseconds, and the playback volume ranges from 0 (silence) to 100. The tricky argument is the tone, a value between 0 to 127 that is the same as a MIDI note number, and has a rather complex relationship to tone frequency.

My `ClipsPlayer` class offers the method:

`static void playTone(String noteStr, int duration)`

The `duration` argument is the same, but the volume is fixed at 100. More importantly, the user specifies the note using piano notation (e.g., C4, B#5, etc.). This is a simpler interface than `Manager.playTone()`, but requires some background musical knowledge, which I'll now supply.

A piano has a mix of black and white keys, as in Figure 6-16.

Figure 6-16. *Part of a piano keyboard*

Keys are grouped into octaves, each octave consisting of 12 consecutive white and black keys. The white keys are labeled with the letters *A* to *G* and an octave number. For example, the note named C4 is the white key closest to the center of the keyboard, often referred to as *middle C*. The "4" means that the key is in the fourth octave, counting from the left of the keyboard.

A black key is labeled with the letter of the preceding white key and a sharp (#). For instance, the black key following C4 is known as C#4.

A note for musicians: for simplicity's sake, I'll be ignoring flats in this discussion.

Figure 6-17 shows the keyboard fragment of Figure 6-16 labeled with note names. I've assumed that the first white key is C4.

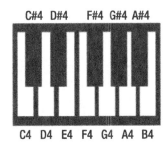

Figure 6-17. *Piano keyboard with note names*

Figure 6-17 utilizes the C major scale, where the letters appear in the order C, D, E, F, G, A, and B. There's a harmonic minor scale that starts at A, but I'll not be using it here.

After B4, the fifth octave begins, starting with C5 and repeating the same sequence as in the fourth octave. Before C4 is the third octave, which ends with B3.

The note names can be mapped to tone frequencies or pitches, but that's not particularly useful for `Manager.playTone()`, which uses MIDI note numbers.

MIDI note numbers can range between 0 and 127, extending well beyond the piano's scope, which only includes 88 standard keys. This means that the note naming scheme gets a little strange below note 12 (C0), since we have to start talking about octave −1 (e.g., see the table at www.harmony-central.com/MIDI/Doc/table2.html). Additionally, a maximum value of 127 means that note names only go up to G9; there is no G#9. Table 6-1 shows the mapping of MIDI numbers to notes for the fourth octave.

Table 6-1. *MIDI Note Numbers and Note Names*

MIDI Number	Note Name
60	C4
61	C#4
62	D4
63	D#4
64	E4
65	F4
66	F#4
67	G4
68	G#4
69	A4
70	A#4
71	B4

A table showing the correspondence between all MIDI note numbers and note names can be found at www.phys.unsw.edu.au/jw/notes.html.

From Note Name to MIDI Note Number

The note name syntax used by `ClipsPlayer.playTone()` is simple, albeit nonstandard. Only a single letter–single octave combination is allowed (e.g., C4, A0), so it's not possible to refer to the −1 octave. A sharp can be included, but only after the octave number (e.g., G4#); the normal convention is that a sharp follows the note letter. No notation for flats is included here, although you can represent any flatted note with the *sharped* version of the note following it; for example, D-flat is equivalent to C-sharp.

playTone() is defined as

```
public static void playTone(String noteStr, int duration)
{
  int note = convertToNote(noteStr);
  try {
    Manager.playTone(note, duration, 100);    // play at max volume
  }
  catch(Exception e) {}
}  // end of playTone()
```

convertToNote() uses several constants:

```
private static final int[] cOffsets = {9, 11, 0, 2, 4, 5, 7};
                            // A   B  C  D  E  F  G
```

```
private static final int C4_KEY = 60;
      // C4 is the "C" in the 4th octave on a piano
```

```
private static final int OCTAVE = 12;    // note size of an octave
```

The note offsets in cOffsets[] use the C major scale, which is ordered C D E F G A B, but the offsets are stored in A B C D E F G order to simplify their lookup by convertToNote().

convertToNote() calculates a MIDI note number by examining the note letter, octave number, and optional sharp character in the supplied string:

```
private static int convertToNote(String noteStr)
// Convert a note string (e.g. "C4", "B5#") into a note.
{
  char[] letters = noteStr.toCharArray();

  if (letters.length < 2) {
    System.out.println("Incorrect note syntax; using C4");
    return C4_KEY;
  }

  // look at note letter in letters[0]
  int c_offset = 0;
  if ((letters[0] >= 'A') && (letters[0] <= 'G'))
    c_offset = cOffsets[letters[0] - 'A'];
  else
    System.out.println("Incorrect letter: " + letters[0] + ", using C");

  // look at octave number in letters[1]
  int range = C4_KEY;
  if ((letters[1] >= '0') && (letters[1] <= '9'))
    range = OCTAVE * (letters[1] - '0' + 1);  // plus 1 for midi
  else
    System.out.println("Incorrect number: " + letters[1] + ", using 4");

  // look at optional sharp in letters[2]
  int sharp = 0;
  if ((letters.length > 2) && (letters[2] == '#'))
    sharp = 1;    // a sharp is 1 note higher
```

```
                    // (represented by the black keys on a piano)
    int key = range + c_offset + sharp;

    return key;
}   // end of convertToNote()
```

The piano notation understood by `ClipsPlayer.playTone()` could easily be enlarged. For example, David Flanagan's PlayerPiano application from *Java Examples in a Nutshell* (O'Reilly, 2004) covers similar ground to `playTone()`, but also supports flats, chords (combined notes), volume control, and the damper pedal (`www.onjava.com/pub/a/onjava/excerpt/jenut3_ch17/index1.html`). The resulting sequence can be played or saved to a file.

Playing Tone Sequences

`Manager.playTone() ()` (and `ClipsPlayer.playTone()`) is only really useful for playing individual tones. A tone sequence (e.g., a ringtone) should be passed to a MMAPI Player as a JTS file, with the content type `audio/x-tone-seq`.

I was unable to find any application that can directly compose MMAPI JTS files. The simplest approach seems to be to create a ringtone masterpiece using MIDI (or RTTTL), and convert it (via several tortuous steps) into JTS, as shown in Figure 6-18.

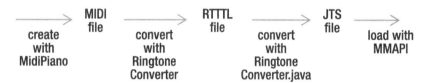

Figure 6-18. *From MIDI to JTS ringtones*

Since MMAPI can play MIDI files directly, these translation steps may seem a little pointless. One reason for the conversion might be that the intended device doesn't support multiple MIDI file playing but does offer concurrent tone sequences.

There's a wealth of MIDI creation tools available, many of them freeware or shareware. Here are some packages that I've tinkered with:

- The free version of Anvil Studio (`www.anvilstudio.com`), which supports the capture, editing, and direct composing of MIDI. It also handles WAV files.

- MidiPiano 1.8.3 (or later), which emulates a standard keyboard synthesizer, and is simpler to use than most tools of this type (`http://midipiano.googlepages.com`).

Once you have a MIDI file, the next step is to convert it to the RTTTL (Ring Tone Transfer Language) format developed by Nokia. Alternatively, there are many sites that host RTTTL files (e.g., `http://merwin.bespin.org/db/rts` and `www.zedge.net/ringtones`), but they tend to be snippets of pop music.

One MIDI-to-RTTTL conversion tool I've used is Ringtone Converter, which also includes a piano keyboard for composing RTTTL tunes directly (www.codingworkshop.com/ringtones). It's a free download, but some features, such as saving, are disabled. However, you can paste the textual RTTTL output into a file.

The last stage is to translate an RTTTL text file into a JTS file understood by MMAPI. I couldn't find a tool that does this, but there is a converter example that comes with Sun's Java ME SDK 3.0 (formerly the Wireless Toolkit) (http://java.sun.com/javame/downloads/sdk30.jsp). The source can be found in the apps\MMAPIDemos\src\example\mmademo\ subdirectory as RingToneConverter.java. I made a few minor modifications to this code to make it work with Java SE rather than Java ME, and my version can be found with the rest of the code for this chapter at the book's web site (http://frogparrot.net/blackberry/ch06/).

Porting SwingSaber to an Earlier Operating System

As an experiment, I compiled SwingSaber on a BlackBerry supporting a popular, earlier operating system, version 4.2. Naturally, I received numerous error messages for methods employing the accelerometer and touchscreen, which first appeared in operating system v4.7.

The touchscreen errors disappeared after I removed the overridden touchEvent() method from IntroScreen and SaberScreen. This meant that LightSaber.setClickAngle() was no longer called from SaberScreen. I also deleted the uses of the accelerometer channel (accelChannel) in SaberScreen's constructor, finalUpdates(), and processShakes(). This meant that LightSaber.shake() was no longer called. There were three remaining errors.

The first was for MathUtilities.atan2(), called in LightSaber.setClickAngle(), but not recognized because it was only added in operating system v4.6. Fortunately, I no longer needed atan2() since it appeared in a method triggered by touch events. Otherwise, I would have had to code a version for myself, or "borrow" one from the Web, such as the atan() method by Stephen Zimmerman, at http://manlyignition.blogspot.com/2008/11/arctan-in-j2me.html.

The second error was caused by Graphics.create() called in ExplodingSprite.loadImagesStrip(), which appeared in v4.7. Fixing this problem was achieved by going back to the deprecated way of creating a Graphics object. Instead of

```
Graphics stripG2D = Graphics.create(newIm);
```

I called

```
Graphics stripG2D = new Graphics(newIm);
```

The third error appeared in SwingSaber.java, when I stopped device tilting from affecting SwingSaber's orientation:

```
Ui.getUiEngineInstance().setAcceptableDirections(
                              Display.DIRECTION_PORTRAIT);
```

The `UiEngineInstance` class was added in 4.7, along with `Ui.getUiEngineInstance()`. The class utilizes the accelerometer to determine how a device is being held, so it's not supported by earlier operating systems.

After I got the code to compile, I tested it on an old device, which highlighted a couple of design weaknesses. Figure 6-19 shows the light saber in action, and illustrates one of the problems.

Figure 6-19. *SwingSaber on an older BlackBerry*

The screen is quite a bit smaller than newer BlackBerrys, but no adjustment is made to the size of the light saber. In fact, its dimensions are hardwired into the code, as highlighted in Figure 6-7, making the saber too long for the screen.

Another problem is the loud music; it would be nice to have a way to reduce the game's volume without affecting the entire device.

Summary

You've been introduced to the BlackBerry Saber, the weapon of a RIM-i Knight. Not as clumsy or as random as a blaster—an elegant device for a more civilized age.

Along the way, I discussed game animation employing an update-draw-sleep loop running in its own thread; reusable `Sprite` and `ExplodingSprite` classes, which aren't based on MIDP 2.0's `Sprite`; and a MMAPI clip player that can handle MIDI, MP3, AU, and tones.

The saber can be swung about by shaking the BlackBerry, touching the screen on the left or right, moving the trackball, or pressing the left and right arrow keys. The BlackBerry vibrates a little whenever you destroy a laser blast.

Now that you've seen how to create and distribute a complete BlackBerry game, it's time to move on to more advanced gaming topics. In the next chapters, you'll see communications programming with HTTP, Bluetooth, and SMS; 2D and 3D graphics techniques using SVG and OpenGL ES; and some extra fun stuff with toy cars and GPS!

Chapter 7

Play a Live Opponent with SMS

Short Message Service (SMS) is a relatively primitive technology, originally designed in the late 1980s for devices with a lot less computing power than a BlackBerry smartphone. BlackBerry users can access their e-mail on their smartphones and typically have phone service contracts that include data transfer measured in megabytes. So it seems crazy to bother with tiny packets containing only 140 bytes of data! But there's a reason why SMS is still a good choice for game communications: it has enormous and widespread support.

By some estimates, the SMS protocol has well over 2 billion active users, making it the most widely used data application on the planet. So when you base your game on SMS, you know that it will work for users all over the world without any unpleasant surprises, despite the fact that operator networks may differ from each other in terms of some of their more advanced offerings.

In this chapter, you'll create the SMS Checkers game shown in Figure 7-1. Since a move on a checkerboard can be easily described in a few bytes, each move can be sent in an SMS message, with plenty of room left over for one player to send a message to the other player along with the move.

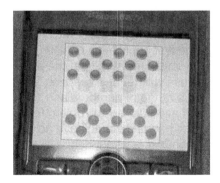

Figure 7-1. *The SMS Checkers game running on the BlackBerry Curve 8320*

Since the advantage of SMS is universal compatibility, the SMS Checkers game will be optimized for cross-platform compatibility. The Maze Deluxe game from Chapter 4 had graphics that needed to be carefully optimized for each device's particular screen size, so naturally, a host of different versions needed to be built. But for Checkers, the graphics are very simple, and—since the only image files we need are a handful of checkers—there's no harm in making a single version that can calculate the board size (and draw the corresponding board) at runtime.

Similarly, the BlackBerry platform uses the standard Wireless Messaging API (defined in JSR 120) and the standard Personal Information Management API (defined in JSR 75). So there's not much advantage in writing the game to be BlackBerry-only when we can just as easily write the game to run on practically any MIDP handset as well—allowing a BlackBerry user to play the game with an opponent who has a different type of phone, as shown in Figure 7-2. However, in this example, you'll see the specific techniques and special points to keep in mind when implementing and debugging applications that use BlackBerry's particular implementation of SMS and PIM.

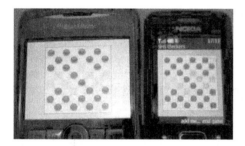

Figure 7-2. *The SMS Checkers game played between a BlackBerry and a Nokia handset*

Sending and Receiving SMS Messages

Your cell phone (BlackBerry or not) already has built-in software for sending and receiving SMS text messages, and that's where standard incoming messages are automatically routed. However, you can send an SMS message to a different application on the handset by adding a port number to the end of the telephone number. Naturally, the application needs to be listening for messages on that port.

An application can select a port number at runtime and then open a message connection to listen for messages on that port. According to JSR 120, the first application to claim a given port (by opening a corresponding `MessageConnection` object for it) will get the port, and later applications that attempt to open a port that is in use will get an exception. An application can dynamically select a port number (by trying a range of numbers and keeping the first one that doesn't throw an exception), but that would be a problem for a game like SMS Checkers because the game instance on one handset would have no way of knowing which port the game instance on another handset is using, hence it couldn't direct messages to it.

There are various strategies for dealing with this problem, but the simplest is just to pick one port number for the game—hard-code it in—and hope that no other popular program is competing for the same port number. The Internet Assigned Numbers Authority (http://iana.org) is in charge of assigning port numbers to registered applications (and you can contact them if you'd like to see about getting an assigned port number for an application). Otherwise, you can just select a port number in the free range: 16000 to 16999. With 1,000 port numbers to choose from, you have a good chance of picking one that doesn't have too much competition for it.

Using a MessageConnection

Listing 7-1 shows how to open a MessageConnection and use it to send and receive messages. Both sending and receiving are operations that need to be run on a separate thread, *not* the event thread. As you can see in Listing 7-1, when a new message arrives for the MessageConnection, the BlackBerry platform uses the event thread to call notifyIncomingMessage() on the connection's MessageListener (which this class has been set to be), indicating which MessageConnection has a new message waiting. This class starts a new thread to receive and handle the message, though, because MessageConnection.receive() is a blocking method, and blocking the event thread will cause the program to throw and Exception or crash. Similarly, the SMSMessage class extends Thread (as shown in Listing 7-2), to avoid blocking the event thread with the sending operation.

Listing 7-1. *SMSManager.java*

```java
package net.frogparrot.net;

import java.io.*;

import javax.wireless.messaging.*;
import javax.microedition.io.*;
import javax.microedition.io.PushRegistry;

import net.frogparrot.smscheckers.Main;

/**
 * Sends and receives binary SMS messages.
 */
public class SMSManager implements Runnable, MessageListener {

//------------------------------------------------------------
//  static fields

  /**
   * The protocol string.
   */
  public static final String SMS_PROTOCOL = "sms://";

  /**
   * The instance of this class.
   */
```

```
      static SMSManager theInstance = null;

//--------------------------------------------------------
//   instance fields

  /**
   * The connection to listen for messages on.
   */
  private MessageConnection myConnection;

  /**
   * The phone number to send to and receive from.
   */
  private String myPhoneNum = null;

  /**
   * The port number to send to.
   */
  private String myPortNum = null;

  /**
   * The listener to send message data to.
   */
  private SmsDataListener myListener;

  /**
   * Whether the current incoming message launched the application.
   */
  private boolean myIsInitialMessage = false;

//--------------------------------------------------------
//   life cycle

  /**
   * Create and start the singleton instance.
   */
  public static void startup(String portNum, SmsDataListener listener) {
    theInstance = new SMSManager(portNum, listener);
  }

  /**
   * Get the singleton instance.
   */
  public static SMSManager getInstance() {
    return theInstance;
  }

  /**
   * Find the push registry connection and start up the listener thread.
   */
  private SMSManager(String portNum, SmsDataListener listener) {
    theInstance = this;
    myPortNum = portNum;
    myListener = listener;
    // We start by checking for a connection with data to read
```

```
    // to see if the application was launched because of
    // receiving an invitation:
    try {
      String[] connections = PushRegistry.listConnections(true);
      if (connections != null && connections.length > 0) {
        myConnection = (MessageConnection)Connector.open(connections[0]);
        myIsInitialMessage = true;
        myConnection.setMessageListener(this);
        // Start by reading the invitation:
        Thread thread = new Thread(this);
        thread.start();
      } else {
        // The application wasn't launched by an incoming SMS
        // but the application should still have a push registry
        // connection to listen for SMS messages on:
        connections = PushRegistry.listConnections(false);
        if (connections == null || connections.length == 0) {
          // if there's no connection to listen on, then
          // that means that no push port was registered.
          // Instead, we start listening on an sms port:
          myConnection = (MessageConnection)Connector.open(
              SMS_PROTOCOL + ":" + myPortNum);
        } else {
          // if the game has a connection (via the push port)
          // listen on it for messages:
          myConnection = (MessageConnection)Connector.open(connections[0]);
        }
        myConnection.setMessageListener(this);
        myListener.noInitialMessage();
      }
    } catch(Exception e) {
      Main.postException(e);
    }
  }

  /**
   * Clean up all of the listening resources.
   * For use when the application closes.
   */
  public static void cleanup() {
    if(theInstance != null) {
      // close the connection:
      try {
        theInstance.myConnection.close();
      } catch(Exception e) {
        Main.postException(e);
      }
      theInstance = null;
    }
  }

//----------------------------------------------------------
// listen for messages

  /**
```

```
 * Implementation of MessageListener. Handle messages
 * when they arrive.
 *
 * @param conn the connection with messages available.
 */
public void notifyIncomingMessage(MessageConnection conn) {
  Main.setMessage("notification!");
  // This isn't the message that launched the game because
  // the game had to be already running to receive this notification
  myIsInitialMessage = false;
  Thread thread = new Thread(this);
  thread.start();
}

/**
 * Load the message from a new thread.
 */
public void run() {
  try {
    Message msg = myConnection.receive();
    byte[] data = null;
    if((msg != null) && (msg instanceof BinaryMessage)) {
      String senderAddress = msg.getAddress();
      if(checkPhoneNum(senderAddress)) {
        data = ((BinaryMessage)msg).getPayloadData();
        if(myIsInitialMessage) {
          myListener.initialMessage(data, senderAddress);
        } else {
          myListener.message(data, senderAddress);
        }
      } else {
        // ignore messages from other people
      }
    } // if (msg != null) {
  } catch (IOException e) {
    Main.postException(e);
  }
}

//-------------------------------------------------------------
//   SMS sending

/**
 * Send an SMS message to the chosen opponent.
 */
public void sendMessage(byte[] data) {
  // for BlackBerry the message address doesn't include
  // the leading protocol information (because it's
  // already in the connection information.
  // So for BlackBerry, the address format is
  // "//phonenum:portnum" when for other MIDP devices
  // it's "sms://phonenum:portnum"
  SMSMessage message = new SMSMessage("//" + myPhoneNum + ":"
      + myPortNum, myConnection, data, myListener);
  message.start();
```

```
    }

//----------------------------------------------------------
// utilities

  /**
   * Reformats and sets the current opponent phone number
   * if none is set, and verifies that subsequent messages
   * came from the right opponent.
   *
   * @returns true if the message can be accepted.
   */
  public boolean checkPhoneNum(String phoneNumber) {
    if(myPhoneNum == null) {
      myPhoneNum = stripPhoneNum(phoneNumber);
      return true;
    } else if (myPhoneNum.endsWith(phoneNumber)) {
      return true;
    } else {
      // This should return false for security,
      // but because of differing phone number formats
      // we have to be a little bit lenient.
      //return false;
      return true;
    }
  }

  /**
   * Strips leading and trailing data off the phone number.
   */
  public static String stripPhoneNum(String phoneNumber) {
    if(phoneNumber.startsWith("sms://")) {
      phoneNumber = phoneNumber.substring(6);
    }
    if(phoneNumber.indexOf(':') != -1) {
      phoneNumber = phoneNumber.substring(0, phoneNumber.indexOf(':'));
    }
    return phoneNumber;
  }

}
```

The reformatting code in Listing 7-1 is merely intended to make the code as robust as possible when dealing with different implementations of the WMA classes.

The SMSMessage class in Listing 7-2 is a simple little class that uses the MessageConnection opened by the SMSManager to send a message. This class wraps the SMS message data with the Thread (and functionality) to send it. In this case it creates a BinaryMessage (instead of a TextMessage) in order to simplify coding the numerical data that describes a move in the SMS Checkers game. Figure 7-3 shows how the classes fit together.

::net.frogparrot.net

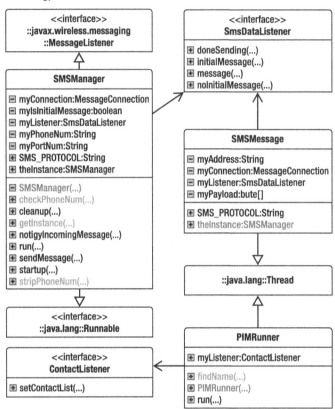

Figure 7-3. *The classes and interfaces of the net.frogparrot.net package*

The SMSManager class and the SMSMessage class work together, with the SMSManager class handling the incoming messages and the SMSMessage class representing each outgoing message. As you can see in Figure 7-3, they each have a handle to the SmsDataListener interface, which is implemented by the CheckersGame class (Listing 7-7 later in this chapter). Naturally, this design separates the SMS routing functionality from the game logic.

Listing 7-2. *SMSMessage.java*

```java
package net.frogparrot.net;

import java.io.*;
import javax.microedition.io.*;
import javax.wireless.messaging.*;

import net.frogparrot.smscheckers.Main;

/**
 * This class holds the data of a binary SMS message
 * and the functionality to send it.
 */
public class SMSMessage extends Thread {
```

```java
//----------------------------------------------------------
//  data fields

  /**
   * The string with the routing information to send an
   * SMS to the right destination.
   */
  private String myAddress;

  /**
   * The data to send.
   */
  private byte[] myPayload;

  /**
   * The connection object that routes the message.
   */
  private MessageConnection myConnection;

  /**
   * The listener to notify when the message has been sent.
   */
  private SmsDataListener myListener;

//----------------------------------------------------------
//  initialization

  /**
   * Set the data and prepare the address string.
   */
  public SMSMessage(String address, MessageConnection conn,
                    byte[] data, SmsDataListener listener) {
    myPayload = data;
    myAddress = address;
    myConnection = conn;
    myListener = listener;
  }

//----------------------------------------------------------
//  business methods.

  /**
   * Sends the message.
   */
  public void run() {
    try {
      BinaryMessage msg = (BinaryMessage)myConnection.newMessage(
          MessageConnection.BINARY_MESSAGE);
      msg.setAddress(myAddress);
      msg.setPayloadData(myPayload);
      myConnection.send(msg);
      if(myListener != null) {
        myListener.doneSending();
      }
```

```
    } catch(Exception e) {
      Main.postException(e);
    }
  }

}
```

The `MessageConnection` instance in Listing 7-1 is returned by the call to the static method `Connector.open()` using the appropriate *uniform resource identifier* (URI) string as an argument. The URI in this case is `sms://:16027`, where `sms://` indicates the SMS protocol and `:16027` indicates that the port number is 16027. When sending an SMS, the destination phone number goes between the protocol part (the URI scheme plus `://`) and the port number part, but to open a receiving connection (as in this case), there's nothing between the protocol/scheme prefix and the port number suffix. To send a message to someone's normal inbox, put the phone number just after the protocol/scheme prefix, and leave off the port number suffix entirely.

To get the formatting exactly right and be sure that the game can send and receive SMS messages correctly, you'll naturally want to do some testing on the simulator. Testing SMS code on the BlackBerry simulator is a little tricky, but not impossible, as explained in the "Testing SMS on the BlackBerry Simulator" sidebar. It's a lot easier, though, on the simulator that's bundled with Sun's Wireless Toolkit (WTK), and for a game that doesn't rely heavily on BlackBerry-specific APIs (like this one), you can actually do much of the testing on the Sun WTK. In the WTK, all you need to do when testing SMS is to be sure that you build a JAD and JAR file (with **Project ↗ Package ↗ Create Package**, for example), and then run it using **Project ↗ Run via OTA** instead of just clicking the Run button. The WTK will allow you to run (via OTA) multiple instances of the simulator simultaneously, and the phone number each one is using will appear in the header of the simulator's window, as shown in Figure 7-4.

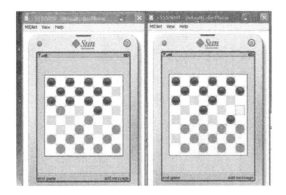

Figure 7-4. *Launching two instances of the WTK simulator on the same computer*

TESTING SMS ON THE BLACKBERRY SIMULATOR

The BlackBerry simulator can't send or receive real SMS messages, but it can simulate them. The SMS port numbers are among the possible launch parameters for the `fledge` executable, described in the "Installing and Distributing Your Game" section of Chapter 2.

Unfortunately, when running the simulator from the BlackBerry JDE, you don't have access to the simulator's launch parameters, so it's not terribly convenient to test an SMS application when running the simulator from the JDE. And since you have to launch two of them to test the exchange of SMS messages, you might as well write a batch file or an Ant script to do it. For example, you can add a target such as the following to the build script given in Chapter 2:

```
<target name="sms-run">
    <!-- run two simulators that can communicate with one another via sms -->
    <mkdir dir="${build.root}\sms-simu-1"/>
    <exec executable="${jde.home}\simulator\fledge.exe"
            dir="${build.root}\sms-simu-1"
            spawn="true">
        <arg value="/app=${jde.home}\simulator\Jvm.dll"/>
        <arg value="/handheld=${model}"/>
        <arg value="/app-param=DisableRegistration"/>
        <arg value="/app-param=JvmAlxConfigFile:${model}.xml"/>
        <arg value="/pin=0x2100000A"/>
        <arg value="/sms-source-port=5000"/>
        <arg value="/sms-destination-port=5001"/>
    </exec>
    <mkdir dir="${build.root}\sms-simu-2"/>
    <exec executable="${jde.home}\simulator\fledge.exe"
            dir="${build.root}\sms-simu-2"
            spawn="true">
        <arg value="/app=${jde.home}\simulator\Jvm.dll"/>
        <arg value="/handheld=${model}"/>
        <arg value="/app-param=DisableRegistration"/>
        <arg value="/app-param=JvmAlxConfigFile:${model}.xml"/>
        <arg value="/pin=0x2100000B"/>
        <arg value="/sms-source-port=5001"/>
        <arg value="/sms-destination-port=5000"/>
        <arg value="/data-port=19781"/>
    </exec>
</target>
```

You can experiment with different arguments to the fledge executable. (To find a list of them, run fledge with the /help option.) The critical arguments in this Ant target are the /sms-source-port and the /sms-destination-port. Note that I've set them opposite to one another. This causes the simulated SMS messages to be sent from one to the other (regardless of what number you use as a telephone number in the URI you use to send the message, a message sent by one will be received by the other).

With this script, you can use the smsdemo (bundled with the samples of the BlackBerry JDK) to send SMS messages from one simulator to the other, without using the provided server program.

There are two main problems when you try to run two instances of the simulator simultaneously. The first problem is that when the simulator is run, it creates a set of files in the directory it was launched from. These files unfortunately don't contain human-readable information that you can use to view and tweak your simulator settings and/or the contents of your simulator's filesystem. They also ensure that it is impossible to run two instances of the simulator simultaneously from the same directory. The preceding sms-run Ant target gets around this problem by specifying an execution directory in the exec task that is used to launch the simulator executable (fledge.exe). Note that the exec task also has the spawn attribute set to true so that the Ant script will return immediately after launching the first instance, so that the second one can be launched without waiting for the execution of the first one to terminate.

The second problem is that the two instances both try to use the same port to connect to the debugger. It appears that there's no way to tell `fledge` to try to connect to the debugger on another port, so you just have to click Ignore for the error message that pops up (as shown in Figure 7-5), and accept that you can't connect them both to the debugger.

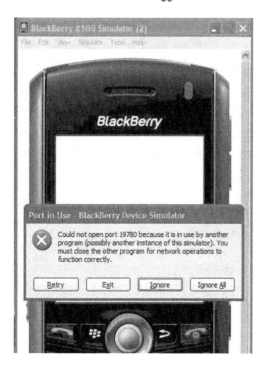

Figure 7-5. *Launching two instances of the BlackBerry simulator on the same computer*

Naturally, this makes it inconvenient to read your debug messages. When you run the simulator from the JDE, the `System.out` calls write to the console. But when you run the simulator by calling the `fledge` executable yourself (from a script or from the command line), it's not clear there's any way to access the `System.out` output. Instead, you should use the `EventLogger` class, as explained in the "Logging Messages with the `EventLogger`" sidebar.

Using the Push Registry

When opening the `MessageConnection`, Listing 7-1 also supports getting the connection from the *push registry*. The push registry is MIDP's way of allowing applications to get their messages even when they're not running.

An application can register itself on the push registry either by using the `MIDlet-Push-1` attribute in the JAD file (e.g., `MIDlet-Push-1: sms://:16027, net.frogparrot.smscheckers.Main, *`) or by dynamically registering itself using the `PushRegistry` class. Normally an application needs to register itself only once, and as long as it doesn't unregister itself from the push registry, it will be launched every time an SMS message arrives on its chosen port. Then, as you can see in Listing 7-1, you can get a handle to the corresponding `MessageConnection` by calling `PushRegistry.listConnections()`. If you give `false` as an argument, it will return all of the connections registered to the MIDlet, and giving `true` causes it to return only those with messages waiting on them.

Unfortunately, the only way to tell if the application was launched by the user or by an incoming SMS is by checking the push registry's connection list. That's why I like to create my own listener interface, `SmsDataListener`, with the four methods shown in Figure 7-3. You can see from the implementation in Listing 7-1 that any class that implements `SmsDataListener` will be notified not only about incoming SMS messages, but will be specially informed about whether the incoming message prompted the MIDlet to launch. If the application was launched with an empty message queue, the `SMSManager` informs the `SmsDataListener` by calling `noInitialMessage()`, whereas if the MIDlet was launched by a message, the `SMSManager` calls `initialMessage()`. All other messages are sent to the listener with a call to `message()`.

Using the push registry for this game is nice because as soon as the urge to play checkers strikes, you can just open up the checkers game, send your friend an invitation to play, and then your friend's checkers game will automatically open up with your invitation in it even if he's on the other side of the world. Unfortunately, the BlackBerry implementation of the `PushRegistry` has some strange behaviors when it comes to passing the port access back and forth between the game application and the platform's push registry application (including unexpectedly unbinding or double-binding the port). The push registry isn't even implemented for RIMlets, only for MIDlets, and I get the strong impression that RIM put in just enough effort so that their push registry implementation would be able to hobble through the TCK for MIDP compliance, but that this feature really isn't very high on their priority list. For that reason, the SMS Checkers game is also designed to allow the user to launch the game and wait for an invitation from another user (instead of assuming that either the game was launched by an invitation or the user will be sending an invitation). Without the push registry, the players have to externally agree to launch the game and agree on who will invite whom to play. It's inelegant, but has the advantage that it works. And a player playing this game on BlackBerry could send a game-launching invitation to a player using another handset.

To enable or disable the push registry feature of this game, you merely need to include (or not include) the `MIDlet-Push-1` JAD attribute mentioned previously. Unfortunately, the BlackBerry build process also makes it inconvenient to add custom attributes in the JAD file. The BlackBerry JDE creates the JAD file using the project properties, and there's no property for adding custom JAD attributes. If you edit the JAD file, your changes will be overwritten at the next build instead of being taken into account. The trick is that (in the JDE) you can add the JAD file to the project just as you would add a source file or a resource. But once the JAD file is added to the project, the JDE is no longer able to correctly update it if you make changes in the project properties. So it's better not to have to add custom JAD attributes if you can avoid it. Hence, the push registry feature is included in this game as a nice-to-have, but use it at your own risk.

Admittedly, on BlackBerry it's possible to write the game as an application that launches at startup and runs constantly in the background waiting for incoming invitation SMS messages. But to keep the game running all the time seems an even more inelegant solution to impose on your users than making them launch the game on their own in order to receive a game invitation.

Finding the Phone Number with PIM

The next question is how to get the destination phone number. Typical mobile phone users—if they memorize their friends' phone numbers at all these days—aren't used to having to type numbers in over and over. That's no problem, because the Personal Information Management (PIM) API allows your application to access the same address book data that the user uses when making a call. PIM also allows you access to the user's calendar and to-do list, which might have some game application if you're creative. (It's also possible to abuse this access in ways that your users won't like—such as sending SMS spam to their friends—which is why the MIDlet needs permission to use the PIM API.)

Since the application may need the user's permission to access the address book (as explained in Chapter 5), the PIM methods can block. So, as with sending or receiving an SMS, you need to be sure to avoid accessing the address book from the event thread. In Listing 7-3 you'll see the PIMRunner utility, which is a Thread subclass that gathers up all of the name and phone number pairs to present to the player to select an opponent. Since it performs this task on a new thread, it can't return the results to the calling method. So you include an interface that it can call back with the data (ContactListener), as you can see in Figure 7-3.

It also has a second utility function that allows the application to use the phone number of the incoming message to identify who invited the local player to play checkers (if the invitation came from someone listed in the address book) in order to tell the local player who the opponent is. Note that the findName() method doesn't spawn (or require) a new thread because it's called from the same thread that was created for reading the incoming SMS message, not from the event thread.

Listing 7-3. *PIMRunner.java*

```
package net.frogparrot.net;

import java.util.Enumeration;
import java.util.Vector;

import javax.microedition.pim.*;

/**
 * A simple PIM utility to load a list of contacts.
 */
public class PIMRunner extends Thread {

  /**
   * A callback listener for this
   * class to call when the PIM list is filled.
   */
  ContactListener myListener;
```

```java
/**
 * The constructor just sets the callback listener for this
 * class to call when the PIM list is filled.
 */
public PIMRunner(ContactListener listener) {
  myListener = listener;
}

/**
 * The method that fills the data fields.
 */
public void run() {
  ContactList addressbook = null;
  Contact contact = null;
  Enumeration items = null;
  Vector names = new Vector();
  Vector phoneNumbers = new Vector();
  try {
    addressbook = (ContactList)(PIM.getInstance(
        ).openPIMList(PIM.CONTACT_LIST, PIM.READ_ONLY));
    items = addressbook.items();
  } catch(Exception e) {
    // if the addressbook can't be opened, then we're done.
    myListener.setContactList(names, phoneNumbers);
  }
  // Now load the contents of the addressbook:
  while(items.hasMoreElements()) {
    try {
      contact = (Contact)(items.nextElement());
      // only continue if the contact has at least one
      // phone number listed:
      int phoneNumCount = contact.countValues(Contact.TEL);
      if(phoneNumCount > 0) {
        String phoneNum = null;
        for(int i = 0; i < phoneNumCount; i++) {
          int attr = contact.getAttributes(Contact.TEL, i);
          // look for a MOBILE number if there is one,
          // otherwise just take the first phone number:
          if(i == 0 || attr == Contact.ATTR_MOBILE) {
            phoneNum = contact.getString(Contact.TEL, i);
          }
        }
        // If we didn't find a mobile number, we skip
        // this contact:
        if(phoneNum != null) {
          // now try to find the name.
          int fieldIndex = Contact.NAME;
          // BlackBerry stores the name in an array of Strings.
          String[] nameArray = contact.getStringArray(fieldIndex, 0);
          // elements 1 and 0 give the first and last name on BlackBerry
          String formattedName = nameArray[1] + " " + nameArray[0];
          names.addElement(formattedName);
          phoneNumbers.addElement(phoneNum);
        }
      }
```

```
    } catch(Exception e) {
      //Main.postException(e);
      // if an individual contact provokes an exception,
      // we skip it and move on.
    }
  } // while(items.hasMoreElements())
  myListener.setContactList(names, phoneNumbers);
}

/**
 * Finds the contact corresponding to the phone number.
 * This is called from the SMS listener thread, hence
 * doesn't need to be run from another thread.
 * If no name corresponds to the phone number, then
 * just send back the number.
 */
public static String findName(String phoneNumber) {
  ContactList addressbook = null;
  Contact contact = null;
  Enumeration items = null;
  try {
    addressbook = (ContactList)(PIM.getInstance(
        ).openPIMList(PIM.CONTACT_LIST, PIM.READ_ONLY));
    items = addressbook.items();
  } catch(Exception e) {
    // if the addressbook can't be opened, then we're done.
    return phoneNumber;
  }
  // Now load the contents of the addressbook:
  while(items.hasMoreElements()) {
    try {
      contact = (Contact)(items.nextElement());
      // only continue if the contact has at least one
      // phone number listed:
      int phoneNumCount = contact.countValues(Contact.TEL);
      for(int i = 0; i < phoneNumCount; i++) {
        if(phoneNumber.endsWith(contact.getString(Contact.TEL, i))) {
          String[] nameArray = contact.getStringArray(Contact.NAME, 0);
          return nameArray[1] + " " + nameArray[0];
        }
      }
    } catch(Exception e) {
      //Main.postException(e);
      // if an individual contact provokes an exception,
      // we skip it and move on.
    }
  } // while(items.hasMoreElements())
  return phoneNumber;
}

}
```

Since the SMS Checkers game is a MIDlet, it uses LCDUI components for its user interface. As explained in Chapters 3 and 4, you would normally avoid using LCDUI components in a professional game (even when using MIDlets). However, creating a custom user interface for a MIDlet is complex enough that it would be a distraction from the point of this chapter. You can see my book *Creating Mobile Games* (Apress, 2007) for more information on the subject. To select your opponent, the SMS Checkers game has two user interface screens: the list of friends' names that the PIMRunner read from the user's address book (shown in Figure 7-6), and a TextBox that the user can type the number into in the case where the game was unable to load any phone numbers from the address book.

Figure 7-6. *The contact list screen of the SMS Checkers game running on the BlackBerry 8100 simulator*

In either case, the entire screen is devoted to the user's input. Listing 7-4 shows how to implement the List that displays the contacts and handle the user's selection with commands that appear on the screen as menu items. The PhoneNumberScreen (where the user can enter a phone number) is very similar—it has the same commands and callbacks since it's a replacement for the PimScreen. You can see it in the source code of this chapter (available for free download on this book's page on the Apress site: www.apress.com).

Listing 7-4. *PimScreen.java*

```java
package net.frogparrot.smscheckers;

import javax.microedition.lcdui.*;
import java.util.Vector;

/**
 * This is a screen that allows the user to select an opponent
 * from the contacts in the address book.
 */
public class PimScreen extends List implements CommandListener {

  /**
   * The phone numbers corresponding to the names.
   */
  private Vector myNumbers;
```

```java
/**
 * Once the user has selected a number, the Main class is called back.
 */
private Main myListener;

/**
 * The menu command that indicates that the user is done entering the
 * opponent's number and is ready to play.
 */
private Command mySelectCommand
    = new Command("Send invitation", Command.SCREEN, 1);

/**
 * The menu command that indicates that the user is waiting for an invitation
 * from another opponent.
 */
 private Command myWaitCommand
     = new Command("Wait for invitation", Command.SCREEN, 1);

/**
 * The menu item to close this application.
 */
private Command myExitCommand
    = new Command("End Game", Command.EXIT, 99);

/**
 * Build the screen.
 */
PimScreen(String[] names, Vector numbers, Main listener) {
  super("Select opponent or wait", List.EXCLUSIVE, names, null);
  addCommand(mySelectCommand);
  addCommand(myWaitCommand);
  addCommand(myExitCommand);
  setCommandListener(this);
  myListener = listener;
  myNumbers = numbers;
}

/**
 * User is done, call back with the response.
 */
public void commandAction(Command c, Displayable s) {
  if(c == mySelectCommand) {
    Main.setMessage("select command");
    int index = getSelectedIndex();
    myListener.setOpponentPhoneNumber((String)(myNumbers.elementAt(index)));
  } else if(c == myWaitCommand) {
    Main.displayMessage("Waiting for an opponent");
    Main.getGame().setWaiting();
  } else if(c == myExitCommand) {
    Main.quit();
  }
}
```

}

When this screen appears, the SMS Checkers game waits idle until the user enters input, and then calls back the game's Main class with the result. You could create a listener interface for this class—as for the PIMRunner and SMSManager—but in this case it's not worth the bother since the class is game-specific (normally the UI would be customized for the game) instead of being a generic utility class.

Building the Checkers Game

Most of what you've done so far can be applied to any multiplayer game where the players communicate via SMS. Now let's see how to apply it to the specific example of SMS Checkers. Figure 7-7 shows how the classes fit together.

Handling the Application Life Cycle

The central command of the SMS Checkers game is handled by the Main class (Listing 7-5), which extends MIDlet, just like the MIDlet class of the MIDP Maze example from Chapter 3.

In addition to the obvious life cycle events (starting and stopping the game), this class handles the logic of the initial handshake of the two players finding each other and agreeing to start a game. It starts by constructing the game data framework in the constructor, and then when the platform launches the game with the call to startApp(), this class calls its startSMS() method, which launches the SMSManager (Listing 7-1), sending it the CheckersGame class (which you'll see in Listing 7-7 in the section "Understanding the SMS Checkers Game Logic") as its SmsDataListener. The reason for setting the CheckersGame class as the SmsDataListener is that once the game begins, that's the class that handles encoding and interpreting move data in SMS messages. But during the initial invitation handshake phase, if the game wasn't launched by an invitation from the remote player, the CheckersGame class merely calls back the Main class's startPIM() method to prompt the local player to send an invitation or to wait for one.

The startPIM() method launches the PIMRunner (Listing 7-3), as explained in the section on "Finding the Phone Number with PIM." When the PIMRunner is done loading the contact list, it calls back the Main class's setContactList() method with the result (because the Main class is set as the PIMRunner's ContactListener). The setContactList() method then displays either the PimScreen (Listing 7-4) or the PhoneNumberScreen, depending on whether the PIMRunner found any contacts or not. Once the player has entered or selected an opponent's phone number, the data entry screen calls back Main's setOpponentPhoneNumber() method to send the invitation, or—if the player has chosen to wait for an invitation from another player—it informs the CheckersGame class that the local player is waiting (in order to keep track of the game state, as you'll see in the section "Understanding the SMS Checkers Game Logic").

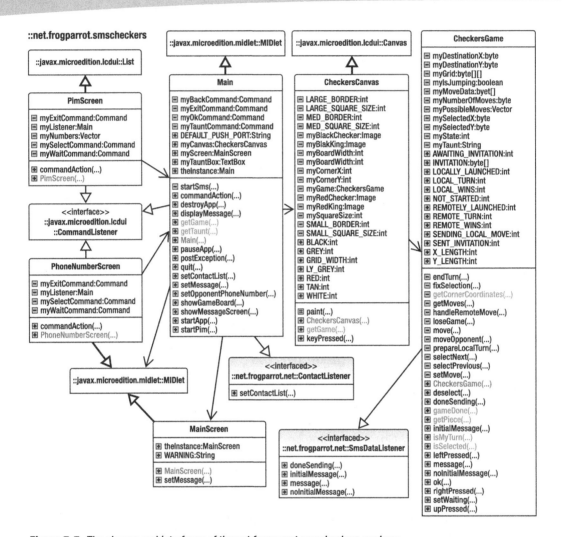

Figure 7-7. *The classes and interfaces of the net.frogparrot.smscheckers package*

Listing 7-5. *Main.java*

```java
package net.frogparrot.smscheckers;

import javax.microedition.midlet.*;
import javax.microedition.lcdui.*;
import net.rim.device.api.system.EventLogger;
import java.util.Vector;

import net.frogparrot.net.*;

/**
 * This class controls the life cycle of the MIDlet.
 */
public class Main extends MIDlet implements CommandListener, ContactListener {
```

```java
//-------------------------------------------------------------------
//   static fields

  /**
   * The sms port to listen on by default.
   */
  public static final String DEFAULT_PUSH_PORT = "16027";

  /**
   * Only one instance of this class should exist.
   */
  static Main theInstance;

  /**
   * The Screen displays messages to the user.
   */
  MainScreen myScreen;

  /**
   * The playing field.
   */
  CheckersCanvas myCanvas;

  /**
   * The text field where the player can add a message
   * for the opponent.
   */
  TextBox myTauntBox;

//-------------------------------------------------------------------
//   instance fields

  /**
   * The menu item to close this application.
   */
  private Command myExitCommand
      = new Command("end game", Command.EXIT, 99);

  /**
   * The menu item to confirm the message.
   */
  private Command myOkCommand
      = new Command("OK", Command.OK, 1);

  /**
   * The menu item to add a message for the remote player.
   */
  private Command myTauntCommand
      = new Command("add message", Command.OK, 2);

  /**
   * The menu item for the taunt box, to remove it.
   */
  private Command myBackCommand
      = new Command("back to game", Command.OK, 2);
```

```java
//-------------------------------------------------------------------
//  initialization and accessors

  /**
   * Initialize the Screen and the commands.
   */
  public Main() {
    try {
      // each BlackBerry application that wants to log
      // messages must register with a unique ID:
      EventLogger.register(0x62e74ebe294681cL, "smscheckers",
          EventLogger.VIEWER_STRING);
      // initialize the instance data:
      theInstance = this;
      myScreen = new MainScreen();
      myScreen.addCommand(myExitCommand);
      myScreen.addCommand(myOkCommand);
      myScreen.setCommandListener(this);
      myCanvas = new CheckersCanvas();
      myCanvas.addCommand(myExitCommand);
      myCanvas.addCommand(myTauntCommand);
      myCanvas.setCommandListener(this);
      myTauntBox = new TextBox("message for opponent",
          "", 50, TextField.ANY);
      myTauntBox.addCommand(myExitCommand);
      myTauntBox.addCommand(myBackCommand);
      myTauntBox.setCommandListener(this);
    } catch(Exception e) {
      postException(e);
    }
  }

/**
 * Return the associated game logic.
 */
public static CheckersGame getGame() {
  return theInstance.myCanvas.getGame();
}

//-------------------------------------------------------------------
//  implementation of MIDlet

  /**
   * The AMS calls this method to start the application.
   */
  public void startApp() throws MIDletStateChangeException {
    try {
      // display my Screen on the screen:
      Display.getDisplay(this).setCurrent(myScreen);
      // this application starts by listening for a message:
      startSms();
    } catch(Exception e) {
      postException(e);
    }
```

```
}

/**
 * If the MIDlet was using resources, it should release
 * them in this method.
 */
public void destroyApp(boolean unconditional)
    throws MIDletStateChangeException {
  SMSManager.cleanup();
  System.gc();
}

/**
 * This closes the game.
 */
public static void quit() {
  // The MIDlet calls these two methods to exit:
  try {
    theInstance.destroyApp(false);
    theInstance.notifyDestroyed();
  } catch (Exception e) {
  }
}

/**
 * If the game is sent to the background, just exit.
 */
public void pauseApp() {
  quit();
}

/**
 * Place the game board on the screen.
 */
public static void showGameBoard() {
  try {
    Display.getDisplay(theInstance).setCurrent(theInstance.myCanvas);
    theInstance.myCanvas.repaint();
  } catch(Exception e) {
    postException(e);
  }
}

/**
 * Place the message display on the screen.
 */
public static void showMessageScreen() {
  try {
    Display.getDisplay(theInstance).setCurrent(theInstance.myScreen);
  } catch(Exception e) {
    postException(e);
  }
}

/**
```

```
  * display the message for the user.
  */
 public static void displayMessage(String message) {
   theInstance.myScreen.setMessage(message);
   showMessageScreen();
 }


//------------------------------------------------------------------
//   implementation of CommandListener

  /*
   * The AMS calls this method to notify the MIDlet of user
   * command input. This class is listening for command
   * input on all of its instance screens.
   */
  public void commandAction(Command c, Displayable s) {
    if(c == myOkCommand) {
      myCanvas.getGame().ok();
    } else if(c == myTauntCommand) {
      Display.getDisplay(this).setCurrent(myTauntBox);
    } else if(c == myBackCommand) {
      Display.getDisplay(this).setCurrent(myCanvas);
    } else if(c == myExitCommand) {
      // if the game is not done, we first
      // inform the other player before exiting:
      if(myCanvas.getGame().gameDone()) {
        quit();
      }
    }
  }


//------------------------------------------------------------------
//   debug logging utilities

  /**
   * A utility to log debug messages.
   */
  public static void setMessage(String message) {
    EventLogger.logEvent(0x62e74ebe294681cL, message.getBytes());
    System.out.println(message);
    //theInstance.myScreen.setMessage(message);
  }

  /**
   * A utility to log exceptions.
   */
  public static void postException(Exception e) {
    System.out.println(e);
    e.printStackTrace();
    String exceptionName = e.getClass().getName();
    EventLogger.logEvent(0x62e74ebe294681cL, exceptionName.getBytes());
    if(e.getMessage() != null) {
      EventLogger.logEvent(0x62e74ebe294681cL, e.getMessage().getBytes());
    }
    theInstance.myScreen.setMessage(exceptionName);
```

```
    }
//-----------------------------------------------------------------
//  SMS initialization

  /**
   * This game starts by listening for incoming SMS messages.
   * The MIDlet checks which push port is registered in the JAD
   * file, and passes this information to the SMSManager so that
   * the SMSManager will know to contact the opponent on the
   * same port.
   */
  private void startSms() {
    try {
      String pushInfo = getAppProperty("MIDlet-Push-1").trim();
      if(pushInfo.startsWith("sms://:")) {
        int comma = pushInfo.indexOf(',');
        String portNum = pushInfo.substring(7, comma);
        // Send the SmsDataListener
        // to be notified when any messages arrive:
        SMSManager.startup(portNum, myCanvas.getGame());
      } else {
        // if there's no push port property in the JAD,
        // then select a port to listen on:
        SMSManager.startup(DEFAULT_PUSH_PORT, myCanvas.getGame());
      }
    } catch(Exception e) {
      SMSManager.startup(DEFAULT_PUSH_PORT, myCanvas.getGame());
    }
  }

//-----------------------------------------------------------------
//  PIM (contact list) methods

  /**
   * Launch the PIM functionality to read the user's address book
   * to populate the list of possible opponents.
   */
  static void startPim() {
    PIMRunner pr = new PIMRunner(theInstance);
    pr.start();
  }

  /**
   * This is the callback method that returns the PIM contact list.
   * The next step is to display the list to the user to allow the
   * user to select an opponent.
   */
  public void setContactList(Vector names, Vector phoneNumbers) {
    if((names == null) || (names.size() == 0)) {
      // no contacts were found, so the user will
      // enter the opponent's number manually:
      Display.getDisplay(this).setCurrent(new PhoneNumberScreen(this));
    } else {
      // select the opponent from the contact list:
```

```
        String[] choices = new String[names.size()];
        names.copyInto(choices);
        Display.getDisplay(this).setCurrent(new PimScreen(choices, phoneNumbers, this));
    }
}

/**
 * The PimScreen or PhoneNumber screen calls this method
 * when the user is done selecting the opponent's phone number.
 */
public void setOpponentPhoneNumber(String number) {
    //Display.getDisplay(this).setCurrent(myScreen);
    displayMessage("waiting for remote player");
    SMSManager.getInstance().checkPhoneNum(number);
    byte[] invitation = new byte[4];
    System.arraycopy(CheckersGame.INVITATION, 0, invitation, 0, 4);
    SMSManager.getInstance().sendMessage(invitation);
}

//-----------------------------------------------------------------
//  taunt methods

/**
 * Return and clear the message in the taunt box.
 */
public static String getTaunt() {
    String retString = theInstance.myTauntBox.getString();
    theInstance.myTauntBox.setString("");
    return retString;
}

}
```

The Main class also handles which screen is displayed to the user at any given time. The possible choices are the two phone number entry screens explained previously, the MainScreen (shown in Listing 7-6), which displays messages to the user, the CheckersCanvas (the game board, as explained following in the "Painting the Checkers Game Graphics" section), and the TauntBox, which is the screen that the player uses to add a message (to "taunt" the opponent) to send along with each move. Since the TauntBox is a generic TextBox with no special functionality, it's merely constructed in the Main class (without requiring a subclass).

Note that the PimScreen and the PhoneNumberScreen are just created as local method variables because they're discarded after use, but the other three screens are held as fields because they're used throughout the game. The screens don't really have a logical sequence as a screen stack, so it's not a problem that we lose the BlackBerry screen stack functionality by creating this game as a MIDlet instead of a RIMlet. The Main class shuffles among these three screens according to incoming SMS input and input from the user. It displays the TauntBox when the user has chosen to enter a message, the MainScreen when the remote player's move was an invitation or contained a message, and the CheckersCanvas when the user dismisses the other screens.

Listing 7-6. *MainScreen.java*

```java
package net.frogparrot.smscheckers;

import javax.microedition.lcdui.*;

/**
 * This class displays the information for the user.
 */
public class MainScreen extends TextBox {

//-----------------------------------------------------------
//   fields

  /**
   * The disclaimer message.
   */
  public static final String WARNING
          = "\n\n* WARNING *\nThis game sends each move in an SMS message. "
          + "Your operator will charge you for one text message for each move.";

  /**
   * The singleton instance.
   */
  static MainScreen theInstance;

//-----------------------------------------------------------
//     initialization and accessors

  /**
   * Set this as the singleton instance.
   */
  public MainScreen() {
    super("Checkers", "please wait" + WARNING, 500, TextField.UNEDITABLE);
    theInstance = this;
  }

  /**
   * Set the message to display.
   */
  public static void setMessage(String message) {
    theInstance.setString(message + WARNING);
  }

}
```

You can see that this class displays a warning message below the current message to display. This is redundant because the BlackBerry smartphone—like all other MIDP devices—displays its own warning screen before sending each SMS, as explained in Chapter 5. I just wanted to be doubly sure that there's absolutely no chance a user will mistakenly run up a huge SMS bill and attempt to sue me for it. The trouble is that on a smartphone, it's possible to have a mobile plan with unlimited Internet access, yet—ironically—have to pay individually for each tiny little SMS message you send! The game is intended for the many people who send text messages all the time, hence are sure that they have mobile phone contracts allowing them to send lots of SMS messages cheaply.

The MainScreen can also be used to display debug messages during the debug phase. If you look in the debug utility methods of Listing 7-5, you'll see that the postException() method writes the error message to the MainScreen, and that the setMessage() method can display debug messages on the MainScreen as well (although the line to do it is commented out in the final version). As explained previously in the "Testing SMS on the BlackBerry Simulator" sidebar, you have to do a little work to get debug/log messages when running the BlackBerry simulator outside of the BlackBerry JDE. These two debug utilities are intended to centralize the handling of debug messages so that you can add debug messages throughout the code with one standardized method call, and you can easily tweak how these messages are displayed depending on which phase of development, testing, or production you're at.

This message-logging feature is the one place where this game is dependent on RIM's proprietary API. (Of course, this call can be easily commented out in order to build the game separately for other platforms.) To get log messages either on the BlackBerry simulator or the device, you need to use the EventLogger, as explained in the "Logging Messages with the EventLogger" sidebar.

LOGGING MESSAGES WITH THE EVENTLOGGER

If you run the BlackBerry simulator or a BlackBerry smartphone with the JDE, anything written to System.out will appear on the console. When you're debugging outside the JDE, however, the output of System.out is not accessible or written to a file. It's lost. The standard way of generating log messages on the BlackBerry is to use the EventLogger class.

All of the applications on the BlackBerry device share the same static EventLogger. To write a message to the EventLogger, your application must first register itself with the EventLogger, providing a long UID, a displayable name, an error level (for message filtering), and a code indicating what type of messages you'd like to log (e.g., Strings or ints). The long UID is used to find the application display name to write to the log for messages set with EventLogger.logEvent(), so each application needs a unique UID (hence the "U").

The BlackBerry JDE provides a simple utility for generating the UID. Just highlight a string in the code (usually the application's name) and then right-click it. The context menu gives you the option of transforming the String into a long, which you can use as the application's UID.

The event log is stored in a file on the device, which you can load onto your PC using the JavaLoader executable (discussed in the "Installing and Distributing your Game" section of Chapter 2). For example, if your device is connected to your computer via USB, you can write the event log to a file using the following command:

```
JavaLoader.exe -u eventlog > eventlog.txt
```

It would be convenient if the simulator were to write the event log to a simple text file, but it doesn't. To get the simulator's event log as a file, you have to simulate a USB connection to it and then use the JavaLoader.

Fortunately there's a much simpler way to view the event log. Just type Alt+L, Alt+G, Alt+L, Alt+G on the keyboard. It works both on the simulator and on the real device. Figure 7-8 shows what it looks like.

Figure 7-8. *Viewing the event log*

Since the keyboard input is routed to your application while it's running, this normally means that you have to exit your application before using the standard shortcut to view the event log. You can also launch the event log viewer from within your application by using the `EventLog.startEventLogViewer()` method.

Since all of the applications share a single event log, you'll see your own messages on it as well as event messages generated by the platform. Each event is given a single line on a scrollable list, and you can see the details of the event by selecting it.

Understanding the SMS Checkers Game Logic

The `CheckersGame` class in Listing 7-7 handles both the game state and the underlying game logic.

When controlling the game state, the `CheckersGame` class works in cooperation with the `Main` class. As explained in the "Handling the Application Life Cycle" section, the `Main` class controls the initialization stage and launches the `SMSManager` to check for messages. The `Main` class also handles the functionality to send an invitation to another user, plus it controls which screen is currently displayed. The `CheckersGame` class does the rest.

The `CheckersGame` keeps track of the game state using a state code, stored in the field `myState`. As you can see in Listing 7-7, the state is mostly used to decide how input should be interpreted. It especially determines whether the application should currently be listening for keyboard input (during the local user's turn) or whether it should be listening for a message from the opponent (during the opponent's turn). Input that isn't relevant to the current state is ignored. The original version of this game—in my earlier book *Creating Mobile Games* (Apress, 2007)—had some rather complex threading and synchronization, but since each turn is so lengthy and discrete, I've since concluded that the synchronization isn't really necessary, so I completely refactored the game state logic, simplifying it by grouping all of the possible game states at the top of this class.

Listing 7-7. *CheckersGame.java*

```
package net.frogparrot.smscheckers;
```

```java
import java.util.Vector;

import net.frogparrot.net.*;

/**
 * This class takes care of the game state and logic,
 * including where all of the pieces are on the board
 * and where it is OK for them to move to.
 */
public class CheckersGame implements SmsDataListener {

//-----------------------------------------------------------
//   game state fields

  /**
   * Possible game states.
   */
  public static final int NOT_STARTED = 0;
  public static final int LOCALLY_LAUNCHED = 1;
  public static final int SENT_INVITATION = 2;
  public static final int REMOTELY_LAUNCHED = 3;
  public static final int AWAITING_INVITATION = 4;
  public static final int LOCAL_TURN = 5;
  public static final int SENDING_LOCAL_MOVE = 6;
  public static final int REMOTE_TURN = 7;
  public static final int LOCAL_WINS = 8;
  public static final int REMOTE_WINS = 9;

  /**
   * A code to identify an invitation SMS (so that
   * it won't be confused with some other type of message).
   */
  public static final byte[] INVITATION = { 8, 1, 9, 7 };

/**
 * The code for the state the game is currently in.
 */
  private int myState = NOT_STARTED;

/**
 * The current message from the local player
 * to the remote player.
 */
  private String myTaunt;

/**
 * The data array that is sent in the binary SMS message.
 */
  private byte[] myMoveData = new byte[140];

/**
 * How many moves are contained in myMoveData.
 * Usually it will be 1, but it can be more if the player
 * is jumping multiple times.
 */
```

```
    private byte myNumberOfMoves = 0;

//-----------------------------------------------------------
//  game logic fields

    /**
     * The length of the checkerboard in the x direction.
     */
    public static final int X_LENGTH = 4;

    /**
     * The length of the checkerboard in the y direction.
     */
    public static final int Y_LENGTH = 8;

    /**
     * This array represents the black squares of the
     * checkerboard. The two dimensions of the array
     * represent the two dimensions of the checkerboard.
     * The value represents what type of piece is on
     * the square.
     * 0 = empty
     * 1 = local player's piece
     * 2 = local player's king
     * -1 = remote player's piece
     * -2 = remote player's king
     */
    private byte[][] myGrid;

    /**
     * If the user has currently selected a piece to move,
     * this is its x grid coordinate. (-1 if none selected)
     */
    private byte mySelectedX = -1;

    /**
     * If the user has currently selected a piece to move,
     * this is its y grid coordinate.(-1 if none selected)
     */
    private byte mySelectedY = -1;

    /**
     * If the user has currently selected a possible
     * destination square for a move, this is its x-coordinate.
     * (-1 if none selected)
     */
    private byte myDestinationX = -1;

    /**
     * If the user has currently selected a possible
     * destination square for a move, this is its y-coordinate.
     * (-1 if none selected)
     */
    private byte myDestinationY = -1;
```

```java
  /**
   * This Vector contains the coordinates of all of the
   * squares that the player could currently move to.
   */
  private Vector myPossibleMoves = new Vector(4);

  /**
   * This is true if the player has just jumped and can
   * jump again.
   */
  private boolean myIsJumping = false;

//--------------------------------------------------------
//  Update the state based on user commands

  /**
   * The user is waiting for an invitation from a remote player.
   */
  public void setWaiting() {
    myState = AWAITING_INVITATION;
  }

  /**
   * Main calls this method when the user selects "OK" on the main
   * message screen. Updates the screen and state accordingly.
   */
  public void ok() {
    switch(myState) {
      case NOT_STARTED:
      case LOCALLY_LAUNCHED:
      case AWAITING_INVITATION:
      case SENT_INVITATION:
        // ignore the OK command if we're not ready for it
        break;
      case REMOTELY_LAUNCHED:
        // start the game.
        Main.showGameBoard();
        myState = LOCAL_TURN;
        break;
      default:
        Main.showGameBoard();
        break;
    }
  }

  /**
   * Main calls this method to handle the case when the local user quits.
   * If the game is not done, it attempts to notify the other player.
   */
  public boolean gameDone() {
    if((myState == LOCAL_TURN) || (myState == REMOTE_TURN)) {
      // the game is not done, so we end it by having the
      // local player lose:
      loseGame();
      return false;
```

```java
    } else {
      return true;
    }
  }

//------------------------------------------------------------------
//  Update the state based on SMS information
//  (implementation of SmsDataListener)

  /**
   * Inform the user of the incoming invitation.
   * If the game was launched by an incoming SMS message,
   * this method will be called with the message data.
   */
  public void initialMessage(byte[] payload, String phoneNumber) {
    if((payload[0] == INVITATION[0]) &&
       (payload[1] == INVITATION[1]) &&
       (payload[2] == INVITATION[2]) &&
       (payload[3] == INVITATION[3])) {
      String name = PIMRunner.findName(SMSManager.stripPhoneNum(phoneNumber));
      Main.displayMessage(name + " invites you to play checkers!\n");
      myState = REMOTELY_LAUNCHED;
    } else {
      // not an invitation to play
      Main.quit();
    }
  }

  /**
   * The application was not launched by receiving a message, so
   * the user launched it. The next step is to call the PIM
   * functionality to allow the user to select an opponent from
   * the address book.
   */
  public void noInitialMessage() {
    myState = LOCALLY_LAUNCHED;
    Main.startPim();
  }

  /**
   * Receive a standard message from the opponent.
   * Handle the message and update the state accordingly.
   */
  public void message(byte[] payload, String phoneNumber) {
    // ignore invitation messages unless
    // awaiting an invitation
    if((payload[0] == INVITATION[0]) &&
       (payload[1] == INVITATION[1]) &&
       (payload[2] == INVITATION[2]) &&
       (payload[3] == INVITATION[3])) {
      if(myState == AWAITING_INVITATION) {
        String name
            = PIMRunner.findName(SMSManager.stripPhoneNum(phoneNumber));
        myState = REMOTELY_LAUNCHED;
      }
```

```java
      } else {
        switch(myState) {
          case SENT_INVITATION:
          case LOCALLY_LAUNCHED:
            handleRemoteMove(payload);
          break;
          case REMOTE_TURN:
          case SENDING_LOCAL_MOVE:
            handleRemoteMove(payload);
          break;
          case LOCAL_TURN:
            // during the local turn, the other player
            // is allowed to quit and end the game:
            myState = LOCAL_WINS;
          break;
          case REMOTE_WINS:
            Main.quit();
          break;
          default:
          break;
        }
      }
    }

  /**
   * A message-sending request has completed.
   * (This is the callback.)
   */
  public void doneSending() {
    switch(myState) {
      case REMOTE_WINS:
        // done informing the remote user
        // so the application can close
        Main.quit();
      break;
      case LOCALLY_LAUNCHED:
        myState = SENT_INVITATION;
      break;
      case SENDING_LOCAL_MOVE:
        myState = REMOTE_TURN;
      break;
      default:
      break;
    }
  }

//---------------------------------------------------------
//    internal game state methods

  /**
   * Interpret one move by the remote player.
   */
  private void handleRemoteMove(byte[] payload) {
    byte numMoves = payload[0];
    int tauntIndex = 1 + numMoves*4;
```

```
  byte tauntLength = payload[tauntIndex];
  String taunt = new String(payload, tauntIndex + 1, tauntLength);
  if(numMoves == 0) {
    Main.displayMessage("You Win!\n" + taunt);
    myState = LOCAL_WINS;
    Main.setMessage("done local win");
  } else {
    for(byte i = 0; i < numMoves; i++) {
      int os = i*4;
      moveOpponent(payload[os+1], payload[os+2], payload[os+3], payload[os+4]);
    }
    prepareLocalTurn();
    if(taunt.length() == 0) {
      Main.showGameBoard();
    } else {
      Main.displayMessage(taunt);
    }
    myState = LOCAL_TURN;
  }
}

/**
 * The game logic of this class calls this method when
 * the user has selected a move.
 */
private void setMove(byte sourceX, byte sourceY, byte destinationX,
                     byte destinationY) {
  int index = (myNumberOfMoves*4) + 1;
  myMoveData[index] = sourceX;
  index++;
  myMoveData[index] = sourceY;
  index++;
  myMoveData[index] = destinationX;
  index++;
  myMoveData[index] = destinationY;
  myNumberOfMoves++;
  myMoveData[0] = (byte)myNumberOfMoves;
}

/**
 * Send the move data to the remote player and
 * advance the internal game state.
 * The game logic of this class calls this method
 * when the local player's turn is over.
 */
private void endTurn() {
  myState = SENDING_LOCAL_MOVE;
  // add the taunt to the move data:
  String taunt = Main.getTaunt();
  byte[] tauntData = taunt.getBytes();
  int index = myNumberOfMoves*4 + 1;
  if(index + tauntData.length < 139) {
    // copy the message into the payload:
    myMoveData[index] = (byte)(tauntData.length);
    System.arraycopy(tauntData, 0, myMoveData, index+1, tauntData.length);
```

```java
    } else {
      // if it's too long to fit into the SMS, just skip it:
      myMoveData[index] = (byte)0;
    }
    SMSManager.getInstance().sendMessage(myMoveData);
    myNumberOfMoves = 0;
  }

  /**
   * Stop the game entirely. Notify the remote player that
   * the user is exiting the game.
   */
  private void loseGame() {
    myState = REMOTE_WINS;
    Main.displayMessage("remote player wins!");
    // sending an empty move indicates
    // that the game is over
    myMoveData[0] = 0;
    myNumberOfMoves = 0;
    String taunt = Main.getTaunt();
    byte[] tauntData = taunt.getBytes();
    if(tauntData.length < 138) {
      // copy the message into the payload:
      myMoveData[1] = (byte)(tauntData.length);
      System.arraycopy(tauntData, 0, myMoveData, 2, tauntData.length);
    } else {
      // if it's too long to fit into the SMS, just skip it:
      myMoveData[1] = (byte)0;
    }
    SMSManager.getInstance().sendMessage(myMoveData);
  }

//----------------------------------------------------------
//   initialization

  /**
   * Constructor puts the pieces in their initial positions:
   */
  CheckersGame() {
    myGrid = new byte[X_LENGTH][];
    for(byte i = 0; i < myGrid.length; i++) {
      myGrid[i] = new byte[Y_LENGTH];
      for(byte j = 0; j < myGrid[i].length; j++) {
        if(j < 3) {
          // fill the top of the board with remote players
          myGrid[i][j] = -1;
        } else if(j > 4) {
          // fill the bottom of the board with local players
          myGrid[i][j] = 1;
        }
      }
    }
    mySelectedX = 0;
    mySelectedY = 5;
    getMoves(mySelectedX, mySelectedY, myPossibleMoves, false);
```

```
    }

//----------------------------------------------------------
//    game logic accessors

  /**
   * get the piece on the given grid square.
   */
  byte getPiece(byte x, byte y) {
    return(myGrid[x][y]);
  }

  /**
   * This is called by CheckersCanvas to determine if
   * the square is currently selected (as containing
   * a piece to move or a destination square).
   */
  boolean isSelected(byte x, byte y) {
    boolean retVal = false;
    if((x == mySelectedX) && (y == mySelectedY)) {
      retVal = true;
    } else if((x == myDestinationX) && (y == myDestinationY)) {
      retVal = true;
    }
    return(retVal);
  }

  /**
   * This tells whether or not the keystrokes should currently
   * be taken into account.
   */
  boolean isMyTurn() {
    return(myState == LOCAL_TURN);
  }


//----------------------------------------------------------
//    internal game logic

  /**
   * Once the opponent's move data has been received,
   * this method interprets it.
   * @param ooix = opponent's initial X coordinate
   * @param ooiy = opponent's initial Y coordinate
   * @param oodx = opponent's destination X coordinate
   * @param oody = opponent's destination Y coordinate
   */
  private void moveOpponent(byte ooix, byte ooiy, byte oodx, byte oody) {
    // since both players appear on their own screens
    // as the red side (bottom of the screen), we need
    // to invert the opponent's move:
    int oix = X_LENGTH - ooix - 1;
    int odx = X_LENGTH - oodx - 1;
    int oiy = Y_LENGTH - ooiy - 1;
    int ody = Y_LENGTH - oody - 1;
```

```
      myGrid[odx][ody]
        = myGrid[oix][oiy];
      myGrid[oix][oiy] = 0;
      // deal with an opponent's jump:
      if((oiy - ody > 1) ||
         (ody - oiy > 1)) {
        int jumpedY = (oiy + ody)/2;
        int jumpedX = oix;
        int parity = oiy % 2;
        if((parity > 0) && (odx > oix)) {
          jumpedX++;
        } else if((parity == 0) && (oix > odx)) {
          jumpedX--;
        }
        myGrid[jumpedX][jumpedY] = 0;
      }
      // if the opponent reaches the far side,
      // make him a king:
      if(ody == Y_LENGTH - 1) {
        myGrid[odx][ody] = -2;
      }
    }

  /**
   * Once the opponent's turn has been interpreted,
   * this method prepares the data for the local turn.
   */
  private void prepareLocalTurn() {
    // Now begin the local player's turn:
    // First select the first local piece that can be
    // moved. (rightPressed will select an appropriate
    // piece or end the game if the local player has
    // no possible moves to make)
    mySelectedX = 0;
    mySelectedY = 0;
    myDestinationX = -1;
    myDestinationY = -1;
    rightPressed();
  }

//---------------------------------------------------------
//    handle user input on the game board

  /**
   * If the left button is pressed, this method takes
   * the correct course of action depending on the situation.
   */
  void leftPressed() {
    // in the first case the user has not yet selected a
    // piece to move:
    if(myDestinationX == -1) {
      // find the next possible piece (to the left)
      // that can move:
      selectPrevious();
      // if selectPrevious fails to fill myPossibleMoves, that
```

```java
      // means that the local player cannot move, so the game
      // is over:
      if(myPossibleMoves.size() == 0) {
        loseGame();
      }
    } else {
      // if the user has already selected a piece to move,
      // we give the options of where the piece can move to:
      for(byte i = 0; i < myPossibleMoves.size(); i++) {
        byte[] coordinates = (byte[])myPossibleMoves.elementAt(i);
        if((coordinates[0] == myDestinationX) &&
           (coordinates[1] == myDestinationY)) {
          i++;
          i = (new Integer(i % myPossibleMoves.size())).byteValue();
          coordinates = (byte[])myPossibleMoves.elementAt(i);
          myDestinationX = coordinates[0];
          myDestinationY = coordinates[1];
          break;
        }
      }
    }
  }
}

/**
 * if the left button is pressed, this method takes
 * the correct course of action depending on the situation.
 */
void rightPressed() {
  // in the first case the user has not yet selected a
  // piece to move:
  if(myDestinationX == -1) {
    // find the next possible piece that can
    // move:
    selectNext();
    // if selectNext fails to fill myPossibleMoves, that
    // means that the local player cannot move, so the game
    // is over:
    if(myPossibleMoves.size() == 0) {
      loseGame();
    }
  } else {
    // if the user has already selected a piece to move,
    // we give the options of where the piece can move to:
    for(byte i = 0; i < myPossibleMoves.size(); i++) {
      byte[] coordinates = (byte[])myPossibleMoves.elementAt(i);
      if((coordinates[0] == myDestinationX) &&
         (coordinates[1] == myDestinationY)) {
        i++;
        i = (new Integer(i % myPossibleMoves.size())).byteValue();
        coordinates = (byte[])myPossibleMoves.elementAt(i);
        myDestinationX = coordinates[0];
        myDestinationY = coordinates[1];
        break;
      }
    }
```

```
    }
  }

  /**
   * If no piece is selected, we select one. If a piece
   * is selected, we move it.
   */
  void upPressed() {
    // in the first case the user has not yet selected a
    // piece to move:
    if(myDestinationX == -1) {
      fixSelection();
    } else {
      // if the source square and destination square
      // have been chosen, we move the piece:
      move();
    }
  }

  /**
   * If the user decided not to move the selected piece
   * (and instead wants to select again), this undoes
   * the selection. This corresponds to pressing the
   * DOWN key.
   */
  void deselect() {
    // if the player has just completed a jump and
    // could possibly jump again but decides not to
    // (i.e., deselects), then the turn ends:
    if(myIsJumping) {
      mySelectedX = -1;
      mySelectedY = -1;
      myDestinationX = -1;
      myDestinationY = -1;
      myIsJumping = false;
      endTurn();
    } else {
      // setting the destination coordinates to -1
      // is the signal that the the choice of which
      // piece to move can be modified:
      myDestinationX = -1;
      myDestinationY = -1;
    }
  }

//----------------------------------------------------------
//   internal square selection methods

  /**
   * When the player has decided that the currently selected
   * square contains the piece he really wants to move, this
   * is called. This method switches to the mode where
   * the player selects the destination square of the move.
   */
  private void fixSelection() {
```

```
      byte[] destination = (byte[])myPossibleMoves.elementAt(0);
      // setting the destination coordinates to valid
      // coordinates is the signal that the user is done
      // selecting the piece to move and now is choosing
      // the destination square:
      myDestinationX = destination[0];
      myDestinationY = destination[1];
}

/**
 * This method starts from the currently selected square
 * and finds the next square that contains a piece that
 * the player can move.
 */
private void selectNext() {
    // Test the squares one by one (starting from the
    // currently selected square) until we find a square
    // that contains one of the local player's pieces
    // that can move:
    byte testX = mySelectedX;
    byte testY = mySelectedY;
    while(true) {
      testX++;
      if(testX >= X_LENGTH) {
        testX = 0;
        testY++;
        testY = (new Integer(testY % Y_LENGTH)).byteValue();
      }
      getMoves(testX, testY, myPossibleMoves, false);
      if((myPossibleMoves.size() != 0) ||
          ((testX == mySelectedX) && (testY == mySelectedY))) {
        mySelectedX = testX;
        mySelectedY = testY;
        break;
      }
    }
}

/**
 * This method starts from the currently selected square
 * and finds the next square (to the left) that contains
 * a piece that the player can move.
 */
private void selectPrevious() {
    // Test the squares one by one (starting from the
    // currently selected square) until we find a square
    // that contains one of the local player's pieces
    // that can move:
    byte testX = mySelectedX;
    byte testY = mySelectedY;
    while(true) {
      testX--;
      if(testX < 0) {
        testX += X_LENGTH;
        testY--;
```

```java
      if(testY < 0) {
        testY += Y_LENGTH;
      }
    }
    getMoves(testX, testY, myPossibleMoves, false);
    if((myPossibleMoves.size() != 0) ||
       ((testX == mySelectedX) && (testY == mySelectedY))) {
      mySelectedX = testX;
      mySelectedY = testY;
      break;
    }
  }
}

/**
 * Once the user has selected the move to make, this
 * updates the data accordingly.
 */
private void move() {
  // the piece that was on the source square is
  // now on the destination square:
  myGrid[myDestinationX][myDestinationY]
    = myGrid[mySelectedX][mySelectedY];
  // the source square is emptied:
  myGrid[mySelectedX][mySelectedY] = 0;
  if(myDestinationY == 0) {
    myGrid[myDestinationX][myDestinationY] = 2;
  }
  // Store the move data so that it can be sent
  // to the remote player.
  setMove(mySelectedX, mySelectedY,
      myDestinationX, myDestinationY);
  // deal with the special rules for jumps::
  if((mySelectedY - myDestinationY > 1) ||
     (myDestinationY - mySelectedY > 1)) {
    int jumpedY = (mySelectedY + myDestinationY)/2;
    int jumpedX = mySelectedX;
    int parity = mySelectedY % 2;
    // the coordinates of the jumped square depend on
    // what row we're in:
    if((parity > 0) && (myDestinationX > mySelectedX)) {
      jumpedX++;
    } else if((parity == 0) && (mySelectedX > myDestinationX)) {
      jumpedX--;
    }
    // remove the piece that was jumped over:
    myGrid[jumpedX][jumpedY] = 0;
    // now get ready to jump again if possible:
    mySelectedX = myDestinationX;
    mySelectedY = myDestinationY;
    myDestinationX = -1;
    myDestinationY = -1;
    // see if another jump is possible.
    // The "true" argument tells the program to return
    // only jumps because the player can go again ONLY
```

```
    // if there's a jump:
    getMoves(mySelectedX, mySelectedY, myPossibleMoves, true);
    // if there's another jump possible with the same piece,
    // allow the player to continue jumping:
    if(myPossibleMoves.size() != 0) {
      myIsJumping = true;
      byte[] landing = (byte[])myPossibleMoves.elementAt(0);
      myDestinationX = landing[0];
      myDestinationY = landing[1];
    } else {
      // since there are no further jumps, we just end the turn
      // by deselecting everything.
      mySelectedX = -1;
      mySelectedY = -1;
      myDestinationX = -1;
      myDestinationY = -1;
      myIsJumping = false;
      myPossibleMoves.removeAllElements();
      endTurn();
    }
  } else {
    // since it's not a jump, we just end the turn
    // by deselecting everything.
    mySelectedX = -1;
    mySelectedY = -1;
    myDestinationX = -1;
    myDestinationY = -1;
    myPossibleMoves.removeAllElements();
    // tell the other player we're done:
    myIsJumping = false;
    endTurn();
  }
}

/**
 * Given a square on the grid, get the coordinates
 * of one of the adjoining (diagonal) squares.
 * 0 = top left
 * 1 = top right
 * 2 = bottom left
 * 3 = bottom right.
 * @return the coordinates or null if the desired corner
 * is off the board.
 */
private byte[] getCornerCoordinates(byte x, byte y, byte corner) {
  byte[] retArray = null;
  if(corner < 2) {
    y--;
  } else {
    y++;
  }
  // Where the corner is on the grid depends on
  // whether this is an odd row or an even row:
  if((corner % 2 == 0) && (y % 2 != 0)) {
    x--;
```

```java
  } else if((corner % 2 != 0) && (y % 2 == 0)) {
    x++;
  }
  try {
    if(myGrid[x][y] > -15) {
      // we don't really care about the value, this
      // if statement is just there to get it to
      // throw if the coordinates aren't on the board.
      retArray = new byte[2];
      retArray[0] = x;
      retArray[1] = y;
    }
  } catch(ArrayIndexOutOfBoundsException e) {
    // this throws if the coordinates do not correspond
    // to a square on the board. It's not a problem,
    // so we do nothing--we just return null instead
    // of returning coordinates since no valid
    // coordinates correspond to the desired corner.
  }
  return(retArray);
}

/**
 * Determines where the piece in the given
 * grid location can move. Clears the Vector
 * and fills it with the locations that
 * the piece can move to.
 * @param jumpsOnly if we should return only moves that
 *         are jumps.
 */
private void getMoves(byte x, byte y, Vector toFill, boolean jumpsOnly) {
  toFill.removeAllElements();
  // if the square does not contain one of the local player's
  // pieces, then there are no corresponding moves and we just
  // return an empty vector.
  if(myGrid[x][y] <= 0) {
    return;
  }
  // check each of the four corners to see if the
  // piece can move there:
  for(byte i = 0; i < 4; i++) {
    byte[] coordinates = getCornerCoordinates(x, y, i);
    // if the coordinate array is null, then the corresponding
    // corner is off the board and we don't deal with it.
    // The latter two conditions in the following if statement
    // ensure that either the move is a forward move or the
    // current piece is a king:
    if((coordinates != null) &&
       ((myGrid[x][y] > 1) || (i < 2))) {
      // if the corner is empty (and we're not looking
      // for just jumps), then this is a possible move
      // so we add it to the vector of moves:
      if((myGrid[coordinates[0]][coordinates[1]] == 0) && (! jumpsOnly)) {
        toFill.addElement(coordinates);
        // if the space is occupied by an opponent, see if we can jump it:
```

```
        } else if(myGrid[coordinates[0]][coordinates[1]] < 0) {
            byte[] jumpLanding = getCornerCoordinates(coordinates[0],
                                              coordinates[1], i);
            // if the space on the far side of the opponent's piece
            // is on the board and is unoccupied, then a jump
            // is possible, so we add it to the vector of moves:
            if((jumpLanding != null) &&
                (myGrid[jumpLanding[0]][jumpLanding[1]] == 0)) {
                toFill.addElement(jumpLanding);
            }
        }
    }
  }
} // end for loop
}

}
```

In addition to handling the game state, the CheckersGame class also handles the logic describing where the pieces are placed on the board and how they can move. The locations of the pieces are held in the 4×8-byte array field called myGrid. It's 4×8 because the black squares are the only squares that are relevant to the game, so if we remove the other squares (normally red, but gray in this game to be easier on the eyes) and then compress the board, what remains is a 4×8 grid.

Unfortunately, this compressed grid doesn't reflect the possible moves in a natural way. Which square is accessible from which other square depends on which row you're on. In the getCornerCoordinates() method of Listing 7-7, you can see how the row is taken into account when deciding which moves are possible from a given square.

When it's the local player's turn, the game logic needs to determine which moves are possible. The selectNext() and selectPrevious() methods are the starting point to the procedure of finding a piece that the local player can move. These methods go through the squares of the grid one by one to find the next one that contains a local checker that has legal moves. The possible moves are found in the getMoves() method, which uses the getCornerCoordinates() method to find which grid squares are accessible from the current square, and then checks whether they're vacant. If a given square is occupied, the getMoves() method then checks if it's possible to jump the occupant of the square.

The player navigates through the choices of pieces to move by pushing the trackball left or right, and then fixes that selection by pushing up, and can deselect the choice by pushing down, as you can see in the keyPressed() method of Listing 7-8, which calls the navigation methods of Listing 7-7. Once the selection has been fixed, the player can navigate through the possible choices of moves for that piece, as implemented in the rightPressed() and leftPressed() methods. Then the player pushes up once more to send the move to the remote player, as shown in the upPressed() method, which calls the move() method.

The real complexity arises when dealing with multiple jumps. Once the player has jumped once, the game logic has to check whether it's possible to jump again and then allow the player the option of jumping again or of ending the turn after one jump. That logic is handled in the move() method, with help from the getMoves() method, which has special functionality to return only jumps if the player is currently jumping.

The multiple jumps also add complexity to how the move data is interpreted. If a player could only move one space per turn, it would be simple enough to just give the source and destination coordinates of the move. However, since a multiple jump may entail a sequence of simple moves, the move data structure starts by giving the number of atomic moves, as you can see in the setMove() and endTurn() methods of Listing 7-7. Each of the simple moves making up the player's turn are coded as source and destination coordinates in the array myMoveData, which is sent as the payload (data content) of the SMS message that is sent to the opponent. Each call to setMove() writes one simple move to the array of move data and then increments the field myNumberOfMoves. Once the turn is completely finished, the endTurn() method writes the number of moves as the first byte of the payload data, and writes the player's taunt message after the move data.

The taunt message also uses the simple formula of leading with its length (this time in bytes) so that the receiving application will know how many bytes to read and convert into a String. Transforming the String to a byte array (and giving its length) is necessary because the game sends a BinaryMessage instead of a TextMessage. Then, once the data is ready, the endTurn() method resets the local data and calls the SMSManager (Listing 7-1) to send the move to the remote player.

When the game receives the opponent's move data, it is interpreted in the handleRemoteMove() and moveOpponent() methods. Note that the opponent's move data is inverted (so that the local player always appears to be the red pieces and always sees the opponent as the black pieces), as shown in Figure 7-9. If the opponent's move data contains a message, it is posted to the MainScreen (Listing 7-6), which takes the foreground until the local player dismisses it with the OK command.

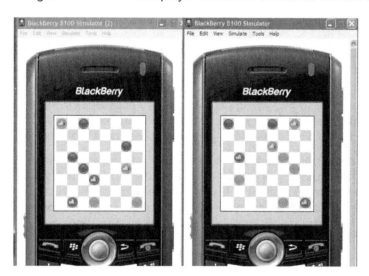

Figure 7-9. *Two instances of the BlackBerry 8100 simulator playing each other*

Painting the Checkers Game Graphics

The checkerboard is a very simple geometric object that changes very little during the game, so it's easy to set up one Canvas class that is appropriate for any screen size, as shown in Listing 7-8. There are three possible board sizes, and (for compatibility) the corresponding checker images are loaded using the standard MIDP Image class rather than RIM's Bitmap class.

For the checker image, I simply drew it in GIMP using circles and gradients, the same way I drew the ladybug image from Chapter 4 (only simpler). When it came to the crown image—to indicate which pieces are "kings"—I didn't feel like I could draw something quite nice enough for the look I wanted for this game. So I did a search for royalty-free crown images, and bought access to one from dreamstime: www.dreamstime.com. Figure 7-10 shows the checker with its crown.

Figure 7-10. *The crowned checker image*

Looking in the paint() method, you can see that the pieces are placed according to the data in the CheckersGame grid, with the user's selected source and destination squares outlined in red.

Listing 7-8. *CheckersCanvas.java*

```java
package net.frogparrot.smscheckers;

import javax.microedition.lcdui.*;
import java.io.IOException;

/**
 * This class is the display of the game.
 */
public class CheckersCanvas extends Canvas {

//-------------------------------------------------------------
//   graphics constants

  /**
   * color constants.
   */
  public static final int BLACK = 0;
  public static final int WHITE = 0xffffff;
  public static final int RED = 0xf96868;
  public static final int GREY = 0xc6c6c6;
  public static final int LT_GREY = 0xe5e3e3;
  public static final int TAN = 0xf9b97b;
```

```java
/**
 * how many rows and columns the display is divided into.
 */
public static final int GRID_WIDTH = 8;

/**
 * Dimensions for the different board sizes and their borders.
 */
private static int SMALL_SQUARE_SIZE = 24;
private static int SMALL_BORDER = 6;
private static int MED_SQUARE_SIZE = 36;
private static int MED_BORDER = 9;
private static int LARGE_SQUARE_SIZE = 48;
private static int LARGE_BORDER = 12;

//------------------------------------------------------------
//    instance fields

/**
 * a handle to the object that stores the game logic
 * and game data.
 */
private CheckersGame myGame;

/**
 * The images of the checkers.
 */
private Image myBlackChecker;
private Image myRedChecker;
private Image myBlackKing;
private Image myRedKing;

/**
 * Checkerboard dimensions and coordinates.
 */
private int mySquareSize;
private int myCornerX;
private int myCornerY;
private int myBorderWidth;
private int myBoardWidth;

//------------------------------------------------------
//    gets / sets

/**
 * @return a handle to the class that holds the logic of the
 * checkers game.
 */
public CheckersGame getGame() {
  return(myGame);
}

//------------------------------------------------------
//    initialization and game state changes
```

```java
/**
 * Constructor performs size calculations.
 */
CheckersCanvas() throws IOException {
  // create the game logic class:
  myGame = new CheckersGame();
  // a few calculations to make the right checkerboard
  // for the current display.
  int width = getWidth();
  int height = getHeight();
  int smBoardSize = SMALL_SQUARE_SIZE*8 + SMALL_BORDER*2;
  int medBoardSize = MED_SQUARE_SIZE*8 + MED_BORDER*2;
  int lgBoardSize = LARGE_SQUARE_SIZE*8 + LARGE_BORDER*2;
  if((width < smBoardSize) || (height < smBoardSize)) {
    Main.setMessage("screen too small");
    Main.quit();
  } else if((width < medBoardSize) || (height < medBoardSize)) {
    mySquareSize = SMALL_SQUARE_SIZE;
    myBorderWidth = SMALL_BORDER;
    myBoardWidth = smBoardSize;
    myBlackChecker = Image.createImage("/img/black_checker_24.png");
    myRedChecker = Image.createImage("/img/red_checker_24.png");
    myBlackKing = Image.createImage("/img/black_king_24.png");
    myRedKing = Image.createImage("/img/red_king_24.png");
  } else if((width < lgBoardSize) || (height < lgBoardSize)) {
    mySquareSize = MED_SQUARE_SIZE;
    myBorderWidth = MED_BORDER;
    myBoardWidth = medBoardSize;
    myBlackChecker = Image.createImage("/img/black_checker_36.png");
    myRedChecker = Image.createImage("/img/red_checker_36.png");
    myBlackKing = Image.createImage("/img/black_king_36.png");
    myRedKing = Image.createImage("/img/red_king_36.png");
  } else {
    mySquareSize = LARGE_SQUARE_SIZE;
    myBorderWidth = LARGE_BORDER;
    myBoardWidth = lgBoardSize;
    myBlackChecker = Image.createImage("/img/black_checker_48.png");
    myRedChecker = Image.createImage("/img/red_checker_48.png");
    myBlackKing = Image.createImage("/img/black_king_48.png");
    myRedKing = Image.createImage("/img/red_king_48.png");
  }
  myCornerX = (width - mySquareSize*8)/2;
  myCornerY = (height - mySquareSize*8)/2;
  if((myBlackChecker == null) || (myRedChecker == null) ||
     (myBlackKing == null) || (myRedKing == null)) {
    Main.setMessage("failed to load images");
    Main.quit();
  }
}

//---------------------------------------------------------
// graphics methods

  /**
```

```
     * Repaint the checkerboard.
     */
    protected void paint(Graphics g) {
      int width = getWidth();
      int height = getHeight();
      // clear the board (including the region around
      // the board, which can get menu stuff and other
      // garbage painted onto it...)
      g.setColor(TAN);
      g.fillRect(0, 0, width, height);
      g.setColor(WHITE);
      g.fillRect(myCornerX - myBorderWidth, myCornerY - myBorderWidth,
                 myBoardWidth, myBoardWidth);
      g.setColor(BLACK);
      g.drawRect(myCornerX - myBorderWidth, myCornerY - myBorderWidth,
                 myBoardWidth, myBoardWidth);
      // now draw the checkerboard:
      // first the dark squares:
      byte offset = 0;
      for(byte i = 0; i < 4; i++) {
        for(byte j = 0; j < 8; j++) {
          // the offset is used to handle the fact that in every
          // other row the dark squares are shifted one place
          // to the right.
          if(j % 2 != 0) {
            offset = 1;
          } else {
            offset = 0;
          }
          // calculate the top-left corner of the current square:
          int xCoord = myCornerX + (2*i + offset)*mySquareSize;
          int yCoord = myCornerY + j*mySquareSize;
          // now if this is a selected square, we draw it lighter
          // and outline it:
          if(myGame.isSelected(i, j)) {
            g.setColor(LT_GREY);
            g.fillRect(xCoord, yCoord,
                       mySquareSize, mySquareSize);
            g.setColor(RED);
            g.drawRect(xCoord, yCoord,
                       mySquareSize - 1, mySquareSize - 1);
          } else {
            // if it's not selected, we draw it dark gray:
            g.setColor(GREY);
            g.fillRect(xCoord, myCornerY + j*mySquareSize,
                       mySquareSize, mySquareSize);
          }
          // now put the pieces in their places:
          int piece = myGame.getPiece(i, j);
          int center = mySquareSize/2;
          if(piece == -1) {
            g.drawImage(myBlackChecker,
                        xCoord + center,
                        yCoord + center,
                        Graphics.VCENTER|Graphics.HCENTER);
```

```
        } else if(piece == -2) {
          g.drawImage(myBlackKing,
                      xCoord + center,
                      yCoord + center,
                      Graphics.VCENTER|Graphics.HCENTER);
        } else if(piece == 1) {
          g.drawImage(myRedChecker,
                      xCoord + center,
                      yCoord + center,
                      Graphics.VCENTER|Graphics.HCENTER);
        } else if(piece == 2) {
          g.drawImage(myRedKing,
                      xCoord + center,
                      yCoord + center,
                      Graphics.VCENTER|Graphics.HCENTER);
        }
      }
    }
  }

  //----------------------------------------------------------
  //  handle keystrokes

  /**
   * Move the player.
   */
  public void keyPressed(int keyCode) {
    if(myGame.isMyTurn()) {
      int action = getGameAction(keyCode);
      switch (action) {
      case LEFT:
        myGame.leftPressed();
        break;
      case RIGHT:
        myGame.rightPressed();
        break;
      case FIRE:
      case UP:
        myGame.upPressed();
        break;
      case DOWN:
        myGame.deselect();
        break;
      }
      repaint();
    }
  }

}
```

And that class is the last class needed to complete the game. Since there is only one version to build, it can be built in the BlackBerry JDE or with a very simple Ant build file.

Of course, as widespread (and fun!) as SMS communication may be, this simple technology has its limitations, and a BlackBerry smartphone can do better. For example, it can access the Internet to play a networked social game. You'll see examples of how to do that in Chapters 9 and 11.

Summary

SMS is a widely supported transport protocol that is convenient for a game where the players take turns. Since SMS messages are delivered by the operator's network, the game can read the list of potential opponents right out of the user's address book. Using standard Java ME classes, the game can manage threads to send and receive SMS messages to exchange data for the players' turns. Tweaking a cross-platform game to run on BlackBerry can be an adventure (since RIM has spent more effort on the proprietary RIMlet profile), but it's doable.

Chapter 8

Using Scalable Vector Graphics

A BlackBerry smartphone has a lot more computing power than the average handset, so you can't help but want to see what kinds of spectacular graphics effects you can create. In Chapter 12 you'll see how to use the OpenGL ES API to create 3D scenes for the latest and greatest models. But before version 5.0, BlackBerry smartphones didn't have a 3D graphics engine built-in. This is probably because BlackBerry devices are optimized for business, not pleasure. But on earlier models—starting from operating system version 4.6.0—BlackBerry devices have scalable vector graphics (SVG) capabilities (as defined in JSR 226). And that same SVG engine that so beautifully renders a corporate logo at just the right scale can also be used to add some pizzazz to your game!

The main application of SVG for the gaming world is to create a fun opening video sequence for your game—or a little short to play between levels—without having to fit a ton of per-pixel movie data in your JAR or COD file. You can use SVG for fixed animations on pre-4.6.0 BlackBerry smartphones by using the BlackBerry Theme Studio Composer to convert them to the Plazmic Media Engine (PME) format.

It's also possible to create a game with graphics implemented entirely in SVG. SVG isn't always a practical choice for a game implementation because it takes quite a lot of computing power to create effects that are rather limited compared to what you can do with a real 3D engine. But once you understand how it works, with a little creativity you can use its strengths to come up with a game that's quite out of the ordinary.

Additionally, SVG tools like Inkscape can be helpful for creating game graphics even if you ultimately decide to export your images to a pixel-based format like PNG and implement your game with the standard graphics API.

You'll see how to do all three of these applications—and more—in this chapter.

Understanding Scalable Vector Graphics

On a small device, most graphics data is described on a pixel-by-pixel basis. Even formats that are compressed and optimized are fundamentally lists, mapping pixels to their colors. A lot of drawings, however, can be described far more efficiently in terms of lines and curves. For example, if you draw a simple circle in a 2000×2000-pixel PNG file, it takes more than 8KB to store it (if you optimize by using an indexed color palette as explained in the next chapter, and nearly 36KB if you don't). But if you need to display the circle at that size, you can't just store a smaller version and enlarge it, because the image quality would suffer. It would be nice just to describe the circle in mathematical terms and then let the platform decide how to render it in pixels at display time. The SVG format does just that.

SVG is an XML-based language specified by the World Wide Web Consortium (W3C). It's designed to express 2D images (and animations) in terms of paths. The paths are described in terms of Bézier curves, which pack complex information about location and curvature into a handful of points.

Drawing with Bézier Curves

The math behind Bézier curves isn't too difficult, but in practice it's even simpler just to think of them in intuitive terms. At each endpoint of each segment of the curve, you have a tangent segment defined by an additional point, as shown in Figure 8-1. Moving the endpoint of the tangent segment allows you to change the curve. Lengthening and shortening the tangent segment affects how quickly the curve turns away from the tangent.

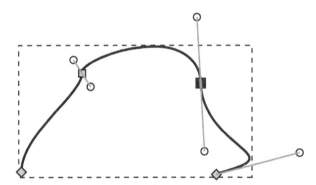

Figure 8-1. *A path defined in terms of Bézier curves*

If you try out an SVG graphics program (such as Inkscape, available free from www.inkscape.org), you'll quickly see how simple and intuitive it is. Just draw a quick scribble with the pencil tool, and then select the "edit paths by nodes" tool to move the points of the drawing around and modify their curvature, as shown in Figure 8-2.

Figure 8-2. *Modifying a path in Inkscape*

While the lines and curves form the basis of an SVG image, the SVG format allows you to define more interesting details than just plain lines. For example, you can define the color, style, and thickness of each drawn line, and you can fill enclosed regions with colors or gradients. Naturally, my first thought was to draw a spaceship for a Space Explorer game, shown in Figure 8-3.

Figure 8-3. *The spaceship for the Space Explorer game*

As you can see from Figure 8-3, a simple gradient fill can give the illusion of three dimensions. And since the SVG drawing is defined in terms of curves that are easy to grab and move around, I only had to draw the hull of the ship once—then I used shrunken copies of it as the engines. I placed them by drawing a guide ellipse (using the ellipse tool), which I later deleted.

Moving the engines around the guide ellipse, I created four versions of the spaceship, as shown in Figure 8-4. These four images—used as animation frames—give the illusion that the spaceship is spinning. In order to use them in a sprite-based game (which you'll see in Chapter 9), I exported them from Inkscape as PNG files, and then merged them all into a single PNG file—along with versions showing flames coming out of the engines—using GIMP (see the "Creating Icon Image Files" sidebar from Chapter 2).

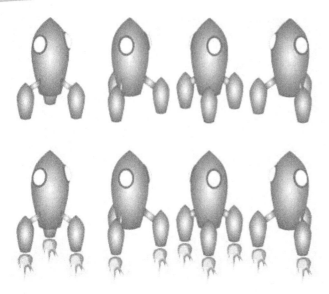

Figure 8-4. *The spaceship sprite animation file, created with Inkscape and GIMP*

While this spaceship illustration is perfect for use as a game sprite, it's not quite right for use in an SVG-based animation, for several reasons.

The first problem is that SVG animations aren't defined as a series of still frames. The animation is defined in terms of *paths*—just like the outline of the drawing. So instead of saying, "Show this frame for X milliseconds, then show this next frame," an SVG animation says, "Move this object along this path so that it takes X seconds to reach the destination." And the path of motion can be defined in terms of lines and Bézier curves just like the lines in the drawing, as you'll see later in this chapter. The animation is ultimately rendered as a series of frames, but the platform can decide at runtime exactly where the individual frames are drawn from the timeline.

The obvious solution for the spaceship animation is to throw away the three extra frames and add animation paths for the engines. That's essentially what I did, but there was a little bit more to it than that.

For one thing, the objects making up an SVG image are painted in the order in which they appear in the SVG file, and the animation can't change that ordering. That means that an object can't go from being in front of another object to being behind that object. So, in particular, the spaceship engines can't go all the way around the hull. Fortunately, you can fake it with a little sleight of hand, as you'll see in the "Creating SVG Animations" section.

The cute bubble windows pose a similar problem. They're supposed to look like elliptical spheroids sticking halfway out of raised ellipses sticking out of the hull of the spaceship. But since SVG can't even handle the idea of one shape going around behind another, it certainly doesn't support instructions like, "This shape cuts through (and obscures) this other shape along this curve." It's possible to create such instructions through path clipping or by creating a 3D animation in a 3D graphics program and then exporting it as a 2D SVG animation, but that's a little more complicated than what I wanted to do with this example. So I just replaced the bubble windows with flat oval windows.

Lastly, while the standard SVG format supports gradient fills, the SVG Tiny format doesn't. And JSR 226—which is the SVG API implemented on the BlackBerry platform—only supports SVG Tiny, as explained in the "Creating SVG and SVG Tiny Files" section. So I replaced the gradients with solid fills and added a shadow to give some cartoonish approximation of depth. Figure 8-5 shows the spaceship that can be animated with SVG.

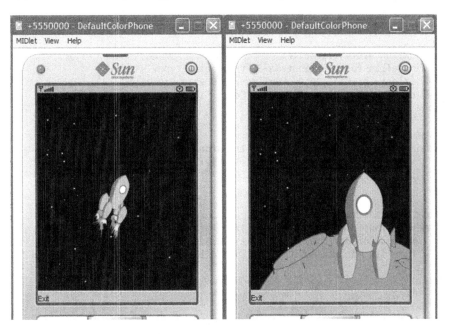

Figure 8-5. *The SVG Space Explorer animation running on the WTK emulator*

Understanding the SVG Format

SVG files are quite readable and intuitive as long as you have a basic familiarity with XML.

The drawing is organized as a tree of data where the different branches represent groups of objects that can be transformed together. For example, in the SVG Space Explorer animation, the entire ship is grouped in one g element because it moves as a unit around the screen. The ship object is divided into smaller units—such as the engines and the windows—which move as independent units within the spaceship branch. These units are again defined as g elements that are children of the g element of the ship.

You can branch this data tree down to as many levels as you like. For example, the patch of flame coming out of each engine is made of three closed paths that are grouped so that they can be made visible and invisible together, and the flame grouping is a subset of the engine's group, so that the flames move with the corresponding engine around the spaceship's hull. Then, to avoid repeating the path data, you can define paths in the top section of the SVG file, and reuse them as many times as you like in the body of the image. Listing 8-1 shows how one engine and its flames appear in the body of the image file.

Listing 8-1. *The Element That Describes nacelle-4 from space-animation.svg*

```
<g id="nacelle-4">
  <g transform="scale(.5)">
    <g transform="translate(-226.07577 -37.878232 )">
      <use xlink:href="#mainhull"/>
    </g>
  </g>
  <g transform="translate(-45 260)">
    <g>
      <use xlink:href="#flame1"/>
      <animateTransform attributeName="transform" type="skewY"
          values="0;60;15;20;0" keyTimes="0;0.25;0.5;0.75;1"
          dur="1s" fill="remove" repeatCount="15"/>
    </g>
    <g>
      <use xlink:href="#flame2"/>
      <animateTransform attributeName="transform" type="scale"
          values="1,1;1.5,0.75;1,1.75;1,1" keyTimes="0;0.33;0.66;1"
          dur="1s" fill="remove" repeatCount="15"/>
    </g>
    <g>
      <use xlink:href="#flame3"/>
      <animateTransform attributeName="transform" type="skewX"
          values="0;60;-20;45;0" keyTimes="0;0.25;0.5;0.75;1"
          dur="1s" fill="remove" repeatCount="15"/>
    </g>
    <set attributeName="visibility" to="hidden" begin="15s"/>
  </g>
  <g id="bar-4">
    <path d="M -108,0 L -123,50 L -55,75 L -50,50 z"
        fill="#666666" stroke="#000000" />
    <animateTransform attributeName="transform" type="scale"
        from="0.05,1" to="1,1" dur="1s" fill="freeze" repeatCount="10.5"/>
  </g>
  <animateMotion
      path="M 225.20966,363.24139
          C 338.591,363.24139 435.74974,388.50383 435.80808,419.19913"
      dur="1s" fill="freeze" repeatCount="10.5"/>
</g>
```

(I looked up the word *nacelle* when creating this animation, and it turns out that it's a real word—not just something they made up for Star Trek!)

From Listing 8-1, you can see how to use a reference to a predefined grouping such as `mainhull` or `flames2` in the body of a data grouping. You can also see how simple it is to apply a transformation at any level in the data tree. The engine is just a copy of the hull shape, translated to a different set of coordinates within the drawing and then shrunk by half. All you have to do is put the `use` element inside two g elements, each of which has a `transform` attribute. The transformations are applied starting from the leaves and moving toward the root of the data tree. So in this example, the SVG interpreter will start with the `mainhull` data (which is actually two paths because the hull has a shaded part; see Listing 8-2), and then apply the translation to the path coordinates, followed by the scaling transformation to shrink it down.

The possible transformations are translate, scale, rotate, skewX, and skewY. Translation, scaling, and rotation are self-explanatory, and the two types of skew aren't too much more difficult. Essentially, they modify the image by changing the angle between the coordinate axes. You can see in Listing 8-1 that the flames are distorted using skew transformations during the course of the animation to create a flaming effect.

Some other straightforward SVG path attributes illustrated in Listing 8-1 are fill and stroke. These just give the color of the path outline and the color to use to fill the interior. The colors are written in standard RGB format as #rrggbb, where the first two digits give the amount of red in the color, the second two give the amount of green, and the third two give the amount of blue. To draw a path that is either not filled in or not outlined, just leave off the fill or stroke attribute.

The only difficult part of the SVG file is the path element, and especially its d attribute. To explain it, let's look at the paths that make up the mainhull from the defs section of space animation (Listing 8-2).

Listing 8-2. *The Element Defining mainhull from space-animation.svg*

```
<g id="mainhull">
  <!-- the basic shape of the outer hull of both the rocket and its engines -->
  <path fill="#666666" stroke="#000000"
      d="M 102.94913,233.23945
          C 92.641524,327.40192 128.53432,437.75419 154.6246,540.01215
          C 178.17206,550.92937 197.5947,557.08734 226.0811,556.61989
          C 251.382,557.11835 274.03246,549.86652 297.16791,540.01215
          C 323.25819,437.75419 356.8766,336.10688 348.84338,233.23945
          C 340.81015,130.37202 284.27986,89.162454 226.07577,37.878232
          C 158.44358,89.245831 113.25675,139.07699 102.94913,233.23945 z"
  />
  <path fill="#bbbbbb" stroke="#000000"
      d="M 153.99244,233.93746
          C 152.89743,308.1412 174.55661,455.16902 188.50074,552.6608
          C 199.86064,555.50651 211.8379,556.92914 226.0811,556.69541
          C 251.382,557.19387 274.03246,549.94205 297.16791,540.08768
          C 323.25819,437.82971 356.8766,336.18241 348.84338,233.31498
          C 340.81015,130.44755 284.27986,89.237979 226.07577,37.953751
          C 178.36292,81.851599 155.1058,158.48903 153.99244,233.93746 z"
  />
</g>
```

As mentioned previously, SVG paths are drawn in *painter's order*, which means that the SVG interpreter draws and fills the paths in the order in which they appear in the SVG file. In this case, the dark part of the hull is drawn and painted first, and then the lighter part—given by the second path in Listing 8-2—is drawn on top of it, obscuring most of it.

The value of the d element is a list of commands and points that define the path. The command is given first by a single letter, and the following numbers are the command's arguments. A path generally starts with the M command—to move to the starting point—and then has a sequence of L and C commands giving line segments and curves. Then, if it's a closed path, it ends with a Z command to close the path, drawing a straight line segment if the first and last points are not the same.

The L command simply draws a line segment from the previous point on the list to the point following the L command. You can see an example in Listing 8-1 as the bar-4 element is just a diamond-shaped quadrilateral (which holds the engine onto the hull of the spaceship).

The C command draws a cubic Bézier curve. The curve extends from the previous command's endpoint to the C command's endpoint. You can see in Listing 8-2 that each C is followed by three points given as coordinate pairs. The first two are the control points of the Bézier curve, and the third one is the endpoint of the curve. Figure 8-6 shows how a cubic Bézier curve is defined by four points.

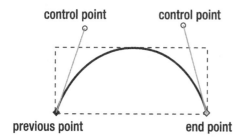

Figure 8-6. *The four points that define a cubic Bézier curve*

There are a few other possible command letters that are essentially variants of the preceding commands. The H, V, and S commands are shorthand versions of L and C (taking fewer arguments) for cases where some information can be copied from the previous segment. There's also a Q command to create a quadratic Bézier curve, which is like a cubic Bézier curve, only simpler—with just one control point that gives the tangent at both endpoints.

All of these commands also have lowercase versions. For the lowercase commands, the coordinates of the argument points are considered to be relative to the coordinates of the previous point (rather than being standard, absolute coordinates).

Creating SVG and SVG Tiny Files

Even if you understand how to read and modify the SVG file yourself, you'll probably want to use a tool to create the paths. Inkscape (available from www.inkscape.org) is a good choice—it's easy, fun, and free. Inkscape, however, has one unfortunate flaw: it creates files in the Full SVG format, not SVG Tiny. At the time of this writing, it doesn't even offer an option to *export* the files in SVG Tiny format. But it's useful to understand how the SVG language works, and manipulating these files by hand (as we'll do in this chapter) is a good way to learn. The conversion is pretty simple—the trick is to eliminate any items that SVG Tiny doesn't support.

The W3C provides a document listing the different feature sets of SVG Basic and SVG Tiny at the following web address:

http://www.w3.org/TR/SVGMobile/

This page provides a good starting point for items to eliminate. For example, it mentions that SVG Tiny doesn't support gradient fills, so you can start your SVG-to–SVG Tiny procedure right in Inkscape by eliminating gradient fills. It also mentions that SVG Tiny doesn't support the A command in the `path` element (which gives elliptical arcs). Unfortunately, if you create an ellipse in Inkscape, it creates a path made of elliptical arcs by default. They're easy to fix, though, again right in Inkscape. Just select the ellipse, select **Path ↗ Object to Path**, fix the endpoints a bit if Inkscape hasn't closed the ellipse properly, and you're done—the offending A command will be eliminated from your file.

The biggest change I had to make to the SVG file was to eliminate the use of the `style` attribute. The W3C document lists `style` in the attribute table as not available for SVG Tiny. In a nutshell, SVG allows you to group style attributes in a single attribute as follows:

```
style="fill:#666666;fill-opacity:1;stroke:#000000; ↵
stroke-width:1.62334483000000000; ↵
stroke-miterlimit:4;stroke-dasharray:none;stroke-dashoffset:0;stroke-opacity:1"
```

However, this type of grouping isn't supported by SVG Tiny. The style data needs to be listed in separate attributes, as shown in the `path` elements of Listings 8-1 and 8-2. Inkscape also added a number of attributes from the `sodipodi` namespace and a bunch of other elements and attributes of questionable provenance. Since the SVG Tiny file is readable enough that I can recognize the crucial data in it, I just used a when-in-doubt, throw-it-out policy and deleted everything that didn't have a purpose I could identify.

If you have to create a number of SVG Tiny files, you'll obviously want to automate some of these steps with a script. Once I got the hang of the SVG Tiny format, though, I found it was simple enough just to create the file structure by hand and use Inkscape to generate the paths, which I merely copied and pasted from Inkscape's file into mine. And the nice thing about Inkscape is that—even if it won't generate the file in SVG Tiny for you—at least it will let you open and view your SVG Tiny file so that you can confirm that you got it right. Listing 8-3 shows the SVG Space Explorer animation that I created with a little help from Inkscape.

Listing 8-3. *space-animation.svg*

```
<?xml version="1.0" encoding="UTF-8" standalone="no"?>
<!-- Created manually by Carol Hamer (with some assistance from Inkscape to↵
 generate paths) -->
<svg width="240" height="320" viewBox="0 0 480 640" stroke-miterlimit="2"
    xmlns="http://www.w3.org/2000/svg" xmlns:xlink="http://www.w3.org/1999/xlink"
    xml:space="preserve" version="1.1" baseProfile="tiny">
  <defs>
    <g id="mainhull">
      <!-- the basic shape of the outer hull of both the rocket and its engines -->
      <path fill="#666666" stroke="#000000"
        d="M 102.94913,233.23945
           C 92.641524,327.40192 128.53432,437.75419 154.6246,540.01215
           C 178.17206,550.92937 197.5947,557.08734 226.0811,556.61989
           C 251.382,557.11835 274.03246,549.86652 297.16791,540.01215
           C 323.25819,437.75419 356.8766,336.10688 348.84338,233.23945
           C 340.81015,130.37202 284.27986,89.162454 226.07577,37.878232
           C 158.44358,89.245831 113.25675,139.07699 102.94913,233.23945 z"
      />
```

```
        <path fill="#bbbbbb" stroke="#000000"
           d="M 153.99244,233.93746
              C 152.89743,308.1412 174.55661,455.16902 188.50074,552.6608
              C 199.86064,555.50651 211.8379,556.92914 226.0811,556.69541
              C 251.382,557.19387 274.03246,549.94205 297.16791,540.08768
              C 323.25819,437.82971 356.8766,336.18241 348.84338,233.31498
              C 340.81015,130.44755 284.27986,89.237979 226.07577,37.953751
              C 178.36292,81.851599 155.1058,158.48903 153.99244,233.93746 z"
        />
    </g>
    <!-- the flames coming out of the engine are defined separately -->
    <!-- because they move independently -->
    <g id="flame1">
      <path fill="#de422d" stroke="#000000"
         d="M 44.285715,0.93361156
            C 34.850224,2.1830519 21.583854,5.9982466 14.285715,14.50504
            C 6.9875754,23.011833 5.382605,35.920611 7.142857,50.219325
            C 8.903109,64.518038 7.1428573,73.790751 7.1428573,73.790751
            C 7.1428573,73.790751 21.153463,53.520997 35,54.50504
            C 48.846537,55.489083 47.857144,178.79075 47.857144,178.79075
            C 47.857144,178.79075 48.276474,87.742027 65.714286,82.362182
            C 83.152098,76.982337 91.428577,153.79076 88.571427,142.36218
            C 85.714287,130.93361 87.029909,74.942848 92.857143,60.933611
            C 98.938578,46.313251 101.27236,36.504612 98.571429,28.076468
            C 95.870503,19.648324 87.807944,6.993361 80.714286,4.5050398
            C 73.620628,2.0167188 53.721206,-0.31582874 44.285715,0.93361156 z"
      />
    </g>
    <g id="flame2">
      <path fill="#f36a1b" stroke="#000000"
         d="M 44.285715,7.362183
            C 34.850224,8.6116233 23.012425,12.426818 15.714286,20.933611
            C 8.4161468,29.440404 10.382605,38.777754 12.142857,53.076468
            C 13.903109,67.375181 22.857143,112.36218 22.857143,112.36218
            C 22.857143,112.36218 15.439177,64.949568 29.285714,65.933611
            C 43.132251,66.917654 57.142858,129.50504 57.142858,129.50504
            C 57.142858,129.50504 48.276474,80.59917 65.714286,75.219325
            C 83.152098,69.83948 114.28572,135.21933 111.42857,123.79075
            C 108.57143,112.36218 84.887052,76.371419 82.857143,60.933611
            C 80.827234,45.495803 91.272355,35.076041 88.571429,26.647897
            C 85.870503,18.219753 78.52223,11.993361 71.428572,9.5050398
            C 64.334914,7.0167188 53.721206,6.1127427 44.285715,7.362183 z"
      />
    </g>
    <g id="flame3">
      <path fill="#f3db1b" stroke="#000000"
         d="M 34.908948,15.842559
            C 24.536318,22.871778 23.862981,20.556401 19.194662,33.335491
            C 14.416814,46.414407 5.0000001,130.93361 5.0000001,130.93361
            C 5.0000001,130.93361 15.439177,64.949568 29.285714,65.933611
            C 43.132251,66.917654 36.428572,102.36218 36.428572,102.36218
            C 36.428572,102.36218 48.276474,72.742027 65.714286,67.362182
            C 83.152098,61.982337 81.43842,79.824223 82.142856,88.076464
            C 88.839253,67.034613 71.969434,52.101962 71.313274,32.362183
            C 70.657115,12.622404 45.281577,8.8133395 34.908948,15.842559 z"
```

```
            />
        </g>
        <g id="planet">
            <!-- the planet is just a big circle with some craters drawn on it -->
            <path id="the-planet-itself" fill="#659a72" stroke="#000000"
                d="M 711.42279,559.50388 C 711.42279,755.06959 552.70856,915.2193↵
357.14285,915.2193 C 161.57714,915.2193 2.8571472,756.4993 2.8571472,560.93359 C↵
2.8571472,365.36788 161.57714,206.64789 357.14285,206.64789 C 551.70371,206.64789↵
709.8525,364.94936 711.42279,559.50388 z"
                />
            <path id="crater-filler-1" fill="#659a72"
                d="M 93.210334,321.98754 L 96.453561,323.21997 L 94.248167,325.3605 L↵
93.210334,321.98754 z"
                />
            <path id="crater-filler-2" fill="#659a72"
                d="M 268.04179,212.91988 L 278.40754,218.79075 L 264.55596,223.37737 L↵
268.04179,212.91988 z"
                />
            <path id="crater-1" fill="#659a72" stroke="#000000"
                d="M 296.81843,316.44258
                    C 296.81843,329.6189 250.55769,340.40906 193.55577,340.40906
                    C 136.55385,340.40906 90.291428,329.71523 90.291428,316.53891
                    C 90.291428,303.36259 136.55385,292.66876 193.55577,292.66876
                    C 250.2648,292.66876 296.36074,303.33438 296.81843,316.44258 z"
                transform="matrix(0.8474231,-0.5309182,0.5309182,0.8474231,↵
-153.05378,99.167179)" />
            <!-- To save paper, some planet strokes are not printed here -->
            <!-- Download the complete source code from apress.com -->
            <path d="M 266.39061,244.75099
                    C 271.06828,245.1408 278.83241,249.15414 285.83785,249.15414
                    C 286.57171,249.15414 287.30557,249.15414 288.03943,249.15414" />

        </g>
        <g id="star">
            <path fill="#ffffff" d="M 1,1 L -1,1 L -1,-1 L 1,-1 z"/>
        </g>
    </defs>
    <g id="whole-scene">
      <g id="background">
        <!-- paint the entire background black -->
        <rect x="-240" y="0" width="960" height="640" fill="#000000"/>
        <!-- paint on a field of fainter background stars -->
        <!-- spaced to fill the viewBox -->
        <g id="stars-1">
          <use xlink:href="#star" transform="translate(50 50)"/>
          <use xlink:href="#star" transform="translate(5 600)"/>
          <use xlink:href="#star" transform="translate(68 346)"/>
          <use xlink:href="#star" transform="translate(456 500)"/>
          <use xlink:href="#star" transform="translate(333 111)"/>
          <use xlink:href="#star" transform="translate(351 253)"/>
          <use xlink:href="#star" transform="translate(400 98)"/>
          <use xlink:href="#star" transform="translate(111 333)"/>
          <use xlink:href="#star" transform="translate(120 437)"/>
          <use xlink:href="#star" transform="translate(298 267)"/>
          <use xlink:href="#star" transform="translate(12 185)"/>
```

```xml
    <use xlink:href="#star" transform="translate(283 573)"/>
    <use xlink:href="#star" transform="translate(366 44)"/>
    <use xlink:href="#star" transform="translate(50 555)"/>
    <!-- paint some on the edges -->
    <use xlink:href="#star" transform="translate(-235 140)"/>
    <use xlink:href="#star" transform="translate(560 50)"/>
    <use xlink:href="#star" transform="translate(680 427)"/>
    <use xlink:href="#star" transform="translate(703 505)"/>
    <use xlink:href="#star" transform="translate(-56 112)"/>
    <use xlink:href="#star" transform="translate(-22 429)"/>
    <use xlink:href="#star" transform="translate(-107 1)"/>
    <use xlink:href="#star" transform="translate(619 589)"/>
    <use xlink:href="#star" transform="translate(495 490)"/>
    <use xlink:href="#star" transform="translate(522 630)"/>
    <use xlink:href="#star" transform="translate(-99 15)"/>
    <use xlink:href="#star" transform="translate(-201 253)"/>
    <use xlink:href="#star" transform="translate(715 147)"/>
    <use xlink:href="#star" transform="translate(555 333)"/>
  </g>
  <!-- paint on a field of foreground stars (scaled to be larger) -->
  <!-- you might potentially add a motion animation to this set -->
  <!-- spaced to fill the viewBox after scaling -->
  <g id="stars-2" transform="scale(2)">
    <use xlink:href="#star" transform="translate(50 50)"/>
    <use xlink:href="#star" transform="translate(5 100)"/>
    <use xlink:href="#star" transform="translate(68 306)"/>
    <use xlink:href="#star" transform="translate(156 200)"/>
    <use xlink:href="#star" transform="translate(33 111)"/>
    <use xlink:href="#star" transform="translate(51 253)"/>
    <use xlink:href="#star" transform="translate(30 98)"/>
    <use xlink:href="#star" transform="translate(111 233)"/>
    <use xlink:href="#star" transform="translate(120 37)"/>
    <use xlink:href="#star" transform="translate(208 267)"/>
    <use xlink:href="#star" transform="translate(12 185)"/>
    <use xlink:href="#star" transform="translate(223 73)"/>
    <use xlink:href="#star" transform="translate(6 44)"/>
    <use xlink:href="#star" transform="translate(50 155)"/>
  </g>
  <g>
    <use xlink:href="#planet"/>
    <!-- the planet slides into view in time for the landing -->
    <animateTransform attributeName="transform" type="translate"
            values="0,1000;0,1000;-40,250" keyTimes="0;0.75;1"
            dur="10s" fill="freeze" repeatCount="1"/>
  </g>
</g>
<g id="spaceship">
  <!-- the entire spaceship is rotated by 90% so that the rotate(auto) -->
  <!-- of the animateMotion element will cause the spaceship to point -->
  <!-- in the direction of the path of motion -->
  <g transform="rotate(90)">
    <!-- two of the four rocket engines are behind the main hull -->
    <g id="nacelle-3">
      <!-- the engines are just the same shape as the hull, scaled by half -->
      <g transform="scale(.5)">
```

```
    <g transform="translate(-226.07577 -37.878232 )">
      <use xlink:href="#mainhull"/>
    </g>
</g>
<!-- the flame is translated into position below the engine -->
<!-- after the distorting animations are performed. -->
<g id="flames-3" transform="translate(-45 260)">
  <!-- each flame layer is animated individually -->
  <g>
    <use xlink:href="#flame1"/>
    <animateTransform attributeName="transform" type="skewX"
        values="0;20;-45;0" keyTimes="0;0.33;0.66;1"
        dur="1s" fill="remove" repeatCount="15"/>
  </g>
  <g>
    <use xlink:href="#flame2"/>
    <animateTransform attributeName="transform" type="scale"
        values="1,1;1.5,0.75;1,1.75;2,2;1,1"
        keyTimes="0;0.25;0.5;0.75;1"
        dur="1s" fill="remove" repeatCount="15"/>
  </g>
  <g>
    <use xlink:href="#flame3"/>
    <animateTransform attributeName="transform" type="skewY"
        values="0;60;15;20;0" keyTimes="0;0.25;0.5;0.75;1"
        dur="1s" fill="remove" repeatCount="15"/>
  </g>
  <!-- the flames must disappear after the spaceship lands -->
  <set attributeName="visibility" to="hidden" begin="15s"/>
</g>
<g id="bar-3">
  <!-- the bar holding the engine to the hull is a quadrilateral -->
  <!-- which is scaled in the X-direction so that it appears to turn -->
  <path d="M 110,0 L 125,50 L 55,75 L 50,50 z"
      fill="#bbbbbb" stroke="#000000" />
  <animateTransform attributeName="transform" type="scale"
      from="1,1" to="0.05,1" dur="1s" fill="freeze" repeatCount="10.5"/>
</g>
<!-- the entire engine (including bar and flame) follows -->
<!-- an elliptical path around the main hull -->
<animateMotion
    path="M 14.529648,420.32217
        C 14.529648,388.81358 108.91429,363.24139 225.20966,363.24139"
    dur="1s" fill="freeze" repeatCount="10.5"/>
</g>
<g id="nacelle-4">
  <g transform="scale(.5)">
    <g transform="translate(-226.07577 -37.878232 )">
      <use xlink:href="#mainhull"/>
    </g>
  </g>
  <g id="flames-4" transform="translate(-45 260)">
    <g>
      <use xlink:href="#flame1"/>
      <animateTransform attributeName="transform" type="skewY"
```

```
              values="0;60;15;20;0" keyTimes="0;0.25;0.5;0.75;1"
              dur="1s" fill="remove" repeatCount="15"/>
        </g>
        <g>
          <use xlink:href="#flame2"/>
          <animateTransform attributeName="transform" type="scale"
              values="1,1;1.5,0.75;1,1.75;1,1" keyTimes="0;0.33;0.66;1"
              dur="1s" fill="remove" repeatCount="15"/>
        </g>
        <g>
          <use xlink:href="#flame3"/>
          <animateTransform attributeName="transform" type="skewX"
              values="0;60;-20;45;0" keyTimes="0;0.25;0.5;0.75;1"
              dur="1s" fill="remove" repeatCount="15"/>
        </g>
        <set attributeName="visibility" to="hidden" begin="15s"/>
      </g>
      <g id="bar-4">
        <path d="M -108,0 L -123,50 L -55,75 L -50,50 z"
            fill="#666666" stroke="#000000" />
        <animateTransform attributeName="transform" type="scale"
            from="0.05,1" to="1,1" dur="1s" fill="freeze" repeatCount="10.5"/>
      </g>
      <animateMotion
          path="M 225.20966,363.24139
                C 338.591,363.24139 435.74974,388.50383 435.80808,419.19913"
          dur="1s" fill="freeze" repeatCount="10.5"/>
    </g>
    <g id="hull">
      <!-- the main hull itself doesn't have any separate animation -->
      <use xlink:href="#mainhull"/>
    </g>
    <g id="window">
      <!-- the window is two concentric ellipses -->
      <g>
        <path fill="#666666" stroke="#000000"
          d="M 52.342524,249.14996
             C 52.342524,285.47603 28.437894,314.95808 -1.016016,314.95808
             C -30.469926,314.95808 -54.374546,285.47603 -54.374546,249.14996
             C -54.374546,212.82387 -30.469926,183.34183 -1.016016,183.34183
             C 28.357674,183.34183 52.216364,212.64161 52.342034,248.86842"
          />
        <!-- the window pane is grouped separately because it has a transformation
  -->
        <!-- it darkens as the window turns towards the shadow -->
        <g id="pane">
          <path d="M 41.468204,249.92805
              C 41.468204,279.47839 22.504994,303.46127 -0.860386,303.46127
              C -24.225766,303.46127 -43.188976,279.47839 -43.188976,249.92805
              C -43.188976,220.37771 -24.225766,196.39483 -0.860386,196.39483
              C 22.441354,196.39483 41.368124,220.22944 41.467814,249.69903"
            />
          <animateColor attributeName="fill" values="#ffffff;#ffffff;#666666"
            keyTimes="0;0.5;1" dur="1s" fill="freeze" repeatCount="10.5"/>
        </g>
```

```
        <!-- the motion and width scaling are computed -->
        <!-- according to a spline -->
        <!-- to give the illusion of a circular path -->
        <animateTransform attributeName="transform" type="scale"
            values="0.05,1;1,1;0.05,1" calcMode="spline"
            keySplines="0 .75 .25 1; .75 0 1 .25"
            dur="1s" fill="freeze" repeatCount="10.5"/>
    </g>
    <animateMotion path="M 350,0 L 225,0 L 100,0"
        calcMode="spline" keySplines="0 .1 .9 1; .1 0 1 .9"
        dur="1s" fill="freeze" repeatCount="10.5"/>
</g>
<g id="nacelle-1">
    <!-- for the front engines the bar is drawn first -->
    <!-- because it appears behind the engine -->
    <g id="bar-1">
        <path fill="#666666" stroke="#000000"
            d="M -108,0 L -123,50 L -55,75 L -50,50 z" />
        <animateTransform attributeName="transform" type="scale" from="1,1"
            to="0.05,1" dur="1s" fill="freeze" repeatCount="10.5"/>
    </g>
    <g transform="scale(.5)">
        <g transform="translate(-226.07577 -37.878232 )">
            <use xlink:href="#mainhull"/>
        </g>
    </g>
    <g id="flames-1" transform="translate(-45 260)">
        <g>
            <use xlink:href="#flame1"/>
            <animateTransform attributeName="transform" type="skewY"
                values="0;60;15;0" keyTimes="0;0.33;0.66;1"
                dur="1s" fill="remove" repeatCount="15"/>
        </g>
        <g>
            <use xlink:href="#flame2"/>
            <animateTransform attributeName="transform" type="skewX"
                values="0;-30;20;45;0" keyTimes="0;0.25;0.5;0.75;1"
                dur="1s" fill="remove" repeatCount="15"/>
        </g>
        <g>
            <use xlink:href="#flame3"/>
            <animateTransform attributeName="transform" type="scale"
                values="1,1;1,1.75;2,0.75;1,1" keyTimes="0;0.33;0.66;1"
                dur="1s" fill="remove" repeatCount="15"/>
        </g>
        <set attributeName="visibility" to="hidden" begin="15s"/>
    </g>
    <animateMotion path="M 435.80808,419.19913
        C 435.80808,450.70773 341.50502,477.40296 225.20966,477.40296"
        dur="1s" fill="freeze" repeatCount="10.5"/>
</g>
<g id="nacelle-2">
    <g id="bar-2">
        <path d="M 110,0 L 125,50 L 55,75 L 50,50 z"
            fill="#bbbbbb" stroke="#000000" />
```

```
          <animateTransform attributeName="transform" type="scale" from="0.05,1"
              to="1,1" dur="1s" fill="freeze" repeatCount="10.5"/>
        </g>
        <g transform="scale(.5)">
          <g transform="translate(-226.07577 -37.878232 )">
            <use xlink:href="#mainhull"/>
          </g>
        </g>
        <g id="flames-2" transform="translate(-45 260)">
          <g>
            <use xlink:href="#flame1"/>
            <animateTransform attributeName="transform" type="skewX"
                values="0;-60;20;45;0" keyTimes="0;0.25;0.5;0.75;1"
                dur="1s" fill="remove" repeatCount="15"/>
          </g>
          <g>
            <use xlink:href="#flame2"/>
            <animateTransform attributeName="transform" type="skewY"
                values="0;60;20;0" keyTimes="0;0.33;0.66;1"
                dur="1s" fill="remove" repeatCount="15"/>
          </g>
          <g>
            <use xlink:href="#flame3"/>
            <animateTransform attributeName="transform" type="scale"
                values="1,1;1.5,0.75;1,1.75;2,2;1,1" keyTimes="0;0.25;0.5;0.75;1"
                dur="1s" fill="remove" repeatCount="15"/>
          </g>
          <set attributeName="visibility" to="hidden" begin="15s"/>
        </g>
        <animateMotion path="M 225.20966,477.40296
            C 108.91429,477.40296 14.529648,451.83077 14.529648,420.32217"
            dur="1s" fill="freeze" repeatCount="10.5"/>
      </g>
    </g>
    <!-- the whole spaceship grows as it travels -->
    <animateTransform attributeName="transform" type="scale" values="0.1;0.25;0.5"
        keyTimes="0;0.66;1" dur="15s" fill="freeze" repeatCount="1"/>
    <!-- the spaceship flies along this curve -->
    <animateMotion path="M -47.685323,118.797
        C -8.6903733,199.6092 35.366396,272.0702 81.614203,290.70558
        C 128.73236,309.69166 240,320 240,160"
        rotate="auto" dur="10s" fill="freeze" repeatCount="1"/>
    <!-- the landing is given as a separate animate command -->
    <!-- because the orientation changes. -->
    <!-- it flies nose-first and lands feet-first -->
    <animateMotion path="M 240 160 L 240 240" begin="10s"
        rotate="270" dur="5s" fill="freeze" repeatCount="1"/>
  </g>
 </g>
</svg>
```

Creating SVG Animations

Inkscape won't help you create (or play) your SVG animations. For that, the obvious choice is the BlackBerry Theme Studio. It's available for free download from the BlackBerry developer web site:

`http://na.blackberry.com/eng/developers/themes/devtools.jsp`

The BlackBerry Theme Studio comes with a Composer application that allows you to import, create, and modify SVG images and animations. It allows you to select different components of the image and move them around, defining your animation frames as you go. Figure 8-7 shows what it looks like.

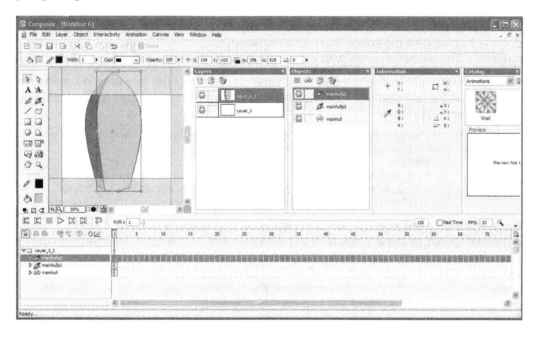

Figure 8-7. *The BlackBerry Theme Studio Composer*

Naturally, you can create the entire animation in Composer if you like. I found that it wasn't as versatile or helpful as Inkscape for creating the original drawing. Probably the simplest strategy is to create the original drawing in Inkscape and then import it into Composer in order to animate it. This procedure unfortunately isn't as simple as it could be since Composer prefers the different nodes to have id tags, which Inkscape doesn't add by default. This is another reason why it's a good idea to understand the SVG/SVG Tiny language—so you can just troubleshoot the animation itself when the tools don't do exactly what you want. To illustrate how the SVG/SVG Tiny language works, I developed the Space Explorer animation by hand instead of generating it with a tool.

Fortunately, the animations are based on the same type of path and transformation data as the components of still SVG images. So what you've read in the previous section (assuming you weren't thinking you could just skip to the animations section) will help you understand how the animation works.

> **Note** The BlackBerry Theme Studio 5.0 Composer can import Flash (SWF) animations and convert them to SVG. This is the standard way of playing SWF files on the BlackBerry platform since even BlackBerry 5.0 doesn't support playing SWF files directly. The Composer can also convert either animation type to PME files that can be played by the Plazmic Media Engine on BlackBerry smartphones with earlier operating systems (as early as 4.1.0) that don't support SVG.

In the SVG Space Explorer animation in Listing 8-3, the spaceship expands as it flies into view along a curved path (for 10.5 seconds), spinning with flickering flames coming out of its engines. After 10.5 seconds, it starts to land on the planet. During the landing, the planet moves into view from below, and the spaceship expands further as it descends, engines first. The spaceship doesn't spin during the landing, but the engines continue flaming until the spaceship has completed its landing (15 seconds into the animation). The animation ends with the still shot shown on the right of Figure 8-5.

The fundamental idea is illustrated in the animation of each of the four engines, shown in Listing 8-3 as the last element contained inside the g groupings of nacelle-1, nacelle-2, nacelle-3, and nacelle-4:

```
<!-- the entire engine (including bar and flame) follows -->
<!-- an elliptical path around the main hull -->
<animateMotion
    path="M 14.529648,420.32217
          C 14.529648,388.81358 108.91429,363.24139 225.20966,363.24139"
    dur="1s" fill="freeze" repeatCount="10.5"/>
```

The path attribute of the animateMotion element uses the same command-and-coordinate format as the d attribute of the path element. In this case, I started with the guide ellipse I originally used to place the engines, and used Inkscape to convert it to a path. Since Inkscape converted the ellipse to sequence of four cubic Bézier curves, the simplest way to animate their motion around the hull was to add a fourth engine and have each engine follow one of the four curved segments.

The dur, fill, and repeatCount attributes tell the engine to take 1 second to travel along the curved path and to repeat this motion 10.5 times. Then the engine freezes (remains stationary) *with respect to the rest of the ship*—although it continues moving along with the rest of the spaceship, as a subcomponent of the spaceship grouping (which has its own animateMotion and animateTransform elements, shown at the end of Listing 8-3). Since the engine's path is not closed with a Z command, it immediately returns to its starting point after each 1-second motion. But since the starting point of one engine's path is exactly the endpoint of the next engine's path—and they're identical—they do a little relay race that gives the illusion that each engine is spinning all the way around the hull.

If you're doing an animation with one single object that has to go from behind another object to being in front of that object, you can use a variant of this same trick: you can create two copies of an object—one in a later layer and one in an earlier layer—and then use the set element to make one copy visible for part of the animation and the other copy visible for the rest. In Listing 8-3, you can see how to set an object's visibility, as each of the four sets of flames (coming out of the four engines) has a set element to make it disappear after 15 seconds of animation time.

Whichever type of animation you're using, the change is continuous—not a set of discrete frames. Most types of animation allow you to specify a simple to and from, along with the start time and the duration (using begin and dur), and the platform will ensure a smooth transition at a constant speed over the desired duration. To vary the speed, you can define a series of transformations given by values and keyTimes. For example, the spaceship grows according to a scale transformation (given near the bottom of Listing 8-3) in which it grows from 0.1 of its size to 0.25 of its size during the first 66 percent of the animation duration, and grows from 0.25 of its size to 0.5 of its size during the rest of the animation duration (which is spread over 15 seconds):

```
<animateTransform attributeName="transform" type="scale" values="0.1;0.25;0.5"
    keyTimes="0;0.66;1" dur="15s" fill="freeze" repeatCount="1"/>
```

You may notice that the spaceship is animated with two consecutive animateMotion elements at the bottom of Listing 8-3: one for flying onto the scene, and a second one for landing. If it were merely a question of changing the speed, I could have used keyPoints, which would allow me to break up the path into segments corresponding to keyTimes. In this case, however, the spaceship changes orientation as it comes in for a landing, engines first. The rotate="auto" attribute ensures that the spaceship will be pointing its nose in the same direction that it's flying along the path. Of course I ended up having to add a 90-degree rotation to the spaceship grouping since the rotate="auto" feature can't automatically guess which end of the object is meant to be the nose. Then, to descend in an upright position, the landing animation has a rotate attribute of 270 degrees to compensate for the earlier 90-degree rotation.

> **Note** Coordinates (and other numerical values) within SVG attributes can be separated either by commas or whitespace. Even whitespace is not technically necessary in cases where there's no ambiguity, and the command letter can be left off of repeated commands (in order to condense the file by eliminating redundant information). So, d="M 0, -3 L 0.4, 0.5 L 0.75 0.2" is the same as d="M0-3L.4.5.75.2". By contrast, the semicolons separating the various key values are not optional.

The most interesting part of the animation in Listing 8-3 is probably the window grouping. Even though the hull of the spaceship does not really spin, you can give the illusion that it's spinning by moving its surface features, such as the windows. Naturally, the shadow doesn't move, because the surface is meant to be made of smooth metal, with regions moving in and out of the light as it spins. Since the window is supposed to be part of the surface of the hull, it should appear to widen as it comes into view and contract as it goes out of view—but not at a constant rate. It needs to travel along the ship's surface (and expand and contract) as though it were moving along a circular path that bulges out toward the viewer. This can be easily accomplished by timing the animation with keySplines instead of keyTimes. In essence, the motion-to-*time* relation is curved instead of linear. So instead of moving along a path at a constant rate, the rate of motion varies according to a curve.

A *spline* is similar to a Bézier curve, with tangent segments given by critical points. The width of the window in Listing 8-3 is animated as follows:

```
<animateTransform attributeName="transform" type="scale"
    values="0.05,1;1,1;0.05,1" calcMode="spline"
    keySplines="0 .75 .25 1; .75 0 1 .25"
    dur="1s" fill="freeze" repeatCount="10.5"/>
```

The values attribute tells how much the object should be scaled in the x and y directions at the three key moments: the beginning, the middle, and the end. Note that the y-coordinate is always scaled by a factor of 1 (in other words not scaled at all) while the x-coordinate goes from 5 percent of the width to being full width to being 5 percent of the width again. The keySplines values describe the time curve between each set of values in the values attribute. There's one fewer set of keySplines values than values values because the values values are the endpoints, while the keySplines values describe the segments between them.

The keySplines values give only the critical points of the motion-to-time curve—the endpoints of the curve are assumed to be (0,0) and (1,1). So the two key spline curves in the preceding scaling animation are shown in Figure 8-8.

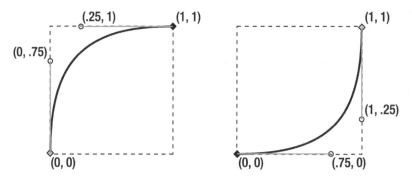

Figure 8-8. *The spline curves of the window-scaling transformation*

The window grouping also illustrates the fact that you can animate almost any attribute that you can draw in SVG. Just use the animate and animateColor elements. You can see (in Listing 8-3) that as the window pane moves from the light to the shadow, its color changes from white to dark gray.

Naturally, lighting effects can be done more realistically with a real 3D engine. But if you watch the animation, you'll see that using ad hoc tricks in 2D can give you a pretty reasonable approximation of 3D.

Adding an Animation to Your Game

If your animation is defined completely in SVG (like the spaceship animation in Listing 8-3), then it's quite simple to play it. You include the SVG file as a resource in your JAR/COD file and load it as you would any other resource. Then you instantiate the corresponding SVGAnimator and get its target component—which is a Canvas or Field that can be displayed on the device's screen—and set the animation to play.

To use the RIM graphics classes on the BlackBerry platform, just create the SVGAnimator with net.rim.device.api.ui.Field as an argument to get a Field target component, as shown in Listing 8-4. (The SVGAnimator is implemented behind the scenes by the Plazmic media engine.)

Listing 8-4. *SvgFieldAnimator.java*

```java
package net.frogparrot.svgmovie;

import java.io.InputStream;
import javax.microedition.m2g.*;

import net.rim.device.api.ui.Field;

import net.frogparrot.ui.*;

/**
 * This is a wrapper class for the SVGAnimator to make it
 * behave like other animated fields (for modularity).
 */
public class SvgFieldAnimator implements FieldAnimator {

//------------------------------------------------------------
//   fields

  /**
   * The underlying SVGFieldAnimator.
   */
  SVGAnimator myAnimator;

//------------------------------------------------------------
//   data initialization and cleanup

  /**
   * Load the animations.
   * @param viewportWidth width in pixels of the visible area.
   * @param viewportHeight height in pixels of the visible area.
   */
  public SvgFieldAnimator(int viewportWidth, int viewportHeight) {
    try {
      InputStream inputStream
          = getClass().getResourceAsStream("/space-animation.svg");

      // Load our svg image from the input stream:
      SVGImage animation = (SVGImage)SVGImage.createImage(inputStream, null);
      animation.setViewportWidth(viewportWidth);
      animation.setViewportHeight(viewportHeight);

      // The second argument tells the animator what type of object to return
      // as its "targetComponent" to draw on.
      myAnimator = SVGAnimator.createAnimator(animation,
          "net.rim.device.api.ui.Field");

      myAnimator.setTimeIncrement(0.05f);
    } catch(Exception e) {
```

```java
      // for debug
      System.out.println(e);
    }
  }

//----------------------------------------------------------
//    implementation of FieldAnimator

  /**
   * @see FieldAnimator#getField()
   */
  public Field getField() {
    return (Field)(myAnimator.getTargetComponent());
  }

  /**
   * @see FieldAnimator#frameAdvance()
   */
  public boolean frameAdvance() {
    return false;
  }

  /**
   * @see FieldAnimator#play()
   */
  public void play() {
    myAnimator.play();
  }

  /**
   * @see FieldAnimator#pause()
   */
  public void pause() {
    myAnimator.pause();
  }

  /**
   * @see FieldAnimator#stop()
   */
  public void stop() {
    myAnimator.stop();
  }

  /**
   * @see FieldAnimator#setTimeIncrementMillis(long)
   */
  public void setTimeIncrementMillis(long timeIncrement) {
    myAnimator.setTimeIncrement(timeIncrement/1000);
  }

  /**
   * @see FieldAnimator#keyChar(char, int, int)
   */
  public boolean keyChar(char key, int status, int time) {
    return false;
```

```
}

/**
 * @see FieldAnimator#navigationMovement(int, int, int, int)
 */
public boolean navigationMovement(int dx, int dy, int status, int time) {
    return false;
}

}
```

The main points to notice in Listing 8-4 are the lines where you set the viewport width and height. The coordinate system within the SVG file has nothing to do with the pixel-based coordinate system of your device's screen. As mentioned previously, the beauty of SVG is that images can be naturally rendered at any size. But there's a little bit of work to do to tell the SVG engine exactly how big you want the image.

The first step is found in the svg element at the very top of Listing 8-3. Its viewBox attribute tells which part of the SVG image/animation is the visible region *with respect to the coordinate system of the SVG file*. In this case, the value is "0 0 480 640", which means that the part of the SVG image/animation to show is the rectangle of width 480 and height 640 with (0,0) as its top-left corner. The svg element's width and height attributes, by contrast, are meant to give a hint about how big to make the image *in terms of pixels on the device display*. If you do nothing to modify the viewport width and height, then the target component's dimensions in pixels will match the svg element's width and height attribute values.

> **Note** Unlike many timer functions, the SVGAnimator class's setTimeIncrement() method takes an argument in seconds (given as a float) rather than in milliseconds (given as an int). This method sets the delay between frames rendered, so the time increment of 0.05f (used in the constructor of Listing 8-4) gives a frame rate of 20 frames per second.

If you'd like to use the same SVG file on screens of different sizes, however, you can override the suggested width and height using the methods setViewportWidth() and setViewportHeight(), as shown in the constructor of Listing 8-4. The one thing to beware of is that if your new width/height ratio is different from the width/height ratio found in the file, the SVG engine may show parts of the image that were not meant to be visible. In this example, the viewbox is a lot taller than it is wide. If you try to set it to fill the whole screen on a widescreen BlackBerry device, the SVGAnimator will show the whole viewbox—centered in the middle of the screen—plus some additional regions on either side of the viewbox. That's why if you look at the background grouping of Listing 8-3, you'll see that a rectangle much wider than the viewbox is painted black and filled with stars. I just did that so that it wouldn't be a problem to play the animation on a wide screen as well as on a narrow screen (to allow more flexibility in screen layout).

The SVGFieldAnimator class in Listing 8-4 is essentially just a wrapper for the SVGAnimator class to make it behave like other types of animated fields. It implements a general FieldAnimator interface so that different types of animated game screens can be placed in the same Manager, as you'll see later in this chapter and the next. Figure 8-9 shows the structure of the little package that helps keep the animation code modular so that it can be reused.

::net.frogparrot.ui

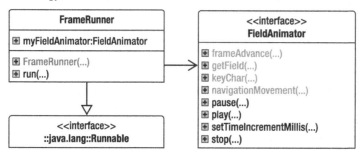

Figure 8-9. *The structure of the net.frogparrot.ui package*

The Screen that actually displays the animation is less generic, so it goes in this application's own special package, shown in Figure 8-10. As usual, the Main life cycle class has to be in the application's own package as well to distinguish it from the other Main classes in BlackBerry's global namespace. (Since there are no surprises in this Main class, it's not reprinted here—download the complete source code from www.apress.com.)

The SvgScreen class (Listing 8-5) is a typical RIM Screen, specially implemented to display a Field that is controlled by a net.frogparrot.ui.FieldAnimator. Looking in the constructor, you can see how it works together with the SVGFieldAnimator class from Listing 8-4: the SvgScreen creates an SVGFieldAnimator of the right size to fill the display, it gets the underlying Field from the SVGFieldAnimator, it fills the display with it, and it starts it up with a call to play().

::net.frogparrot.svg

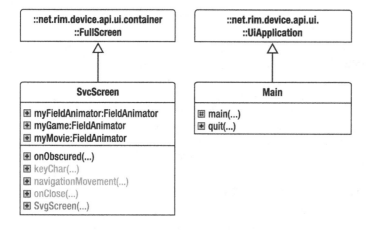

Figure 8-10. *The structure of the net.frogparrot.svg package*

The reason for extending RIM's `FullScreen` class (instead of the usual `MainScreen`) is that this simple application doesn't need the added menu functionality of the `MainScreen`. With only one screen and no danger of having a menu pop up, you can have the application quit and clean up in the `onObscured()` method. It's a fairly simple way of handling the different ways the user can exit the application (such as by pressing the red key, which is dealt with in different ways in Chapters 6 and 9).

Listing 8-5. *SvgScreen.java*

```java
package net.frogparrot.svg;

import net.rim.device.api.ui.Screen;
import net.rim.device.api.ui.container.FullScreen;
import net.rim.device.api.ui.Field;
import net.rim.device.api.ui.Graphics;
import net.rim.device.api.system.Display;

import net.frogparrot.svggame.SvgController;
import net.frogparrot.svgmovie.SvgFieldAnimator;

import net.frogparrot.ui.FieldAnimator;

/**
 * A Simple screen to paint the SVG opening animation and
 * the SVG game on.
 */
public class SvgScreen extends FullScreen {

//-----------------------------------------------------------
//   fields

  /**
   * The opening animation runner.
   */
  FieldAnimator myMovie;

  /**
   * The game runner.
   */
  FieldAnimator myGame;

  /**
   * Whichever animator is current.
   */
  FieldAnimator myFieldAnimator;

//-----------------------------------------------------------
//   data initialization and cleanup

  /**
   * Initialize the screen.
   */
  SvgScreen() {
    super();
    try {
```

```java
      int screenWidth = Display.getWidth();
      int screenHeight = Display.getHeight();
      myMovie = new SvgFieldAnimator(screenWidth, screenHeight);
      myFieldAnimator = myMovie;
      add(myMovie.getField());
      myMovie.play();
    } catch(Exception e) {
      System.out.println(e);
    }
  }

  /**
   * This is called by the BlackBerry platform when
   * the screen is popped off the screen stack.
   */
  public boolean onClose() {
    if(myMovie != null) {
      myMovie.stop();
      myMovie = null;
      int screenWidth = Display.getWidth();
      int screenHeight = Display.getHeight();
      myGame = new SvgController(screenWidth, screenHeight);
      deleteAll();
      add(myGame.getField());
      myFieldAnimator = myGame;
      myGame.play();
      // the screen is not removed:
      return false;
    } else if(myGame != null) {
      myGame.stop();
      myGame = null;
      myFieldAnimator = null;
    }
    // end the program.
    Main.quit();
    // confirm that the screen has been removed:
    return true;
  }

  /**
   * This is to end the game if the game is sent to the
   * background for any reason (such as red key or green key).
   * If the game has more than one screen, use keyDown()
   * instead, as illustrated in the Swinging Saber game.
   */
  protected void onObscured() {
    if(myMovie != null) {
      myMovie.stop();
      myMovie = null;
    }
    if(myGame != null) {
      myGame.stop();
      myGame = null;
    }
    myFieldAnimator = null;
```

```
    // end the program.
    Main.quit();
  }

//--------------------------------------------------------
//   user input

  /**
   * Override keyChar to direct key input to the animator.
   * @return Whether the key input was used.
   */
  public boolean keyChar(char key, int status, int time) {
    return myFieldAnimator.keyChar(key, status, time);
  }

  /**
   * Override navigationMovement to direct key input to the animator.
   * @see net.rim.device.api.ui.Screen#navigationMovement(int, int, int, int)
   */
  public boolean navigationMovement(int dx, int dy, int status, int time) {
    return myFieldAnimator.navigationMovement(dx, dy, status, time);
  }

}
```

You can see in the keyChar() and navigationMovement() methods at the bottom of Listing 8-5 that this screen just passes the user input along to the FieldAnimator to handle it. The SVG animation has no use for this input, but it's used by the new implementation of FieldAnimator that you'll see in the next section. If you look at the onClose() method—which the platform calls when the user presses Esc—you'll see that the SvgScreen stops the animation, cleans it up, and replaces it with an SVG game.

Creating a Game in SVG

In this section, you'll see the SVG Space Explorer game that lets the user drive the spaceship from the earlier SVG Space Explorer animation. This example is meant to illustrate the theory—to show what's possible with SVG and how to do it. Keep in mind, however, that an SVG-based game is typically far more resource-intensive than a comparable sprite-based game, so choosing to use SVG limits your possible target devices. Only the high-end (4.6.0-plus) BlackBerry devices have the SVG APIs implemented, and even then you still need to be careful to test your game on your target devices during the development phase to be sure that they can handle it.

The starting point for the SVG Space Explorer game was naturally the space-animation.svg file from Listing 8-3. I had to make changes throughout the file, and I think that reprinting the complete new version here would be more confusing than helpful, so I'll just highlight the changes. The complete alternate SVG file for the game is bundled with the source code as space-components.svg.

First of all, I deleted the planet entirely because it isn't needed. Then I deleted the fixed animations for the spaceship (following a set path and growing) because directing the spaceship is the player's job. Naturally, I also eliminated the transformation that rotated the spaceship by 90 degrees (because that was only to compensate for the `rotate="auto"` attribute of the path animation, as explained previously), and instead added a translation to center the spaceship, as explained following. Then I changed the `repeatCount` attributes on all of the spinning and flame-flickering animations to `indefinite` so that the spaceship never stops spinning. Similarly, I deleted the commands that set the flames to invisible after 15 seconds.

Controlling the SVG Animation from the Code

To run the spaceship animation during the game, it's actually possible to use an `SVGAnimator`, as in Listing 8-4. While an `SVGAnimator` is playing, you can modify the image data, and the animator will update the rendered image. But if you want to coordinate the animation updates with the updates from user commands, you need to take a little more hands-on approach to timing.

Since the animation is part of the user interface, updates need to be performed by the event thread. To get your action to be run by the event thread, you need to wrap it an a `Runnable` and pass the `Runnable` to `Application.invokeLater()` or `Application.invokeAndWait()`. If you look at Figure 8-9, you'll see that the `FieldAnimator` interface has a very simple little helper class called `FrameRunner` to allow you to have the `FieldAnimator.frameAdvance()` method called from another thread. All `FrameRunner` does is call `FieldAnimator.frameAdvance()` from its `run()` method.

The game naturally requires a more interesting implementation of the `FieldAnimator` interface, shown in Listing 8-6. You can see that the game animation is launched from the `play()` method, which passes the `FrameRunner` to `Application.invokeLater()` in order to invoke the `SvgController.frameAdvance()` method once every 100 milliseconds. The `invokeLater()` method (with the `repeat` option set to true) acts very much like a `java.util.TimerTask` run by a `java.util.Timer`—just pass it a `Runnable` for it to invoke repeatedly at fixed intervals. (Using a `TimerTask` run by a `Timer` is illustrated in the next chapter.) The problem with using the `invokeLater()` method to repeatedly advance your animation is that it's not necessarily guaranteed to call your animation code at a fixed rate. According to the JavaDoc, "The runnable object will be added to the event queue after each period of milliseconds specified by the time parameter." Basically, the event thread has more important things to do than advance your animation, so when its queue starts getting full, that can throw off the timing. Andrew's game thread implementation from Chapter 6 shows one strategy for getting tighter control over the animation timing. In this case, however, we'll just use the simple solution and optimize it later if tests show that it's necessary.

Listing 8-6. *SvgController.java*

```java
package net.frogparrot.svggame;

import java.io.InputStream;
import javax.microedition.m2g.*;

import org.w3c.dom.*;
```

```java
import org.w3c.dom.svg.*;

import net.rim.device.api.ui.Field;
import net.rim.device.api.ui.Graphics;
import net.rim.device.api.ui.UiApplication;

import net.frogparrot.ui.*;

/**
 * This is an illustration of how an SVG animation
 * can be controlled to form a game.
 */
public class SvgController extends Field implements FieldAnimator {

//-----------------------------------------------------------
//   fields

  /**
   * The SVG image built from the image data in the file.
   */
  SVGImage myImage;

  /**
   * The root element.
   */
  SVGSVGElement mySvgSvg;

  /**
   * Game objects that are described in the SVG file.
   */
  SVGLocatableElement mySpaceship;
  SVGLocatableElement myFlames1;
  SVGLocatableElement myFlames2;
  SVGLocatableElement myFlames3;
  SVGLocatableElement myFlames4;

  /**
   * The Graphics instance that is used for drawing operations.
   */
  ScalableGraphics myScalableGraphics;

/**
 * The width (in screen pixels) of the visible region.
 */
 int myViewportWidth;

/**
 * The height (in screen pixels) of the visible region.
 */
 int myViewportHeight;

/**
 * The spaceship's current location and direction, in terms of SVG coordinates.
 */
 float mySpaceshipX;
```

```
    float mySpaceshipY;
    float mySpaceshipAngle;

  /**
   * The data and objects to control the game animation.
   */
  int myInvokeLaterId = -1;
  long myTimeIncrement = 100;
  FrameRunner myFrameRunner;

  /**
   * The user's latest input data.
   */
  char myInput = (char)-1;


//-----------------------------------------------------------
//    data initialization and cleanup

  /**
   * Load the image data and modify it based on the viewport dimensions.
   * @param viewportWidth width in pixels of the visible area.
   * @param viewportHeight height in pixels of the visible area.
   */
  public SvgController(int viewportWidth, int viewportHeight) {
    super(Field.FOCUSABLE);
    try {
      myScalableGraphics = ScalableGraphics.createInstance();
      myViewportWidth = viewportWidth;
      myViewportHeight = viewportHeight;
      // get the resource from the file:
      InputStream inputStream
          = getClass().getResourceAsStream("/space-components.svg");
      myImage = (SVGImage)SVGImage.createImage(inputStream, null);

      // The SVGSVGElement has some interesting functionality
      // to control the whole image:
      Document doc = myImage.getDocument();
      mySvgSvg = (SVGSVGElement)doc.getDocumentElement();

      // Get handles to the elements that represent components of the image:
      mySpaceship = (SVGLocatableElement)doc.getElementById("spaceship");
      myFlames1 = (SVGLocatableElement)doc.getElementById("flames-1");
      myFlames2 = (SVGLocatableElement)doc.getElementById("flames-2");
      myFlames3 = (SVGLocatableElement)doc.getElementById("flames-3");
      myFlames4 = (SVGLocatableElement)doc.getElementById("flames-4");
      // the engine flames should be invisible except when the rocket is moving:
      myFlames1.setTrait("visibility", "hidden");
      myFlames2.setTrait("visibility", "hidden");
      myFlames3.setTrait("visibility", "hidden");
      myFlames4.setTrait("visibility", "hidden");

      // tell the SVG Image how big to scale itself:
      myImage.setViewportWidth(viewportWidth);
      myImage.setViewportHeight(viewportHeight);
```

```
      // move the animation forward very slightly because it's
      // the animation the puts the engines in place:
      myImage.incrementTime(0.01f);

      // Create the runnable that advances the animation:
      myFrameRunner = new FrameRunner(this);
    } catch(Exception e) {
      // for debug
      System.out.println(e);
    }
  }

//----------------------------------------------------------
//   implementation of Field

  /**
   * When this field is laid out, it merely claims all of the
   * area that it is given.
   */
  protected void layout(int width, int height) {
    setExtent(width, height);
  }

  /**
   * Paint the SVG image onto the field.
   * @param g The Graphics object that draws into the Field.
   */
  protected void paint(Graphics g) {
    myScalableGraphics.bindTarget(g);
    myScalableGraphics.render(0, 0, myImage);
    myScalableGraphics.releaseTarget();
  }

//----------------------------------------------------------
//   implementation of FieldAnimator

  /**
   * @see FieldAnimator#getField()
   */
  public Field getField() {
    return this;
  }

  /**
   * @see FieldAnimator#frameAdvance()
   */
  public boolean frameAdvance() {
    try {
      // advance the animation:
      myImage.incrementTime(0.15f);
      // get the latest user input, and clear the input data:
      char key = (char)-1;
      synchronized(this) {
        key = myInput;
```

```
        myInput = (char)-1;
      }
      // move the spaceship accordingly:
      SVGMatrix spaceshipTransform = mySpaceship.getMatrixTrait("transform");
      if(key == (char)-1) {
        // just turn the flames off:
        myFlames1.setTrait("visibility", "hidden");
        myFlames2.setTrait("visibility", "hidden");
        myFlames3.setTrait("visibility", "hidden");
        myFlames4.setTrait("visibility", "hidden");
      } else if(key == 'd') {
        // scale up
        spaceshipTransform.mScale(1.25f);
      } else if(key == 'x') {
        // scale down
        spaceshipTransform.mScale(0.75f);
      } else if(key == 'f') {
        // rotate clockwise:
        mySpaceshipAngle += 45f;
        // apply the rotation to the current transformation:
        spaceshipTransform.mRotate(45f);
      } else if(key == 'e') {
        // turn the flames on when the ship moves forward:
        myFlames1.setTrait("visibility", "visible");
        myFlames2.setTrait("visibility", "visible");
        myFlames3.setTrait("visibility", "visible");
        myFlames4.setTrait("visibility", "visible");
        // Move the spaceship in the direction it is pointing:
        spaceshipTransform.mTranslate(0f, -100f);
      } else if(key == 's') {
        // rotate counterclockwise:
        mySpaceshipAngle -= 45f;
        // apply the rotation to the current transformation:
        spaceshipTransform.mRotate(-45f);
      }
      // Once the matrix has been modified, it has to be set back
      // into the spaceship element in order to take effect:
      mySpaceship.setMatrixTrait("transform", spaceshipTransform);
      // The call to invalidate forces a repaint operation:
      invalidate(0, 0, myViewportWidth, myViewportHeight);
    } catch(Exception e) {
      System.out.println(e);
    }
    return true;
  }

  /**
   * @see FieldAnimator#play()
   */
  public void play() {
    // Application#invokeLater has a built-in timer function
    // so it can be used to advance an animation from the
    // event thread. Don't forget to save the ID so that
    // you can stop the animation later!
    myInvokeLaterId = UiApplication.getUiApplication().invokeLater(
```

```
      myFrameRunner, myTimeIncrement, true);
}

/**
 * @see FieldAnimator#pause()
 */
public void pause() {
  stop();
}

/**
 * @see FieldAnimator#stop()
 */
public void stop() {
  if(myInvokeLaterId != -1) {
    UiApplication.getUiApplication().cancelInvokeLater(myInvokeLaterId);
    myInvokeLaterId = -1;
  }
}

/**
 * @see FieldAnimator#setTimeIncrementMillis(long)
 */
public void setTimeIncrementMillis(long timeIncrement) {
  if(timeIncrement <= 0) {
    throw new IllegalArgumentException("timeIncrement must be positive");
  }
  myTimeIncrement = timeIncrement;
}

/**
 * @see FieldAnimator#keyChar(char, int, int)
 */
public synchronized boolean keyChar(char key, int status, int time) {
  if((key == 's') || (key == 'd') || (key == 'f') ||
     (key == 'e') || (key == 'x')) {
    myInput = key;
    return true;
  } else {
    // the keystroke was not relevant to this game
    return false;
  }
}

/**
 * @see FieldAnimator#navigationMovement(int, int, int, int)
 */
public synchronized boolean navigationMovement(int dx, int dy,
      int status, int time) {
  // map navigation input to key input for simplicity:
  if(dx < 0) { //left
    myInput = 's';
  } else if(dx > 0) { // right
    myInput = 'f';
  } else if(dy < 0) { // up
```

```
      myInput = 'e';
    } else {
      // the motion was not relevant to this game
      return false;
    }
    // the motion was used by this game
    return true;
  }

}
```

The frameAdvance() method is where the action occurs. The first step is to call the incrementTime() method on the image to advance the spinning/flaming animation. In Listing 8-6 you actually advance the animation by .15f seconds (150 milliseconds) even though there's really only been a 100-millisecond delay since the last call to frameAdvance(). This isn't a problem because the animation can be played at any speed (just like it can be scaled to any size). In this case, you're essentially just applying a scaling factor to the animation's time dimension.

The next step is to read and interpret the user input. The synchronized blocks ensure that each input command is used only once. Synchronization is not technically necessary here since the navigationMovement(), keyChar(), and frameAdvance() methods are all called by the event thread. Still, from this application's perspective, these calls have different entry points, and it's nice to be aware of places like this where threading issues could occur if the platform were to call one of these methods from the wrong thread.

Understanding Coordinates and Transformations

The spaceship and the flames coming out of the engines are transformed based on the user's input. The spaceship and the flames correspond to g groupings from the SVG file. If you look back at Listing 8-3, you can see that some of the elements have id attributes with values like "spaceship" and "flames-1". The constructor in Listing 8-6 shows what those id attributes are good for—they allow you to easily locate interesting branches of your data tree using the getElementById() method.

Once you have a handle to a branch of a data tree, you can transform it. In this case you can see that—in response to user input—you take out the spaceship's transform and modify it by rotating, scaling, or translating it, and then you put it back in. Then you call the Field.invalidate() method to force a repaint. Notice that (unlike in the SVGAnimator case) the SVGImage isn't transparently bound to the Field object behind the scenes. You implement the SVGImage-to-Field binding yourself in the Field.paint() method. It's just a couple of simple lines to tell the Field to render this SVGImage on itself when it gets painted.

In addition to the spaceship's transformations, the flames are only set to be visible when the spaceship is actually moving. I realize that since there's no air resistance in space, the ship wouldn't really just move forward a short distance (and stop!) for each blast of the engines, so this game requires a little bit of artistic license and suspension of disbelief. Figure 8-11 shows the SVG Space Explorer game in action.

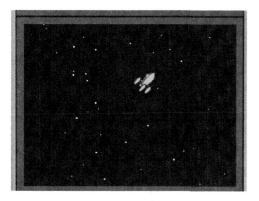

Figure 8-11. *The SVG Space Explorer game*

We need a little bit of background about the SVG coordinate system in order to explain why the transformation `spaceshipTransform.mTranslate(0f, -100f)` is the right transformation to move the ship one step forward in its current direction. It's very similar to the coordinate system used by the `javax.microedition.m3g` package, as you'll see the "2D vs. 3D Graphics in Java ME" sidebar.

2D VS. 3D GRAPHICS IN JAVA ME

The `javax.microedition.m2g` package defined in JSR 226 naturally has a lot in common with the `javax.microedition.m3g` package from JSR 184. If you've got the hang of one of them, it's not too hard to learn the other. (They're also related to the OpenGL ES coordinates that you'll see in Chapter 12.)

Both the 2D and the 3D APIs use matrix multiplication on the position coordinates to perform transformations like rotations and scaling. An additional dimension is included so that translations—which are fundamentally additive—can also be expressed through matrix multiplication. So a 2D point has coordinates (x,y,1) and a 3D point has coordinates (x,y,z,1) when a transformation matrix acts on it. It's very simple to see how this works in two dimensions with a scale transformation, a translation by (t1,t2), and a rotation:

$$\begin{pmatrix} s & 0 & 0 \\ 0 & s & 0 \\ 0 & 0 & 1 \end{pmatrix} \begin{pmatrix} x \\ y \\ 1 \end{pmatrix} = (sx, sy, 1)$$

$$\begin{pmatrix} 1 & 0 & t1 \\ 0 & 1 & t2 \\ 0 & 0 & 1 \end{pmatrix} \begin{pmatrix} x \\ y \\ 1 \end{pmatrix} = (x+t1, y+t2, 1)$$

$$\begin{pmatrix} \cos\theta & -\sin\theta & 0 \\ \sin\theta & \cos\theta & 0 \\ 0 & 0 & 1 \end{pmatrix} \begin{pmatrix} x \\ y \\ 1 \end{pmatrix} = (x\cos\theta - y\sin\theta, x\sin\theta + y\cos\theta, 1)$$

If the rotation isn't immediately obvious, just think of a 90-degree angle (which has cos 0 and sin 1), and you can see how the coordinate axes are rotated in a counterclockwise direction. The skew transformations as well as the scaling in a single direction are equally simple. The corresponding transformations work in fundamentally the same way in 3D (with four-dimensional coordinates and matrices).

In SVG, the transformations are simple enough that you don't generally have to think about how they translate into matrices. To perform multiple transformations on a part of your drawing, you can just nest a series of g elements, each with a simple transformation. Transformation nesting is shown in the nacelle-3 grouping in Listing 8-3. However, if you prefer to define your transformations in terms of matrices, you have that option both in the SVG file and in the code.

In the code, you can use your drawing's root-level SVGSVGElement to create an SVGMatrix using the method createSVGMatrixComponents(float a, float b, float c, float d, float e, and float f). The method creates the corresponding transformation matrix (which can be set as the transformation matrix for any SVGElement in the drawing):

$$\begin{pmatrix} a & c & e \\ b & d & f \\ 0 & 0 & 1 \end{pmatrix}$$

In both 2D and 3D, the image data has a tree structure. The actual coordinates are found at the leaves of the data tree, and the transformations are applied to them successively as the graphics interpreter makes its way to the root. And in both APIs, you can define animations based on smooth transitions framed by "key" times.

Creating a mesh in 3D space and projecting it onto a 2D screen is obviously far more complex than just drawing a 2D polygon. The relative simplicity of 2D graphics gives you some fun advantages in the SVG world that you don't have in M3G. For example, even though M3G files are data trees like SVG files, they're not written in human-readable XML because they would be too big. Similarly, smoothing a 3D surface (as SVG does with Bézier curves) isn't practical on a handset.

So it's not just a matter of "3D is just like 2D, only better." Each API has its advantages and disadvantages that determine which one is the best choice for a given application.

The fundamental point to remember is that the transformations work by applying a transformation matrix to the object's coordinates. That means that a rotation transformation isn't going to automatically rotate an object around its *own* center—it rotates the object around the origin: point (0,0). Similarly, a scaling operation may appear to move an object if the object isn't defined in terms of coordinates that are centered around the origin.

Note that this doesn't mean that the object needs to be at the center of the screen to be scaled or rotated correctly. Each branch of the SVG image tree has its own internal coordinate system. The transformations you find as you go toward the root define how to get from a branch's local coordinates to the overall image coordinates defined at the viewbox level. So you can use the getElementById() method to get a handle to a data leaf defined around its own local origin—and apply a transformation at that stage—before another transformation moves it to its final location.

You might have noticed that the class org.w3g.dom.svg.SVGSVGElement (which represents the whole image) has a whole series of transformation methods of its own.

These are to set transformations that will be applied at the very root of the data tree. So they're useful for things like maps, where you want to be able to scale and pan the whole image without getting into the nitty-gritty data structure, but they're not at all helpful for delicate interactions among different components of the image.

In the SVG Space Explorer game, I mentioned previously that the last change I made when converting the animation SVG file (space-animation.svg) to the game SVG file (space-components.svg, included in the source code) was to translate the spaceship branch so that it's centered around its own origin. That was to simplify the transformations that move the spaceship.

When the spaceship is pointing upward (which is its default position), the move command (char 'e' or the up navigation movement) should make it move a short distance upward on the game screen. So the translation (0f, -100f) makes sense (when you remember that going up means decreasing the y-coordinate).

To see why the same transformation causes the spaceship to move in the direction its pointing—even after a rotation—you just do a quick matrix calculation. Keep in mind that the SVGMatrix.mTranslate() method (like all of its m<Transform> methods) acts by multiplying the new transformation *on the right* of the existing transformation. Here's what happens when you apply a translation to a rotation matrix on the right:

$$
\begin{pmatrix} \cos\theta & -\sin\theta & 0 \\ \sin\theta & \cos\theta & 0 \\ 0 & 0 & 1 \end{pmatrix}
\begin{pmatrix} 1 & 0 & t1 \\ 0 & 1 & t2 \\ 0 & 0 & 1 \end{pmatrix}
= \begin{pmatrix} \cos\theta & -\sin\theta & t1\cos\theta - t2\sin\theta \\ \sin\theta & \cos\theta & t1\sin\theta + t2\cos\theta \\ 0 & 0 & 1 \end{pmatrix}
$$

It applies the rotation to the translation itself! So instead of moving a distance of (0, –100f), the translation vector is rotated in the direction the spaceship is currently pointing before being applied. It's a pretty slick trick for game programmers who are used to having to take into account a sprite's current direction data in order to decide how to move!

The scaling transformation has a similar interaction with the translation, only simpler. You'll see when you play this game that the ship moves a very short distance when it's shrunken down compared to how far it moves when it is enlarged.

The next obvious question is what to do if you want to translate an object but you *don't* want the object's current orientation to affect the translation. You simply apply the translation on the left:

$$
\begin{pmatrix} 1 & 0 & t1 \\ 0 & 1 & t2 \\ 0 & 0 & 1 \end{pmatrix}
\begin{pmatrix} \cos\theta & \sin\theta & 0 \\ \sin\theta & \cos\theta & 0 \\ 0 & 0 & 1 \end{pmatrix}
= \begin{pmatrix} \cos\theta & \sin\theta & t1 \\ \sin\theta & \cos\theta & t2 \\ 0 & 0 & 1 \end{pmatrix}
$$

You can see that the two transformations don't interfere with each other when applied in this order. That's why the rotation and scaling transformations in the frameAdvance() method work as expected even after the user has translated the spaceship around the screen.

The SVGMatrix class doesn't have a built-in function for multiplying a transformation on the left, but it's very easy to improvise one. First, use SVGMatrix.createSVGMatrixComponents(float a, float b, float c, float d, float e, float f) to create your desired matrix. Next get your SVGElement's transform matrix and apply it to your created matrix by sending it as an argument to the right-hand multiplication method mMultiply(). Lastly, set the resulting matrix as your SVGElement's transform matrix. Or—even simpler—grab handles to two nested g elements and transform them individually.

Summary

SVG allows you to create exciting opening sequences and between-level animations for your game—even for older-model BlackBerry smartphones. On more advanced models, SVG can even be used to implement unique and original games. The coordinates and transformations used by SVG are related to those used by 3D graphics, so—once you understand the theory—you're on your way to creating all sorts of exciting game graphics!

The Space Explorer game from this chapter isn't quite a complete game, though, because it doesn't have an object or any way to win. But starting from these raw materials (an object that the user can move around the screen), there are lots of possibilities for how to complete the game. For example, you could add a scoring mechanism (and music!) like the Swinging Saber game of Chapter 6. Or you could turn it into a role-playing game where you interact with other players over the Internet. You'll see how to do that in the next chapter.

Creating Role-Playing Games on the Internet

Internet-friendliness is one of BlackBerry's biggest draws. Being able to access your e-mail (and the rest of the Internet) while you're on the go is essentially the whole point of having a BlackBerry smartphone. So creating a social game (using the Internet) is a fun way to build on the BlackBerry platform's strengths!

The Internet allows you to create a universe for your game where *everyone in the world* who is currently playing the game can (virtually) find each other. Group games of this type have existed practically ever since people figured out how to network two terminals together, and massively multiplayer online role-playing games (MMORPGs) perennially rank among the most popular (and addictive) games on the market! And the really fun part—the social interaction with live, intelligent opponents—is one thing that a BlackBerry smartphone can deliver as well as a PC or a game console.

In this chapter, you'll see how to make the Tweet Space game, which is a game where you explore a virtual asteroid belt in a virtual spaceship and meet *real* people there (flying their own virtual spaceships). The game uses the Twitter social networking platform (http://twitter.com) as the server component to transfer the messages among the players. The game logic builds on the sprite and animation techniques you've seen in Chapters 6 and 8. Figure 9-1 shows what the finished game looks like.

Figure 9-1. *The Tweet Space game running on the BlackBerry 8900 simulator*

Communicating via HTTP

HTTP is probably the most important communication protocol for an application programmer to understand. It's the standard language of the Internet—used by browsers as well as small devices—so it's widely supported. It's also easy to find tools to help you test and troubleshoot communications problems. I assume that most people reading this know HTTP well, but if you don't, it's pretty simple.

At the lowest level, network communications come down to a stream of ones and zeros that are transmitted through a cable or over the airwaves. A protocol is just a language for those bits that expresses how the data should be divided into packets, routed, and interpreted. Different protocols can be built on top of one another by filling the data payload of one protocol with the language of another protocol. For example, Twitter sends data encoded in a format such as XML or JSON, which is sent as the body data of an HTTP request or response, and the HTTP-encoded messages are transported as the data content of transmissions in the TCP/IP protocol.

When programming games and other user applications, you don't usually have to worry about how the TCP/IP protocol routes the messages. (Although with BlackBerry, you do have to worry about it a little bit—see the "HTTP Connections in the BlackBerry World" sidebar.) You normally just have to deal with the HTTP protocol, which is a language for sending requests that (essentially) consist of the following parts:

- An *address*, which may contain additional routing information and other arguments for the destination application to interpret

- A *command* (such as GET or POST), which, naturally, indicates whether you'd like to get data from the remote source or post some there

- A set of *headers*, which are property/value pairs giving information about the sending application/device and the types of data it is sending or can accept

- A *body*, which is the block of data being transferred

HTTP is a two-part protocol in which each request from the client requires a response from the server. The response has almost the same format as the request, except that it has a numerical response code instead of a command. The response codes are three-digit numbers indicating whether the operation succeeded or failed, and giving a hint as to why. A response code of 200 means that the request succeeded, something in the 400 to 499 range indicates a problem with the request, and something in the 500 to 599 range indicates a server error.

Implementing Communications in a Game

BlackBerry uses the standard CLDC javax.microedition.io classes to implement HTTP connections. The HttpConnection implementation handles the grunt work of parsing the data stream into the parts described previously, allowing you to access the data with simple getters and setters.

> **Tip** When you get a cryptic error message in a networked game, it's often difficult to tell whether the problem is in the client or the server or both. You'll save yourself a lot of time when troubleshooting if you use tools like cURL (`http://curl.haxx.se`) and Wireshark (`www.wireshark.org`). cURL allows you to send simple HTTP requests from the command line (and gives you the server's response) so that you can simulate the message your client application is supposed to be sending and confirm that the server responds properly. Wireshark captures (and shows you) the precise data that is sent in each direction so that you can easily trace bugs to their source. For a GET command, you can also test the server by merely typing the URL in your browser, but be aware that if the server component takes into account the client's `User-Agent` header, its behavior with the browser may be different than the behavior when using the actual client.

Sending and receiving data over HTTP is quite simple. You take the *uniform resource locator* (URL)—that is, the Internet address of the server you'd like to connect to—and use it as the argument to the `Connector.open()` method. The `Connector` parses the URL and opens the connection, returning it to you wrapped in the correct type of `Connection` object (`HttpConnection` in this case). A simple example looks like this:

```
public void run() {
  HttpConnection connection
      = (HttpConnection)(Connector.open("http://example.com/servlet/myservlet"));
  connection.setRequestMethod(HttpConnection.GET);
  InputStream is = connection.openInputStream();
  // read the data from the stream
  is.close();
  connection.close;
}
```

I've wrapped the operative code in a `run()` method to emphasize the fact that you have to be careful about threading when programming network communications. Opening the HTTP connection (and reading data from it) is a blocking operation, so it can't be done on the event thread. As discussed in Chapter 7, calling a blocking operation from the event thread can cause the application to freeze and crash. In this case, the platform will probably try to pop up a permission dialog to ask the user if it's OK for your game to communicate via HTTP, *but* it needs to use the event thread to display the dialog (which is a problem if you've instructed the event thread to listen on the connection socket). So you normally have the event thread trigger another thread to handle the communications, as you'll see in Listing 9-1.

There's a little bit of added complexity when programming HTTP on the BlackBerry platform, explained in the "HTTP Connections in the BlackBerry World" sidebar.

HTTP CONNECTIONS IN THE BLACKBERRY WORLD

A typical handset connects to the Internet by passing through the operator's gateway. The handset sends the data over the air to the operator (such as T-Mobile or Orange), and the operator passes it along to the

Internet. BlackBerry is a little more complicated because the route to the Internet might follow the standard path, but it might not. For people using BlackBerry's enterprise solutions, the data channel may pass through the BlackBerry network or through a company intranet instead of passing through the operator's Internet gateway. Additionally, it's possible for a BlackBerry smartphone to connect to the Internet directly using Wi-Fi or through a USB cable that's connected to a PC.

The RIM APIs allow your application to query the device to check its network coverage as well as providing *servicebook* classes to tell you which types of connections are available for the device. Then you can select which type of message routing you'd like by appending special code parameters to your URL when you call `Connector.open()`.Before BlackBerry version 5.0, however, RIM didn't provide a method that allows you to say "just open the cheapest connection that works"—which is what you want in a nonbusiness-related game like Tweet Space.

Fortunately, Marcus Watkins tackled this problem when developing the VersatileMonkey PodTrapper application. You can read the whole story on the Web at `www.versatilemonkey.com/story.html`. He has given his `HttpConnectionFactory` class to the public domain. It's bundled with the source code of Tweet Space, and it's also available for download at the following address:

`www.versatilemonkey.com/blog/index.php/2009/06/24/networking-helper-class`

The `HttpConnectionFactory` class returns an `HttpConnection` just like the one you'd get from `Connector.open()`. And, like the standard `Connector.open()` method, it can be switched from HTTP to HTTPS just by changing the protocol prefix of the URL. To get the most out of the `HttpConnectionFactory`, you need to wrap the code that uses the `HttpConnection` inside a `try...catch` block that's in a loop that will try the next type of connection if the first one fails. This inconvenient trick is necessary because there are some connection problems that can only be detected by catching the `Exception` upon failure. The `httpRequest()` method of Listing 9-1 illustrates a typical use of the `HttpConnectionFactory` class.

You can restrict the types of connections that the `HttpConnectionFactory` class will attempt to make by constructing it with different constants (indicating different classes of connection types). In Chapter 11, Andrew restricts the connection types in order to prevent the Fox and Hounds game from making a connection through the *BlackBerry Internet Service* (BIS). If you're not a member of the BlackBerry Alliance Program, that's what you're supposed to do. However, it's not clear that RIM plans to continue restricting BIS access to Alliance Program members, and it's not even clear that they actually restrict BIS connections at all. The Tweet Space game tries all of the possible connection types (`HttpConnectionFactory.TRANSPORTS_ANY`) because it really doesn't matter to the game which route is used to get the HTTP messages to Twitter and back. In the worst-case scenario, it tries to make a BIS connection, it fails, and then it tries the next connection that the factory provides.

By the 5.0 version of the BlackBerry JDE, RIM finally realized that most third-party applications (like games) have no reason to be concerned with the low-level details of precisely which underlying transport carries the HTTP messages—it's something that should be decided between the user, the operator, and the BlackBerry smartphone. So the 5.0 API includes a built-in `ConnectionFactory` class based on Marcus Watkins' `HttpConnectionFactory` class. If you're targeting the latest BlackBerry smartphones only, you'll probably want to use the new factory class. Otherwise, you can stick with the `HttpConnectionFactory` class for backward compatibility.

The `TweetReader` class reads and interprets the messages (aka *tweets*) that the other players have posted to the Twitter server. The idea is that each player's spaceship has a position in a giant (virtual) map of outer space, and the game automatically tweets the player's position, orientation, ship type, and (optional) text message to Twitter. The TweetReader class periodically downloads all of the latest messages to get the data on how and where to draw the remote ships. A remote player's text message is displayed when her spaceship is close enough to the local player's spaceship to be visible on the screen.

The periodic calls to read the latest messages from Twitter are triggered by the java.util.Timer and TimerTask classes. They work together to call the run() method of a Runnable at fixed intervals in the same way that Application.invokeLater() was used to advance the animation in Chapter 8 (see Listing 8-6). The difference is that Application.invokeLater() uses the event thread to call the run() method, which is exactly what you *don't* want when your repeated action is a network connection. The TimerTask is scheduled in the constructor of Listing 9-1, and the run() method it calls is a little farther down.

Listing 9-1. *TweetReader.java*

```java
package net.frogparrot.tweetspace;

import java.io.*;
import java.util.Timer;
import java.util.TimerTask;
import javax.microedition.io.HttpConnection;

import org.json.me.JSONArray;
import org.json.me.JSONObject;

import com.versatilemonkey.net.*;

/**
 * This class reads tweets from Twitter and uses the data to
 * place the remote players.
 */
public class TweetReader extends TimerTask {

//-----------------------------------------------------------
//  instance fields

  /**
   * The handle to the game board.
   */
  SpaceLayer mySpaceLayer;

  /**
   * The timer that runs this task periodically.
   */
  Timer myTimer;

  /**
   * The Twitter id of the most recent message that has
   * been read by this class.  This is used in the request
   * in order not to get the same messages again.
   */
  long mySinceId = 0;
```

```java
//-----------------------------------------------------------
//  data initialization and accessors

  /**
   * Schedule the task.
   * @param layer a handle to the game board for callbacks
   */
  public TweetReader(SpaceLayer layer) {
    mySpaceLayer = layer;
    myTimer = new Timer();
    // check for messages every 10 seconds:
    myTimer.schedule(this, 10000, 10000);
  }

//-----------------------------------------------------------
//  generic connection utilities

  /**
   * A simple utility to send a BlackBerry HTTP request.
   */
  public static String httpRequest(String url, String credentials,
        String postData) {
    HttpConnection connection = null;
    String retString = null;
    try {
      HttpConnectionFactory factory = new HttpConnectionFactory(url,
          HttpConnectionFactory.TRANSPORTS_ANY);
      while(true) {
        try {
          connection = factory.getNextConnection();
          try {
            if(credentials != null) {
              connection.setRequestProperty("Authorization",
                  "Basic " + credentials);
              OutputStream os = connection.openOutputStream();
              os.write(postData.getBytes());
              os.close();
            }
            if(postData != null) {
              connection.setRequestMethod("POST");
            } else {
              connection.setRequestMethod("GET");
            }
            int responseCode = connection.getResponseCode();
            int length = (int)(connection.getLength());
            InputStream is = connection.openInputStream();
            byte[] data = new byte[length];
            int bytesRead = is.read(data);
            retString = new String(data);
            is.close();
            if(responseCode == 200) {
              break;
            }
          } catch(IOException ioe) {
```

```
            //Log the error:
            Main.postException(ioe);
          }
        } catch(NoMoreTransportsException e) {
          //Log the error:
          Main.postException(e);
          break;
        } finally {
          try {
            connection.close();
          } catch(Exception e) {}
        }
      }
    } catch(Exception e) {
      Main.postException(e);
    }
    return retString;
  }

//------------------------------------------------------------
//  business methods

  /**
   * Get the list of remote player tweets to parse and display.
   */
  public void run() {
    try {
      // all of the game tweets are read from one list on the Twitter server:
      StringBuffer buff
          = new StringBuffer("http://api.twitter.com/1/bbspaceexp/lists/");
      buff.append(Main.theLabels.getString(Main.TWEETSPACE_LISTNAME));
      buff.append("/statuses.json");
      if(mySinceId > 0) {
        buff.append("?since_id=");
        buff.append(mySinceId);
      }
      String url = buff.toString();
      // read the recent tweets from the internet:
      String responseData = httpRequest(url, null, null);
      // parse the tweet data and update the opponent ships accordingly:
      parseJson(responseData);
    } catch(Exception e) {
      Main.postException(e);
    }
  }

  /**
   * Parse and store the remote players' data and messages.
   * @param jsonStr The data block returned by Twitter
   */
  void parseJson(String jsonStr) {
    try {
      JSONArray results = new JSONArray(jsonStr);
      int length = results.length();
      // parse them in reverse order to show the most recent
```

```
      // message from each opponent:
      for(int i = 1; i < length + 1; i++) {
        JSONObject tweet = results.getJSONObject(length - i);
        mySinceId = tweet.getLong("id");
        String text = tweet.getString("text");
        JSONObject user = tweet.getJSONObject("user");
        String name = user.getString("screen_name");
        if(!name.equals(Main.getInstance().getLoginScreen().getUsername())) {
          mySpaceLayer.setAlienShip(name, text);
        }
      }
    } catch(Exception e) {
      Main.postException(e);
    }
  }

}
```

The Twitter API is remarkably user-friendly. By changing your query URL, you can download a batch of tweets by topic or by other criteria. The online documentation (at `http://apiwiki.twitter.com/Twitter-API-Documentation`) tells you what functions are available and how to formulate the calls.

In the Tweet Space game, all of the players' accounts are added to a list administered by the user `bbspaceexp`. There's nothing special about the `bbspaceexp` account—it's a standard Twitter account I created to administer the game lists. When the player enters her Twitter username and password, the game sends Twitter a request to send a direct message to `bbspaceexp` (see the bottom of Listing 9-2). The `TweetReader` class simply requests all of the latest *updates* (another word for tweets) that have been posted by users who are on this list.

Actually, the game has one list for each language supported by the game. The English label corresponding to `Main.TWEETSPACE_LISTNAME` is en01. (The use of language resources is explained in Chapter 2.)

Twitter allows you to request the response data in different standard formats such as XML or JSON by changing the extension on the end of the request URL. Since JSON is a simple and efficient format for arrays of object data, the Tweet Space game uses JSON (see the "JavaScript Object Notation" sidebar).

You can see that the `parseJson()` method of Listing 9-1 extracts the relevant data from each of the tweets on the list and passes it along to the game logic classes using the `setAlienShip()` method, which you'll see in the "Building the Tweet Space Game Logic" section later in this chapter (specifically Listing 9-6).

JAVASCRIPT OBJECT NOTATION

JavaScript Object Notation (JSON) is a simple and intuitive format for expressing object data as text. It's better than XML for communication between Java applications because JSON organizes the data into basic, universal data structures: strings, hashtables, arrays, and primitives.

Have a look at the following JSON-encoded data:

```
{"validated":false,"labels":["OK",null,"Cancel"],"frameseq":[3,2,0,2]}
```

Even if you've never seen JSON before, it's obvious how to interpret the data. It's a hashtable with three key/value pairs, two of which have arrays as values. There's not much more to the JSON format than what's shown in the preceding line.

Strings and numbers are written with almost all of the same formatting conventions (such as escape sequences) in JSON as in Java. A *JSON object* is a hashtable-like data structure enclosed in braces—{ }— and a "JSON array" is a list of values enclosed in brackets—[ ]. JSON objects and JSON arrays can act as values within JSON objects and JSON arrays. That's basically it, but if you need more precision, the entire language is described on a single page at www.json.org.

Even if this format looks easy to parse, there's no need to reinvent the wheel. The JSON web site provides a free, open source library for Java ME. The only restriction on the library is the stipulation that "the Software shall be used for Good, not Evil." You can download it from www.json.org, and it's bundled with the source code of the Tweet Space game.

In addition to the class for reading the remote players' messages, there's naturally a corresponding class that posts the local player's data. It's the TweetField class of Listing 9-2. The use of HTTP is the same as in Listing 9-1, with a simple addition of an authentication step that's explained in the "Logging In" section, which follows.

Listing 9-2. *TweetField.java*

```
//#preprocess
package net.frogparrot.tweetspace;

import java.io.*;
import javax.microedition.io.HttpConnection;

import net.rim.device.api.ui.component.EditField;

import com.versatilemonkey.net.*;

import net.frogparrot.ui.*;

/**
 * An EditField that sends the input to Twitter as tweets.
 */
public class TweetField extends EditField implements MessageField, Runnable {

//-----------------------------------------------------------
//  instance fields

  /**
   * Data to position the cursor.
   */
  int myCursorPosition = 0;
  int mySentPosition = 0;
  int myLabelLength = 0;

  /**
```

```java
    * Whether the user has updated the login credentials since the last post.
    */
   boolean myNewLogin = false;

   /**
    * The string to post to Twitter.
    */
   String mySendString;

   /**
    * A message to display to the local user.
    */
   String myUpdateMessage;

   /**
    * The game board.
    */
   SpaceLayer mySpaceLayer;

   /**
    * A runnable inner class to pass to invokeLater()
    * to ensure that display updates are called from the event thread.
    */
   Runnable myUpdateDisplay = new Runnable() {
       public void run() {
         String displayMessage = myUpdateMessage;
         myUpdateMessage = null;
         if(displayMessage != null) {
           mySentPosition += displayMessage.length();
           myCursorPosition += displayMessage.length();
           insert(displayMessage);
           setCursorPosition(myCursorPosition);
         }
       }
   };

//-----------------------------------------------------------
//  data initialization and access

  /**
   * Initialize the field.
   */
  public TweetField(String label) {
    super(label, "");
    myLabelLength = getLabelLength();
    mySentPosition = myLabelLength;
  }

  /**
   * Give this instance a handle to the game board.
   */
  public void setSpaceLayer(SpaceLayer layer) {
    mySpaceLayer = layer;
  }
```

```java
//------------------------------------------------------------
//  handle user input

  /**
   * @see net.frogparrot.ui.MessageField#keyChar(char, int, int, boolean)
   */
  public boolean keyChar(char key, int status, int time, boolean fromManager) {
    return keyChar(key, status, time);
  }

//#ifdef RIM_4.2.0
  /**
   * @see net.frogparrot.ui.MessageField#navigationMovement
   */
  public boolean navigationMovement(int dx, int dy, int status,
      int time, boolean fromManager) {
    return navigationMovement(dx, dy, status, time);
  }
//#endif

  /**
   * Ensure that the cursor is placed at the end of the field
   * when focus is gained.
   * @see net.rim.device.api.ui.component.EditField#onFocus
   */
  protected void onFocus(int direction) {
    setCursorPosition(myCursorPosition);
  }

  /**
   * Save the cursor location for later use.
   * @see net.rim.device.api.ui.component.EditField#onUnfocus
   */
  protected void onUnfocus() {
    myCursorPosition = getCursorPosition();
  }

  /**
   * @see net.frogparrot.ui.MessageField#loginUpdated
   */
  public void loginUpdated(String username) {
    Thread t = new Thread(this);
    myNewLogin = true;
    t.start();
  }

//------------------------------------------------------------
//  handle the remote player's data

  /**
   * Display the latest message from a remote user.
   * @param name the remote user's screen name
   * @param message the remote user's message
   */
  public void displayRemoteMessage(String name, String message) {
```

```
      String postString = "\n" + name + ": " + message + "\n";
      mySentPosition += postString.length();
      myCursorPosition += postString.length();
      insert(postString);
      setCursorPosition(myCursorPosition);
      // This tells the local spaceship to stop where it is.
      mySpaceLayer.move(SpaceLayer.DOWN);
      // This scrolls the messages to the end and gives the
      // local user the opportunity to respond.
      setFocus();
   }

   //-----------------------------------------------------------
   //   sending methods

   /**
    * Post the local user's data and latest message to Twitter.
    */
   public void sendMessage() {
      // get the user's message input:
      int currentLength = getTextLength() + myLabelLength;
      StringBuffer buff = new StringBuffer("status=");
      buff.append(mySpaceLayer.getPosition());
      if(currentLength > mySentPosition) {
         // update the sent postion so that this data won't be sent twice:
         buff.append(getText(mySentPosition, currentLength - mySentPosition));
         mySentPosition = currentLength + 1;
         insert("\n");
         myCursorPosition++;
      }
      // cache the current message for sending (in case login is needed)
      mySendString = buff.toString();
      // if the user hasn't logged in, then prompt the user to log in
      // (instead of just sending the message):
      if(Main.getInstance().getLoginScreen().getCredentials() == null) {
         Main.getInstance().pushLoginScreen();
      } else {
         Thread t = new Thread(this);
         t.start();
      }
   }

   /**
    * Perform the http POST operation
    */
   public void run() {
      HttpConnection connection = null;
      try {
         HttpConnectionFactory factory = new HttpConnectionFactory(
             "http://twitter.com/statuses/update.json",
             HttpConnectionFactory.TRANSPORTS_ANY);
         String credentials = Main.getInstance().getLoginScreen().getCredentials();
         if(mySendString == null) {
            StringBuffer buff = new StringBuffer("status=");
            buff.append(mySpaceLayer.getPosition());
```

```java
      buff.append(Main.theLabels.getString(Main.TWEETSPACE_TWEETSPACE));
      mySendString = buff.toString();
    }
    while(true) {
      try {
        connection = factory.getNextConnection();
        try {
          connection.setRequestMethod( "POST" );
          connection.setRequestProperty("Authorization", "Basic " + credentials);
          OutputStream os = connection.openOutputStream( );
          os.write(mySendString.getBytes());
          os.close();
          int responseCode = connection.getResponseCode();
          int length = (int)(connection.getLength());
          InputStream is = connection.openInputStream();
          byte[] data = new byte[length];
          int bytesRead = is.read(data);
          String str = new String(data);
          is.close();
          if(responseCode == 200) {
            // if the login succeeded, then send a message to the
            // space explorer list admin to add this player:
            if(myNewLogin) {
              requestListAddition(credentials);
              myNewLogin = false;
            }
            break;
          } else if(responseCode == 401) {
            // login failed, prompt the user to give valid credentials:
            myUpdateMessage
                = Main.theLabels.getString(Main.TWEETSPACE_LOGIN_ERROR);
            Main.getUiApplication().invokeLater(myUpdateDisplay);
            break;
          }
        } catch(IOException ioe) {
          //Log the error:
          Main.postException(ioe);
        }
      } catch(NoMoreTransportsException e) {
        //There are no more transports to attempt
        Main.postException(e);
        break;
      } finally {
        try {
          connection.close();
        } catch(Exception e) {}
      }
    }
  } catch(Exception e) {
    Main.postException(e);
  }
}

/**
 * Posts a request to add this user to the list players (so that
```

```
 * this player's tweets will be visible to other players).
 */
public void requestListAddition(String credentials) {
  TweetReader.httpRequest("http://twitter.com/friendships/create/bbspaceexp.json",
      credentials, "");
  String reqStr = "screen_name=bbspaceexp&text=add me to "
          + Main.theLabels.getString(Main.TWEETSPACE_LISTNAME);
  TweetReader.httpRequest("http://twitter.com/direct_messages/new.json",
      credentials, reqStr);
}

}
```

The TweetField class has the added functionality of acting as an EditField where the user can enter messages and view messages from other players. The RIM EditField implementation takes care of all of the standard text functionality such as interpreting keyboard input as text and breaking the text into lines to display. Posting the remote messages into the same text field where the local user enters text is a little unorthodox, however, which is why there are some extra fields and methods to keep track of where the cursor is supposed to be. You can see that the both the sendMessage() and displayRemoteMessage() methods keep track of how much of the text content has been sent (or was part of the remote message) so that only the user's latest text gets posted each time.

There's no particular error handling for the case where the user enters a message that's too long. If the message is too long, Twitter will automatically truncate it. There's no danger of losing the position data since the local player's position data is prepended to the beginning of the tweet (as you'll see in the "Building the Tweet Space Game Logic" section). You could add extra functionality to warn the user when the message is too long (or send it in two tweets), but given how small the edit field is on the screen, it's unlikely that message truncation will be a serious enough problem to warrant special effort.

As usual, there's a little Runnable to update the display (called myUpdateDisplay in Listing 9-2). Since any updates to the display *must be* performed on the event thread and communications *can't be* performed on the event thread, you need a way to make the one thread trigger an action on the other. In this example, the myUpdateDisplay Runnable is merely used to display a login error message. The displayRemoteMessage() method is actually called from the game animation code (which is obviously run by the event thread) since a remote player's message is displayed only when the corresponding spaceship becomes visible.

Logging In

In any networked game, the server needs to be able to identify the messages from the various players. Figure 9-2 shows the login screen of the Tweet Space game.

The Tweet Space game saves the player's credentials to avoid the annoyance of having to log in every time. If you're writing a high-security application, you might want to include a dialog to ask the user if he wants his credentials saved—and you can even encrypt the data using the encryption APIs discussed in Chapter 5. In that case, you would probably want to use HTTPS instead of HTTP to transmit sensitive data. This game, however, has a simple (and very weak) security model since the worst thing a hacker could do is impersonate another player. It hardly matters that the username and password are stored in the RMS without encryption, since they're also sent to Twitter (across the Internet) without encryption, as explained in the "Base64 Encoding and Basic Access Authentication" sidebar.

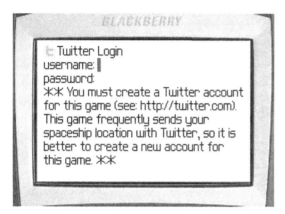

Figure 9-2. *The Tweet Space login screen on the simulator*

BASE64 ENCODING AND BASIC ACCESS AUTHENTICATION

Base64 encoding is the standard way of transforming binary data into text data. It's used as a way to send binary data through a transport protocol that only allows text. HTTP uses Base64 encoding as a way of sending a username and password pair in the header data of a request. Encoding is required because a password could potentially include characters that aren't allowed in the header section of a request.

Base64 encoding is a simple one-to-one encoding like the first secret codes you played with as a kid. Just number the characters in the following string from 0 to 64, and that gives you the mapping between 6-bit data chunks and characters:

`ABCDEFGHIJKLMNOPQRSTUVWXYZabcdefghijklmnopqrstuvwxyz0123456789+/`

Since binary data is normally divided into 8-bit octets (not groups of 6 bits), the binary data is treated as one long stream of bits. The bit stream is then read as 6-bit groups—most significant first—for encoding. If the number of bits isn't a multiple of six, one or two equal signs are added to the end of the string to indicate how much *padding* (with extra zero bits) was added to perform the encoding.

Base64 encoding is not to be confused with encryption. Even if your password looks unfamiliar to you after you encode it this way, it's really equivalent to just typing your password in clear text. When the `TweetField` class sends the user's credentials using `Authorization: Basic` (in the `run()` method of Listing 9-2), that means that the username and password are sent across the open Internet with no security whatsoever (another reason not to use your everyday Twitter account for this game—see Figure 9-2). The Twitter API currently allows basic access authentication, but may phase it out at some point due to its lack of security.

One nice thing about Base64 encoding is that (being a time-worn standard) all of the encoding and decoding classes were developed for you long ago. RIM provides input and output streams to do the job. You can see how to use them in the `setCredentials()` and `getCredentials()` methods of Listing 9-3.

The login functionality is separate enough that it's grouped in its own separate package for modularity. Figure 9-3 shows the structure of the `net.frogparrot.login` package.

::net.frogparrot.login

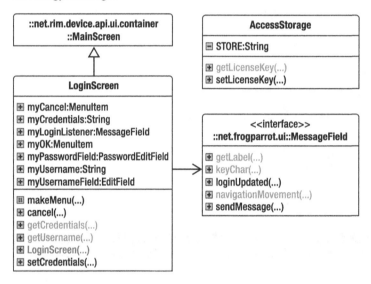

Figure 9-3. *The logic of the net.frogparrot.login package*

The `LoginScreen` is pushed onto the top of the screen stack when the user selects "update login" from the menu of the main game screen. (Figure 9-4 shows where the main game screen, `SimpleScreen`, fits into the package logic. It's called "simple" because it merely handles this one menu item and displays a `Manager` that handles the rest of the game graphics.) When the user is done entering his credentials, he selects the `LoginScreen`'s OK menu item, which calls the `setCredentials()` method. That method encodes and stores the credentials (using the `AccessStorage` class from Chapter 5, Listing 5-6), pops the `LoginScreen` off the screen stack, and notifies the `TweetField` that the user credentials have been updated. The `TweetField` appears in Figure 9-3 as the `net.frogparrot.ui.MessageField` interface. You can see at the top of Listing 9-2 that the `TweetField` implements this interface. This helps keep the code as modular and reusable as possible. As soon as the `LoginScreen` notifies the `TweetField` of the updated login, the `TweetField` tries out the new credentials by tweeting the user's current location (see the `loginUpdated()` method of Listing 9-2). The code for the Base64 encoding is shown in Listing 9-3. The rest of the code of the `LoginScreen` class (building a form with `EditFields` and `MenuItems`) is a simple application of the RIM UI classes demonstrated in Chapter 4. (You can find it in the complete source code for this chapter, which you can download from www.apress.com or http://frogparrot.net/blackberry/.)

Listing 9-3. *Business Methods from LoginScreen.java*

```java
//------------------------------------------------------------------
//  business methods

  /**
   * Called when the user selects "log in", this method
   * launches the action to check and save the user's credentials.
   */
  public void setCredentials() {
    try {
      myUsername = myUsernameField.getText();
      StringBuffer buff = new StringBuffer(myUsername);
      buff.append(":");
      buff.append(myPasswordField.getText());
      // encode the username and password for basic authentication:
      byte[] clearData = buff.toString().getBytes();
      byte[] codedData = Base64OutputStream.encode(clearData, 0,
          clearData.length, false, false);
      // store the encoded username and password in memory:
      AccessStorage.setLicenseKey(codedData);
      myCredentials = new String(codedData);
      UiApplication.getUiApplication().popScreen(this);
      // Tell the message field to try the new credentials:
      myLoginListener.loginUpdated(myUsername);
    } catch(Exception e) {
      Main.postException(e);
    }
  }

  /**
   * Read the user's credentials from the record store.
   * @return The user's (b64) basic-authentication encoded
   * username and password.
   */
  public String getCredentials() {
    if(myCredentials == null) {
      byte[] credentials = AccessStorage.getLicenseKey();
      if((credentials != null) && (credentials.length != 0)) {
        myCredentials = new String(credentials);
      }
    }
    return myCredentials;
  }

  /**
   * @return The current username or null if no valid username is found.
   */
  public String getUsername() {
    if(myUsername == null) {
      try {
        String credentials = getCredentials();
        String clearString = new String(Base64InputStream.decode(credentials));
        int index = clearString.indexOf(':');
        myUsername = clearString.substring(0, index);
      } catch(Exception e) {
```

```
    }
  }
  return myUsername;
}
```

Building the Tweet Space Game Logic

The next step is to design the game itself. For BlackBerry smartphones that have operating system version 4.6.0 and greater, the game will open with the SVG Space Explorer animation from Chapter 8. But to keep this game compatible with the rest of the BlackBerry smartphones out there, the rest of the game will use a more standard, sprite-based implementation (rather than using the SVG Space Explorer game logic).

Let's start with an overview of the net.frogparrot.tweetspace package, shown in Figure 9-4.

To the left, you can see the TweetReader and TweetField classes (Listings 9-1 and 9-2), which receive and send messages. Each instance of the Spaceship class (near the bottom of Figure 9-4) represents an opponent's spaceship. You can see that it holds the ship's position as well as the remote player's name and most recent text message. The Spaceship class holds a handle to the TweetField class to display the message when the ship comes into the local player's viewscreen. Naturally, each opponent's position needs to be expressed as a text string that can be sent in a tweet. The position string has the following format:

`*<x-coordinate> <y-coordinate> <orientation> <sprite code>*<user message>`

The coordinates are integers, the <orientation> is a character indicating which direction (up, down, left, or right) the spaceship is pointing, and the <sprite code> is an integer code indicating which spaceship image should be used for the player's spaceship. Here's a typical example:

`*4501 7987 u 3*Hi, fancy meeting you here in space!`

The parseJson() method (from Listing 9-1) extracts the entire tweet as a String, and then it's up to the game logic to parse the String to get the remote spaceship's latest data. Fortunately, the RIM APIs provide a lot of interesting utilities that are lacking in standard Java ME. For example, RIM provides a StringUtilities class that makes it simple to parse the data string into an array of words, as illustrated in the update() method of Listing 9-4.

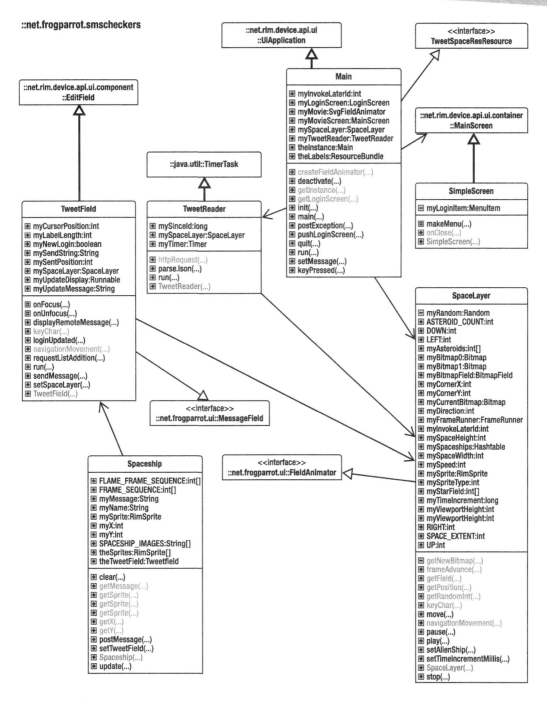

Figure 9-4. *The logic of the net.frogparrot.tweetspace package*

Listing 9-4. *Position String Methods from Spaceship.java*

```java
//----------------------------------------------------------
//  instance data initialization and access

  /**
   * Create a new sprite based on a tweet from a remote user.
   * @param name the remote user's screen name
   * @param tweet the text containing the message and the coordinates.
   * @param id which sprite image to use.
   */
  Spaceship(String name, String tweet) {
    myName = name;
    // parse the message to interpret and set the ship's data:
    update(tweet);
  }

  /**
   * parse the message to interpret and set the ship's data.
   * @param tweet the text containing the message and the coordinates.
   */
  public void update(String tweet) {
    try {
      // first extract and interpret the position data:
      int startIndex = tweet.indexOf('*');
      int endIndex = tweet.indexOf('*', startIndex + 1);
      String infoStr = tweet.substring(startIndex, endIndex);
      // use RIM's string utilities to split the data into an array of Strings
      String[] dst = new String[4];
      StringUtilities.stringToWords(infoStr, dst, 0);
      // Save the user's message for display:
      synchronized(this) {
        myMessage = tweet.substring(endIndex + 1);
      }
      // interpret the data:
      myX = Integer.parseInt(dst[0]);
      myY = Integer.parseInt(dst[1]);
      if(mySprite == null) {
        mySprite = getSprite(dst[3]);
      }
      if("d".equals(dst[2])) {
        mySprite.setTransform(RimSprite.TRANS_ROT180);
      } else if("l".equals(dst[2])) {
        mySprite.setTransform(RimSprite.TRANS_ROT90);
      } else if("r".equals(dst[2])) {
        mySprite.setTransform(RimSprite.TRANS_ROT270);
      } else {
        mySprite.setTransform(RimSprite.TRANS_NONE);
      }
    } catch(Exception e) {
      // if parsing fails, throw the message out:
      Main.postException(e);
      throw new IllegalArgumentException();
    }
  }
}
```

You can see in Listing 9-4 that each `Spaceship` has a corresponding sprite so it can be drawn on the screen. The `getSprite()` method creates a sprite from a list of spaceship images, selecting the image according to the `<sprite code>` from the message. Each of the spaceship image files has eight frames so that it can be animated to appear to spin. You already saw the first one in Figure 8-4 of the previous chapter. Figure 9-5 shows another.

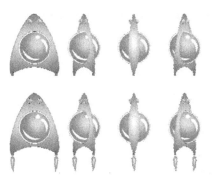

Figure 9-5. *A game sprite image for the Tweet Space game*

In each case, the top four frames make up the animation with the engines turned off, and the bottom four make up the animation with the engines turned on. The frames are numbered in reading order (from left to right and then top to bottom), starting from frame 0 in the top-left corner. The `Spaceship` class has the two frame sequences that correspond to the two animation tracks for either spaceship:

```
public static final int[] FRAME_SEQUENCE = { 3, 2, 1, 0 };
public static final int[] FLAME_FRAME_SEQUENCE = { 7, 6, 5, 4 };
```

All of the sprite image files are saved as indexed PNG images. This saves space in the JAR/COD file, as explained in the "PNG Image Optimization" sidebar.

PNG IMAGE OPTIMIZATION

The Portable Network Graphics (PNG) format is impressively versatile. You can give each pixel 64 bits of data describing its precise color and transparency if you like—or you can shrink your image file by cutting back on frills you don't need.

One way to cut down on your game's JAR/COD file size is to convert the image files from *truecolor* (RGB) mode to *indexed*. The way it works is that the indexed PNG file has a *palette* of all of the colors used by the image, and then for each pixel it stores an index into the palette instead of storing the actual color value to paint the pixel. This can save you quite a lot of data, since an index into a palette of 256 colors requires only 8 bits per pixel. If your original PNG image file encoded 24 bits of truecolor information per pixel, then converting it to an indexed PNG image can cut the file size by nearly two-thirds.

It's easy to convert files to indexed mode using GIMP. Just select **Image ↗ Mode ↗ Indexed**, and GIMP will even generate an optimized palette for you. I used this trick on the Tweet Space game because I had so much fun drawing spaceships that I ended up bloating the JAR file with a ton of image data. Indexing cut my largest sprite image from 64.8KB to 32.0KB, and the image quality wasn't visibly affected.

As with all optimizations, however, there's a trade-off. Some images really do need more than 256 colors. For example, let's look at the background image of the SwingSaber game from Chapter 6. It occupies a whopping 208KB of JAR file real estate. Naturally, you might try to index it to cut it down to size. Figure 9-6 shows the result.

Figure 9-6. *The SwingSaber background image before and after indexing*

As shown, indexing made the image a little choppier throughout, and it eliminated the gradual fade-out that was so nice for helping the image look good on different-size screens. So you have to make the call as to whether a change in file size is worth the price, given the constraints of a particular game.

One more trick you can use to shrink your image file size is to group multiple images in a single PNG file. Each indexed PNG image file needs to contain all of its palette data (as well as some other header data). It's a waste to repeat this data if your game has a consistent color scheme. Instead, you can paste your images into one PNG file, index it (which creates a single palette for the composite image), and then cut the subimages out at runtime as you need them (using `Graphics.drawBitmap()` with coordinate arguments, for example, as illustrated in Listing 9-5).

As you've already seen in Chapters 4 and 6, you unfortunately can't use `javax.microedition.lcdui.game.Sprite` with RIM's UI classes. The problem is that the BlackBerry platform has two different image implementations, corresponding to the two different versions of the `Graphics` class: the `javax.microedition.lcdui.Graphics` class and the `net.rim.device.api.ui.Graphics`. The two `Graphics` classes are very similar to one another, but they're incompatible. The MIDP game API is based on one type of `Graphics`, while the BlackBerry UI API is based on the other. That means that your game can either use BlackBerry's convenient UI functionality *or* it can use MIDP's game API, *but not both*.

Fortunately, it's not too difficult to reimplement the sprite functionality that you need. For the SwingSaber game in Chapter 6, Andrew reimplemented the collision detection functionality. In Tweet Space, you don't need the collision detection—instead you need the image rotation and animation functionality. I deliberately followed the `javax.microedition.lcdui.game.Sprite` class as closely as possible when creating the `net.forgparrot.game.RimSprite` class (to make it easier to port existing games to BlackBerry). So the `RimSprite` class (Listing 9-5) allows you to create an animated game character based on a multiframe image. It also allows you to define the coordinates of a *reference pixel* within the frame that is used when painting the character into a larger image. (The defineReferencePixel() method allows you to set which pixel within the sprite frame is the reference pixel, and then the method setRefPixelPosition() allows you to set where that reference pixel goes with respect to the coordinates of the larger image.) Since the most natural way to rotate an image is around the image's own center, I added a simple method, centerReferencePixel(), which defines the sprite's reference pixel to be the center pixel of its frame. These methods are called by the Spaceship class's getSprite() method.

Listing 9-5. *RimSprite.java*

```java
package net.frogparrot.game;

import net.rim.device.api.system.Bitmap;
import net.rim.device.api.ui.Graphics;

/**
 * This reproduces some of the functionality of the
 * lcdui Sprite class, for use with RIM Graphics objects.
 */
public class RimSprite {

//-----------------------------------------------------------
//    Constants

  public static final int TRANS_NONE = 0;
  public static final int TRANS_ROT90 = 5;
  public static final int TRANS_ROT180 = 3;
  public static final int TRANS_ROT270 = 6;

//-----------------------------------------------------------
//    fields

  /**
   * The underlying image and its rotated versions.
   */
  Bitmap myImage;
  Bitmap myImage90;
  Bitmap myImage180;
  Bitmap myImage270;

  /**
   * The dimensions describing how to cut the individual Sprite out of its image.
   */
  int myFrameWidth;
  int myFrameHeight;
  int myRowLength;
  int myColumnLength;

  /**
   * The reference pixel with respect to the Sprite's internal coordinates.
   */
  int myRefPixelX = 0;
  int myRefPixelY = 0;

  /**
```

```
     * Where the reference pixel is placed
     * with respect to the external graphics object.
     */
    int myXcoordinate = 0;
    int myYcoordinate = 0;

    /**
     * Data to select the correct frame of the correct image to display.
     */
    int myOrientation;
    int[] myFrameSequence;
    int myFrameIndex;

//----------------------------------------------------------
//   data initialization and accessors

    /**
     * Calculate the image and frame data.
     * @param url The name of the Image resource.
     * @param rowLength the number of columns the image is divided into
     * @param columnLength the number of rows the image is divided into
     */
    public RimSprite(String url, int rowLength, int columnLength) {
      try {
        myImage = Bitmap.getBitmapResource(url);
        myImage90 = rotateBitmap(myImage);
        myImage180 = rotateBitmap(myImage90);
        myImage270 = rotateBitmap(myImage180);
        myFrameWidth = myImage.getWidth()/rowLength;
        myFrameHeight = myImage.getHeight()/columnLength;
        myRowLength = rowLength;
        myColumnLength = columnLength;
        int animationLength = myRowLength*myColumnLength;
        myFrameSequence = new int[animationLength];
        for(int i = 0; i < animationLength; i++) {
          myFrameSequence[i] = i;
        }
      } catch(Exception e) {
      }
    }

    /**
     * Creates a new Sprite with the same underlying data as an
     * existing Sprite. This is a memory-saving option to allow
     * multiple Sprites to use the same underlying image files
     * in memory.
     */
    public RimSprite(RimSprite source) {
      myFrameWidth = source.myFrameWidth;
      myFrameHeight = source.myFrameHeight;
      myImage = source.myImage;
      myImage90 = source.myImage90;
      myImage180 = source.myImage180;
      myImage270 = source.myImage270;
      myRowLength = source.myRowLength;
```

```java
    myColumnLength = source.myColumnLength;
    myFrameSequence = source.myFrameSequence;
    myRefPixelX = source.myRefPixelX;
    myRefPixelY = source.myRefPixelY;
  }

  /**
   * Set the order of the frames to create the animation.
   * @param frameSequence An array of indices into the array of frames,
   *    indexed in reading order (left-to-right rows, read from top to bottom).
   */
  public void setFrameSequence(int[] frameSequence) {
    myFrameSequence = frameSequence;
  }

  /**
   * Set where (in the Graphics object's coordinate system) the
   * Sprite's reference pixel is to be painted.
   */
  public void setRefPixelPosition(int x, int y) {
    myXcoordinate = x;
    myYcoordinate = y;
  }

  /**
   * @return The x-coordinate of the Sprite's reference pixel with respect
   * to the painter's coordinate system.
   */
  public int getRefPixelX() {
    return myXcoordinate;
  }

  /**
   * @return The y-coordinate of the Sprite's reference pixel with respect
   * to the painter's coordinate system.
   */
  public int getRefPixelY() {
    return myYcoordinate;
  }

  /**
   * Set the pixel within the Sprite (with respect to the top-
   * left corner of the Sprite) that is used to calculate the
   * placement of the Sprite for painting.
   */
  public void defineReferencePixel(int x, int y) {
    myRefPixelX = x;
    myRefPixelY = y;
  }

  /**
   * Set the center of the Sprite to be the pixel
   * (within the Sprite, with respect to the top-
   * left corner of the Sprite) that is used to calculate the
   * placement of the Sprite for painting.
```

```java
  */
  public void centerReferencePixel() {
    myRefPixelX = myFrameWidth/2;
    myRefPixelY = myFrameHeight/2;
  }

  /**
   * Set the desired orientation of the Sprite image.
   */
  public void setTransform(int orientation) {
    myOrientation = orientation;
  }

//-----------------------------------------------------------
//   business methods

/**
 * A simple utility to take a bitmap image and
 * return a copy of the image, rotated by 90 degrees.
 * @param src <description>
 * @return <description>
 */
  public static Bitmap rotateBitmap(Bitmap src) {
    Bitmap retObj = null;
    try {
      int imageWidth = src.getWidth();
      int imageHeight = src.getHeight();
      int[] dataSrc = new int[imageWidth*imageHeight];
      src.getARGB(dataSrc, 0, imageWidth, 0, 0, imageWidth, imageHeight);
      int[] dataDst = new int[dataSrc.length];
      for(int i = 0; i < imageWidth; i++) {
        for(int j = 0; j < imageHeight; j++) {
          dataDst[(imageWidth - i - 1)*imageHeight + j]
              = dataSrc[j*imageWidth + i];
        }
      }
      retObj = new Bitmap(imageHeight, imageWidth);
      retObj.setARGB(dataDst, 0, imageHeight, 0, 0, imageHeight, imageWidth);
    } catch(Exception e) {
    }
    return retObj;
  }

  /**
   * Paint the Sprite onto the target that is bound to the Graphics object.
   */
  public void paint(Graphics g) {
    myFrameIndex++;
    myFrameIndex %= myFrameSequence.length;
    // compute which part of the image to paint,
    // based on the orientation and the frame index:
    int frame = myFrameSequence[myFrameIndex];
    int gridX = frame % myRowLength;
    int gridY = frame / myRowLength;
    switch(myOrientation) {
```

```
      case TRANS_NONE:
        g.drawBitmap(myXcoordinate - myRefPixelX,
                   myYcoordinate - myRefPixelY,
                   myFrameWidth, myFrameHeight,
                   myImage, gridX*myFrameWidth, gridY*myFrameHeight);
      break;
      case TRANS_ROT90:
        g.drawBitmap(myXcoordinate - myRefPixelY,
                   myYcoordinate - (myFrameWidth - myRefPixelX),
                   myFrameHeight, myFrameWidth,
                   myImage90,
                   gridY*myFrameHeight,
                   (myRowLength - gridX - 1)*myFrameWidth);
      break;
      case TRANS_ROT180:
        g.drawBitmap(myXcoordinate - (myFrameWidth - myRefPixelX),
                   myYcoordinate - (myFrameHeight - myRefPixelY),
                   myFrameWidth, myFrameHeight,
                   myImage180,
                   (myRowLength - gridX - 1)*myFrameWidth,
                   (myColumnLength - gridY - 1)*myFrameHeight);
      break;
      case TRANS_ROT270:
        g.drawBitmap(myXcoordinate - (myFrameHeight - myRefPixelY),
                   myYcoordinate - myRefPixelX,
                   myFrameHeight, myFrameWidth,
                   myImage270,
                   (myColumnLength - gridY - 1)*myFrameHeight,
                   gridX*myFrameWidth);
      break;
    }
  }

}
```

Most of the work in Listing 9-5 is merely a question of computing how to get from a pair of coordinates in an image to the corresponding pair of coordinates when the image is rotated.

The one interesting point to notice is how to modify an image by taking out (and manipulating) its underlying pixel data array, illustrated in the rotateBitmap() method of Listing 9-5. In the javax.microedition.lcdui package (as well as in the net.rim graphical APIs), you can get and set the data of an Image (respectively Bitmap) in terms of an int array that gives the color of each pixel. This technique allows you to do amusing tricks with the pixel data such as swapping colors, modifying transparency, and even transferring image data from one of the two Graphics implementations to the other. (It's a fairly costly operation (in terms of memory), though, so it should be used sparingly.)

The rotateBitmap() method illustrates how to use the array of pixel data. The indices into the pixel data array would be easier to understand if it were a double array where the color value of pixel (i,j) is simply stored at data[i][j]. But creating an array for every scan line of the image would be a huge waste of memory. It's more efficient to put all of the data in a single array, arranged in reading order. So the color value of pixel (i,j) is stored at data[i +

j*w], where w is the width of the image (in pixels), as shown in Figure 9-7. To rotate the image, the trick is to figure out how to rearrange the pixel data in the data array.

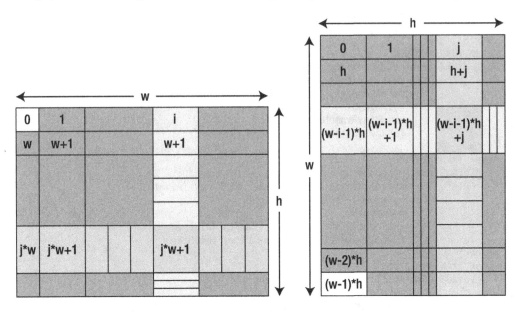

Figure 9-7. *How to map a pixel's index to its new index when an image is rotated*

For each pixel (i,j) in the image, you need to find both its index in the original data array and its index in the data array of the rotated image. That way you can copy the color value of the pixel from data array to the other. To figure out the two indices, I just drew a diagram of how the indices work (see Figure 9-7). You can see how the index of the point (i,j) is mapped from the original image to the destination image, and that mapping is used to copy the data value in the rotateBitmap() method.

There's similar reasoning at work in the paint() method of Listing 9-5. The image is made up of several animation frames (and possibly rotated), so the trick is to figure out exactly which patch of the image needs to be painted onto the bound Graphics instance. The paint() method calls drawBitmap() to render a portion of the image. You can see that the first two arguments indicate where the Bitmap fragment should be placed (with respect to the coordinates of the Graphics instance), the next group gives the size of the animation frame and the Bitmap to copy the image data from, and the last two give the corner of the frame to paint (in terms of the Bitmap's coordinates).

Now that you have the players, you need a universe for them to inhabit. The game universe is an animated field, so it reuses the net.frogparrot.ui package from Chapter 8 (see Figure 8-9). As you saw in Chapter 8, the FieldAnimator interface helps standardize the treatment of net.rim.device.api.ui.Fields that have a corresponding animation that can start, stop, advance one frame at a time, and respond to user input. And FrameRunner is a tiny helper class that wraps the FieldAnimator's frame-advancing functionality in a Runnable so that it can be called by the BlackBerry platform's event thread.

SpaceLayer (Listing 9-6) uses FieldAnimator and FrameRunner in exactly the same way that the SvgController from Listing 8-6 used them. Namely, the FieldAnimator's play() method passes the FrameRunner as an argument to the UiApplication.invokeLater() method. The UiApplication.invokeLater() method acts like a java.util.Timer, telling the platform's event thread to call the FieldAnimator's frameAdvance() method at regular intervals, updating the game animation several times per second. See Figure 9-4 to get an overview of the SpaceLayer class and how it fits into the net.frogparrot.tweetspace package.

Listing 9-6. *SpaceLayer.java*

```java
//#preprocess
package net.frogparrot.tweetspace;

import java.util.Random;
import java.util.Hashtable;
import java.util.Enumeration;

import net.rim.device.api.system.Bitmap;
import net.rim.device.api.ui.component.*;
import net.rim.device.api.ui.*;

import net.frogparrot.ui.*;
import net.frogparrot.game.RimSprite;

/**
 * The animated game board, including graphics and data to
 * place the objects in space.
 */
public class SpaceLayer implements FieldAnimator {

//-----------------------------------------------------------
//    constants

  /**
   * The length (and width) of the underlying space coordinate system.
   */
  public static final int SPACE_EXTENT = 10000;

  /**
   * The number of asteroids to place.
   */
  public static final int ASTEROID_COUNT = 10000;

  /**
   * Navigation constants.
   */
  public static final int UP = 0;
  public static final int DOWN = 1;
  public static final int LEFT = 2;
  public static final int RIGHT = 3;

//-----------------------------------------------------------
//    fields
```

```
/**
 * The size of the visible region in pixels.
 */
int myViewportWidth;
int myViewportHeight;

/**
 * The data and objects to control the game animation.
 */
int myInvokeLaterId = -1;
long myTimeIncrement = 100;
FrameRunner myFrameRunner;

/**
 * The spaceship object and its data.
 */
RimSprite mySprite;
int mySpriteType;
int myCornerX;
int myCornerY;
int myDirection;
int mySpeed;

/**
 * The graphics objects for the field.
 */
Bitmap myCurrentBitmap;
Bitmap myBitmap0;
Bitmap myBitmap1;
BitmapField myBitmapField;

/**
 * The data that describes our area of space.
 * Each two consecutive ints in the array give the x and y
 * coordinates of an object in space.
 */
int[] myStarField = new int[100];
int[] myAsteroids = new int[2*ASTEROID_COUNT];
Hashtable mySpaceships = new Hashtable();
int mySpaceWidth = SPACE_EXTENT;
int mySpaceHeight = SPACE_EXTENT;

/**
 * A utility for randomly filling space with stars, etc.
 */
private Random myRandom = new Random();

//----------------------------------------------------------
//    initialization and accessors

/**
 * Create the underlying data.
 */
public SpaceLayer(int viewportWidth, int viewportHeight) {
```

CHAPTER 9: Creating Role-Playing Games on the Internet 303

```
    try {
      // select the local player's spaceship image based on the
      // BlackBerry version:
//#ifdef RIM_4.1.0
      mySpriteType = 1;
//#endif
//#ifdef RIM_4.2.0
      mySpriteType = 2;
//#endif
//#ifdef RIM_4.3.0
      mySpriteType = 3;
//#endif
//#ifdef RIM_4.6.0
      mySpriteType = 4;
//#endif
      myViewportWidth = viewportWidth;
      myViewportHeight = viewportHeight;
      // the local player's ship is one of the cached ship sprites:
      mySprite = Spaceship.getSprite(mySpriteType);
      // place the spaceship in the middle of the viewscreen:
      mySprite.setRefPixelPosition(myViewportWidth/2, myViewportHeight/2);
      // fill the background with (fixed) randomly placed stars:
      for(int i = 0; i < myStarField.length/2; i+=2) {
        myStarField[i] = getRandomInt(myViewportWidth);
        myStarField[i + 1] = getRandomInt(myViewportHeight);
      }
      // fill the virtual space grid with moveable asteroids:
      for(int i = 0; i < ASTEROID_COUNT; i+=2) {
        myAsteroids[i] = getRandomInt(mySpaceWidth);
        myAsteroids[i+1] = getRandomInt(mySpaceHeight);
      }
      // initialize the two bitmaps for image double-buffering:
      myBitmap0 = new Bitmap(myViewportWidth, myViewportHeight);
      myBitmap1 = new Bitmap(myViewportWidth, myViewportHeight);
      myCurrentBitmap = myBitmap0;
      // get the graphics object to draw on the first bitmap:
      Graphics g = new Graphics(myCurrentBitmap);
      // color the current bitmap black:
      g.pushRegion(new XYRect(0, 0, myViewportWidth, myViewportHeight));
      g.setColor(g.FULL_BLACK);
      g.fillRect(0, 0, myViewportWidth, myViewportHeight);
      // Set the bitmap into a bitmap field so that it can be displayed:
      myBitmapField = new BitmapField(myCurrentBitmap, Field.FOCUSABLE);
      // create the Runnable that is used to advance the game animation:
      myFrameRunner = new FrameRunner(this);
    } catch(Exception e) {
    }
  }

  /**
   * This method keeps track of which buffer is visible
   * and which is being painted.
   * @return the data buffer to paint into
   */
  private Bitmap getNextBitmap() {
```

```java
      if(myCurrentBitmap == myBitmap1) {
        myCurrentBitmap = myBitmap0;
      } else {
        myCurrentBitmap = myBitmap1;
      }
      return myCurrentBitmap;
    }

  /**
   * a randomization utility.
   * @param upper the upper bound for the random int.
   * @return a random nonnegative int less than the bound upper.
   */
  int getRandomInt(int upper) {
    int retVal = myRandom.nextInt() % upper;
    if(retVal < 0) {
      retVal += upper;
    }
    return(retVal);
  }

//------------------------------------------------------------
//    methods for communication with remote players:

  /**
   * Place the remote player's ship and store its message
   * (creating if necessary).
   * @param name the remote player's screen name
   * @param text the tweet containing the ship data and message
   */
  public void setAlienShip(String name, String text) {
    try {
      Spaceship existing = (Spaceship)(mySpaceships.get(name));
      if(existing != null) {
        existing.update(text);
      } else {
        Spaceship ship = new Spaceship(name, text);
        mySpaceships.put(name, ship);
      }
    } catch(IllegalArgumentException iae) {
      // if the tweet is malformed and/or not relevant to
      // the game, it is logged and ignored:
      Main.postException(iae);
    }
  }

  /**
   * Creates a string that encodes the current local
   * player data, to send in the tweet.
   * @return the local player data to tweet
   */
  public String getPosition() {
    StringBuffer buff = new StringBuffer("*");
    buff.append(myCornerX + mySprite.getRefPixelX());
    buff.append(" ");
```

```
      buff.append(myCornerY + mySprite.getRefPixelY());
      buff.append(" ");
      switch(myDirection) {
        case RIGHT:
          buff.append("r ");
        break;
        case DOWN:
          buff.append("d ");
        break;
        case LEFT:
          buff.append("l ");
        break;
        default:
          buff.append("u ");
        break;
      }
      buff.append(mySpriteType);
      buff.append("*");
      return buff.toString();
    }

  //----------------------------------------------------------
  //   implementation of FieldAnimator

    /**
     * @see FieldAnimator#getField()
     */
    public Field getField() {
      return myBitmapField;
    }

    /**
     * @see FieldAnimator#frameAdvance()
     */
    public synchronized boolean frameAdvance() {
      try {
        // decide how far to travel this frame, based on the speed:
        int distance = mySpeed*12;
        // decide where/how to place the spaceship, based on direction:
        switch(myDirection) {
          case UP:
            // rotate the sprite image to the correct direction:
            mySprite.setTransform(RimSprite.TRANS_NONE);
            myCornerY -= distance;
            // handle the wraparound:
            if(myCornerY < 0) {
              myCornerY += mySpaceHeight;
            }
            break;
          case DOWN:
            // rotate the sprite image to the correct direction:
            mySprite.setTransform(RimSprite.TRANS_ROT180);
            myCornerY += distance;
            // handle the wraparound:
            if(myCornerY > mySpaceHeight) {
```

```
        myCornerY -= mySpaceHeight;
      }
      break;
    case LEFT:
      // rotate the sprite image to the correct direction:
      mySprite.setTransform(RimSprite.TRANS_ROT90);
      myCornerX -= distance;
      // handle the wraparound:
      if(myCornerX < 0) {
        myCornerX += mySpaceWidth;
      }
      break;
    case RIGHT:
      // rotate the sprite image to the correct direction:
      mySprite.setTransform(RimSprite.TRANS_ROT270);
      myCornerX += distance;
      // handle the wraparound:
      if(myCornerX > mySpaceWidth) {
        myCornerX -= mySpaceWidth;
      }
      break;
  }
  // now draw all of the graphics onto the next bitmap:
  Bitmap currentBitmap = getNextBitmap();
  Graphics g = new Graphics(currentBitmap);
  // Start by painting the whole region black:
  g.pushRegion(new XYRect(0, 0, myViewportWidth, myViewportHeight));
  g.clear();
  g.setColor(g.FULL_BLACK);
  g.fillRect(0, 0, myViewportWidth, myViewportHeight);
  // Now add the fixed background stars:
  g.setColor(g.FULL_WHITE);
  for(int i = 0; i < myStarField.length/2; i++) {
    g.fillRect(myStarField[2*i], myStarField[2*i+1], 2, 2);
  }
  // Now add the asteriods that are visible nearby:
  int xCoord = 0;
  int yCoord = 0;
  for(int i = 0; i < ASTEROID_COUNT; i+=2) {
    xCoord = myAsteroids[i] - myCornerX;
    if((xCoord < myViewportWidth && xCoord > 0)
          || (mySpaceWidth + xCoord < myViewportWidth)) {
      yCoord = myAsteroids[i+1] - myCornerY;
      if((yCoord < myViewportHeight && yCoord > 0)
            || (mySpaceHeight + yCoord < myViewportHeight)) {
        if(xCoord < 0) {
          xCoord += mySpaceWidth;
        }
        if(yCoord < 0) {
          yCoord += mySpaceHeight;
        }
        g.fillArc(xCoord, yCoord, 8, 8, 0, 360);
      }
    }
  }
}
```

```java
      // now the alien ships that are visible nearby:
      Enumeration elements = mySpaceships.elements();
      while(elements.hasMoreElements()) {
        Spaceship ship = (Spaceship)(elements.nextElement());
        xCoord = ship.getX() - myCornerX;
        if((xCoord < myViewportWidth && xCoord > 0)
               || (mySpaceWidth + xCoord < myViewportWidth)) {
          yCoord = ship.getY() - myCornerY;
          if((yCoord < myViewportHeight && yCoord > 0)
                 || (mySpaceHeight + yCoord < myViewportHeight)) {
            if(xCoord < 0) {
              xCoord += mySpaceWidth;
            }
            if(yCoord < 0) {
              yCoord += mySpaceHeight;
            }
            RimSprite alienSprite = ship.getSprite();
            alienSprite.setRefPixelPosition(xCoord, yCoord);
            alienSprite.paint(g);
            ship.postMessage();
          }
        }
      }
      // now paint the rocket on top:
      mySprite.paint(g);
      // since the region was pushed onto the context stack,
      // it must be popped off:
      g.popContext();
      // set the newly painted bitmap to be visible:
      myBitmapField.setBitmap(currentBitmap);
    } catch(Exception e) {
      // if it doesn't set the bitmap, then the animation didn't advance:
      return false;
    }
    return true;
  }

  /**
   * @see FieldAnimator#play()
   */
  public synchronized void play() {
    // Application#invokeLater has a built-in timer function
    // so it can be used to advance an animation from the
    // event thread.  Don't forget to save the ID so that
    // you can stop the animation later!
    myInvokeLaterId = UiApplication.getUiApplication().invokeLater(
        myFrameRunner, myTimeIncrement, true);
  }

  /**
   * @see FieldAnimator#pause()
   */
  public void pause() {
    stop();
  }
```

```java
/**
 * @see FieldAnimator#stop()
 */
public synchronized void stop() {
  if(myInvokeLaterId != -1) {
    UiApplication.getUiApplication().cancelInvokeLater(myInvokeLaterId);
    myInvokeLaterId = -1;
  }
}

/**
 * @see FieldAnimator#setTimeIncrementMillis(long)
 */
public void setTimeIncrementMillis(long timeIncrement) {
  if(timeIncrement <= 0) {
    throw new IllegalArgumentException("timeIncrement must be positive");
  }
  myTimeIncrement = timeIncrement;
}

/**
 * Handle the user commands.
 * @param direction The input direction (in terms of GameCanvas constants).
 */
void move(int direction) {
  switch(direction) {
    case UP:
      if(mySpeed < 4) {
        mySpeed++;
      }
      mySprite.setFrameSequence(Spaceship.FLAME_FRAME_SEQUENCE);
      break;
    case DOWN:
      mySpeed = 0;
      mySprite.setFrameSequence(Spaceship.FRAME_SEQUENCE);
      break;
    case LEFT:
      switch(myDirection) {
        case UP:
          myDirection = LEFT;
          break;
        case DOWN:
          myDirection = RIGHT;
          break;
        case LEFT:
          myDirection = DOWN;
          break;
        case RIGHT:
          myDirection = UP;
          break;
      }
      break;
    case RIGHT:
      switch(myDirection) {
```

```
                case UP:
                  myDirection = RIGHT;
                  break;
                case DOWN:
                  myDirection = LEFT;
                  break;
                case LEFT:
                  myDirection = UP;
                  break;
                case RIGHT:
                  myDirection = DOWN;
                  break;
            }
          break;
       }
    }

/**
 * Pass user input to the animated field.
 * @see net.rim.device.api.ui.Screen#keyChar(char, int, int)
 */
public boolean keyChar(char key, int status, int time) {
   if((key == 's') || (key == 'd')) { //left
     move(LEFT);
   } else if((key == 'f') || (key == 'j')) { // right
     move(RIGHT);
   } else if((key == 'e') || (key == 't')) { // up
     move(UP);
   } else if((key == 'x') || (key == 'b')) { // down
     move(DOWN);
   } else {
     // the keystroke was not relevant to this game
     return false;
   }
   // the keystroke was used by this game
   return true;
}

/**
 * Pass user input to the animated field.
 * @see net.rim.device.api.ui.Screen#navigationMovement(int, int, int, int)
 */
public boolean navigationMovement(int dx, int dy, int status, int time) {
   if(dx < 0) { //left
     move(LEFT);
   } else if(dx > 0) { // right
     move(RIGHT);
   } else if(dy > 0) { // down
     move(DOWN);
   } else if(dy < 0) { // up
     move(UP);
   } else {
     // the motion was not relevant to this game
     return false;
   }
```

```
      // the motion was used by this game
      return true;
    }

}
```

You can see that when the user selects "up," the spaceship starts moving in the direction that it's facing, and it continues moving until the user selects "down." Selecting "right" or "left" causes the ship to rotate.

Most of the techniques used in the `SpaceLayer` class should be familiar to you by this point. You saw the `#preprocess` directive back in Chapter 4 as a way to create different compiled binaries for different handset models from a single codebase. (Here, it's just used to select the player's spaceship image, but preprocessing is used for backward compatibility later in this example.) Similarly, the use of sprites, animation, and input handling should be familiar from Chapters 6 and 8. This class even uses randomization to generate elements of the game board just like the maze games from Chapters 3 and 4.

The algorithm for placing the objects in space, however, is new. In this case, it's actually kind of nice that you can't use the `javax.microedition.lcdui.game` API, because if you could, you'd probably be tempted to implement this background using a `TiledLayer`. Even though the functionality of `javax.microedition.lcdui.game.Sprite` is almost universally applicable to any game with a character that moves around the screen, `javax.microedition.lcdui.game.TiledLayer` is essentially optimized for Super Mario Brothers, and the more your game diverges from that model, the less clear it is that `TiledLayer` will help you.

In the Tweet Space game, most of the background is just black space with scattered stars. Creating that backdrop by painting it with PNG image files would be a huge waste both of computing power and space in the JAR. Plus, I'd like to capture the feel of space travel by painting both a near background and a far background: a near background full of asteroids that appear to move based on the player's position, and a far background of distant stars that stay fixed. I could implement that by painting two layers of PNG images on top of one another (with transparency), but that would be an incredible waste of computing power just to draw a handful of simple white dots.

You can see what's in the Tweet Space universe from the constants and the "data that describes our area of space" (at the top of Listing 9-6). It's a 10,000×10,000-pixel coordinate grid containing 10,000 asteroids and 50 stars. Each asteroid has a fixed location in the 10,000×10,000-pixel grid of the universe. The viewport is always centered on the local player's ship, so the illusion of movement is created by moving the background. That's where the asteroids come in—they give the player the impression that the spaceship is moving. Unlike the Asteroids game of old, these asteroids are just scenery, so they always pass behind the player's ship without hitting it.

The stars are 50 randomly placed white dots. They're meant to be so distant that they don't appear to move at all as the player's ship travels through the asteroid belt. That's why—in the constructor of `SpaceLayer`—the stars' coordinates are chosen only with respect to the size of the viewport, whereas the asteroids' coordinates are scattered throughout all of the extent of space.

All of the objects in space are positioned and painted in the `frameAdvance()` method. This game uses explicit graphics double-buffering (just like the RIMlet maze games of Chapters 3 and 4). The `frameAdvance()` method works by taking the image buffer (`Bitmap`) that isn't currently displayed, drawing into it (with its `Graphics` instance), and then placing the newly painted `Bitmap` into the `BitmapField` for display.

The two coordinates `myCornerX` and `myCornerY` tell where the top-left pixel of the viewport (visible window) is positioned with respect to the 10,000×10,000-pixel grid of space. When the player's spaceship moves (at the top of the `frameAdvance()` method), the values of `myCornerX` and `myCornerY` are all that really change. In reality, the player's ship sprite was positioned at the center of the viewport—using `setRefPixelPosition()` back in the constructor of `SpaceLayer`—and that is where it is always painted, as the very last step of the `frameAdvance()` method.

The tricky part is placing the asteroids at the right places in the visible region. Most of the time you just subtract the viewport's corner coordinates from the asteroid's coordinates to decide where to place the asteroid in the viewport. There's a little complexity, however, in dealing with wraparound that occurs when the spaceship approaches the bottom and/or right-hand borders of space. You can see how it's dealt with in the `for` loops in the middle of the `frameAdvance()` method.

Figure 9-8 illustrates how the wraparound asteroid locations are computed when the viewport crosses one (or both) of the edges of the space background. If the asteroid's x-coordinate minus the viewport's corner x-coordinate is negative, then the asteroid is to the left of the viewport (hence not visible), *unless* you have the particular situation illustrated in Figure 9-8: the asteroid's (absolute) x-coordinate plus the distance between the right edge of space and the viewport's corner x-coordinate add up to less than the viewport width. The y-coordinates of the wraparound asteroids near the bottom edge of space are computed in exactly the same way.

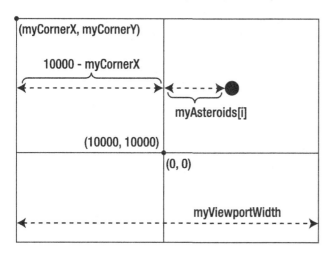

Figure 9-8. *How to compute the asteroid's x-coordinate when the viewport crosses the right-hand edge of space*

Since the remote players' positions (like the asteroids' positions) are given with respect to the 10,000×10,000-pixel space grid, their spaceships are placed using exactly the same algorithm as is used to place the asteroids. The remote ships are placed in the `frameAdvance()` method right after the asteroids are placed.

The final step of painting a remote player's ship is a call to `postMessage()`. The `postMessage()` method of the `Spaceship` class checks whether there's a message from the remote player that hasn't been displayed yet (and, if so, displays it and clears the `Spaceship`'s `myMessage` field).

There are a couple of other methods that facilitate communication between the local player and the other players in the 10,000×10,000-pixel virtual universe. The `setAlienShip()` method takes a tweet string from a remote player and interprets it in order to place or update the corresponding remote ship. This is called by the `TweetReader` class back in Listing 9-1. And the `getPosition()` method computes the local player's current position and orientation data and encodes it in a `String` in the same format that the `update()` method of Listing 9-4 is designed to interpret.

Now that we have the communications code and the game logic, the last step is to piece them together into a complete application.

Putting It Together

A lot of video games don't require complicated page layout logic because they just use the entire screen as the playing field. A social game like this one, however, needs a playing field window and a text window. This is the sort of design where the BlackBerry platform has a big advantage over an ordinary MIDP handset. The checkers game from Chapter 7 also allowed occasional messages, but since that game was implemented as a MIDlet—to optimize cross-platform compatibility—there was no simple way to show the messages and the checkerboard at the same time. In a MIDlet, either the device is displaying a `Canvas` that you can paint however you like *or* it's displaying a `Screen` (that has built-in text functionality such as scrolling), *but not both*. In a RIMlet, a `Screen` can hold `Field`s of any type, arranged however you like. So, unlike the checkers game, where the player has to flip back and forth between the game board and the message functionality, a Tweet Space player gets the whole picture at once.

Designing the Screen Layout

To display the Tweet Space game board and messages at the same time, you need an expanded version of the `net.frogparrot.ui` package from Chapter 8. Figure 9-9 shows the expanded package including the `MessageField` interface (implemented by `TweetField`, Listing 9-2) and a `TwoFieldManager` class (Listing 9-7), designed to hold a `MessageField` and an animated field (controlled by a `FieldAnimator`).Figure 9-10 shows what the completed game looks like live.

::net.frogparrot.ui

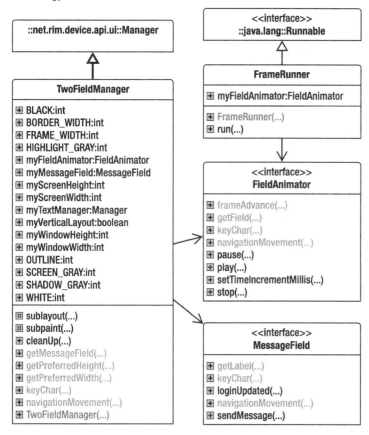

Figure 9-9. *The logic of the expanded net.frogparrot.ui package*

In a nutshell, the TwoFieldManager places the two fields either side by side or one above the other (depending on the device display dimensions). It also paints a frame around the animated window, much like the borders used in the Maze Deluxe game from Chapter 4 (see Listings 4-1 and 4-2). This class uses preprocessing (like the SelectSizeManager class of Listing 4-2), but not to encode information about the screen dimensions. Unlike the SelectSizeManager class, the screen layout for the TwoFieldManager is computed at runtime, in the constructor.

Listing 9-7. *TwoFieldManager.java*

```java
//#preprocess
package net.frogparrot.ui;

import net.rim.device.api.ui.*;
import net.rim.device.api.ui.container.*;
import net.rim.device.api.ui.component.*;
import net.rim.device.api.system.Characters;
import net.rim.device.api.system.Display;
```

```java
import net.frogparrot.tweetspace.Main;

/**
 * This class controls the overall layout of the screen,
 * including an animated window and a message window.
 */
public class TwoFieldManager extends Manager {

//-----------------------------------------------------------
//    constants

  /**
   * Color constants for the frame around the window.
   */
  public static final int BLACK = 0;
  public static final int WHITE = 0xffffff;
  public static final int SCREEN_GRAY = 0x00777777;
  public static final int HIGHLIGHT_GRAY = 0x00cccccc;
  public static final int SHADOW_GRAY = 0x00303030;
  public static final int OUTLINE = 0x00101010;

  /**
   * The number of pixels around the animated window field
   * (including the frame).
   */
  public static final int BORDER_WIDTH = 9;

  /**
   * The number of pixels of the border are used for
   * a frame that is drawn around the window.
   */
  public static final int FRAME_WIDTH = 4;

//-----------------------------------------------------------
//    instance fields

  /**
   * The screen dimensions.
   */
  int myScreenWidth;
  int myScreenHeight;
  int myWindowWidth;
  int myWindowHeight;

  /**
   * Whether the two windows are placed side by side
   * or one above the other.
   */
  boolean myVerticalLayout;

  /**
   * The object that holds and animates the animated window.
   */
  FieldAnimator myFieldAnimator;
```

```java
  /**
   * The editable text field.
   */
  MessageField myMessageField;

  /**
   * The text field has a separate layout manager so that
   * it can scroll separately.
   */
  Manager myTextManager;

//----------------------------------------------------------
//  data initialization and cleanup

  /**
   * Build the two fields based on the screen dimensions.
   */
  public TwoFieldManager(MessageField mf, Main mmain) {
    super(USE_ALL_HEIGHT | USE_ALL_WIDTH);
    myMessageField = mf;
    try {
      // get the font to check its dimensions
      Font font = Font.getDefault();
      // The Graphics class has methods to get the
      // screen dimensions and so does the Display class.
      // One pair is deprecated, the other requires a signature.
      // Take your pick ;^)
      myScreenWidth = Graphics.getScreenWidth();
      myScreenHeight = Graphics.getScreenHeight();
      //myScreenWidth = Display.getWidth();
      //myScreenHeight = Display.getHeight();

      // The text area needs to be at least big enough
      // to fit two lines of text vertically and the
      // game title horizontally:
      boolean screenOK = true;
      if(myScreenWidth > myScreenHeight) {
        int textWidth = font.getAdvance(myMessageField.getLabel());
        myWindowHeight = myScreenHeight - 2*(BORDER_WIDTH);
        myWindowWidth = myScreenHeight - 2*(BORDER_WIDTH);
        if((myScreenWidth - myWindowWidth) < textWidth) {
          myWindowWidth = myScreenWidth - (textWidth + 2*BORDER_WIDTH);
          // handle the case where the screen isn't big enough:
          if(myWindowWidth < 5*BORDER_WIDTH) {
            screenOK = false;
          }
        }
        myVerticalLayout = false;
      } else {
        int textHeight = font.getHeight();
        myWindowWidth = myScreenWidth - 2*(BORDER_WIDTH);
        myWindowHeight = myWindowWidth - 2*(BORDER_WIDTH);
        if((myScreenHeight - myWindowHeight) < 2*textHeight) {
          myWindowHeight = myScreenHeight - 2*(textHeight + BORDER_WIDTH);
          // handle the case where the screen isn't big enough:
```

```java
        if(myWindowHeight < 5*BORDER_WIDTH) {
          screenOK = false;
        }
      }
      myVerticalLayout = true;
    }
    // now that we have the dimensions, build the fields:
    if(screenOK) {
      // Any field animator can be placed in the animated window:
      myFieldAnimator = mmain.createFieldAnimator(myWindowWidth, myWindowHeight);
      add(myFieldAnimator.getField());
      myFieldAnimator.play();
    } else {
      throw new IllegalArgumentException("Screen too small");
    }
    // create and add the scrolling area for the text:
    myTextManager = new VerticalFieldManager(Manager.VERTICAL_SCROLL
            | Manager.VERTICAL_SCROLLBAR | Manager.USE_ALL_HEIGHT);
    myTextManager.add((Field)myMessageField);
    add(myTextManager);
  } catch(Exception e) {
    Main.postException(e);
  }
}

/**
 * Stop the animation and clear the data.
 */
public void cleanUp() {
  if(myFieldAnimator != null) {
    myFieldAnimator.stop();
    myFieldAnimator = null;
  }
  myTextManager = null;
}

/**
 * @return The MessageField displayed by this Manager.
 */
public MessageField getMessageField() {
  return myMessageField;
}

//-----------------------------------------------------------
//   implementation of Manager

/**
 * This Manager prefers to fill the whole display.
 */
public int getPreferredHeight() {
  return myScreenWidth;
}

/**
 * This Manager prefers to fill the whole display.
```

```
    */
    public int getPreferredWidth() {
      return myScreenHeight;
    }

/**
 * Place the fields according to the screen dimensions.
 */
    protected void sublayout(int width, int height) {
      // start by positioning the animated window:
      Field animatedWindow = myFieldAnimator.getField();
      setPositionChild(animatedWindow, BORDER_WIDTH, BORDER_WIDTH);
      layoutChild(animatedWindow, myWindowWidth, myWindowHeight);
      // The dimensions and placement of the text field depend
      // on the screen dimensions and on the position of the
      // animated window:
      int textFieldWidth = 0;
      int textFieldHeight = 0;
      if(myVerticalLayout) {
        textFieldWidth = myScreenWidth;
        textFieldHeight = myScreenHeight - myWindowHeight;
        setPositionChild(myTextManager, 0, myWindowHeight + 2*(BORDER_WIDTH));
      } else {
        textFieldHeight = myScreenHeight;
        textFieldWidth = myScreenWidth - myWindowWidth;
        setPositionChild(myTextManager, myWindowWidth + 2*(BORDER_WIDTH), 0);
      }
      layoutChild(myTextManager, textFieldWidth, textFieldHeight);
      // be sure to tell the platform that this Manager fills the whole screen:
      setExtent(myScreenWidth, myScreenHeight);
    }

/**
 * Paint the two fields with a frame around the animated window.
 */
    protected void subpaint(net.rim.device.api.ui.Graphics g) {
      // choose colors to indicate the focus:
      int background = HIGHLIGHT_GRAY;
      int outline = OUTLINE;
      if(myFieldAnimator.getField().isFocus()) {
        background = SCREEN_GRAY;
        outline = WHITE;
      }
      // clear the screen and paint the animated window:
      g.setColor(background);
      g.fillRect(0, 0, myScreenWidth, myScreenHeight);
      paintChild(g, myFieldAnimator.getField());
      // draw the frame around the animated window:
      int cornerX = BORDER_WIDTH;
      int cornerY = BORDER_WIDTH;
      // first the top:
      int[] xPts = { cornerX - FRAME_WIDTH,
                     cornerX,
                     cornerX + myWindowWidth,
                     cornerX + myWindowWidth + FRAME_WIDTH };
```

```java
int[] yPts = { cornerY - FRAME_WIDTH,
               cornerY,
               cornerY,
               cornerY - FRAME_WIDTH };
// set the colors to create a gradient,
// darker on the inside edge, lighter on the outside
int[] colors = { HIGHLIGHT_GRAY,
                 SHADOW_GRAY,
                 SHADOW_GRAY,
                 HIGHLIGHT_GRAY };
g.drawShadedFilledPath(xPts, yPts, null, colors, null);
// now draw the left side:
xPts[0] = cornerX - FRAME_WIDTH;
xPts[1] = cornerX;
xPts[2] = cornerX;
xPts[3] = cornerX - FRAME_WIDTH;
yPts[0] = cornerY - FRAME_WIDTH;
yPts[1] = cornerY;
yPts[2] = cornerY + myWindowHeight;
yPts[3] = cornerY + myWindowHeight + FRAME_WIDTH;
g.drawShadedFilledPath(xPts, yPts, null, colors, null);
// now the bottom:
// reverse the colors to give more shading to the
// bottom/right sides for a 3D effect:
colors[0] = SHADOW_GRAY;
colors[1] = HIGHLIGHT_GRAY;
colors[2] = HIGHLIGHT_GRAY;
colors[3] = SHADOW_GRAY;
xPts[0] = cornerX - FRAME_WIDTH;
xPts[1] = cornerX;
xPts[2] = cornerX + myWindowWidth;
xPts[3] = cornerX + myWindowWidth + FRAME_WIDTH;
yPts[0] = cornerY + myWindowHeight + FRAME_WIDTH;
yPts[1] = cornerY + myWindowHeight;
yPts[2] = cornerY + myWindowHeight;
yPts[3] = cornerY + myWindowHeight + FRAME_WIDTH;
g.drawShadedFilledPath(xPts, yPts, null, colors, null);
// now the right side:
xPts[0] = cornerX + myWindowWidth + FRAME_WIDTH;
xPts[1] = cornerX + myWindowWidth;
xPts[2] = cornerX + myWindowWidth;
xPts[3] = cornerX + myWindowWidth + FRAME_WIDTH;
yPts[0] = cornerY - FRAME_WIDTH;
yPts[1] = cornerY;
yPts[2] = cornerY + myWindowHeight;
yPts[3] = cornerY + myWindowHeight + FRAME_WIDTH;
g.drawShadedFilledPath(xPts, yPts, null, colors, null);
// Draw a dark or highlighted outline around the window:
g.setColor(outline);
g.drawRect(cornerX, cornerY,
           myWindowWidth, myWindowHeight);
// Draw a dark outline around the frame:
g.setColor(OUTLINE);
g.drawRect(cornerX - FRAME_WIDTH - 1, cornerY - FRAME_WIDTH - 1,
           myWindowWidth + 2*FRAME_WIDTH + 1,
```

```
                myWindowHeight + 2*FRAME_WIDTH + 1);
    // end with the text field:
    paintChild(g, myTextManager);
  }

  /**
   * Override keyChar to direct key input to the active window,
   * and cause the escape key to switch the focus for ease of navigation.
   * @return Whether the key input was used.
   */
  public boolean keyChar(char key, int status, int time) {
    if(myFieldAnimator.getField().isFocus()) {
      if(key == Characters.ESCAPE) {
        // the spaceship stops moving when the player is entering
        // a message:
        myFieldAnimator.keyChar('x', status, time);
        myTextManager.setFocus();
        // force repaint:
        invalidate();
        return true;
      } else {
        return myFieldAnimator.keyChar(key, status, time);
      }
    } else {
      if(key == Characters.ESCAPE) {
        // when the user switches the focus off of the
        // message field, prompt it to send the message:
        myMessageField.sendMessage();
        myFieldAnimator.getField().setFocus();
        // force repaint:
        invalidate();
        return true;
      } else {
        return myMessageField.keyChar(key, status, time, true);
      }
    }
  }

  /**
   * Override navigationMovement to direct key input to the active window.
   * @see net.rim.device.api.ui.Screen#navigationMovement(int, int, int, int)
   */
//#ifdef RIM_4.2.0
  public boolean navigationMovement(int dx, int dy, int status, int time) {
    if(myFieldAnimator.getField().isFocus()) {
      return myFieldAnimator.navigationMovement(dx, dy, status, time);
    } else {
      return myMessageField.navigationMovement(dx, dy, status, time, true);
    }
  }
//#endif

}
```

You can see that the layout and painting functionality in Listing 9-7 is similar to the UI implementation from Chapter 4. As you saw in Listing 4-2, you don't bother with RIM's drawFocus() method to paint some sort of focus indicator around the focused field. The focus painting is handled in the subpaint() method. The animated field is queried with the isFocus() method (to check whether it is the field with the focus), and then the entire TwoFieldManager is painted accordingly: the whole background is painted a lighter shade of gray when the TweetField is focused (see Figure 9-1).

The main point to notice is how user input is handled. The default functionality uses the navigation input (from the trackball) to switch the focus from one Field to another—in addition to allowing a Field to "consume" the navigation input (for navigation inside the Field). In this game, however, the default widget navigation philosophy doesn't really make sense. In the animated game board, all of the navigation directions are used to direct the spaceship (see Listing 9-6), and in a multiline text input field, the navigation movements are important to allow the user to move the cursor around without typing. So you need some other way to switch the focus back and forth between the two Fields.

The simple solution is to use the Esc key (the back arrow) to switch the focus from one to the other. You just need to remember that the Esc key is normally a way for the user to pop the screen or exit the game, so if you override it, then you need to make sure that there's still a menu item to exit the game! (The menu construction takes place in Listing 9-8, which follows.)

The widget navigation using the Esc key is implemented in the keyChar() method in Listing 9-7. Note that this implementation of LayoutManager calls the keyChar() method of the Field that currently has the focus. Don't worry that the Field's keyChar() method would be called twice (since the platform also calls the keyChar() method of the focused Field)—it won't be. When there's user input to interpret, the platform first sends it to the containing Field or Manager (the TwoFieldManager in this case), and once the user input is consumed (by the keyChar() method returning true), the key input information won't be passed any further.

Notice also that when the user switches the focus from the MessageField back to the animated game field, the MessageField immediately posts the player's text to Twitter (see the sendMessage() method of Listing 9-2).

Organizing the Code

If you look at Figure 9-4, you see in the center the Main class, which directs the whole show. Since the various data classes have complex interrelationships, the Main class has all of the code to construct them (and later clean them up) in the right order. Some of the life cycle and error-handling code is the same as you'll find in earlier incarnations of the life cycle class (see Listing 5-3, plus the "Logging Messages with the EventLogger" sidebar from Chapter 7), so those parts aren't reprinted here.

The main point to notice in Listing 9-8 is the two different launch sequences, depending on whether the operating system version number is high enough to handle SVG. The movie that's shown on smartphones with operating system version 4.6.0 or greater is

the Space Explorer animation from Chapter 8 (see Figure 8-11). It requires the
SvgFieldAnimator class from Listing 8-4.

The other thing to notice is how the red key is handled. Any event that sends the game
to the background (the red key, for example) triggers the deactivate() method. Since
this game doesn't make sense running in the background, the deactivate() method is
implemented to stop the game and clean it up. This is the third way you've seen in this
book of handling the red key: in the SwingSaber game, it was handled in the keyDown()
method; and in the SVG game and animation, any action that obscures the screen
causes the application to quit (see Listing 8-5).

Listing 9-8. *Animation-Handling Methods of Main.java*

```
//------------------------------------------------------------
//   static methods

  /**
   * The entry point.
   */
  public static void main(String[] args) {
    // each BlackBerry application that wants to log
    // messages must register with a unique ID:
    EventLogger.register(0xe9d1942bbd3cd08cL, "tweetspace",
        EventLogger.VIEWER_STRING);
    theInstance = new Main();
//#ifdef RIM_4.6.0
    theInstance.showOpeningMovie();
//#else
    theInstance.init();
//#endif
    // Set the current thread to notify this application
    // of events such as user input.
    theInstance.enterEventDispatcher();
  }


//------------------------------------------------------------
//   special code to run the opening movie
//   for version 4.6.0+ only!

//#ifdef RIM_4.6.0
  /**
   * Movie-related data fields
   */
  SvgFieldAnimator myMovie;
  int myInvokeLaterId;
  MainScreen myMovieScreen;

  /**
   * Launch the movie.
   */
  void showOpeningMovie() {
    myMovieScreen = new MainScreen() {
      public boolean onClose() {
        // if the user escapes the movie,
```

```
          // close it up and start the game:
          cancelInvokeLater(myInvokeLaterId);
          run();
          return true;
        }
      };
      myMovie = new SvgFieldAnimator(
          Graphics.getScreenWidth(), Graphics.getScreenHeight());
      myMovieScreen.add(myMovie.getField());
      pushScreen(myMovieScreen);
      myMovie.play();
      myInvokeLaterId = invokeLater(this, 16000, false);
  }

  /**
   * Launch the game at the end of the movie.
   */
  public void run() {
    myMovie.stop();
    popScreen(myMovieScreen);
    myMovie = null;
    myMovieScreen = null;
    init();
  }
//#endif
```

The Tweet Space code actually consists of eight packages:

- net.frogparrot.tweetspace: This is the main package, containing all of the code that's unique to the Tweet Space game. It's shown in Figure 9-4.

- net.frogparrot.ui: This package contains the reusable code to create a user interface that consists of an animated field (such as a game-playing field or a fixed movie animation) and an editable text field. It's shown in Figure 9-9.

- net.frogparrot.login: This package contains generic functionality to handle input, encoding, and storage of login credentials. It's shown in Figure 9-3.

- net.frogparrot.game: This package contains just the RimSprite class from Listing 9-5. It's a generic utility that mimics some of the functionality of the javax.microedition.lcdui.game.Sprite class so that it can be used with RIM UI classes.

- net.frogparrot.svgmovie: This class is just the class from Chapter 8 that runs an SVG animation in a RIM Field. It's given in Listing 8-4.

- com.versatilemonkey.net: This is VersatileMonkey's HttpConnectionFactory class (with a related Exception), explained in the "HTTP Connections in the BlackBerry World" sidebar.

- org.json.me and org.json.me.util: These are the JSON-parsing utilities explained in the "JavaScript Object Notation" sidebar.

I just separated out all of the functionality suites that were reused or potentially reusable and put them in their own separate packages (so that the main functionality wouldn't be drowned in a jumble of peripheral code). Note that on the BlackBerry platform, packages that really are reusable can be built and installed separately as libraries for reuse. In your Ant build file (or in the JDE), just set the project type to library instead of midlet or cldc (application).

Figure 9-10 shows what the completed game looks like live.

Figure 9-10. *The Tweet Space game running on the BlackBerry 8700 smartphone*

Summary

MMORPGs are fun and easy to create by exchanging simple HTTP messages with a server on the Internet. The Tweet Space game also applies and builds on a number of game-programming techniques from previous chapters: game sprites, a custom user interface, and an opening animation.

Now that you've seen the basics of how to create a simple social game, it's time to take these skills to the next level! In the next chapter, you'll learn one last type of communications programming when you use Bluetooth to drive a remote control sports car from your BlackBerry. Then, in Chapter 11, you'll build on the HTTP programming techniques you've seen here and use the BlackBerry smartphone's Global Positioning System (GPS) to make a live-action fox-and-hounds game!

Chapter 10

Remotely Drive a (Toy) Sports Car

Grab your Walther PPK, slip it nonchalantly into Q Branch's specially modified Berns-Martin triple-draw holster. The name's Bond, BlackBerry Bond.

Choosing how to integrate a sophisticated mobile device into the hectic lifestyle of an MI5 agent with a double-0 prefix is surprisingly difficult. Perhaps it could play a dual role as a jet pack, hang glider, or vodka martini flask?

I finally found inspiration in the movie *Tomorrow Never Dies*, where Bond remotely drives his BMW 750iL (modified with rockets, tear gas, and tire spikes) via a mobile phone. He unfortunately didn't choose a BlackBerry for this task, which may explain why the car ended up falling off the roof of a hotel car park.

Sadly, the vast finances of Apress don't stretch to them buying me a BMW, but they promised me something similar, comparable with my status within the company. In due course, I received the *Dream Cheeky USB Remote Control Mini Car*, complete with its own garage (see Figure 10-1).

Figure 10-1. *My Dream Cheeky sports car*

I was somewhat disappointed to note that the car is only 9 centimeters long, but as the Dream Cheeky web site reports (www.dreamcheeky.com), it "performs like a real road car to drive away boredom at home or work."

The black wire coming out the back of the garage in Figure 10-1 is a USB cable that plugs into a PC. Inside the garage is an infrared transmitter that lets the car race around several meters from the garage.

My initial plan for connecting the system to my BlackBerry is summarized by Figure 10-2.

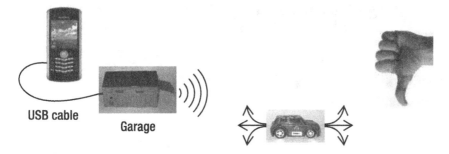

USB cable   Garage

Figure 10-2. *BlackBerry and car: Not possible!*

The "thumbs down" indicates that this configuration is impossible. The BlackBerry does have a USB port, but can only function as a peripheral device for a host controller. Typically, devices are mice and keyboards, and controllers are PCs and consoles. Since the garage is a USB *device*, I need to plug it into a host PC. This is what Dream Cheeky suggests, and they include a device driver and GUI interface for Windows. The GUI is shown in Figure 10-3.

Figure 10-3. *The Dream Cheeky Windows GUI*

The steering wheel doesn't actually turn; instead the car is moved by pressing the six red buttons positioned around the steering column. The GUI emits pleasing car revving noises, and the dashboard lights up.

My second configuration idea is shown in Figure 10-4.

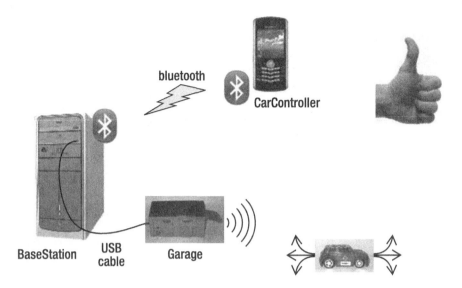

Figure 10-4. *BlackBerry, BaseStation, and car: Now we're smokin'.*

The idea is to use BlackBerry's Bluetooth support to communicate with a PC (the BaseStation) that converts the Bluetooth messages into USB commands sent down the cable to the garage. This configuration offers the user the chance to walk along with his car as it travels around the office, controlling it with the BlackBerry, via the PC.

This approach also offers a few advantages for the developer. One is that the implementation can be split into smaller parts. The GUI interface and client code on the BlackBerry (the CarController in Figure 10-4) can be developed independently of the BaseStation, which consists of a Bluetooth server and a USB command generator. These two components can also be implemented separately, leading to an application constructed from three fairly distinct pieces:

- The CarController—a GUI and Bluetooth client on the BlackBerry

- A Bluetooth server on the PC (part of the BaseStation application)

- A USB controller for the Dream Cheeky car (also part of the BaseStation)

The rest of this chapter describes the application by focusing on each of these parts in turn.

One of the drawbacks of Bluetooth coding on the BlackBerry is that RIM's device simulator doesn't support Bluetooth, and so it's not possible to test an application without employing a real device. I didn't have a BlackBerry during the early stages of my coding, so I implemented a second version of CarController, called BlueCarController, on a netbook (see Figure 10-5).

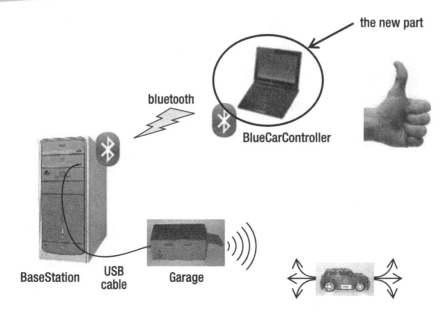

Figure 10-5. *Netbook, BaseStation, and car: Still smokin'.*

This wasn't as much work as I'd thought beforehand, and it meant that I could test out the BaseStation code in a wireless situation without requiring a BlackBerry. Other advantages of this strategy are that porting CarController highlighted a few design problems, and I ended up with a GUI that runs on different devices.

Since this book is about BlackBerry development, I won't describe the netbook BlueCarController in much detail, but the code is available at the book's web site (http://frogparrot.net/blackberry/ch10/).

A Quick Introduction to USB

USB (Universal Serial Bus) communication is carried out between a host and its devices. Usually the host is a PC or laptop, and devices their peripherals, such as printers, hard drives, and keyboards. The host detects devices, manages data flow on the communications bus, carries out error checking, and often provides power to the devices. In this chapter, the host is the PC running the BaseStation application, and the device is the Dream Cheeky garage and car.

A device is uniquely identified by its vendor and product IDs (two hexadecimal digits), which are essential information for USB programming. The Dream Cheeky car comes with very little technical information, so the easiest way to find its IDs is with a USB analysis tool, such as USBDeview (free from www.nirsoft.net/utils/usb_devices_view.html). Figure 10-6 shows USBDeview's brief list of USB devices attached to one of my test machines.

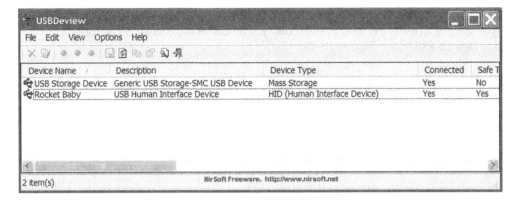

Figure 10-6. *USBDeview's list of USB devices*

The Dream Cheeky vehicle is identified as Rocket Baby, a name that doesn't appear anywhere in the Dream Cheeky documentation. Double-clicking the Rocket Baby row brings up more details, shown in Figure 10-7.

Properties	
Device Name:	Rocket Baby
Description:	USB Human Interface Device
Device Type:	HID (Human Interface Device)
Connected:	Yes
Safe To Unplug:	Yes
Disabled:	No
USB Hub:	No
Drive Letter:	
Serial Number:	
Created Date:	30/07/2009 15:23:16
Last Plug/Unplug Date:	13/12/2009 11:31:34
VendorID:	0a81
ProductID:	0702
USB Class:	03
USB SubClass:	00
USB Protocol:	00
Hub / Port:	Hub 1, Port 2
Computer Name:	
Vendor Name:	
Product Name:	
ParentId Prefix:	6&25352eab&0

OK

Figure 10-7. *USBDeview's details on Rocket Baby*

The important entries for my needs are the VendorID and ProductID hexadecimals: 0a81 and 0702.

A less direct way of finding this information is to browse through Window's Device Manager, via the Control Panel's System utility. The car is registered as a Human Interface Device (HID) (see Figure 10-8).

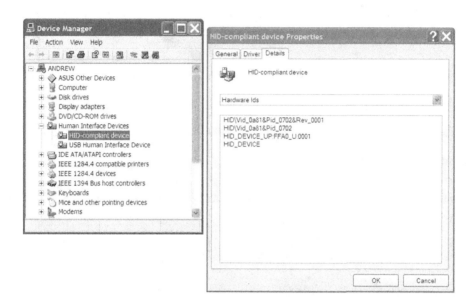

Figure 10-8. *Device manager HID information*

Devices often belong to a particular USB class; for example, the HID class includes keyboards, pointing devices, and game controllers.

When a new device is plugged in, the host enters a discovery phase where it examines and initializes the device. Typically, a device driver is loaded based on the device's USB class, and communication can then begin.

USB supports four forms of communication (called transfer types): control, bulk, interrupt, and isochronous. Fortunately, I only need control transfers to control the Dream Cheeky vehicle. Bulk transfers are intended for applications where the rate of transfer isn't critical, such as sending a file to a printer. Interrupt transfers are for devices that receive the host's attention periodically, such as keyboards and mice. Isochronous transfers have guaranteed delivery time but no error correcting, so are often utilized for streaming audio and video.

A *control transfer* consists of up to three stages: setup, data (which is optional), and status. The setup stage contains a request (e.g., to send information to a device or set its configuration). The data stage transmits data from the host to the device (or device to host depending on the request type). The status stage delivers details about the success of the transfer.

I'll use control writes to send car movement commands from the host (the PC) to the device (the garage).

For a longer introduction to USB, I suggest the USB Made Simple site at www.usbmadesimple.co.uk. A wonderful source for lots more information is Jan Axelson's web site, www.lvr.com. He is also the author of the definitive book on USB, *USB Complete: The Developer's Guide, Fourth Edition* (Lakeview Research, 2009). The USB specification is very readable and can be found at www.usb.org/developers/docs.

The Human Interface Device Class

After installing the Dream Cheeky GUI, a quick look in its code directory (C:\Program Files\keUSBCAR) reveals a library called USBHID.dll. The name is very suggestive, but it's also possible to look inside the DLL using tools such as PE Explorer (www.heaventools.com/overview.htm) to discover that it uses Windows's HID.DLL library (see Figure 10-9).

RVA	Name
100316A6h	KERNEL32.dll
100317A2h	USER32.dll
10031828h	SETUPAPI.dll
100318A0h	HID.DLL

Figure 10-9. *The libraries used by Dream Cheeky's USBHID.dll*

It's not surprising that Dream Cheeky employs the Windows HID API (details at http://msdn.microsoft.com/en-us/library/ms793246.aspx) to interface with the garage. Windows has included HID drivers since the early days of USB, and the HID class is popular for defining nonstandard device drivers (i.e., for USB gadgets that aren't handy drives).

The HID specification is quite small, consisting of just six requests types, and I only need one of them, SET_REPORT, which provides a way for the host to transfer data (called reports) to the device. For details on HID, see www.usb.org/developers/hidpage and www.lvr.com/hidpage.htm. It's also very clearly explained over three chapters in Jan Axelson's *USB Complete* (mentioned previously).

The Windows HID API provides an extensive set of functions for building, sending, and receiving reports. The bad news is that there isn't a Java binding for this API. That's quite a major hole in Java's support for USB, bearing in mind the popularity of the HID class. The good news is that a SET_REPORT request is actually just a control write transfer, and so it's easy to "build" a SET_REPORT using a lower-level USB library that offers control transfers.

A Java USB Library

JSR 80 is the candidate USB extension for Java, located at http://javax-usb.org. The Windows implementation has been in an alpha state for several years, and I had quite a number of problems getting it to transfer data. Instead I went for LibusbJava, available from http://libusbjava.sourceforge.net/wp.

LibusbJava relies on libusb-win32, a Windows port of a widely used USB library for Linux. libusb-win32 can be downloaded from http://libusb-win32.sourceforge.net, as two packages: libusb-win32-filter-bin-0.1.12.1.exe and libusb-win32-device-bin-0.1.12.1.tar.gz.

The executable installs libusb-win32 in C:\Program Files\LibUSB-Win32\, along with various drivers. testlibusb-win.exe, located in C:\Program Files\LibUSB-Win32\bin, can be employed to test the installation by listing out the USB devices linked to the PC.

libusb-win32-device-bin-0.1.12.1.tar.gz contains the inf-wizard.exe tool in libusb-win32-device-bin-0.1.12.1\bin\. It can be used to create a INF file, which specifies how the car will be controlled by libusb-win32 at runtime. inf-wizard.exe starts by listing all the devices connected to the PC, listed by their vendor ID, product ID, and device description (see Figure 10-10).

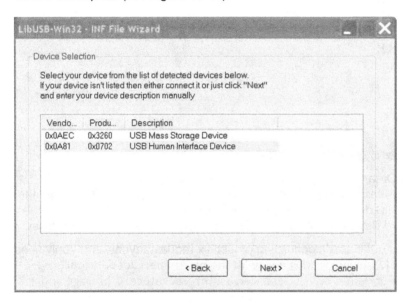

Figure 10-10. *The inf-wizard.exe application*

The output from USBDeview USBDeview (see Figure 10-7) let me identify the second entry in Figure 10-10 as the Dream Cheeky car. After I'd selected that entry, inf-wizard.exe generated an INF file for the vehicle, which I installed in the operating system by right-clicking it.

Once libusb-win32 is installed, the LibusbJava library can be downloaded from http://libusbjava.sourceforge.net/wp. The necessary files are a JAR (ch.ntb.usb-0.5.9.jar) and a zipped DLL (LibusbJava_dll_0.2.4.0.zip). I placed the JAR and unzipped DLL in a directory on my D:\ drive (D:\libusbjava\), but anywhere is fine.

The JAR includes a number of test applications, the simplest being a viewer for all the USB devices connected to the machine. Figure 10-11 shows its output with the Dream Cheeky car IDs highlighted.

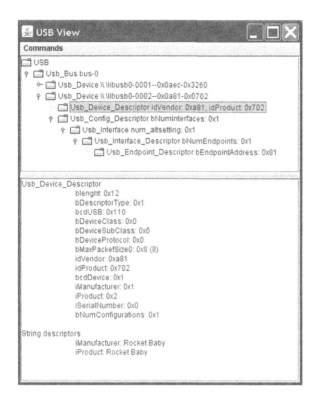

Figure 10-11. *The USB view application*

The viewer (which is inside `ch.ntb.usb-0.5.9.jar`) is started using the command line:

```
java -Djava.library.path="d:\libusbjava"
          -cp "d:\libusbjava\ch.ntb.usb-0.5.9.jar;."
               ch.ntb.usb.usbView.UsbView
```

The paths to the DLL and JAR files need to match their location on your machine.

LibusbJava's API documentation is at `http://libusbjava.sourceforge.net/wp/res/doc`. Of special importance for my needs is the `usb_control_msg()` method in `LibusbJava`, which sends a control transfer to a device.

Analyzing the Dream Cheeky Car Protocol

Before I can start sending control transfers from the PC to the car, I need to know what should go in the messages. Most off-the-shelf USB gadgets don't come with this kind of technical information, so what's to be done? It's time to turn detective, with the help of a USB protocol analyzer.

I decided to use SourceQuest's SourceUSB (`www.sourcequest.com`), a simple-to-use but powerful analyzer that records USB I/O requests and other events. It's not free, but a 30-day trial period is a good way to try out the product. It requires the user to register for a free activation key.

Another popular and free analyzer is SnoopyPro from
http://sourceforge.net/projects/usbsnoop. I tried this tool but found that it interacted
rather strangely with the car device driver, causing the vehicle to behave erratically (e.g.,
start moving but refuse to stop).

The first step in analyzing with SourceUSB is to identify which device should be monitored.
The simplest thing is to look through the detected devices' vendor and product IDs. Figure
10-12 shows the description details for the port 2 HID device, which must be the Dream
Cheeky car because the Vid and Pid values in its Hardware ID are 0a81 and 0702.

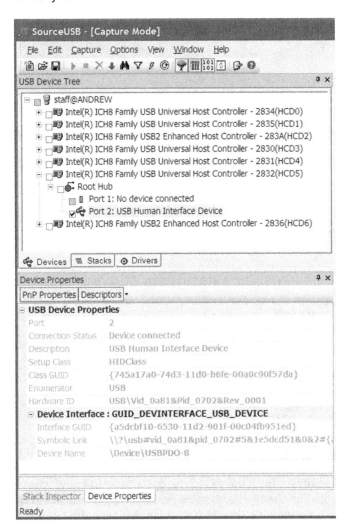

Figure 10-12. *SourceUSB device description details*

The next step is to turn on packet capturing for that device, and fire up the Dream
Cheeky GUI (as shown in Figure 10-3). I pressed the forward and reverse buttons a few
times, and looked at SourceUSB's captured packets (see Figure 10-13).

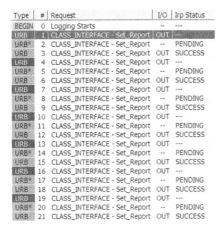

Type	#	Request	I/O	Irp Status
BEGIN	0	Logging Starts	--	---
URB	1	CLASS_INTERFACE - Set_Report	OUT	---
URB*	2	CLASS_INTERFACE - Set_Report	--	PENDING
URB	3	CLASS_INTERFACE - Set_Report	OUT	SUCCESS
URB	4	CLASS_INTERFACE - Set_Report	OUT	---
URB*	5	CLASS_INTERFACE - Set_Report	--	PENDING
URB	6	CLASS_INTERFACE - Set_Report	OUT	SUCCESS
URB	7	CLASS_INTERFACE - Set_Report	OUT	---
URB*	8	CLASS_INTERFACE - Set_Report	--	PENDING
URB	9	CLASS_INTERFACE - Set_Report	OUT	SUCCESS
URB	10	CLASS_INTERFACE - Set_Report	OUT	---
URB*	11	CLASS_INTERFACE - Set_Report	--	PENDING
URB	12	CLASS_INTERFACE - Set_Report	OUT	SUCCESS
URB	13	CLASS_INTERFACE - Set_Report	OUT	---
URB*	14	CLASS_INTERFACE - Set_Report	--	PENDING
URB	15	CLASS_INTERFACE - Set_Report	OUT	SUCCESS
URB	16	CLASS_INTERFACE - Set_Report	OUT	---
URB*	17	CLASS_INTERFACE - Set_Report	--	PENDING
URB	18	CLASS_INTERFACE - Set_Report	OUT	SUCCESS
URB	19	CLASS_INTERFACE - Set_Report	OUT	---
URB*	20	CLASS_INTERFACE - Set_Report	--	PENDING
URB	21	CLASS_INTERFACE - Set_Report	OUT	SUCCESS

Figure 10-13. *Packets caught by SourceUSB*

The volume of data in Figure 10-13 is a bit daunting, but essentially a series of SET_REPORT messages are being sent from the host (the PC) to the device (the car). A message appears in a dark URB row, and is followed by two rows of URB interrupt transfer messages. The transfers, which have PENDING and SUCCESS Irp status values, can be ignored. As a result, Figure 10-13 shows a total of seven SET_REPORT messages.

Figure 10-14 shows the details of the first SET_REPORT packet.

Figure 10-14. *The first SET_REPORT packet*

Figure 10-15 shows the details of the second SET_REPORT packet

Figure 10-15. *The second SET_REPORT packet*

What should be apparent after some examination is that the two packets are identical, except for their data content. The first packet contains 0x01, the second 0xFF. In fact, every SET_REPORT packet is identical except for its data.

Figure 10-16 shows the data in the third SET_REPORT packet.

Figure 10-16. *The third SET_REPORT packet*

Figure 10-17 shows the data in the fourth SET_REPORT packet.

Figure 10-17. *The fourth SET_REPORT packet*

The third packet contained 0x08, and the fourth 0xFF. After several minutes of experimentation, the pattern of data transmission becomes apparent. A forward car movement consists of two messages: 0x01 is sent when the forward button is pressed, and 0xFF is sent when the button is released. A backward movement also consists of two messages: 0x08 is sent when the button is pressed, and 0xFF is sent when the button is released. The 0xFF message is equivalent to "stop."

Playing with the other buttons on the car's GUI reveals the data sent when those buttons are pressed, which is summarized by Figure 10-18.

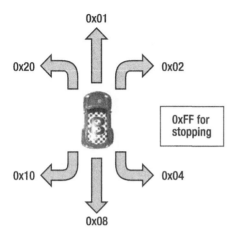

Figure 10-18. *Button presses and their data*

For example, when the user presses the "turn left" button on the GUI, 0x20 is sent in the control transfer. When the button is released, 0xFF is sent.

Using the LibusbJava Library

The LibusbJava web site (http://libusbjava.sourceforge.net) includes a number of general examples, so the following program (CarTester.java) concentrates on how to send control transfers. The LibusbJava API documentation is online at http://libusbjava.sourceforge.net/wp/res/doc.

The main() function of CarTester.java gives a good overview of what the program does: a connection is made to the car based on its version and product IDs, and then the vehicle is sent forward a short distance, and after a brief wait, made to reverse.

```
public static void main(String[] args)
{
  CarTester carDev = new CarTester((short)0x0a81, (short)0x0702);
                      // version and product IDs for the car
  carDev.forward(400);    // move forward for 400ms

  System.out.println("Waiting...");
  try {
    Thread.sleep(2000);
  }
  catch(InterruptedException e) {}

  carDev.backward(400);
  carDev.close();
}  // end of main()
```

The CarTester() constructor initializes the library, finds the device, and opens a connection to it, which is stored as a long integer (called a handle).

```java
// global
private long handle = 0;


public CarTester(short vid, short pid)
{
  LibusbJava.usb_init();

  Usb_Device dev = findDevice(vid, pid);
  if (dev == null) {
    System.out.println("Device not found");
    System.exit(1);
  }

  System.out.println("Found Device. Openning...");
  handle = LibusbJava.usb_open(dev);
  if (handle == 0) {
    System.out.println("Failed to Open");
    System.exit(1);
  }
}  // end of CarTester()
```

findDevice() finds all the communication buses and devices connected to the host, and then searches through them looking for the device with the specified vendor and product IDs.

```java
private Usb_Device findDevice(short vid, short pid)
{
  System.out.println("Looking for device: (vendor: 0x" +
            Integer.toHexString(vid) +
            "; product: 0x" + Integer.toHexString(pid) + ")");
  LibusbJava.usb_find_busses();
  LibusbJava.usb_find_devices();

  Usb_Bus bus = LibusbJava.usb_get_busses();
  while (bus != null) {
    Usb_Device dev = bus.getDevices();
    while (dev != null) {
      Usb_Device_Descriptor desc = dev.getDescriptor();
      System.out.println("  examining device: " + desc);
      if ((desc.getIdVendor() == vid) &&
          (desc.getIdProduct() == pid))
        return dev;
      dev = dev.getNext();
    }
    bus = bus.getNext();
  }
  return null;
}  // end of findDevice()
```

Closing down a device at the end of main() is a matter of calling LibusbJava.usb_close() on the handle.

```
public void close()
{
  System.out.println("Closing");
  if (handle > 0) {
    LibusbJava.usb_close(handle);
    handle = 0;
  }
}  // end of close()
```

Moving the Car

I decided to implement timed forward and reverse operations to allow the car to move for a specified period and then stop.

```
public void forward(int period)
{ System.out.println("  forward");
  sendCommand(0x01, period);
}

public void backward(int period)
{ System.out.println("  backward");
  sendCommand(0x08, period);
}

private void sendCommand(int opCode, int period)
// execute the opCode operation for period ms
{ if (handle > 0) {
    sendControl(opCode);
    wait(period);
    sendControl(0xFF);    // stop the operation
  }
}

private void wait(int ms)
{ try {
    Thread.sleep(ms);
  }
  catch(InterruptedException e) {}
}
```

The movement data is hardwired into the forward() and backward() calls to sendCommand(), which calls sendControl() with the data, waits a set time, and then calls sendControl() again with the 0xFF stop data.

sendControl() uses LibusbJava.usb_control_msg() to build and send a control transfer over to the device.

```
private void sendControl(int opCode)
{
  byte[] bytes = { new Integer(opCode).byteValue() };

  int rval = LibusbJava.usb_control_msg(handle,
              USB.REQ_TYPE_DIR_HOST_TO_DEVICE |
              USB.REQ_TYPE_TYPE_CLASS |
```

```
                           USB.REQ_TYPE_RECIP_INTERFACE,
                           0x09, 0x0200, 0,
                           bytes, bytes.length, 2000);
    if (rval < 0) {
      System.err.println("Control Error: " + LibusbJava.usb_strerror() );
      close();
      System.exit(1);
    }
  }  // end of sendControl()
```

The prototype for LibusbJava.usb_control_msg() is

```
public static int usb_control_msg(long handle, int requesttype,
               int request, int value, int index,
               byte[] bytes, int size, int timeout)
```

The parameters use (almost) the same names as in the USB control transfer specification, and the method returns the number of bytes written (or a negative number if there's an error). The relevant section of the specification (available at www.usb.org/developers/docs) is section 9.3 (in the Revision 2.0 document).

The packet information generated by SourceUSB is a great help for knowing what arguments should be passed to LibusbJava.usb_control_msg(). Figure 10-14 lists the settings for bmRequestType, Request, Value (high and low bytes), Index, and Length.

bmRequestType is a mix of three bit settings, for the data transfer direction, the device type, and the type of the recipient, which Figure 10-14 shows to be 0x22, or a combination of the constants OUT, CLASS, and ENDPOINT. In LibusbJava these constants are called USB.REQ_TYPE_DIR_HOST_TO_DEVICE, USB.REQ_TYPE_CLASS, and USB.REQ_TYPE_RECIP_ENDPOINT. To my dismay, this collection of bits did *not* work when I tried them in LibusbJava.usb_control_msg(). I was forced to try other bit combinations, until I arrived at USB.REQ_TYPE_DIR_HOST_TO_DEVICE, USB.REQ_TYPE_TYPE_CLASS and USB.REQ_TYPE_RECIP_INTERFACE (which is equivalent to 0x21).

> **Note** An endpoint is a device port where data arrives. An interface is a collection of endpoints.

Another tricky argument is the value integer in LibusbJava.usb_control_msg(), which is displayed as two bytes by SourceUSB in Figure 10-14. The two bytes must be combined into a single hexadecimal (i.e., 0x02 and 0x00 become 0x0200).

The timeout value is not part of the USB specification, but is used by libusb to decide how long to wait for a response before signaling an error.

USB Devices Are Temperamental

My experiences with programming USB gadgets have not been too pleasant, so I thought I'd briefly mention some techniques I've developed for avoiding, or at least reducing, headaches.

It helps to have two test machines. In the case of the Dream Cheeky car, I installed the Dream Cheeky GUI on one machine, and the LibusbJava library, libusb-win32 library, and libusb-win32-generated car driver on another. In this way there's no chance of having two device drivers for the same USB gadget interact badly. At the programming level, this kind of interaction problem often shows itself as the informative Windows USB error, "A device attached to the system is not functioning."

If a device driver generates an error, the only certain way to correctly reset it is to reboot the machine. This may eventually add hours to the application's development time.

Although SourceUSB is a great tool, it may not report the full story of what is happening at the operating system kernel and hardware levels. For example, my problem with the control transfer's request type is probably due to the kernel converting it from using an endpoint to using the device's interface.

Always write a simple test rig (e.g., CarTester.java) to test the communication protocol before moving to a more complex application.

The USBCar Class

Once CarTester.java was working, I made a few minor changes to convert it into the USBCar class, whose class diagram is shown in Figure 10-19 (only public methods are shown).

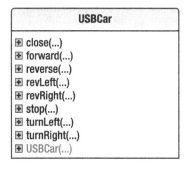

Figure 10-19. *Class diagram for the USBCar class*

The constructor, USBCar(), works in the same way as CarTester's constructor, using version and product IDs to find a device. There are also seven methods that move the car, which differ from CarTester in not having a time period argument:

```
public void forward()
{ sendControl(0x01); }

public void turnRight()
{ sendControl(0x02); }

public void revRight()
{ sendControl(0x04); }

public void reverse()
```

```
{ sendControl(0x08); }

public void revLeft()
{ sendControl(0x10); }

public void turnLeft()
{ sendControl(0x20); }

public void stop()
{ sendControl(0xFF); }
```

sendControl() is unchanged from CarTester.java—it sends a single control transfer to the device.

It's up to the user of the USBCar class to ensure that stop() is called; otherwise, the car will never stop after being sent a movement command.

A Bluetooth Server

The BaseStation application on the PC performs two main tasks: it sends USB movement commands to the garage, and it acts as a Bluetooth server, receiving messages from the BlackBerry (i.e., see Figure 10-4). The USB operations are managed by an instance of the USBCar class, but how is the Bluetooth code implemented?

Before getting down to coding details, I'll supply some background on Bluetooth, JSR 82 (a Java layer over Bluetooth for mobile devices), and BlueCove (a version of JSR 82 for Java SE).

Bluetooth

Bluetooth is a wireless technology for communication over distances of up to 10 meters, offering reasonably fast data transfer rates of around 1 Mbps, principally between battery-powered devices. Bluetooth's primary intent is to support the creation of ad hoc personal area networks (PANs) for small data transfers (or voice communication) between devices such as phones and PDAs.

Bluetooth is ideal as the communications layer for mobile games involving a small number of players, such as sports (e.g., tennis) and networked board games (e.g., Go). An oft-cited drawback that the players must be physically near each other is actually perceived as an advantage by people who enjoy a social element in their gaming.

Bluetooth PANs come in two main configurations: *piconets* and *scatternets*. A piconet is analogous to a client/server application, and is how I'll be using Bluetooth in this chapter. Piconets are so named because they only permit a maximum of seven clients to be connected to a server at a time.

A scatternet lets a server be the client of another piconet, enabling the construction of peer-to-peer networks. Scatternet functionality is not widely supported on phones and PDAs at the moment.

Bluetooth information can be found at www.bluetooth.org and www.bluetooth.com.

JSR 82

JSR 82 is a Java ME layer over a Bluetooth software stack that hides the underlying Bluetooth hardware or firmware in the device. Figure 10-20 shows these layers.

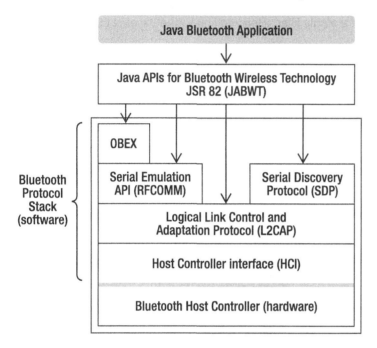

Figure 10-20. *JSR 82 and Bluetooth stack*

L2CAP segments data into packets for transmission and reassembles received packets into larger messages.

RFCOMM provides functionality similar to a standard serial communications port, which is utilized as a stream connection at the Java level. I employ RFCOMM as the communications link between the BlackBerry and the PC.

OBEX (Object Exchange protocol) provides a means of moving data as objects (such as images and files), and is built on top of RFCOMM.

Service Discovery Protocol (SDP) allows a server to register its services with the device, and is also employed by clients looking for devices and services. The Java ME Bluetooth API hides SDP behind a discovery API supported by a DiscoveryAgent class and DiscoveryListener interface.

A good Java ME-plus-Bluetooth site is www.javabluetooth.com, which includes a Bluetooth introduction, information on kits and devices, and a FAQ.

BlueCove

BlueCove is a free implementation of the Bluetooth stack for Java SE on Windows XP, Linux, and the Mac (http://bluecove.org). It implements JSR 82, including SDP, RFCOMM, L2CAP, and OBEX.

My BlueCove needs are quite modest—I want to create a server that can accept a single RFCOMM stream connection from a BlackBerry client. There's no need for the server to be threaded since I only expect a single BlackBerry to link to the BaseStation code (e.g., see Figure 10-4).

Downloading BlueCove is very simple, just a single bluecove-2.1.0.jar JAR file is required. The tricky part is making sure that the Bluetooth device (in my case a dongle connected to a USB port of my PC) utilizes a Bluetooth stack recognized by BlueCove.

The dongle came with a BlueSoleil Bluetooth stack (www.bluesoleil.com), which offers a range of useful services on top of the standard Bluetooth functionality (e.g., file synchronization between machines). A quick look at the BlueCove documentation (http://code.google.com/p/bluecove/wiki/Documentation) seemed to suggest that BlueCove would happily work with BlueSoleil. It was only after receiving some baffling runtime error messages that I reread the documentation and found that BlueCove only supports BlueSoleil versions 1.6.0, 2.3, and 3.2.2.8. My dongle came with BlueSoleil version 6, which isn't recognized. In fact, even BlueSoleil version 3.2.2.8 didn't seem to be agreeable to BlueCove. Finally, I uninstalled all of the BlueSoleil software, and controlled the dongle using Window XP's built-in Bluetooth stack. This only supports RFCOMM connections, but that's all I need for this chapter's application.

The Base Station

A Bluetooth server is identified by a Bluetooth UUID (universally unique identifier) and a service name, which can be anything. In BaseStation.java, I use

```
private static final String UUID_STRING = "11111111111111111111111111111111";
                  // 32 hex digits which will become a 128-bit ID
private static final String SERVICE_NAME = "basestation";
                  // use lowercase
```

The main() method makes the server *discoverable* by a client and begins waiting for a client stream connection:

```
// global
private static USBCar carDev;


public static void main(String args[])
{
  carDev = new USBCar((short)0x0a81, (short)0x0702);
              // the car's vendor and product IDs
  try {
    System.out.println("Setting device to be discoverable...");
    LocalDevice local = LocalDevice.getLocalDevice();
```

```
      local.setDiscoverable(DiscoveryAgent.GIAC);

      /* Create an RFCOMM connection notifier for the server, with
         the given UUID and name. */
      System.out.println("Start advertising BaseStation server...");
      StreamConnectionNotifier server =
         (StreamConnectionNotifier) Connector.open(
            "btspp://localhost:" + UUID_STRING + ";name=" + SERVICE_NAME);

      while (true) {
        System.out.println("Waiting for incoming connection...");
        StreamConnection conn = server.acceptAndOpen();
          // wait for a client connection
          // acceptAndOpen() makes the service visible to clients
        System.out.println("Connection requested...");
        processClient(conn);
      }
    }
    catch (Exception e) {
      System.out.println(e);
    }

    carDev.close();
  }  // end of main()
```

The server's device is made discoverable by a client with the code:

```
LocalDevice local = LocalDevice.getLocalDevice();
local.setDiscoverable(DiscoveryAgent.GIAC);
```

The DiscoveryAgent.GIAC (general/unlimited inquiry access code) constant means that all remote devices (i.e., all the clients) will be able to find the device. There's also a DiscoveryAgent.LIAC constant, which limits the device's visibility.

The RFCOMM stream connection offered by the server requires a suitably formatted URL. The basic format is

```
btspp://<hostname>:<UUID>;<parameters>
```

I use localhost as the hostname, but any Bluetooth address can be employed.

The UUID field is a unique 128-bit identifier representing the service; I utilize a 32-digit hexadecimal string (each hex digit uses 4 bits).

The URL's parameters are <name>=<value> pairs, separated by semicolons. Typical <name> values are name for the service name (used here), and security parameters such as authenticate, authorize, and encrypt. It's best to make the name string all lowercase; otherwise, some JSR 82 clients won't recognize it at discovery time.

The creation of the StreamConnectionNotifier instance, called server, by the Connector.open() call generates a service record. The record is a description of the Bluetooth service as a set of ID/value attributes. It can be accessed by calling LocalDevice.getRecord():

```
ServiceRecord record = local.getRecord(server);
```

The ServiceRecord class offers get/set methods for accessing and changing a record's attributes.

The call to acceptAndOpen() inside the while loop makes the server block until a client connection arrives, and also adds the server's service record to the device's Service Discovery Database (SDDB). When a client carries out device and service discovery, it contacts the SDDBs of the devices that it's investigating.

When a client connection is made, acceptAndOpen() returns a MIDP StreamConnection object, which is passed to processClient() to handle the client communication.

Processing the Client

processClient() converts the connection into input and output streams, and uses processMsgs() to read and write messages between the server and client. When the communication is finished, these streams and connection are closed.

```
private static void processClient(StreamConnection conn)
{
  try {
    reportDeviceName(conn);

    /* Get an InputStream and OutputStream from the
       stream connection, and start processing client messages.
    */
    InputStream in = conn.openInputStream();
    OutputStream out = conn.openOutputStream();
    processMsgs(in, out);

    System.out.println("Close down connection");
    if (conn != null) {
      in.close();
      out.close();
      conn.close();
    }
  }
  catch (IOException e)
  {  System.out.println(e);  }
} // end of processClient()
```

It's possible to map a DataInputStream and DataOutputStream to the StreamConnection instance so that basic Java data types (e.g., ints, floats, doubles, strings) can be read and written. I've used InputStream and OutputStream because their byte-based read() and write() methods can be easily utilized as building blocks for implementing different forms of message processing (as shown following in readData() and sendMessage()).

reportDeviceName() prints the friendly name of the client device.

```
private static void reportDeviceName(StreamConnection conn)
{
  String devName;
  try {
    RemoteDevice rd = RemoteDevice.getRemoteDevice(conn);
```

```
    devName = rd.getFriendlyName(false);   // to reduce connections
  }
  catch (IOException e)
  { devName = "Device ??";   }

  System.out.println("Connection made by device: " + devName);
} // end of reportDeviceName()
```

The information about a remote device (the client in this case) is stored in a RemoteDevice instance. RemoteDevice includes methods for finding the client's Bluetooth address, its friendly device name, and details about its security settings. It also includes a method for verifying those settings.

The handler retrieves the client's device name by calling RemoteDevice.getFriendlyName():

```
devName = rd.getFriendlyName(false);
```

The false argument stops the handler from obtaining the name by contacting the client via a new connection. Instead, information present in the RemoteDevice object (rd) is utilized.

If true is used, it's possible for an IOException to be raised on certain platforms, because the requested connection may take the total number of connections past the maximum allowed.

Processing Messages

The processMsgs() method waits for a message to arrive from the client and passes it to processMsg(). The message bye$$ is treated specially since it denotes that the client wants to close the link.

```
private static void processMsgs(InputStream in, OutputStream out)
{
  boolean isRunning = true;
  String line;
  while (isRunning) {
    if((line = readData(in)) == null)   // there's a problem
      isRunning = false;
    else {   // there was some input
      if (line.equals("bye$$")) {
        isRunning = false;
        sendMessage(out, "ok: exiting");
      }
      else
        processMsg(out, line);
    }
  }
} // end of processMsgs()
```

The messy details of reading a message are hidden inside readData(), which either returns the message as a string, or null if there's been a problem. A message is transmitted with sendMessage().

A message from the CarController client consists of two words. The first is a direction, which can be left, fwd, right, revLeft, rev, or revRight. The word carHorn can also be received, but is currently ignored. The direction word is followed by the string `true` or `false`—`true` means that the car should start moving in that direction, while `false` tells it to stop. On the client side, `true` indicates that a direction button has been pressed, while `false` means that the button has been released.

```java
// global
private static USBCar carDev;


private static void processMsg(OutputStream out, String line)
{
  System.out.println("Processing message: " + line);

  String[] tokens = line.split("\\s+");
  if (tokens.length != 2) {
    System.out.println("error: wrong no. of tokens");
    sendMessage(out, "error: wrong no. of tokens");
    return;
  }

  if (tokens[1].equals("false")) {  // button released
    carDev.stop();
    sendMessage(out, "ok: stopped");
  }
  else {    // pressed a direction button
    if (tokens[0].equals("left")) {
      carDev.turnLeft();
      sendMessage(out, "ok: turned left");
    }
    else if (tokens[0].equals("fwd")) {
      carDev.forward();
      sendMessage(out, "ok: forward");
    }
    else if (tokens[0].equals("right")) {
      carDev.turnRight();
      sendMessage(out, "ok: turned right");
    }
    else if (tokens[0].equals("revLeft")) {
      carDev.revLeft();
      sendMessage(out, "ok: reversed left");
    }
    else if (tokens[0].equals("rev")) {
      carDev.reverse();
      sendMessage(out, "ok: reversed");
    }
    else if (tokens[0].equals("revRight")) {
      carDev.revRight();
      sendMessage(out, "ok: reversed right");
    }
    else if (tokens[0].equals("carHorn")) {  // no direction action
      sendMessage(out, "ok: horn ignored");
    }
    else {
      System.out.println("Did not recognize direction; stopping");
      carDev.stop();
```

```
      sendMessage(out, "error: unknown direction");
    }
  }
}  // end of processMsg()
```

A direction string is converted into a USB command that is sent to the car using the USBCar instance, carDev, and a message is sent back to the client indicating what the server has done.

Reading a Message

When a client sends a message to the server (e.g., left true), it's actually sent as a stream of bytes prefixed with its length (e.g., 9left true). The number is encoded in a single byte, which puts an upper limit on the message's length at 255 characters.

Since a message always begins with its length, readData() can use that value to constrain the number of bytes it reads from the input stream.

```
private static String readData(InputStream in)
{
  byte[] data = null;
  try
    int len = in.read();      // get the message length
    if (len <= 0) {
      System.out.println("Message Length Error");
      return null;
    }

    data = new byte[len];
    len = 0;
    // read the message, perhaps requiring several read() calls
    while (len != data.length) {
      int ch = in.read(data, len, data.length - len);
      if (ch == -1) {
        System.out.println("Message Read Error");
        return null;
      }
      len += ch;
    }
  }
  catch (IOException e)
  {  System.out.println("readData(): " + e);
     return null;
  }

  // convert byte[] to trimmed String
  return new String(data).trim();
} // end of readData()
```

InputStream.read() is called repeatedly until the necessary number of bytes have been obtained. The bytes are converted into a String and returned; the message length is discarded.

Sending a Message

sendMessage() () adds the message's length to the front of a message, and the result is sent out as a sequence of bytes:

```
private static boolean sendMessage(OutputStream out, String msg)
{
  try {
    out.write(msg.length());
    out.write(msg.getBytes());
    return true;
  }
  catch (Exception e)
  {  System.out.println("sendMessage(): " + e);
     return false;
  }
}  // end of sendMessage()
```

The Car Controls

The CarControls RIMlet performs two main tasks: it presents a GUI for controlling the car, and it functions as a Bluetooth client for sending car commands over to the BaseStation on the PC (see Figure 10-4 for the configuration). It also has a third, minor, role, of playing car-revving sound clips when a button is pressed.

The GUI is shown in Figure 10-21 as it appears in the BlackBerry 9530 simulator.

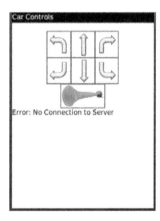

Figure 10-21. *The CarControls GUI*

The seven picture buttons change color when pressed. When a button is pressed, a sound is emitted until the button is released.

The status message Error: No Connection to Server is also accompanied by a dialog box message (see Figure 10-22), which can be dismissed.

Figure 10-22. *Dialog box concerning Bluetooth support*

A drawback of RIM's simulator is that it doesn't support Bluetooth, and so a Bluetooth client can only be properly tested on a real device.

Figure 10-23 shows the class diagram for the CarControls RIMlet, with private methods hidden.

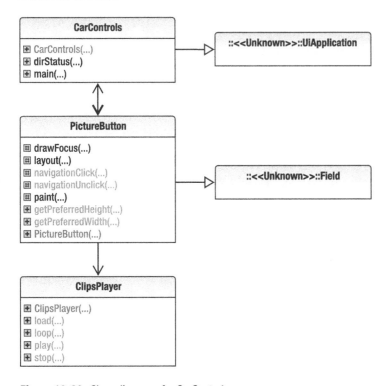

Figure 10-23. *Class diagrams for CarControls*

CarControls is the top-level application that manages the Bluetooth connection to the BaseStation. Each picture button is implemented as an instance of PictureButton, and ClipsPlayer loads and plays car sounds. ClipsPlayer is a simplified version of the same-named class from Chapter 6. The original ClipsPlayer stores a collection of MMAPI (Mobile Media API) player objects in a Hashtable whose keys are their file names. The clips can be MIDI, MP3, WAV, or AU files, or tone sequences (JTS files). There's also a static method for playing a note for a certain period. The version used in this chapter can only play WAV files.

Initializing the Car Controls

The CarControls () constructor initializes the ClipsPlayer, creates the GUI, and sets up the Bluetooth connection with the server:

```
public CarControls()
{
  ClipsPlayer player = new ClipsPlayer();
  player.load("ignition");

  MainScreen mainScreen = new MainScreen();
  mainScreen.setTitle( new LabelField("Car Controls",
                    LabelField.ELLIPSIS | LabelField.USE_ALL_WIDTH));

  makeGUI(mainScreen, player);
  pushScreen(mainScreen);

  player.play("ignition");

  makeConnection();    // to the Bluetooth server
} // end of CarControls()
```

makeGUI() creates several rows of PictureButton objects and an uneditable text field to report status messages:

```
// global
private EditField statusEF;


private void makeGUI(MainScreen mainScreen, ClipsPlayer player)
{
  VerticalFieldManager vfm = new VerticalFieldManager();
  vfm.add( new RichTextField(Field.NON_FOCUSABLE) );    // a blank row

  HorizontalFieldManager rowMan2 =                new
 HorizontalFieldManager(Field.FIELD_HCENTER);
  rowMan2.add( new PictureButton(this, player, "left") );
  rowMan2.add( new PictureButton(this, player, "fwd") );
  rowMan2.add( new PictureButton(this, player, "right") );
  vfm.add(rowMan2);

  HorizontalFieldManager rowMan3 =                new
 HorizontalFieldManager(Field.FIELD_HCENTER);
  rowMan3.add( new PictureButton(this, player, "revLeft") );
  rowMan3.add( new PictureButton(this, player, "rev") );
  rowMan3.add( new PictureButton(this, player, "revRight") );
  vfm.add(rowMan3);

  HorizontalFieldManager rowMan4 =                new
 HorizontalFieldManager(Field.FIELD_HCENTER);
  rowMan4.add( new PictureButton(this, player, "carHorn") );
  vfm.add(rowMan4);

  statusEF = new EditField(Field.READONLY);    // status text field
  vfm.add(statusEF);
```

```
   mainScreen.add(vfm);
}    // end of makeGUI()
```

Each `PictureButton` object is passed a reference to the top-level `UIApplication`, the `ClipsPlayer`, and the name of image that should appear on the button. The buttons use the this reference to call `dirStatus()`:

```
// global
private String response;

public void dirStatus(String buttonName, boolean isPressed)
// called by the buttons
{ response = contactServer(buttonName+ " " + isPressed);
  invokeLater( new Runnable() {
    public void run()
    {   statusEF.setText(response); }
  });
} // end of dirStatus()
```

`dirStatus()` is called with the button name and whether it has been pressed or released. This information is sent to the `BaseStation` and its response is placed in the status field.

Pairing with Bluetooth Devices

Before two Bluetooth devices can communicate, they must be paired. This is frankly a bit of a pain but is a good security measure. A pairing is made when you *discover* another Bluetooth device on your BlackBerry (in my case, the `BaseStation` server running on the PC) and enter a passkey, which the server checks before *authenticating* the partnership.

Bluetooth must be enabled on your BlackBerry (it's disabled by default to extend battery life). The discovery phase is entered by you clicking Add Device on the Bluetooth settings screen.

Discovery can be a lengthy process if there's a lot of devices nearby, but look for a device named basestation (the service name used by `BaseStation.java`). After selecting the device, the BlackBerry will prompt you for a passkey, which will be passed to the server. On the server, Windows will ask for a passkey and check that the client has supplied the correct one. Any series of digits will do (I used 1234). If the two keys match, then a communication's link is set up and the pairing will appear in the BlackBerry's Paired Devices list.

Information about the services offered by the server will be made available under the **Properties** menu item. Since my server is using the Windows Bluetooth stack, which only supports RFCOMM, the only service listed is a serial port, but that's what I need.

The pairing and service selection interface on BlackBerry replaces the need to support SDP on the device. In JSR 82, SDP allows a client application to look for devices and services by itself.

Connecting to the Base Station

The CarControls() constructor calls makeConnection() to connect to the server. It determines if there is an available serial port (which there should be after the user has paired with the BaseStation server). The port is opened, and input and output streams are connected to it.

```
// globals
private StreamConnection blueConn;  // for the server
private InputStream in;      // stream from server
private OutputStream out;    // stream to server
private boolean isClosed = true;    // is the connection to the server closed?

private void makeConnection()
{
  try {
    BluetoothSerialPortInfo[] info = BluetoothSerialPort.getSerialPortInfo();
    if ((info == null) || (info.length == 0))
      closeConnection("No bluetooth serial ports available for connection");

    // connect to the server, and extract IO streams
    blueConn = (StreamConnection) Connector.open(
                        info[0].toString(), Connector.READ_WRITE);
    out = blueConn.openOutputStream();
    in = blueConn.openInputStream();
    isClosed = false;    // i.e. the connection is open
  }
  catch (IOException e) {
    closeConnection("Unable to open serial port");
  }
  catch (UnsupportedOperationException e) {
    closeConnection("This handheld or simulator does not support bluetooth");
  }
}  // end of makeConnection()
```

When something goes wrong in makeConnection(), it calls closeConnection():

```
private void closeConnection(final String message)
{
  invokeLater( new Runnable() {
    public void run()
    { Dialog.alert(message);
      closeDown();
    }
  });
}  // end of closeConnection()
```

Bluetooth isn't supported by the simulator, so an UnsupportedOperationException will be raised in makeConnection(). The resulting dialog displayed by closeConnection() is shown in Figure 10-22.

closeDown() sends bye$$ to the server, which signals link closure, and then closes the link:

```
private void closeDown()
{
```

```
      if (!isClosed) {
        sendMessage("bye$$");   // tell the server that the client is leaving
        try {
          if (blueConn != null) {
            in.close();
            out.close();
            blueConn.close();
          }
        }
        catch (IOException e)
        {  System.out.println(e);  }
        isClosed = true;
      }
}  // end of closeDown();
```

Communicating with the Base Station

When a button is pressed or released in CarControls, dirStatus() is called, which in turn calls contactServer() to send a message to the server and get a response:

```
private String contactServer(String msg)
{
  if (isClosed)
    return "Error: No Connection to Server";

  if ((msg == null) || (msg.trim().equals("")))
    return "Empty input message";
  else {
    if (sendMessage(msg)) {     // message sent ok
      String response = readData();  // wait for response
      if (response == null) {
        isClosed = true;
        return "Error: Server Terminated Link";
      }
      else  // there was a response
        return response;
    }
    else {   // unable to send message
      isClosed = true;
      return "Error: Connection Lost";
    }
  }
}  // end of contactServer()
```

readData() and sendMessage() are essentially the same as the same-named methods in the BaseStation server.

A Picture Button

As Figure 10-23 indicates, PictureButton is a subclass of Field. I want the button to display a picture that changes its appearance when the button is pressed, and then changes back to its original image when released. I call Bitmap.getBitmapResource() to

load the two pictures, whose names are built from a string passed to the
PictureButton() constructor.

```
// globals
private final static String IMAGE_DIR = "images/";

private CarControls top;
private ClipsPlayer player;
private String dir;
private Bitmap inActiveIm, activeIm;


public PictureButton(CarControls pb, ClipsPlayer p, String d)
{
  super(Field.FOCUSABLE); // the field will be focusable
  top = pb;
  player = p;
  dir = d;
  activeIm = Bitmap.getBitmapResource(IMAGE_DIR+dir+"On.png");
  inActiveIm = Bitmap.getBitmapResource(IMAGE_DIR+dir+"Off.png");
  player.load(dir);
} // end of PictureButton()
```

For example, calling the constructor with the string fwd will make it load
images/fwdOn.png and images/fwdOff.png.

The constructor is also passed references to the top-level UIApplication and the
ClipsPlayer, which plays a sound when the button is pressed.

When Field is overridden, it's usual to redefine getPreferredWidth() and
getPreferredHeight() to ensure that the field is properly positioned by layout
managers. I use the active image's dimensions to set the field's dimensions, but I
could have employed the inactive image since both pictures are the same size.

```
public int getPreferredHeight()
{  return activeIm.getHeight();  }

public int getPreferredWidth()
{  return activeIm.getWidth();  }
```

A custom field must include implementations of the layout() and paint() abstract
methods. The layout is based on the field's preferred dimensions.

```
protected void layout(int width, int height)
{  setExtent( Math.min(width, getPreferredWidth()),
             Math.min(height, getPreferredHeight()) );
}
```

Painting the button is a matter of drawing the active image when the button is pressed,
or drawing the inactive image when it's released, which depends on the value of an
isPressed boolean.

```
// global
private boolean isPressed = false;

protected void paint(Graphics graphics)
```

```
{
  int w = getWidth();
  int h = getHeight();
  // draw the background color and picture
  graphics.setColor(Color.WHITE);
  graphics.fillRect(0, 0, w, h);

  if (isPressed) {
    graphics.drawBitmap(0, 0, w, h, activeIm, 0, 0);
    graphics.setColor(Color.BLUE);
  }
  else {    // not pressed
    graphics.drawBitmap(0, 0, w, h, inActiveIm, 0, 0);
    graphics.setColor(Color.BLACK);
  }
  graphics.drawRect(0, 0, w, h);

  top.dirStatus(dir, isPressed);
} // end of paint()
```

Figure 10-24 shows how a pressed forward-direction button is rendered.

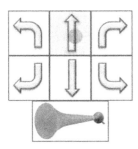

Figure 10-24. *The pressed forward button*

At the end of `paint()`, `dirStatus()` is called in the top-level application, which causes a Bluetooth message to be sent over to the `BaseStation`.

Implementing Button Presses and Releases

A natural way of handling button presses and releases is through the touchscreen support available on some BlackBerry devices. But I also want the GUI to work on devices that only have keyboard, trackball, or trackwheel capabilities. In that case, it's better to monitor navigation clicks, since they're generated by all those input mechanisms. For example, when a `TouchEvent.Click` is delivered to an application, a `navigationClick` event is also sent.

Navigation clicks and releases are caught by overriding `navigationClick()` and `navigationUnclick()`.

```
protected boolean navigationClick(int status, int time)
{ isPressed = true;
```

```
    player.loop(dir);
    invalidate();
    return true;
}

protected boolean navigationUnclick(int status, int time)
{ isPressed = false;
  player.stop(dir);
  invalidate();
  return true;
}
```

navigationClick() sets the isPressed boolean to true so that the active image will be drawn when paint() is trigged by invalidate(). In addition, the sound clip starts playing continuously while the button is pressed. navigationClick() returns true so that the click event isn't passed on to the screen where it would activate the context menu.

navigationUnclick() is similar, causing the inactive image to be rendered, and stops the clip from playing when the button is released.

The Netbook Version of CarControls

As explained at the start of this chapter, there's no real need for a Java SE version of the CarControls client, but it's useful for debugging and testing the server. Figure 10-25 shows the GUI for BlueCarControls (the Java SE code), which replicates the look of CarControls fairly closely (see Figure 10-21).

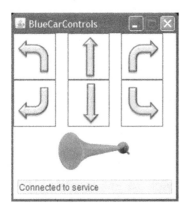

Figure 10-25. *The BlueCarControls GUI*

Class diagrams for BlueCarControls are shown in Figure 10-26, and should be compared to the diagrams for CarControls in Figure 10-23.

The top-level UIApplication on BlackBerry has become a JFrame in Java SE, while the Field subclass is now a JPanel called ButtonPanel.

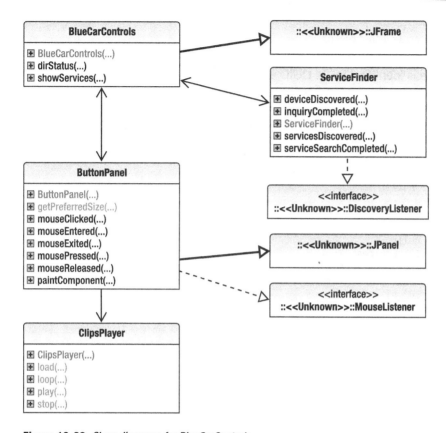

Figure 10-26. *Class diagrams for BlueCarControls*

ButtonPanel draws active and inactive button images by overriding paintComponent(), while the BlackBerry version overrides paint(). The main difference in ButtonPanel is the use of MouseEvents to govern the changing of the images, while PictureButton utilizes RIM's navigationClick events.

The public methods in ClipsPlayer look unchanged between the two clients, but the Java SE version uses a HashMap of AudioClips internally rather than a Hashtable of Player objects in the BlackBerry code.

Using ServiceFinder

The biggest change is the addition of a ServiceFinder class, which employs the BlueCove library to implement Bluetooth's SDP. BlueCarControls creates an instance of ServiceFinder to carry out devices and services searches.

```
// globals
private static final String UUID_STRING = "11111111111111111111111111111111";
private static final String SERVICE_NAME = "basestation";

private ServiceFinder serviceFinder;
```

```
// in the BlueCarControls constructor
serviceFinder = new ServiceFinder(this, UUID_STRING, SERVICE_NAME);
```

The required service is identified by its UUID and service name, so they're passed to
ServiceFinder. When ServiceFinder finishes, it returns control to BlueCarControls by
calling showServices(), which displays the matching services (stored in searchTable)
and asks the user to pick one. If the table only contains one entry, then its
ServiceRecord is used by default.

```
public void showServices(Hashtable<String,ServiceRecord> searchTable)
{
  if (searchTable == null)
    System.exit(1);

  int keysCount = 0;
  String firstKey = null;
  System.out.println("\nDevices:");
  for (Map.Entry e : searchTable.entrySet()) {
    System.out.println("   " + e.getKey()); // + " Value=" + e.getValue());
    if (keysCount == 0)
      firstKey = (String) e.getKey();
    keysCount++;
  }

  ServiceRecord servRec;
  if (keysCount == 1) {
    System.out.println("Using " + firstKey);
    servRec = (ServiceRecord) searchTable.get(firstKey);
  }
  else
    servRec = selectRecord(searchTable);

  if (servRec == null) {
    System.out.println("No matching service found");
    System.exit(1);
  }
  else
    makeConnection(servRec);
} // end of showServices()
```

makeConnection() utilizes the ServiceRecord to open a URL connection to the server,
and layers an input and output stream on top of the connection:

```
// globals
private StreamConnection blueConn;  // for the server
private InputStream in;      // stream from server
private OutputStream out;   // stream to server

private JTextField statusTF;   // status text field in GUI

private boolean isClosed = true;  // is the connection to the server closed?


private void makeConnection(ServiceRecord servRecord)
{
```

```
// get a URL for the service
String servURL = servRecord.getConnectionURL(
                        ServiceRecord.NOAUTHENTICATE_NOENCRYPT, false);
if (servURL != null) {
  System.out.println("Found service");
  try {
    // connect to the server, and extract IO streams
    blueConn = (StreamConnection) Connector.open(servURL);
    out = blueConn.openOutputStream();
    in = blueConn.openInputStream();

    System.out.println("Connected to service");
    isClosed = false;    // i.e. the connection is open
    SwingUtilities.invokeLater( new Runnable() {
      public void run()
      {  statusTF.setText("Connected to service");  }
    });
  }
  catch (Exception ex)
  {  System.out.println(ex);   }
}
else
  System.out.println("No service found");
}  // end of makeConnection()
```

From this point on, BlueCarControls uses I/O methods similar to those in the BlackBerry CarControls class (e.g., contactServer(), readData(), sendMessage(), and closeDown()).

Finding a Device, Finding a Service

The ServiceFinder class encapsulates the most complex aspects of writing a Bluetooth application—having a client search for devices and then search each of those devices for relevant services. The details aren't relevant to BlackBerry programming since service discovery is carried out by the device rather than by code. But if you're interested, then please read "An Echoing Client/Server Application Using Bluetooth," available at my *Killer Game Programming in Java* web page (http://fivedots.coe.psu.ac.th/~ad/jg), as Chapter B1 near the bottom of the page. The example code is a Java ME MIDlet, but its ServiceFinder class is very similar to the one I've used in BlueCarControls.

The device part of the search restricts itself to PCs and phones, so Bluetooth hardware such as printers are skipped. The service search looks only for RFCOMM (i.e., serial port support) with the same UUID as the UUID_STRING global defined in BlueCarControls.

Summary

This chapter detailed how I got a BlackBerry to send driving instructions to a PC via Bluetooth, and made the PC pass those instructions on to a toy car through a USB interface. I had to involve a PC since a BlackBerry is a USB *device* rather than a *host controller*, so it can't manage communication with the car directly.

The application employs the BlackBerry's built-in support for Bluetooth, while the Java code on the PC accesses Windows XP's Bluetooth stack via the BlueCove library.

Developing the USB software on the PC required a modicum of detective work using the USBDeview, SourceUSB, and PE Explorer tools. The implementation utilizes the LibusbJava and libusb-win32 libraries to communicate through one of the machine's USB ports with the car.

The BlackBerry client couldn't be tested on the device simulator, so I found it useful to develop a version of the client on a netbook running Windows XP.

The GUI on the BlackBerry illustrates the use of custom picture button fields.

Chapter 11

Fox and Hounds

As a formerly renowned Professor of Symbological Noetics, it was natural that I be asked to unravel the riddle, "7,000 Hollywood thanks to he who rests close to the leukodystrophies."

Little did I realize that it would lead to me being chased through the streets and vaulted archways of my hometown, Hat Yai. I'd become a wily fox tracked by four tenacious hounds:

- *Sir Tetley Teabag*: A scholar of BlackBerry lore and tea cozy semiotics. The sound of his aluminum crutches a welcome echo in any reverberant space.

- *Silo Malarkey*: The tattoo-covered, albino postman, a devotee of the Hopeless Day organization, and severe corporeal mortification.

- *Max Caller*: The wheelchair-bound director of HERN-IA; his wheeled mobility device containing a Sinclair ZX-81 supercomputer, surface-to-air FIM-92 Stingers, and a toaster.

- *Beau Jeste*: The Gallic savoir-vivre and captain of the Central Region Armored Police. His dark eyes scorched the earth before him, radiating a fiery clarity that forecast his reputation for unblinking severity in all matters.

I'm staggering from street to street, learning the ropes in the trenches, aided by my Fox and Hounds GPS application, but for how much longer?

And then suddenly it all became clear.

GPS Gaming

The Global Positioning System (GPS) is a network of US navigational satellites that broadcast signals worldwide containing latitude, longitude, altitude, and time data. Aside from its original role as a navigational aid, it's at the heart of a growing collection of location-based services. These include such essential mobile applications as finding the nearest coffee shop, gathering shopping discount coupons based on the user's current location, personalized weather services, and location-based games involving geocaching and hide-and-seek.

Geocaching is a modern-day take on treasure hunts, played using handheld GPS receivers. Unfortunately, the treasures (or *caches*) aren't brimming kegs of doubloons and pieces of eight; they're more likely to be plastic boxes containing notebooks and knickknacks (if you're lucky).

GPS-based hide-and-seek and chase games are growing in popularity, as typified by Fast Foot Challenge (`www.fastfoot.mobi`). Several runners try to catch the elusive player X within a specified outdoor playing area and time (e.g., a 1-kilometer radius circle in 30 minutes). There's also Catch&Run (`www.catchandrun.com`), based on David Vavra's thesis, "GPS game for mobile framework Locify," available at `http://edux2.felk.cvut.cz/car/car_bachelors_thesis.pdf`.

Fox and Hounds is a simple chase game, inspired by the author's enjoyment of Fast Foot Challenge.

Playing Fox and Hounds

The game organizer generates five IDs, which he prints on large sheets of paper (see Figure 11-1) and hands out to the players. One ID starts with an *F* (for the fox), and the other four with an *H* (for the hounds).

Figure 11-1. *A player ID sheet for the fox*

It's important that the fox and hounds are kept separate at this stage since a fox can "kill" a hound by sending its ID to the Fox and Hounds server, and the hounds can win by killing the fox in the same way.

The organizer tells the fox to log into the game server at a particular time and place, which will start the game's clock ticking; the server responds by the sending a map of the playing area to the fox's BlackBerry. The hounds must also log in to get their copies of the map, but starting from a different location (or locations).

The fox will receive roughly 30-second updates to his map, which will display icons indicating the players current positions. Figure 11-2 shows that the fox is represented by a green fox head, and the hounds by red dog heads.

Figure 11-2. *The Fox and Hounds map showing three players*

The hounds' maps will also be periodically updated, but less frequently—once every 2 minutes. This time difference gives the fox an advantage to offset the number of hounds chasing him.

The fox wins if he can stay alive for 30 minutes, or can kill all the hounds in that time. A hound wins if he can kill the fox before the 30 minutes has passed.

A kill request is sent to the server by a player typing in an opponent's ID. This requires the player to get close enough to the other person to see their printed ID sheet (see Figure 11-1), while avoiding being seen themselves (lest they be killed first). Figure 11-3 shows the kill screen on the fox's BlackBerry who is entering the ID of a hound he has seen.

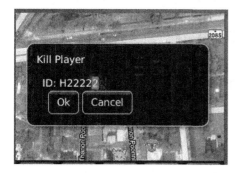

Figure 11-3. *Trying to kill a hound*

A dead hound is shown on the map with an *X* through his icon; that player can no longer kill the fox, but will still receive updates of the player's positions.

Figure 11-4 shows one of the possible game-over messages, indicating that the fox has won.

Figure 11-4. *The fox wins*

Once the game is over, the server will no longer accept kill requests or logins.

Setting up a new game requires the organizer to place a new map and list of player IDs in the server's home directory, and then restart the server.

An Overview of the Fox and Hounds Implementation

The game is a web-based client/server networking application, with the five players running the client software (called FHClient) on their BlackBerrys. They communicate through HTTP with the Fox and Hounds server implemented as a Java EE servlet. A simplified view of this configuration is shown in Figure 11-5.

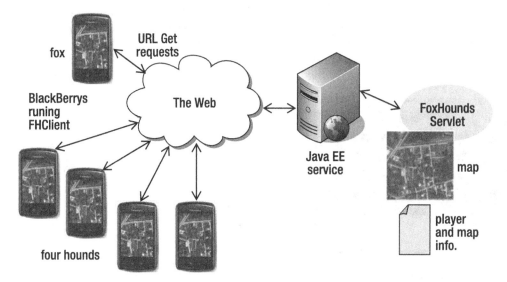

Figure 11-5. *The Fox and Hounds client/server application*

The client devices must include GPS support, which is rapidly becoming a standard part of BlackBerry, dating from the 8100 Pearl and OS 4.2. It may be possible to use an external GPS receiver with older devices, attached via Bluetooth.

The server-side machine can be any PC running Java EE (the current name for Java's Enterprise Edition). Java EE is a framework for the construction of web-based client/server applications, supporting simplified networking, concurrency, transactions, easy access to databases, and much more (http://java.sun.com/j2ee). Aside from Sun's reference implementation, Glassfish (https://glassfish.dev.java.net), there are many other Java EE–compatible systems, including Tomcat from the Jakarta project (http://jakarta.apache.org/tomcat) and Adobe JRun (www.adobe.com/products/jrun). In my tests, I used Apache Tomcat.

Java EE is a complex development environment, centered around servlets, JavaServer Pages (JSPs), and Enterprise JavaBeans (EJBs). *Servlets* are objects specialized for the serving of web content, typically web pages, in response to client requests. JSPs are web pages that may contain embedded Java. EJBs focus on server-side processing, including the connection of server-side applications to other Java functionality, such as JTA (Java Transaction API), JMS (Java Message Service), and JDBC (Java Database Connectivity).

Servlets deal with client requests using the HTTP protocol, which thankfully only contains a few commands; the two principal ones are the GET method and the POST method. A GET method (request) is usually sent by a web browser when it asks for a page from a server. A POST method (request) is more typically associated with the submission of details taken from a web page form.

One advantage of using the HTTP protocol rather than TCP/IP or UDP to communicate between the clients and the server is its ability to bypass firewall restrictions, which is known as *HTTP tunneling* (http://en.wikipedia.org/wiki/HTTP_tunnel_(software)). Another is that a servlet can be tested using an ordinary browser, by manually typing in the GET requests as URL addresses.

A downside is that HTTP is purely a request/response protocol—the client must initiate the communication to receive a reply. It's not at all easy for the server to send a message to a client without first receiving one from it. This means that a web-based server cannot easily broadcast (multicast) a message received from one client to all the others (a common requirement of multiplayer games).

One possible solution is the BlackBerry Push Service, formerly known as the BlackBerry Push API (http://na.blackberry.com/eng/developers/javaappdev/pushapi.jsp).

Push services have been used widely for applications that deliver time-important data, such as stock information, news bulletins, and banking details, to BlackBerry client devices.

The Fox and Hounds server could send push messages, using the WAP PAP 2.2 or RIM formats, to a BlackBerry Enterprise Server or BlackBerry Push Server. The server automatically delivers the messages to registered clients, which should be listening for them.

There's an example push client in the JDE, called HTTPPushDemo.java, that waits for image data on a specified port and renders the data when it arrives.

The drawback with push for Fox and Hounds is the introduction of another server. It seems easier to use a polling thread on the client side rather than a push thread and server, especially for a gaming application where fast message delivery isn't that crucial.

> **Note** An excellent book on servlets and JSPs is *Core Servlets and Java Server Pages: Core Technologies, Vol. 1 (Second Edition)*, by Marty Hall and Larry Brown (Prentice Hall, 2003). This edition is available for free at `http://pdf.coreservlets.com`.

Time for an Example: CurrentTime

The CurrentTime servlet implements a time-of-day service. A browser or stand-alone application can contact it by referring to the servlet's URL, which is converted into a GET request sent to the Java EE server managing the servlet. The situation is illustrated by Figure 11-6.

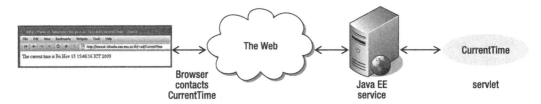

Figure 11-6. *Calling CurrentTime from a browser*

My departmental Java EE server (Apache Tomcat) stores my servlets at `http://tomcat.takasila.coe.psu.ac.th/~ad`. The CurrentTime servlet can be reached with the URL `http://tomcat.takasila.coe.psu.ac.th/~ad/CurrentTime`, as shown in Figure 11-7.

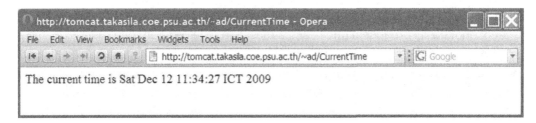

Figure 11-7. *CurrentTime in the browser*

The simplest way of writing a servlet is to inherit Java EE's HttpServlet class, which offers all the necessary basic support. When a GET request arrives, the Java EE service automatically calls the servlet's doGet() method. There's also a doPost() method for processing POST requests.

All that CurrentTime requires is doGet() code that returns the time, wrapped up as simple HTML:

```
public class CurrentTime extends HttpServlet
{
```

```
public void doGet(HttpServletRequest request,
                  HttpServletResponse response)
                      throws ServletException, IOException
{
  response.setContentType("text/html"); // use HTML output
  PrintWriter out = response.getWriter();
  out.println("<p>The current time is " + new java.util.Date());
  out.close(); // Close stream
}  // end of doGet()

} // end of CurrentTime class
```

Various client and request information is available in the HttpServletRequest object passed to doGet(), but CurrentTime doesn't need it.

The other doGet() argument is an HttpServletResponse object that permits various forms of output to be delivered to the client. CurrentTime creates an output stream and transmits an HTML-formatted date and time.

A servlet can output a stream of HTML that is displayed nicely in a browser, but can deliver almost anything, such as text and images.

The Game Organizer Gets Organized

Due to the real-world nature of Fox and Hounds, there's a need for an organizer who prepares IDs for the players, creates a map, initializes the game server, and acts as a referee during the game. The refereeing job involves making sure that the fox and hounds start from different locations and keep their ID sheets visible. The other tasks can be automated to some degree.

ID Creation

The IDs are randomly generated six-letter strings, which should start with F or H. A small piece of Java is required for doing this:

```
private static String generateID(boolean isFox)
{
  if (isFox)
    System.out.println("Generating a Fox ID");
  else
    System.out.println("Generating a Hound ID");

  String lets = "ABCDEGJKLMNPQRSTUVWXYZ0123456789"; //no F,H,I,O
  Random rand = new Random();

  StringBuffer sb = (isFox) ? new StringBuffer("F"): new StringBuffer("H");
  for (int i=0; i < ID_LEN; i++)
    sb.append( lets.charAt( rand.nextInt(lets.length())) );

  return sb.toString();
}  // end of generateID()
```

If generateID(true) is called, then a fox ID is returned; otherwise, a hound ID is returned. The ID only uses uppercase letters and numbers, and excludes easy-to-mistake characters such as *O* and *I*.

The generation of a large image like the one in Figure 11-1 can be done by hand, or managed by another bit of code that creates a banner image containing the ID on a yellow background with a black border, and the Fox and Hounds logo.

```
private static BufferedImage drawBanner(String idStr)
{
  BufferedImage image = new BufferedImage(IM_WIDTH,IM_HEIGHT,
                              BufferedImage.TYPE_INT_ARGB);
  Graphics2D g2d = image.createGraphics();
  g2d.setRenderingHint(RenderingHints.KEY_TEXT_ANTIALIASING,
                    RenderingHints.VALUE_TEXT_ANTIALIAS_ON);
      // smoothly draw the big letters

  g2d.setColor(Color.YELLOW);
  g2d.fillRect(0, 0, IM_WIDTH, IM_HEIGHT);     // yellow background

  g2d.setColor(Color.BLACK);
  g2d.drawRect(0, 0, IM_WIDTH-1, IM_HEIGHT-1);   // black border

  drawLogo(g2d);
  drawID(g2d, idStr);

  return image;
}  // end of drawBanner()
```

drawLogo() adds in a Fox and Hound image, while drawID() writes out the ID in bold, 184-point SansSerif.

```
private static void drawID(Graphics2D g2d, String idStr)
{
  Font font = new Font("SansSerif", Font.BOLD, 184);
  g2d.setFont(font);

  FontMetrics metrics = g2d.getFontMetrics(font);
  int height = metrics.getHeight();
  int ascent = metrics.getAscent();    // where is font baseline
  int width = metrics.stringWidth(idStr);

  if (height > IM_HEIGHT)
    System.out.println("Height of ID is too large;some text lost");
  if (width > IM_WIDTH)
    System.out.println("Width of ID is too large; some text lost");

  g2d.drawString(idStr, (IM_WIDTH- width)/2,     // centered text
                    (IM_HEIGHT-height)/2 + ascent);
}  // end of drawID()
```

generateID() and drawBanner() can be combined with a piece of code to save the resulting image into a PNG file:

```
String idStr = generateID(isFox);
System.out.println("ID: " + idStr);
```

```
BufferedImage image = drawBanner(idStr);

try {   // save the image to a file
  ImageIO.write(image, "png", new File(ID_FNM));
  System.out.println("Saved ID to " + ID_FNM);
}
catch (IOException e)
{  System.out.println("Could not save ID to " + ID_FNM);  }
```

The complete program, called IDCreator.java, can be found in the online code for this chapter at the book's website (`http://frogparrot.net/blackberry/ch11/`).

Making a Map

There are many tools for creating maps, not least the low-tech solution of drawing one with a pencil. However, the Fox and Hounds server must be able to convert the latitude and longitude positions of the players into coordinates on the image so that the fox and dog icons can be correctly positioned. For this reason, I decided to use Google Static Maps, a URL-based API for generating map images (`http://code.google.com/apis/maps/documentation/staticmaps`), which requires the user to sign up for a free API key.

The API returns an image (either GIF, PNG, or JPG) in response to an HTTP request via a URL. For each request, you can specify the geographical center of the map, the size of the image, the zoom level, the type of map, and the placement of location markers on the map.

The terms-of-use for a Google static map state that a map should only be displayed within browser content, as part of a web page. This is not the case with Fox and Hounds, which might be a problem with a commercial game. However, the map contains a Google copyright notice, which is quite visible within the Fox and Hounds client.

A typical static map URL has the following form:

```
http://maps.google.com/maps/api/staticmap?
    center= <LATITUDE>,<LONGITUDE>&
    zoom=<ZOOM_FACTOR>&
    size=<IMAGE_WIDTH>x<IMAGE_HEIGHT>&
    format=JPG&
    maptype=hybrid&
    sensor=false&
    key=<API_KEY>
```

The center coordinates specify the latitude and longitude at the center of the image. A zoom factor of 0 shows the entire world on one map, with each succeeding zoom level doubling the horizontal and vertical dimensions. A zoom factor of 21 shows details on individual buildings.

The size parameter gives the dimensions of the image (640×640 is the largest size). The format is the image type (JPG, GIF, and PNG are supported). `maptype` defines the map content, including `roadmap`, `satellite`, `hybrid`, and `terrain`. `sensor` specifies whether the application is using a sensor to determine the user's location. `key` is the user's Maps API key (which is free from Google).

For example, the following URL

```
http://maps.google.com/maps/api/staticmap?
    center=7.000556,100.491943&
    size=256x256&
    zoom=0&
    format=jpg&
    maptype=hybrid&
    sensor=false&
    key=<API_KEY>
```

produces a 256×256 JPG image of the entire world (with a zoom value of 0) centered on latitude 7.000556, longitude 100.491943 (see Figure 11-8). (The coordinate [7.000556,100.491943] is the location of my home in Thailand.)

Figure 11-8 shows that a static map omits parts of the polar regions. This is due to Google Maps using a Mercator projection, a widely used cylindrical map projection (think of the world as a balloon inflated until it presses against a cylinder, which records the earth's surface features and is then unrolled).

Figure 11-8. *A static map of the world*

A Mercator projection preserves the angles and the shapes of small objects, but distorts the size and shape of large objects. The scaling increases at greater distances from the equator toward the poles, where it becomes infinite. For that reason, Mercator is only used for latitudes ranging between ±85.05113 degrees, even though the longitude values surround the earth between ±180 degrees around Greenwich, United Kingdom.

Changing the zoom factor allows us to close in on the specified location. For example, the following produces Figure 11-9:

```
http://maps.google.com/maps/api/staticmap?
    center=7.000556,100.491943&
    size=256x256&
```

```
zoom=18&
format=jpg&
maptype=hybrid&
sensor=false&
key=<API_KEY>
```

Figure 11-9. *Same location as Figure 11-8, but at zoom 18*

The difference between each zoom level is a factor of 2 increase in the dimensions of the world's image. For example, it starts at 256×256 at zoom 0, becomes 512×512 at zoom 1, becomes 1024×1024 at zoom 2, and so on.

Attempting to increase the zoom factor beyond 18 leads to a blank picture for this example location, since more detailed satellite images aren't available. However, if the map type is changed to roadmap and the zoom factor to 19, as follows:

```
http://maps.google.com/maps/api/staticmap?
    center=7.000556,100.491943&
    size=256x256&
    zoom=19&
    format=jpg&
    maptype=roadmap&
    sensor=false&
    key=<API_KEY>
```

then the rather uninteresting Figure 11-10 is generated.

The use of Mercator projection by Google Maps means that it's relatively simple to write code that translates a latitude-and-longitude coordinate into a pixel coordinate in the image.

Thanon Poonnakan Soi 2

POWERED BY
Google   Map data ©2009 AND, Tele Atlas

Figure 11-10. *Empty streets in my hometown*

What About BlackBerry Maps?

Users familiar with BlackBerry GPS may be wondering why I didn't use the built-in BlackBerry Maps API to display the map information. The main reason is that I wanted the option to create my own maps, rather than use only those offered by BlackBerry. Another reason is that I wanted to perform map calculations on the server side. As you'll see, each client is passed image coordinates for the players by the server, and only has to draw the fox and hound icons at those positions.

Also, it's only since version 4.5 that BlackBerry maps can be embedded inside an application's UI, which is necessary for building a game around map functionality.

Initializing the Game Server

Once the IDs have been generated (one for the fox, four for the hounds) and a map created, the server must be initialized. As Figure 11-5 suggests, this involves putting a copy of the map in a standard location on the server, so the Fox and Hounds servlet can load it. Also, configuration details are placed in a text file called players.txt. For example:

```
7.000556
100.491943
18
F11111
H22222
H33333
H44444
H55555
```

The first three lines are the latitude, longitude, and zoom factor used in the map, while the last five lines are the IDs of the players.

The exact location of these files depends on how Apache Tomcat is configured on your machine, but I'm placing mine in the webapps/ directory, where web pages are stored.

The Server Side

Figure 11-5 shows a single oval of the server side called FoxHoundsServlet. A more detailed overview is given in Figure 11-11, which highlights the classes and public methods in the servlet.

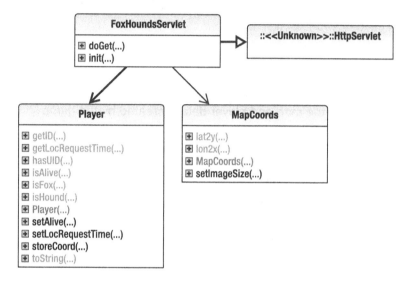

Figure 11-11. *The Fox and Hounds servlet*

As with the CurrentTime servlet described earlier, FoxHoundsServlet receives most of its functionality from inheriting HttpServlet, and implements the doGet() method to handle GET messages from the clients. The servlet maintains an array of Player objects, one for each player, and uses the MapCoords class to convert latitudes and longitudes into image coordinates.

A client sends a message to FoxHoundsServlet as a URL GET request, with arguments added to the URL after a ?. Each argument takes the form name=value, with multiple name/value pairs separated by &.

The three types of message are as follows:

- FoxHoundsServlet?cmd=hi&uid=??: A "hi" message is used by a client to join the game. The uid parameter value (represented by ??) holds the client's ID. If the ID is valid, then a map is returned to the client by the server.

- FoxHoundsServlet?cmd=loc&uid=??&lat=??&long=??: A "loc" message sends the client's current latitude and longitude to the server. The server's response is a string of players' details, including their image coordinates and whether they are alive or dead.

- FoxHoundsServlet?cmd=kill&uid=??&kid=??: A "kill" message tells the server that the player wants to kill the player specified in the kid field. The server's response indicates whether the kill was successful or not.

A serious drawback of this protocol is that it's carried out in plain text and is attached to URLs, and is therefore open to interception. Encryption would safeguard the IDs, possibly by using HTTPS instead of HTTP.

Initializing the Server

FoxHoundsServlet's init() method is called when the servlet is loaded (or reloaded) into the server. It is utilized to load the map and player details created by the game organizer.

```
// globals
private static final String PLAYERS_FNM = "players.txt";
private static final String MAP_FNM = "map.jpg";

private String imMimeType = null;   // mime type of the image


public void init() // throws ServletException
{
  ServletContext sc = getServletContext();

  //load player info and the map
  String playersFnm = sc.getRealPath(PLAYERS_FNM);
  loadPlayersInfo(playersFnm);

  String mapFnm = sc.getRealPath(MAP_FNM);
  loadMap(mapFnm);
  imMimeType = sc.getMimeType(mapFnm);
} // end of init()
```

ServletContext lets the servlet communicate with the Java EE server. ServletContext.getRealPath() returns the specified file's location in the server so that the servlet can load its contents. loadPlayersInfo() is a standard line-by-line parser that assumes that the player information has the following format:

```
map center latitude
map center longitude
map zoom
player id1    //if id starts with 'H' then is hound; 'F' means fox
player id2    //one fox, 4 hounds
   :
player id5
```

Here is the code for loadPlayersInfo():

```
// globals
private static final int MAX_PLAYERS = 5;

private Player[] players;      // for storing player information
private MapCoords mapCoords;   // (lat,long) into image coords


private void loadPlayersInfo(String playersFnm)
{
  try {
    BufferedReader in = new BufferedReader( new FileReader( playersFnm ));
    // load map details
    String latStr = in.readLine();    // latitude
    String lonStr = in.readLine();    // longitude
    String zoomStr = in.readLine();   // zoom factor
    mapCoords = new MapCoords(latStr, lonStr, zoomStr);

    // store player IDs
    players = new Player[MAX_PLAYERS];
    String line;
    int i = 0;
    while (((line = in.readLine()) != null) && (i < MAX_PLAYERS)) {
      players[i] = new Player(line.trim());
      i++;
    }
    in.close();
  }
  catch (IOException e)
  {  System.out.println("Problem reading " + playersFnm);  }
}  // end of loadPlayersInfo()
```

A Player object is created for each player, and the map details (the latitude and longitude of the center point, and the zoom factor) are used to initialize a MapCoords object. MapCoords will be used to convert player positions into image coordinates during the game.

loadMap() loads the map and uses its dimensions to further initialize the MapCoords object:

```
// globals
private BufferedImage mapIm = null;


private void loadMap(String mapFnm)
{
  try {
    mapIm = ImageIO.read( new File(mapFnm) );
  }
  catch(IOException e)
  {  System.out.println("Could not read map from " + mapFnm);  }

  if (mapIm != null)
    mapCoords.setImageSize( mapIm.getWidth(), mapIm.getHeight() );
}  // end of loadMap()
```

Reinitializing the Servlet

How is the game changed to use a different map and/or players? The simplest solution is to have the organizer change the map and players.txt files, and then force the Java EE server to reload the servlet. This will restart the servlet and cause init() to be called again. The details of servlet reloading depend on the configuration of the Java EE system.

Processing a Client Message

The three types of client message ("hi," "loc," and "kill") all arrive at the doGet() method in FoxHoundsServlet, and are delegated to other methods for processing. However, before this separation occurs, the servlet needs to check if the game is over.

```
// globals
private static final long GAME_TIME_LENGTH = 30*60;    // 30 minutes in seconds
private boolean isGameOver = false;
private String gameOverMessage;
private long startTime = -1;      // in secs; set when fox says hi


public void doGet( HttpServletRequest request,
                   HttpServletResponse response ) throws IOException
{  if (isGameOver) {
     PrintWriter output = response.getWriter();
     output.println("GAME_OVER " + gameOverMessage);
     output.close();
   }
   else {    // game isn't over
     // check if game-playing time has expired
     long currTime = System.currentTimeMillis()/1000;    // in secs
     if ((startTime > -1) && ((currTime - startTime) > GAME_TIME_LENGTH)) {
       isGameOver = true;
       gameOverMessage = "Playing time ended:\nfox wins";
       PrintWriter output = response.getWriter();
       output.println("GAME_OVER " + gameOverMessage);
       output.close();
     }
     else    // still time to play
       processCmd(request, response);
   }
}  // end of doGet()
```

If the game's current running time has exceeded the maximum game running time (GAME_TIME_LENGTH), then the fox has won, and a game-over message is transmitted back to the client. All game-over messages start with a GAME_OVER string to allow them to be easily identified when they arrive at a client.

Processing a command always involves a user ID, so processCmd() only proceeds if the uid value matches an ID read from players.txt.

```
private void processCmd(HttpServletRequest request,
                        HttpServletResponse response)  throws IOException
/*  Cmd formats:
```

```
      FoxHoundsServlet?cmd=hi&uid=??
      FoxHoundsServlet?cmd=loc&uid=??&lat=??&long=??
      FoxHoundsServlet?cmd=kill&uid=??&kid=??
*/
{ // check the player ID first, which is used by all the commands
  String uid = request.getParameter("uid");
  Player p = findPlayer(uid);
  if (p == null) {
    PrintWriter output = response.getWriter();
    output.println("Player ID not found");  // request rejected
    output.close();
  }
  else {    // player was found, now process command
    String command = request.getParameter("cmd");
    if (command.equals("hi"))
      processHi(p, response);
    else if (command.equals("loc"))
      processLoc(p, request, response);
    else if (command.equals("kill"))
      processKill(p, request, response);
    else {
      PrintWriter output = response.getWriter();
      output.println("Command not understood: " + command);
      output.close();
    }
  }
}  // end of processCmd()
```

findPlayer() cycles through the Player objects until it finds the ID or runs out of players:

```
private Player findPlayer(String uid)
// return the player with ID == uid, or null
{
  for (Player p : players)
    if (p.hasUID(uid))
      return p;
  return null;
}  // end of findPlayer()
```

Saying Hi

Processing a "hi" message involves sending back a map, delivered as an image/JPG web page containing the image in byte form; the client must reassemble it into an image. When the fox first says "hi," the game officially starts, and the hounds have 30 minutes to kill him.

```
private void processHi(Player p, HttpServletResponse response)
                                     throws IOException
{ sendMap(response);
  if (p.isFox() && (startTime == -1))    //set when fox first says hi
    startTime = System.currentTimeMillis()/1000;
}
```

```
private void sendMap(HttpServletResponse resp) throws IOException
{
  if ((mapIm == null) || (imMimeType == null)) {
    PrintWriter output = resp.getWriter();
    output.println("Map not found");  // request rejected
    output.close();
  }
  else {
    resp.setContentType(imMimeType);
    // image ==> byte array
    ByteArrayOutputStream baos = new ByteArrayOutputStream();
    ImageIO.write(mapIm, "jpg", baos);
    byte[] buf = baos.toByteArray();

    resp.setContentLength((int) buf.length);  // set content size
    OutputStream out = resp.getOutputStream();
    out.write(buf);
    out.flush();
    out.close();
  }
}  // end of sendMap()
```

Processing a "loc" Message

A "loc" message contains the client's current latitude and longitude, which must be stored in its Player details. The server responds by returning position details for all the players, which the client uses to update their map display.

```
private void processLoc(Player p, HttpServletRequest request,
                        HttpServletResponse response) throws IOException
// Message format: FoxHoundsServlet?cmd=loc&uid=??&lat=??&long=??
{
  // convert (lat,long) to map image coordinates
  double lat = getGPSCoord( request.getParameter("lat"));
  int yCoord = mapCoords.lat2y(lat);

  double lng = getGPSCoord( request.getParameter("long"));
  int xCoord = mapCoords.lon2x(lng);

  PrintWriter output = response.getWriter();
  if ((xCoord < 0) || (xCoord >= mapIm.getWidth()) ||
      (yCoord < 0) || (xCoord >= mapIm.getHeight()) ) {
    output.println("You've dropped off the map");
    output.println("lat: " + lat);
    output.println("long: " + lng);
  }
  else {
    p.storeCoord(xCoord, yCoord);  // store new coords for player
    sendLocations(p, output);       // send back all players details
  }
  output.close();
}  // end of processLoc()
```

The hard work of converting the player's latitude and longitude into image coordinates is done by the MapCoords object, which I'll explain later.

sendLocations() sends the players positions, with each position using the following format:

```
        id-type x y player-state
```

The id-type is the letter *F* or *H*; full IDs aren't sent back to a client since a naughty user might utilize that information to kill a player without first finding them.

```
// globals
private static final int MIN_REQUEST_PERIOD = 2*60;
                                        // 2 minutes in seconds

private void sendLocations(Player p, PrintWriter output)
{
  if (p.isFox()) {
    output.println("LOCS");
    for (Player pl : players)     // always send info to the fox
      output.println( pl.toString() );
  }
  else {   // p is a hound, so check request interval
    long requestTime = System.currentTimeMillis()/1000; //in secs
    if ((requestTime - p.getLocRequestTime()) > MIN_REQUEST_PERIOD) {
      output.println("LOCS");
      for (Player pl : players)
        output.println( pl.toString() );
      p.setLocRequestTime(requestTime);
    }
    else
      output.println("TOO SOON");   // loc request is too soon
  }
} // end of sendLocations()
```

sendLocations() always lets the fox receive player locations, but a hound must wait MIN_REQUEST_PERIOD seconds between location requests.

The position details are preceded by a LOCS string to make the information easy to distinguish from error messages when it arrives on the client side.

Killing a Player

The difficult thing about killing another player is dealing with all the situations when the request should be denied. For example, only the fox can kill a hound, and both the fox and hound must be alive at the time!

```
private void processKill(Player p, HttpServletRequest request,
                     HttpServletResponse response) throws IOException
// Message format: FoxHoundsServlet?cmd=kill&uid=??&kid=??
{
  Player target = findPlayer( request.getParameter("kid") );
                        // get the player who is meant to be killed
  PrintWriter output = response.getWriter();
```

```
    if (target == null)
      output.println("Target not found");
    else if (!p.isAlive())
      output.println("Zombie player not allowed");
    else if (!target.isAlive())
      output.println("Target already dead");
    else
      killPlayer(p, target, output);
    output.close();
  }  // end of processKill()
```

killPlayer() checks that the players are a fox and hound, and then kills the target. It must then check for various game-over scenarios: if the fox has killed all the hounds, then it has won, while if a hound has successfully killed the fox, then that hound is the winner.

```
private void killPlayer(Player p, Player target, PrintWriter output)
{
  synchronized(target) {
    // target can only be killed by one thread at a time
    if (p.isFox() && target.isHound()) {    // fox can kill hound
      target.setAlive(false);    // kill hound
      if (allHoundsDead()) {
        isGameOver = true;
        gameOverMessage = "Fox wins";
        output.println("GAME_OVER " + gameOverMessage);
      }
      else
        output.println("Hound killed");
    }
    else if (p.isHound() && target.isFox()) {    // hound can kill fox
      target.setAlive(false);    // kill fox
      isGameOver = true;
      gameOverMessage = "Hound " + p.getID() + " wins";
      output.println("GAME_OVER " + gameOverMessage);
    }
    else
      output.println("Kill rejected");
  }
}  // end of killPlayer()
```

Since multiple clients can communicate with the servlet at the same time, it's possible that two or more hounds will try to kill the fox at the same time. Their requests are sequentialized by synchronizing on the target at the start of killPlayer().

Player Information

A Player object stores information about a single player, including his ID, his current (x,y) pixel location on the map, whether he's alive, and the time (in seconds) of his last "loc" request.

```
public class Player
{
  private String id;    // hound ID starts with 'H', a fox with 'F'
  private int x, y;
```

```
    private boolean isAlive = true;
    private long locRequestTime;      // seconds
        // time when locations were last requested


    public Player(String uid)
    { id = uid;
      x = -1;        // location unknown
      y = -1;
      locRequestTime = -1;
    }

    // more methods

} // end of Player class
```

The code assumes that if the ID starts with an *H*, then the player is a hound, or a fox if the letter is a *F*—for example:

```
public boolean isHound()
{   return (id.charAt(0) == 'H');   }

public boolean isFox()
{   return (id.charAt(0) == 'F');   }
```

The locRequestTime value is used to decide if a client's "loc" request should be answered. The fox is always sent the current player information, but a hound must wait roughly 2 minutes between player updates.

The toString() method is unusual in that it doesn't return the player's complete ID:

```
public String toString()
{   return (id.charAt(0) + " " + x + " " + y + " " + isAlive);   }
```

The first letter of the ID (*F* or *H*) is enough to identify the player type without revealing enough to kill the player.

Manipulating Map Coordinates

The main duty of MapCoords is to convert latitude and longitude positions into (x, y) coordinates on the map image.

The MapCoords object requires five initial values: the map center's latitude and longitude, the static map's zoom factor, and the image's pixel width and height. The first three are supplied in the constructor call, and the image information arrives via the setImageSize() method:

```
// globals
private double lonCenter, latCenter; //(lat,long) of image center
private int zoom;
private int imWidth, imHeight;


public MapCoords(String latStr, String lonStr, String zoomStr)
```

```
{
  try {
    latCenter = Double.parseDouble(latStr);
  }
  catch (Exception ex){
    latCenter = 0;
  }

  try {
    lonCenter = Double.parseDouble(lonStr);
  }
  catch (Exception ex){
    lonCenter = 0;
  }

  try {
    zoom = Integer.parseInt(zoomStr);
  }
  catch (Exception ex){
    zoom = 0;
  }

  imWidth = 0; imHeight = 0;

  // calculate the scaling factors for the
  // latitude and longitude calculations (see below)
}  // end of MapCoords()


public void setImageSize(int w, int h)
{ imWidth = w;
  imHeight = h;
}
```

From Mercator to Image Coordinates

Google maps use a Mercator cylindrical projection to flatten the earth's surface onto a 2D map, as illustrated by Figure 11-12.

Longitudes are mapped linearly to the x-axis, but latitudes are increasingly spaced out the further they are from the equator. This increasing distortion means that Google Maps only utilizes the Mercator projection between latitudes 85.05113 degrees north and south, which explains why some parts of the polar regions are missing in Figures 11-8 and 11-12.

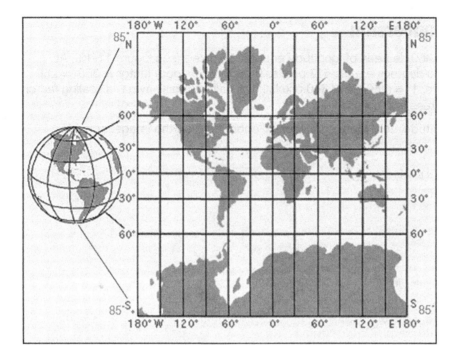

Figure 11-12. *The Mercator projection*

When a static map is displayed with a zoom factor of 0, the earth's projection is displayed as a 256×256-pixel image, as in Figure 11-13.

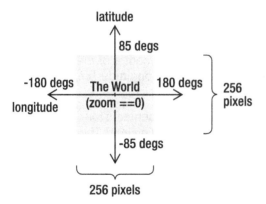

Figure 11-13. *A static map at zoom factor 0*

As the zoom factor increases, the size of the earth image doubles.

Longitude Conversion

At zoom factor 0, 360 degrees of longitude equals 256 pixels (see Figure 11-13). At zoom factor 1, 360 degrees equals 512 pixels. Therefore, at zoom factor n, $360° = 256 * 2^n$ pixels. Therefore, $1° = (256 * 2^n) / 360$ pixels (I will call this lonConvert, a scaling factor that converts degrees into pixels.)

To convert a longitude, lon, to its equivalent x-coordinate on the image, consider Figure 11-14.

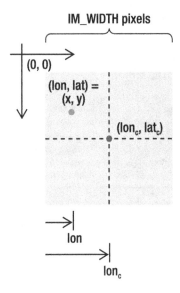

Figure 11-14. *Converting longitude to an x-coordinate*

In Figure 11-14, lon_c and lat_c are the longitude and latitude at the center of the image, while IM_WIDTH is the width of the image. A player is currently at longitude lon and latitude lat.

The number of longitudinal degrees between the player and the center is $lon_c - lon$. This is equivalent to the pixel distance on the image: $(lon_c - lon) *$ lonConvert. Therefore, $x = $ IM_WIDTH $/ 2 - (lon_c - lon) *$ lonConvert. This calculation is implemented in the MapCoords class as the method lon2x():

```
// global
private double lonConvert;

// in the constructor
lonConvert = (256.0 * Math.pow(2, zoom)) / 360.0;


public int lon2x(double lon)
// convert a longitude to a x-coordinate pixel in the image
{
    if ((lon < -180) || (lon > 180))
```

```
      return -1;
   if (imWidth <= 0)
      return -1;

   return (int) (imWidth/2 - (lonCenter - lon)*lonConvert);
} // end of lon2x()
```

Latitude Conversion

A latitude can be converted into a y-coordinate on a Mercator map by using an inverse Gudermannian function, invGud(), defined in http://en.wikipedia.org/wiki/Mercator_projection as follows:

$$
y = \frac{1}{2} \ln \left(\frac{1 + \sin(\varphi)}{1 - \sin(\varphi)} \right)
$$

where φ is the latitude. Let the maximum latitude on a Mercator projection, LAT_MAX, equal 85.05113 degrees. Then, at zoom factor 0, there will be 2 * invGud(LAT_MAX) y-coordinates spanning 256 pixels (see Figure 11-13 for an illustration of this idea). This means that a single y-coordinate spans 256 / (2 * invGud(LAT_MAX)) pixels. Therefore, at zoom factor n, a single y-coordinate spans (256 / (2 * invGud(LAT_MAX))) *2^n pixels. In the following code, I call this pixel value latConvert, and use it as a scaling factor to convert y-coordinates on a Mercator map into pixels.

To convert a latitude, lat, to its equivalent y-axis pixel position on the image, consider Figure 11-15.

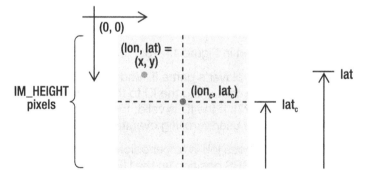

Figure 11-15. *Converting latitude to a y-coordinate*

In Figure 11-15, the y-axis Mercator map distance between the player coordinate and the center is invGud(lat) − invGud(lat$_c$). This is equivalent to the pixel distance (invGud(lat) − invGud(lat$_c$)) * latConvert. Therefore, the y-axis distance from the top of the image down to the coordinate is IM_HEIGHT / 2 − (invGud(lat) − invGud(lat$_c$)) * latConvert. This calculation is implemented in the MapCoords class as the method lat2y():

```java
// globals
private static final double LAT_MAX = 85.05113;
                            // max latitude where Mercator works
private double latConvert;

// in the constructor
latConvert = (256.0 / (2*invGud(LAT_MAX))) * Math.pow(2, zoom);


public int lat2y(double lat)
// convert a latitude to a y-coordinate pixel in the image
{
  if ((lat < -LAT_MAX) || (lat > LAT_MAX))
    return -1;
  if (imHeight <= 0)
   return -1;

  double worldDist = invGud(lat) - invGud(latCenter);
  int yDist = (int)(worldDist * latConvert);
  return (imHeight/2 - yDist);
}  // end of lat2y()


private double invGud(double latitude)
/* Calculates the y-value for a latitude in degrees
   An inverse Gudermannian function for a Mercator map. */
{
  double sign = Math.signum(latitude);
  double sin = Math.sin( Math.toRadians(latitude) * sign);
  return sign * (Math.log((1.0 + sin)/(1.0 - sin)) / 2.0);
}
```

The Client Side

The Fox and Hounds client, FHClient, is illustrated in Figure 11-16.

FHClient starts with IDScreen, which obtains the player's game ID and passes it to ImageScreen. ImageScreen sends a "hi" message containing the ID to the servlet (inside a URL of the form FoxHoundsServlet?cmd=hi&uid=??). If the ID is valid, then the game map is returned; ImageScreen displays it and manages user-scrolling over it.

Concurrently, a LocUpdater thread is created, whose job is to periodically send "loc" messages to the servlet containing the player's GPS position (in the URL FoxHoundsServlet?cmd=loc&uid=??&lat=??&long=??). The latitude and longitude are obtained from GPSLocator, attached to the device's GPS receiver. The servlet returns player coordinates, which are passed to ImageScreen for rendering as icons on top of the map.

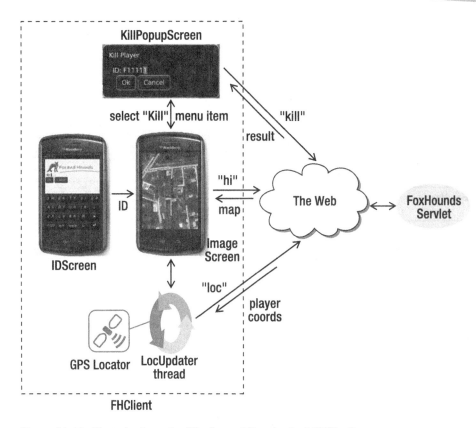

Figure 11-16. *The main elements of the Fox and Hounds client (FHClient)*

A Kill menu item, available on ImageScreen, presents KillPopupScreen, where the player can enter the ID of a target. This is passed to the servlet inside a "kill" message (the URL FoxHoundsServlet?cmd=kill&uid=??&kid=??) with the target's ID given in the kid field. The server's response indicates whether the kill was successful, which KillPopupScreen passes to ImageScreen, which may then finish the game.

Figure 11-17 shows the class diagrams for FHClient, with only public methods visible.

I won't describe the details of FHClient and IDScreen since they're quite standard UIApplication and MainScreen subclasses. IDScreen displays an image header, an edit field, and OK and Cancel buttons. If the user clicks OK, then ImageScreen is started, and the input ID is passed to it.

The PlayerLoc class stores information about a player, including his ID letter (*H* or *F*), his current (x,y) location on the map, and whether he is alive. This information, together with player icon images, are used to draw the players on top of the map.

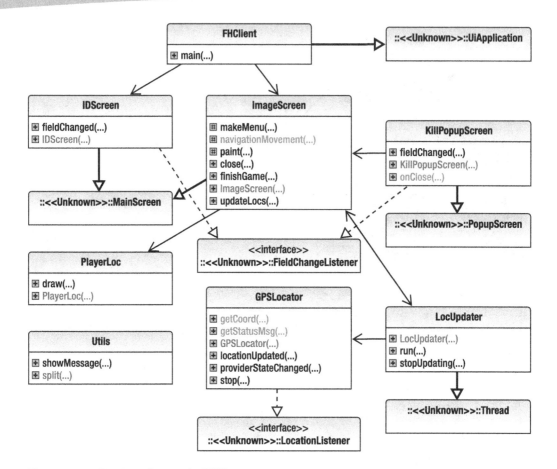

Figure 11-17. *The class diagrams for FHClient*

Playing the Game

ImageScreen is the heart of the Fox and Hound client, managing the following tasks:

- Saying hi to the server in order to get a copy of the game map.
- Starting the LocUpdater thread. The thread sends "loc" messages to the server periodically, and receives player coordinates in return.
- Drawing player icons (a green fox and red dogs) on top of the map.
- Processing player input to scroll the map.
- Finishing the game when either a fox or hound wins.

I'll look at each of these tasks in turn.

Saying Hi to the Server

The ImageScreen constructor calls sayHiToServer() to send a "hi" message to the server containing the ID obtained from IDScreen. It then waits for a map or error message to be returned. If a map arrives, the ID has been accepted, and game play can begin.

```
// globals
private Bitmap mapIm = null;
private boolean mapLoaded = false;

private String uid;   // ID obtained from IDScreen
private LocUpdater locUpdater = null;    // thread for obtaining location info


private void sayHiToServer()
{ Thread t = new Thread( new Runnable() {
    public void run()
    {
      String hiReply = requestHi(uid);
      if (hiReply.equals("Map received")) {
        mapLoaded = true;
        drawImage(mapIm);

        // start polling for locations
        locUpdater = new LocUpdater(uid, imScr);
        locUpdater.start();
      }
      else if (hiReply.startsWith("GAME_OVER"))
        finishGame( hiReply.substring(10) );
      else  // report error
        Utils.showMessage("Error", hiReply);
    }
  });
  t.start();
}  // end of sayHiToServer()
```

All the communication between the client and server is carried out in a separate thread since we don't want the client's user interface to freeze while an answer arrives from the server.

There are several possible replies that might turn up, but "Map received" means that the map has arrived, and so location updating should commence in the LocUpdater thread.

Utils.showMessage() is a useful method for displaying a message dialog from anywhere in the application:

```
// in the Utils class
public static void showMessage(String title, String message)
{
  synchronized(Application.getEventLock()) {
    UiEngine ui = Ui.getUiEngine();
    Dialog dialog = new Dialog( Dialog.D_OK, title + "\n\n" + message, Dialog.OK,
                      Bitmap.getPredefinedBitmap(Bitmap.INFORMATION),
                      Manager.VERTICAL_SCROLL);
    ui.pushGlobalScreen(dialog, 1, UiEngine.GLOBAL_QUEUE);
```

```
    }
} // end of showMessage()
```

The code comes from a BlackBerry knowledge base article at
www.blackberry.com/knowledgecenterpublic/livelink.exe/fetch/2000/348583/800332/
800505/800608/How_To_-
_Alert_a_user_from_a_Background_application.html?nodeid=820551&vernum=0.

requestHi() adds ;deviceside=true to the URL, which tells the device to employ a
direct TCP connection for the HttpConnection to the servlet. If the connection is
successfully opened, then the method must examine the data that's returned to
distinguish between receiving a map (a JPG image) or text containing an error message.

```
// global
private static final String SERVER =
                "http://tomcat.takasila.coe.psu.ac.th/~ad/FoxHoundsServlet";


private String requestHi(String id)
{
  String hiReply = "Hi failed";
  String hiDirect = SERVER + "?cmd=hi&uid=" + id + ";deviceside=true";
  HttpConnection conn = null;
  InputStream inStream = null;
  try {
    conn = (HttpConnection) Connector.open(hiDirect, Connector.READ, true);
    inStream = conn.openInputStream();
    if (conn.getResponseCode() == HttpConnection.HTTP_OK) {
      if (isJPG(conn)) {        // a map is returned (a JPG)
        mapIm = downloadImage(inStream);
        hiReply = "Map received";
      }
      else   // read text response
        hiReply = downloadReply(inStream);
    }
  }
  catch (IOException ex)
  { System.out.println(ex); }
  finally {
    try {
      inStream.close();
      inStream = null;
      conn.close();
      conn = null;
    }
    catch (Exception e) {}
  }
  return hiReply;
} // end of requestHi()
```

requestHi() checks the HttpConnection's response code (which should be
HttpConnection.HTTP_OK) if the server has been successfully contacted. Then the MIME
type of the response is examined by isJPG() to see if it is image/jpeg.

```
private boolean isJPG(HttpConnection conn) throws IOException
```

```
// is the content of the response a JPG?
{
  String contentType = conn.getHeaderField("content-type");
  if (contentType == null)
    return false;
  if (contentType.startsWith("image/jpeg"))
    return true;
  return false;
}  // end of isJPG
```

Creating an HTTP Connection

As mentioned, requestHi() uses direct TCP to create its HTTP connection, by adding ;deviceside=true to the URL:

```
String hiDirect = SERVER + "?cmd=hi&uid=" + id + ";deviceside=true";
```

It's called "direct" TCP in the BlackBerry documentation because the connection is made through the wireless carrier without involving any BlackBerry service. Direct TCP should be available on almost all BlackBerry devices, although sometimes a user must grapple with Access Point Name (APN) configuration. APNs vary from carrier to carrier, but are usually preconfigured on the device. This should mean that a programmer can forget about them, unless a particular APN requires a username and password.

You can explicitly specify an APN by adding an apn parameter to the URL, as in ;deviceside=true;apn=internet.com. Having to supply a username and password means adding two further parameters, as in apn=wap.cinqular;TunnelAuthUsername=WAP@CINGULARGPRS.COM;TunnelAuthPassword=CINGULAR1.

Aside from direct TCP, BlackBerry offers a bewildering number of other ways to create an HTTP connection, including via the BlackBerry Enterprise Server/BlackBerry Mobile Data System (BES/MDS), the BlackBerry Internet Service (BIS), and Wi-Fi, and by employing two kinds of Wireless Access Protocol (WAP): 1.0 and 2.0.

For a gaming application like Fox and Hounds, it's unlikely you'll use BES/MDS, which is aimed at secure communication within a business network.

The main advantage of BIS over direct TCP/IP is that some BlackBerry wireless plans don't include direct TCP, but almost all offer BIS. However, a BIS-based client/server application must be approved by the BlackBerry Alliance Program.

Wi-Fi's advantages for web communication are better speed, lower latency, and the lovely fact that there aren't any carrier data charges for using it. A possible disadvantage for Fox and Hounds, which is meant to be an outdoor game, is that Wi-Fi coverage tends to be best inside buildings, and rather spotty outside.

WAP 2.0 is probably the best alternative to direct TCP for Fox and Hounds (let's forget v1.0, which is on its way to joining the dinosaurs). WAP connects through the wireless carrier without employing any BlackBerry infrastructure, just like direct TCP. WAP is supported by all BlackBerry devices, and doesn't require any pesky APN configuration, but does need the UID of the WAP 2.0 service record on the device.

Service records are held in the BlackBerry service book, a configuration store for various aspects of the device, including information about different connection mechanisms.

A WAP 2.0 HTTP connection to the Fox and Hounds servlet would need a ConnectionUID parameter, such as ;deviceside=true;ConnectionUID=WAP2. You can find your device's real WAP 2.0 ID by looking through the service book (open Options and click Advanced Options ➤ Service Book).

As Carol explained in Chapter 9, Marcus Watkins' HttpConnectionFactory class is a great way of hiding all the messiness of trying different transport protocols. It's possible to restrict the protocols to direct TCP and WAP 2.0 by including the HttpConnectionFactory.TRANSPORTS_CARRIER_ONLY constant in the factory constructor:

```
HttpConnectionFactory connFactory =
    new HttpConnectionFactory( SERVER + "?cmd=hi&uid=" + id,
                            HttpConnectionFactory.TRANSPORTS_CARRIER_ONLY);
boolean isMsgSent = false;
while(!isMsgSent) {
  try {
    HttpConnection conn = connFactory.getNextConnection();
    try {
      InputStream is = conn.openInputStream();
      // send the request; process the answer
      if(the transport worked)
        msgSent = true;
    }
    catch(IOException) {
      // transport didn't work
    }
  }
  catch(NoMoreTransportsException e) {  // no more transports left
    Utils.showMessage("Error", "Network request failed");
    break;
  }
}
```

HttpConnectionFactory is available from www.versatilemonkey.com/blog/index.php/2009/06/24/networking-helper-class.

Downloading the Map

Downloading the map means downloading its bytes, storing them in an array, and converting that to a Bitmap:

```
private Bitmap downloadImage(InputStream inStream) throws IOException
{
  byte[] buffer = new byte[256];
  ByteArrayOutputStream baos = new ByteArrayOutputStream();
  while (inStream.read(buffer) != -1)
    baos.write(buffer);
  baos.flush();
  baos.close();
  byte[] imageData = baos.toByteArray();
```

```
    return Bitmap.createBitmapFromBytes(imageData, 0, imageData.length, 1);
}  // end of downloadImage()
```

If the data offered up by the server isn't a JPG, then it's a text message, which means the incoming bytes must be converted to a string:

```
private String downloadReply(InputStream inStream) throws IOException
{
  byte[] buffer = new byte[256];
  StringBuffer sb = new StringBuffer();
  int len = 0;
  while ((len = inStream.read(buffer)) != -1)
    sb.append(new String(buffer, 0, len));
  return sb.toString();
}  // end of downloadReply()
```

Positioning the Map

The map is painted onto the device's screen by having sayHiToServer() call drawImage(). One issue in the design of ImageScreen is that the image is much bigger (640×640 pixels) than the screen. Rather than resizing the map and thereby losing lots of detail, the map is drawn centered on the screen, and the user can press keys (or use the trackwheel) to scroll it horizontally and vertically.

Figure 11-18 shows the relative dimensions of the screen and map.

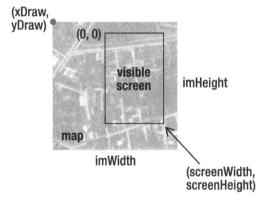

Figure 11-18. *The map drawn to the screen*

The crucial calculation is of the (xDraw,yDraw) coordinate, two negative integers that specify how far the top-left corner of the image is to the left and above the visible screen.

The initial (xDraw,yDraw) value is calculated in drawImage(), which aligns the center of the image with the center of the screen.

```
// globals
private int imWidth, imHeight;
private int screenWidth, screenHeight;
private int xDraw, yDraw;    // top-left corner of image on screen
```

```
private void drawImage(Bitmap im)
{
  imWidth = im.getWidth();
  imHeight = im.getHeight();

  // center the image in the center of the screen
  xDraw = (screenWidth - imWidth)/2;
  yDraw = (screenHeight - imHeight)/2;
  limitMovement();
        /* xDraw and yDraw should be -ve or 0
           since the image is bigger than the screen */
  invalidate();          // draw the screen in its initial state
}  // end of drawImage()
```

limitMovement() adjusts the xDraw and yDraw values so that none of the screen's background is visible, but that may not be possible if the image is smaller than the screen in one of its dimensions.

```
private void limitMovement()
{
  // prevent map's right edge from moving left of the right screen edge
  if (xDraw < (screenWidth-imWidth))
    xDraw = screenWidth-imWidth;

  // prevent map's left edge from moving right of the left screen edge
  if (xDraw > 0)
    xDraw = 0;

  // prevent map's bottom edge from moving above the bottom screen edge
  if (yDraw < (screenHeight-imHeight))
    yDraw = screenHeight-imHeight;

  // prevent map's top edge from moving below the top screen edge
  if (yDraw > 0)
    yDraw = 0;
}  // end of limitMovement()
```

xDraw and yDraw are used to control the scrolling of the image by modifying their values via the keypad or trackwheel. Since ImageScreen is a subclass of MainScreen, this is done by overriding navigationMovement().

```
// global
private static int STEP = 8;  // step increment for moving image

protected boolean navigationMovement(int dx,int dy, int status, int time)
{ xDraw -= (STEP*dx);
  yDraw -= (STEP*dy);
  limitMovement();
  invalidate();          // redraw the screen
  return true;
}  // end of navigationMovement()
```

After a change to xDraw and yDraw, limitMovement() is called to stop the screen's background from being exposed.

Storing Player Details

ImageScreen stores player information in a `PlayerLoc[]` array:

```
// globals
private static final int MAX_PLAYERS = 5;    // one fox, four hounds
private PlayerLoc[] playerLocs;              // player location details

// in the constructor
playerLocs = new PlayerLoc[MAX_PLAYERS];
```

PlayerLoc stores information about a single player, including his ID letter (*H* or *F*), his current (x,y) location on the map, and whether he's alive. PlayerLoc's main job is to draw a player on the map.

The `playerLocs[]` array gets initialized (and updated) by the LocUpdater thread calling `ImageScreen.updateLocs()`. The method is passed a string of player information consisting of fives lines (one for each player), with the following format:

```
first-letter-of-id x y player-state
```

updateLocs() extracts each player's substring and updates the `playerLocs[]` array:

```
public void updateLocs(String playerLocsStr)
{
  Vector lines = Utils.split(playerLocsStr, "\n");
                            // split according to new lines
  int numPlayers = 0;
  for(int i=0; i < lines.size(); i++) {
    if (numPlayers == MAX_PLAYERS)
      break;
    if (lines.elementAt(i) == null)  // ignore empty lines
      continue;
    String line = ((String) lines.elementAt(i)).trim();
    if (line.equals(""))              // ignore blank lines
      continue;
    synchronized(playerLocs) {
      playerLocs[numPlayers] = new PlayerLoc(line);
      numPlayers++;
    }
  }
  invalidate();  // redraw
} // end of updateLocs()
```

The array update is performed in a synchronized block since updateLocs() is called by the LocUpdater thread, which may try to modify the array while ImageScreen is using it.

The invalidate() call at the end of updateLocs() requests a repaint of the screen since the player details have changed.

Rendering the Map and the Players

ImageScreen's paint() method draws the map first, then the player icons, and finally a game-over message if the game is over.

```
// globals
private Bitmap mapIm;
private PlayerLoc[] playerLocs;       // player location details
private boolean isGameOver = false;

protected void paint(Graphics g)
{
  // a black background
  g.setColor(Color.BLACK);
  g.fillRect (0, 0, screenWidth, screenHeight);

  if (mapIm != null)     // draw the map
    g.drawBitmap(0, 0, screenWidth, screenHeight, mapIm, -xDraw, -yDraw);
  // draw player locations
  if (mapLoaded)
    synchronized(playerLocs) {
      for(int i=0; i < MAX_PLAYERS; i++)
        if (playerLocs[i] != null)
          playerLocs[i].draw(g, screenWidth, screenHeight, xDraw, yDraw);
    }

  if (isGameOver)
    showGameOver(g);
}  // end of paint()
```

The first four arguments of Graphics.drawBitmap() specify the drawing region, which is the entire screen (see Figure 11-18). The final two arguments give the top-left visible corner of the image on the screen, which is (–xDraw,–yDraw) since (xDraw,yDraw) is the screen coordinate of the top-left corner of the entire image.

The drawing of the player icons is delegated to the PlayerLoc objects and surrounded by a synchronized block. This prevents the objects from being modified by the LocUpdater thread calling ImageScreen.updateLocs() while they are being painted.

Finishing the Game

There are several ways for the game to finish:

- It may never get started since the initial "hi" message results in a server message saying that the game is already over.

- The LocsUpdater may get a game-over reply when it sends the player's location information to the server, because another player has won.

- The KillPopupScreen may get a game-over message from the server after it sends it a "kill" request.

In all three cases, ImageScreen.finishGame() is called:

```
// globals
private boolean isGameOver = false;
private String gameOverMsg;

public void finishGame(String msg)
```

```
{
  isGameOver = true;
  gameOverMsg = msg;
  invalidate();      // redraw the screen
}  // end of finishGame()
```

The setting of the isGameOver boolean causes paint() to call showGameOver(), which draws the game-over message at the center of the screen, spread over two lines.

Managing Player Location Information

PlayerLoc performs two main tasks: storing information about a player, (including his ID letter, his current location, and whether he's alive), and drawing a player icon.

The player information comes from the LocUpdater thread calling ImageScreen.updateLocs(), supplying it with information sent by the server. updateLocs() creates a PlayerLoc object:

```
// globals
private static final int FOX = 0;    // player types
private static final int HOUND = 1;

private int playerType;
private int x = -1;
private int y = -1;
private boolean isAlive;


public PlayerLoc(String playerInfo)
{
  Vector words = Utils.split(playerInfo, " ");
        // split up the player info string based on its spaces

  if (words.size() == 4) {     // ID-letter x y alive
    String typeStr = (String) words.elementAt(0);
    playerType = typeStr.trim().equals("F") ? FOX : HOUND;
    try {
      x = Integer.parseInt( (String)words.elementAt(1) );
      y = Integer.parseInt( (String)words.elementAt(2) );
    }
    catch (NumberFormatException e) {}

    String aliveStr = (String) words.elementAt(3);
    isAlive = aliveStr.trim().equals("true") ? true : false;
  }
}  // end of PlayerLoc()
```

Drawing the players requires fox and hound images representing when they're alive or dead. These are loaded by the PlayerLoc class rather than by each PlayerLoc object to save unnecessary duplication of effort.

```
// globals
private static final String IMAGES_DIR = "images/";
```

```
// bitmaps used when drawing the players -- loaded by the class
private static final Bitmap foxAlive = loadImage("foxAlive.png");
private static final Bitmap foxDead = loadImage("foxDead.png");
private static final Bitmap houndAlive = loadImage("dogAlive.png");
private static final Bitmap houndDead = loadImage("dogDead.png");


private static Bitmap loadImage(String fnm)
// static image loading carried out by the class
{
  Bitmap im = null;
  System.out.println("Loading image in " + IMAGES_DIR+fnm);
  try {
    im = Bitmap.getBitmapResource(fnm);
  }
  catch (Exception e) {
    System.out.println(e);
    System.exit(1);
  }
  if (im == null) {
    System.out.println("Image is empty");
    System.exit(1);
  }
  return im;
}  // end of loadImage()
```

The drawing of an image is carried out when ImageScreen's paint() calls
PlayerLoc.draw(). The tricky part is calculating the position of the image, which
depends on the current position of the map, as shown in Figure 11-19.

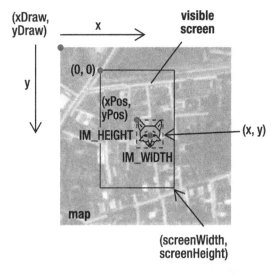

Figure 11-19. *Drawing a player icon*

The draw() call supplies the (xDraw,yDraw) screen coordinate for the top-left of the
image (see Figure 11-19). PlayerLoc already contains the current player position (x,y) on

the image, which must be converted into a screen coordinate (xPos,yPos) for positioning the top-left corner of the player icon. Ignoring error checking, the calculation is

```
int xPos = x + xDraw - IM_WIDTH/2;
int yPos = y + yDraw - IM_HEIGHT/2;
```

xPos and yPos are used to draw the icon, as shown in draw():

```
// globals
private static final int IM_WIDTH = 25;   // size of all images
private static final int IM_HEIGHT = 25;


public void draw(Graphics g, int screenWidth, int screenHeight,
                                      int xDraw, int yDraw)
{  if ((x == -1) || (y == -1))   // error in location info
     return;

  // calculate position on screen of top-left corner of image
  int xPos = x + xDraw - IM_WIDTH/2;
  int yPos = y + yDraw - IM_HEIGHT/2;

  if ((xPos < -IM_WIDTH) || (xPos > screenWidth) ||
      (yPos < -IM_WIDTH) || (yPos > screenHeight))
     return;        // location not visible

  // select image for the player
  Bitmap im = null;
  if (playerType == FOX)
     im = isAlive ? foxAlive : foxDead;
  else if (playerType == HOUND)
     im = isAlive ? houndAlive : houndDead;

  if (im != null)
     g.drawBitmap(xPos, yPos, IM_WIDTH, IM_HEIGHT, im, 0, 0);
} // end of draw()
```

Killing Another Player

The KillPopupScreen class sends a "kill" request to the server, with the following format

FoxHoundsServlet?cmd=kill&uid=??&kid=??

The user ID (uid) comes from the ImageScreen, and the target player ID (kid) is obtained from the user via an edit field when he presses an OK button (see Figure 11-3).

If the reply is a game-over message, then the ImageScreen is informed; otherwise, the message is displayed in a dialog box.

KillPopupScreen is a subclass of PopupScreen and implements FieldChangeListener to respond to the button presses:

```
// globals GUI elements
private ButtonField okButton, cancelButton;
private EditField idEditField;
```

```
public void fieldChanged(Field field, int context)
{
  if (field == okButton) {     // send a "kill" request to server
    String targetID = idEditField.getText();
    sayKillToServer(targetID);
    onClose();
  }
  if (field == cancelButton)
    onClose();
}  // end of fieldChanged()
```

sayKillToServer() sends a "kill" request and deals with the server's response inside a separate thread so the device's event thread isn't forced to wait.

```
private void sayKillToServer(final String targetID)
{
  Thread t = new Thread( new Runnable() {
    public void run()
    {
      String killReply = requestKill(targetID);
      if (killReply.startsWith("GAME_OVER"))
              // the kill means the game is finished
        imageScreen.finishGame(killReply.substring(10));
              // tell the ImageScreen
      else
        Utils.showMessage("Kill Reply", killReply);
    }
  });
  t.start();
}  // end of sayKillToServer()
```

requestKill() creates a FoxHoundsServlet?cmd=kill&uid=??&kid=?? URL and sends it to the server using a direct TCP connection. The coding is similar to the requestHi() method in ImageScreen, but the response can only be textual.

```
// global
private String uid;


private String requestKill(String targetID)
{
  String killReply = "Kill Request failed";
  String hiDirect = SERVER + "?cmd=kill&uid=" + uid + "&" +
                              "kid=" + targetID + ";deviceside=true";

  HttpConnection conn = null;
  InputStream inStream = null;
  try {
    conn = (HttpConnection) Connector.open(hiDirect, Connector.READ, true);
    inStream = conn.openInputStream();
    if (conn.getResponseCode() == HttpConnection.HTTP_OK)
      killReply = downloadReply(inStream);
  }
  catch (IOException ex)
```

```
  { System.out.println(ex); }
  finally {
    try {
      inStream.close();
      inStream = null;
      conn.close();
      conn = null;
    }
    catch (Exception e) {}
  }
  return killReply;
}  // end of requestKill()


private String downloadReply(InputStream inStream)
                                      throws IOException
// extract reply from text sent along stream from server
{
  byte[] buffer = new byte[256];
  StringBuffer sb = new StringBuffer();
  int len = 0;
  while ((len = inStream.read(buffer)) != -1)
    sb.append(new String(buffer, 0, len));
  return sb.toString();
}  // end of downloadReply()
```

The Location Updater Thread

As depicted in Figure 11-16, the location updater thread is started by ImageScreen to periodically send a "loc" message to the server containing the player's current latitude and longitude:

FoxHoundsServlet?cmd=loc&uid=??&lat=??&long=??

The latitude and longitude are supplied by the GPSLocator object, acting as an interface to the device's GPS.

The response from the server is a string of player details, with each player represented by the substring:

first-letter-of-id x y player-state

The details are passed to ImageScreen via its updateLocs().

The heart of LocUpdater is a loop executed in its run() method, which retrieves the device's GPS position, sends a "loc" request, processes the response, and sleeps a bit to slow down the polling of the GPS receiver.

```
// globals
private static final int SLEEP_TIME = 35*1000;    // 35 secs between polling
private volatile boolean isRunning = true;
private String uid;
private GPSLocator gpsLocator;
```

```
public void run()
{
  while(isRunning) {
    Coordinates coord = gpsLocator.getCoord();
    if (coord == null)
      System.out.println("No GPS coordinate found");
    else
      requestLoc(uid, coord);     // send a "loc" request
    try {
      Thread.sleep(SLEEP_TIME);
    }
    catch(InterruptedException ex){}
  }
  gpsLocator.stop();
} // end of run()
```

requestLoc() send a "loc" request to the server using direct TCP in much the same way that a "hi" request is sent by ImageScreen.requestHi() and "kill" by KillPopupScreen.requestKill().

```
// globals
private static final String SERVER =
                    "http://tomcat.takasila.coe.psu.ac.th/~ad/FoxHoundsServlet";

private void requestLoc(String uid, Coordinates coord)
{
  // send the GPS-supplied lat and long
  String locDirect = SERVER + "?cmd=loc&uid=" + uid + "&" +
                "lat=" + coord.getLatitude() + "&" +
                "long=" + coord.getLongitude() +
                ";deviceside=true";
  HttpConnection conn = null;
  InputStream inStream = null;
  try {
    conn = (HttpConnection) Connector.open(locDirect, Connector.READ, true);
    inStream = conn.openInputStream();
    if (conn.getResponseCode() == HttpConnection.HTTP_OK)
      downloadReply(inStream);     // extract answer
  }
  catch (IOException ex)
  { Utils.showMessage("Error", "Location update failed"); }
  finally {
    try {
      inStream.close();
      inStream = null;
      conn.close();
      conn = null;
    }
    catch (Exception e) {}
  }
}  // end of requestLoc()
```

downloadReply() must deal with three cases:

- The arrival of a game-over message, which must be passed to ImageScreen

- The receipt of player location details, which must also be passed to ImageScreen so that they can be displayed on the map

- A "too soon" message, which indicates that the server isn't going to supply player details just yet

```
private void downloadReply(InputStream inStream) throws IOException
{
  byte[] buffer = new byte[256];
  StringBuffer sb = new StringBuffer();
  int len = 0;
  while ((len = inStream.read(buffer)) != -1)
    sb.append(new String(buffer, 0, len));
  String reply = sb.toString();

  if (reply.startsWith("GAME_OVER")) {
    // tell ImageScreen that the game is over
    imageScreen.finishGame(reply.substring(10));
    isRunning = false;
  }
  else if (reply.startsWith("LOCS"))
    // pass location info to ImageScreen
    imageScreen.updateLocs(reply.substring(5));
  else if (reply.startsWith("TOO SOON"))
    {} // request was too soon, so no player info was supplied
  else
    Utils.showMessage("Location Error", reply);
}  // end of downloadReply()
```

GPS and the BlackBerry

A BlackBerry can support GPS through a built-in GPS chip or via a receiver attached using Bluetooth. The device's current latitude and longitude will be available, and perhaps also its altitude, speed, and route information. GPS programming is done through Java ME's Location API (JSR 179) and BlackBerry's JSR 179 extensions.

Startup times for a GPS application (i.e., the time it takes for the first piece of location data to arrive) and data accuracy depend on several factors, such as the location mode being employed and the GPS signal strength. For this reason, GPS coordinate data comes with latitude and longitude accuracy estimates in meters.

There are three basic location modes:

Cell site: The location is calculated from the position of nearby cell towers and their signal strengths. It's the fastest mode, and guaranteed to be offered by wireless carriers. However, it offers poor location accuracy (anywhere from 2 to 20 kilometers away from your actual location), and doesn't provide speed or route information.

Autonomous (also called stand-alone and unassisted): The location information comes solely from the GPS receiver without any assistance from the wireless carrier.

This is the most accurate data source (the supplied position may only be between 4 and 40 meters away from where you're actually standing), but it is slower than other modes. It performs very poorly indoors, close to large obstructions, and in cloudy weather, and takes several minutes to start since it must synchronize with four or more satellites. This "cold-start" cost is a major drawback, and an important programming aim is to keep the receiver "hot" after its startup (i.e., keep the satellite connection open) to ensure that subsequent location requests will be answered almost instantly. The simplest way of doing this is to request data frequently, at 10-second intervals or less. The need to keep the GPS receiver in near-constant operation means that autonomous mode can be a severe drain on the device's battery. GPS is a free service, unlike cell site and assisted modes, which incur data transfer costs. Some carriers—most notably Verizon—either haven't supported autonomous mode in the past or require the user to sign up to a special data plan.

Assisted. The location information utilizes GPS and a variety of other techniques to deal with GPS's drawbacks (and so is sometimes called Assisted-GPS or A-GPS). Position hints may be obtained by triangulating on nearby cell towers or from Wi-Fi base stations, or by querying information stored on servers maintained by the carrier. A Position Determination Entity (PDE) controls and manages the resources required to calculate the position. Startup time is typically less than 30 seconds (much better than autonomous mode), and the position data is more accurate than cell site location details. The requirements for utilizing assisted mode vary from carrier to carrier. Many employ their own PDE configurations, which are only available through special data programs.

Other modes that combine elements of the three basic modes are possible. For example, *MS-based* relies on assisted mode for the first satellite fix, and then switches over to autonomous mode for subsequent location requests.

The choice of mode often depends on your BlackBerry model and carrier, as explained in BlackBerry knowledge base article DB-00615, "What Is - The BlackBerry Smartphone Models and Their Corresponding GPS Capabilities" (www.blackberry.com/knowledgecenterpublic/livelink.exe/fetch/2000/348583/80 0332/800703/What_Is_- _The_BlackBerry_smartphone_models_and_their_corresponding_GPS_capabilities .html?nodeid=1371352&vernum=0).

Prior to BlackBerry OS 5.0, the selection of a location mode was done indirectly by setting criteria in a `Criteria` object. For example, the following settings will cause cell site mode to be utilized by the device:

```
Criteria criteria = new Criteria();
criteria.setHorizontalAccuracy(NO_REQUIREMENT);
criteria.setVerticalAccuracy(NO_REQUIREMENT);
    // longitudinal and latitudinal accuracy not required
criteria.setCostAllowed(true);
criteria.setPreferredPowerConsumption(POWER_USAGE_LOW);
```

Cell site and assisted modes both use wireless networking, and therefore have data costs associated with them, as allowed by the call to `Criteria.setCostAllowed()`.

Autonomous mode doesn't use the wireless network, so `setCostAllowed()` can be set to false, as shown below.

`Criteria.setPreferredPowerConsumption()` specifies a power consumption level permitted when returning a location. Cell site mode requires the least power, assisted mode the highest, and autonomous somewhere in between.

Autonomous mode is specified with

```
Criteria criteria = new Criteria();
criteria.setHorizontalAccuracy(10);
criteria.setVerticalAccuracy(10);
criteria.setCostAllowed(false);        // carrier not used
   // no requirement for power consumption
```

`Criteria.setHorizontalAccuracy()` sets a longitudinal accuracy in meters, while `setVerticalAccuracy()` does the same for latitude. If any accuracy value is supplied in the criteria, then cell site mode is immediately ruled out.

Here is an assisted mode example:

```
Criteria criteria = new Criteria();
criteria.setHorizontalAccuracy(NO_REQUIREMENT);
criteria.setVerticalAccuracy(NO_REQUIREMENT);
criteria.setCostAllowed(true);
criteria.setPreferredPowerConsumption(POWER_USAGE_MEDIUM);
```

Here is another:

```
Criteria criteria = new Criteria();
criteria.setHorizontalAccuracy(50);
criteria.setVerticalAccuracy(50);
criteria.setCostAllowed(true);
criteria.setPreferredPowerConsumption(Criteria.POWER_USAGE_HIGH);
```

Accuracy is required in the second example, so the power consumption level is set higher.

Many carriers, such as Verizon, require a connection to a PDE server for assisted mode, in addition to any `Criteria` settings. The server is specified by its IP address and port number in a call to `GPSSettings.setPDEInfo()`:

```
GPSSettings.setPDEInfo("127.0.0.1", 80);  //address and port no
```

Some carriers also require username and password parameters for the server.

Since Fox and Hounds in an outdoor game, autonomous mode is probably the best choice since it doesn't incur carrier data charges.

On BlackBerry OS 5.0, `BlackBerryCriteria` extends the `Criteria` class to allow a programmer to more directly set the initial location mode, a failover mode, and even a mode to use during execution after GPS contact has been made. The following sets the mode to be autonomous:

```
BlackBerryCriteria myCriteria =
                new BlackBerryCriteria(GPSInfo.GPS_MODE_AUTONOMOUS);
```

However, I've used the Criteria class in my code to increase its portability across different BlackBerry operating systems.

A Criteria object is used to obtain a location provider, which supplies location details:

```
LocationProvider lp = LocationProvider.getInstance(criteria);
Location loc = lp.getLocation(120);     // max wait time (in secs)
```

The first call to LocationProvider.getLocation() may suspend for a considerable amount of time (e.g., 2 minutes or more), especially for an autonomous mode cold-start. Therefore, it's important to move GPS processing into a separate thread from the rest of the application. This is done in FHClient by using the LocUpdater thread to call GPSLocator.

Since most applications require a steady stream of locations (as in our game), it's common to obtain location information through a LocationListener, which provides two methods—locationUpdated() and providerStateChanged(). The location provider calls locationUpdated() whenever the location changes, while providerStateChanged() is called whenever the state of the provider changes.

There's also a ProximityListener interface, which triggers method calls when the device approaches a specified location (or locations), which isn't used in GPSLocator.

Useful Location methods include

- getQualifiedCoordinates(): Returns the coordinates of the location.

- isValid(): Returns true if the location contains valid coordinates.

- getTimestamp(): Returns the time when the location data was obtained.

- getAddressInfo(): Returns the street address, phone number, country, URL, and other data (as an AddressInfo object); otherwise returns null.

- getCourse(): Returns the heading in degrees relative to true north.

- getSpeed(): Returns the device's current ground speed in meters per second.

- getLocationMethod(): Returns a bit mask describing how the location was obtained. The bit constants include MTA_ASSISTED, MTA_UNASSISTED, MTE_CELLID, and MTE_SATELLITE, and can be used like so:

```
if ((loc.getLocationMethod() & Location.MTA_UNASSISTED) > 0)
    System.out.println("Autonomous mode used");
```

The latitude, longitude, altitude, direction, and speed values can be extracted from a QualifiedCoordinates object:

```
QualifiedCoordinates coord = loc.getQualifiedCoordinates();
if (coord != null)  {
  double lat = coord.getLatitude();
  double long = coord.getLongitude();
   :
```

JSR 179 offers two coordinate classes: Coordinates and QualifiedCoordinates. A Coordinates instance contains the latitude, longitude, and elevation with no associated accuracy information; QualifiedCoordinates includes horizontal and vertical uncertainties in meters, accessible via getHorizontalAccuracy() and getVerticalAccuracy().

A major aspect of JSR 179 not utilized in GPSLocator is a *landmark*. A landmark is a location associated with a name and a description, stored in a database on the device (available via the LandmarkStore class). This offers a way for GPS applications to store frequently used locations, such as the boundaries of a game area, or points of interest in a tourist application.

In OS 5.0, the BlackBerryLocationProvider class extends LocationProvider to handle BlackBerryCriteria, pause and resume a location listener, and supply information on the GPS receiver (i.e., whether it's internal or a Bluetooth device). The BlackBerryLocation class extends Location to give access to GPS satellite details, the GPS data source, and the location mode being employed.

Using GPS in Fox and Hounds

GPSLocator starts by defining a Criteria object for autonomous GPS data retrieval, and then creates a location provider and listener.

```
public class GPSLocator implements LocationListener
{
  private static final int DIST_ACCURACY = 10;  // meters
  private static final int LOC_INTERVAL = 10;  // secs between location requests

  private LocationProvider locProvider = null;


  public GPSLocator()
  {
    Criteria cr = new Criteria();       // define autonomous mode
    cr.setHorizontalAccuracy(DIST_ACCURACY);  // longitude
    cr.setVerticalAccuracy(DIST_ACCURACY);    // latitude
    cr.setCostAllowed(false);

    // start location provider and set up its listener
    try {
      locProvider = LocationProvider.getInstance(cr);
      if (locProvider != null)
        locProvider.setLocationListener(this, LOC_INTERVAL,-1,-1);
                          // listener, interval, timeout, maxAge
      else
        Utils.showMessage("GPS Error", "GPS not supported");
    }
    catch (LocationException e) {
      Utils.showMessage("GPS Error", "Location Exception");
    }
  } // end of GPSLocator()
```

GPSLocator is registered as a LocationListener by calling
LocationProvider.setLocationListener(). Aside from the listener reference (this), the
other arguments are the time interval between location requests, the waiting time for a
location to be supplied, and the maximum timestamp age of a returned location. The -1
values mean that default values will be utilized for those arguments. As mentioned, the
interval between location requests should be fairly short so that the GPS device stays
hot while running in autonomous mode.

When a location arrives at the device, locationUpdated() is called:

```
// globals
private double lat, lon;
private boolean hasCoord = false;


public void locationUpdated(LocationProvider lp, Location location)
{
  if (location == null) {
    Utils.showMessage("Location Error", "Location is null");
    return;
  }

  if (!location.isValid()) {
    String errMsg = getErrorMsg( GPSInfo.getLastGPSError() );
    Utils.showMessage("Location Invalid", errMsg);
    return;
  }

  QualifiedCoordinates coord = location.getQualifiedCoordinates();
  if ((coord.getHorizontalAccuracy() > DIST_ACCURACY) ||
      (coord.getVerticalAccuracy() > DIST_ACCURACY))
    return;    // too inaccurate to store

  lat = coord.getLatitude();
  lon = coord.getLongitude();
  hasCoord = true;
}  // end of locationUpdated()
```

Although there should be a Location object available if locationUpdated() is called,
several BlackBerry programmers have reported that the location argument may be null,
which explains the first test in locationUpdated(). Even is there is an object, the latitude
and longitude are only stored if the data is valid and sufficiently accurate.

The latitude and longitude are passed to the LocUpdater thread when it calls
GPSLocator.getCoord():

```
// globals
private double lat, lon;
private boolean hasCoord = false;

public Coordinates getCoord()
// called by the LocUpdater thread
{
  if (!hasCoord)
    return null;
```

```
    else
      return new Coordinates(lat, lon, 0);
                            // don't return altitude or accuracy data
}  // end of getCoord()
```

Thread contention is an issue since getCoord() may be called at the same time that locationUpdated() is changing the lat and lon doubles. However, since they are both basic types, assignments to them will be atomic, so there's no likelihood of data corruption. There's a slim chance that the player will receive slightly out-of-date information, but that doesn't really matter for this game.

The other reason for storing lat and lon is to allow the LocationListener to progress at a fast rate (a location fix is attempted every LOC_INTERVAL seconds [10 seconds]) to ensure that the autonomous mode remains hot. However, LocUpdater progresses at a slower rate, so the players are left a little in the dark about the current positions of other participants.

Location Provider Changes

LocationListener offers providerStateChanged(), which is called when the status of the location provider changes. GPSLocator includes a simple implementation:

```
public void providerStateChanged(LocationProvider lp, int state)
{
  switch (state) {
  case LocationProvider.TEMPORARILY_UNAVAILABLE:
    Utils.showMessage("Location Provider", "Temporarily unavailable");
    break;

  case LocationProvider.OUT_OF_SERVICE:
    Utils.showMessage("Location Provider", "Out of service");
    break;

  case LocationProvider.AVAILABLE:
    Utils.showMessage("Location Provider", "Available");
    break;

  default:
    return;
  }
}  // end of providerStateChanged()
```

The state codes passed to providerStateChanged() have the following meanings:

- TEMPORARILY_UNAVAILABLE: The location provider has stopped working. In autonomous mode, this usually occurs when the user goes indoors or the open sky is obscured by large buildings or cloud cover.

- OUT_OF_SERVICE: This indicates that the chosen location mode isn't available, or the GPS receiver isn't responding. Some developers have reported this state occurring when autonomous mode is specified, since some carriers don't support it.

■   AVAILABLE: This state is only set after a preceding problem has been fixed. Some devices don't report this state, as a way of reducing battery drain.

If a TEMPORARILY_UNAVAILABLE state is triggered, an application can attempt to reset the LocationProvider:

```
// close down the provider
locProvider.setLocationListener(null, 0, 0, 0);
locProvider.reset();
locProvider = null;

// restart the provider
locProvider = LocationProvider.getInstance(cr);
locProvider.setLocationListener(this, LOC_INTERVAL, -1, -1);
```

It's a good idea to leave at least 3 minutes between resets due to the time it takes for the autonomous mode to carry out a cold-start.

Some older BlackBerry operating system versions don't correctly trigger TEMPORARILY_UNAVAILABLE. In those cases, the only way to detect GPS loss is by comparing the current time with the timestamp of the last location received. If the difference is more than 3 minutes, then the satellite link has probably been lost.

Stopping the Location Provider

Stopping the provider, and therefore stopping the GPS device, involves a reset without a subsequent restart:

```
// globals
private LocationProvider locProvider = null;

public void stop()
{
  if (locProvider != null) {
    locProvider.setLocationListener(null, 0, 0, 0);
    locProvider.reset();
    locProvider = null;
  }
}  // end of stop()
```

stop() is called from the LocUpdater thread when it's about to exit its run() method.

Summary

This chapter describes a simple GPS-based hide-and-seek game. Five players run GPS-enabled client software on their BlackBerrys, communicating through HTTP with a Java EE servlet. Each client displays a map of the playing area and icons showing player locations. A separate thread in each client periodically sends GPS information to the server and receives back the locations of the other players.

Chapter 12

Introducing 3D with JSR 239

Agent Psmith: Did you know that our first 3D application, the Beatrix, was designed to be a perfect world? Where none suffered, where everyone would be happy. Jemima Puddle-Duck, Squirrel Nutkin, Benjamin Bunny. It was a disaster. No one would accept the program. Entire crops were lost. Some believed we lacked the programming language to describe your perfect world. Then came Java ME, JSR 239, and Khronos.

Oreo: Isn't that from *The Incredibles*?

Agent Psmith. We succeeded with our second 3D world—the Dominatrix. She's all around us. Even now, in this very room. You can see her when you look out your window or when you turn on your television, if you have the right cable package.

Drano: That sounds like a really good deal.

Agent Psmith: Choose to take this blue berry, the story ends, you wake up in your bed and believe whatever you want to believe. You take the BlackBerry, you stay in Wonderland, and I show you how deep the rabbit hole goes.

Bozo: Whoa.

With the release of the BlackBerry Java Application Development v5.0 beta 5 software, we finally get to play with a 3D API—a Java binding for OpenGL ES, called JSR 239. In this chapter, I'll describe a simple 3D scene coded with JSR 239, grandly termed the *BoxTrix*. Don't get your hopes up too high; it's essentially an animation loop inside a thread, which repeatedly updates the application's state, renders the 3D scene, and perhaps sleeps for a while so the animation can maintain the desired frame rate. The rendering is done to an offscreen buffer that is painted to the BlackBerry's screen using the familiar `paint()` method. This chapter also shows how to

- Initialize JSR 239.
- Create a 3D textured floor.

- Create rotating textured cubes.

- Mix 3D and 2D rendering (for drawing 2D textual overlays at the front of the 3D scene).

- Control a moveable camera. The camera can translate forward, backward, left, right, up, and down, and rotate around the x- and y-axes.

- Display billboards—images that automatically rotate to always face the camera.

- Utilize lighting.

- Shut down JSR 239 at termination time.

Unfortunately, no one can be told what the *BoxTrix* is. You have to see it for yourself. Figure 12-1 shows a screenshot.

Figure 12-1. *BoxTrix: A JSR 239 example*

Two textured boxes continuously rotate around the y-axis; the one with the green lines is centered at the origin, while the metallic cube orbits some distance above the floor. A cube's texture is repeated on each of its faces.

The floor is covered with a grass texture. The figure and tree are billboards that always stay facing the camera.

The text at the top left is drawn as a 2D overlay, which keeps it "pinned" to the screen in front of the changing 3D scene. The red text is positional and rotational information about the camera, the blue text is the camera's current mode (there are three possibilities), and the black number is how long the current frame took to render in milliseconds.

A Brief Introduction to OpenGL ES

JSR 239 is a Java binding around OpenGL ES; before I get stuck into JSR 239 coding, I should explain OpenGL ES.

OpenGL ES (OpenGL for Embedded Systems) is a subset of OpenGL aimed at smaller devices such as mobile phones, PDAs, and games consoles (the official web site is at www.khronos.org/opengles). It only requires around 50KB of memory, and yet its capabilities are very similar to OpenGL's.

The most obvious loss of functionality is probably the OpenGL `glBegin()`/`glEnd()` technique for grouping instructions for shape creation. In OpenGL ES, the programmer defines arrays for a shape's vertices, normals, colors, and texture coordinates.

Another significant loss concerns the GLU and GLUT utility libraries. GLU includes convenience functions for tasks such as positioning the camera, setting up the viewing volume, generating basic shapes, and texture mipmapping (multiple versions of a texture, at reduced levels of detail). RIM comes to the rescue here with its `GLUtils` class, which adds back a few of those methods, including camera positioning. GLUT is mainly utilized in OpenGL applications for its I/O support; on the BlackBerry, that's handled by the `Screen` subclasses.

OpenGL ES differs from OpenGL in its support for fixed-point numbers in addition to floats, to better match the limited computational hardware of smaller devices. Its fixed-point data type utilizes the first 16 bits for a signed two's compliment integer, and the other 16 bits for a fractional part. A shape defined using fixed-point vertices should render more quickly than one employing floats.

OpenGL ES employs profiles—the Common profile has both the float and fixed-point types, and is aimed at more powerful devices such as consoles and mobile phones. The Common Lite profile only offers fixed-point data, and is intended for more basic devices, but I'll build my shapes using floats. There's also a third profile, Safety Critical, for safety-critical embedded applications where testability and certification are crucial.

OpenGL ES only has primitives for creating shapes out of points, lines, or triangles; polygon and quadrilateral (quad) primitives are missing. The shapes in this chapter utilize triangle strips.

OpenGL ES is a "moving" specification, with three incarnations at the moment. OpenGL ES 1.0 is based upon OpenGL 1.3, OpenGL ES 1.1 is defined relative to OpenGL 1.5, and OpenGL ES 2.0 is derived from the OpenGL 2.0 specification.

OpenGL ES 1.1 includes support for multitexturing, mipmap generation, and greater control over point rendering (useful for particle systems). OpenGL ES 2.0 is a more radical change that uses a programmable rendering model based around shaders, with only floating-point operations. The motivation behind this design is the belief that mobile devices will very shortly have the rendering power of today's desktop and laptop machines.

All my coding will be done with the BlackBerry Java Application Development v5.0 beta 5 JDE, since at present (December 2009) JSR 239 is not supported by any BlackBerry devices. BlackBerry's JSR 239 packages provide bindings for OpenGL ES 1.0 and 1.1, and their extensions.

More Information on OpenGL ES

The Khronos Group is in charge of OpenGL ES, so its web site (www.khronos.org/opengles) is an excellent starting point for more details about the technology.

A good beginner's tutorial on OpenGL ES programming is offered by ZeusCMD at
`www.zeuscmd.com/tutorials/opengles/index.php`. It's structured into 25 parts, starting
with the basics, and becoming progressively more advanced. The focus is on
programming in Windows and the Pocket PC.

A collection of presentations from SIGGRAPH 2005 giving an overview of OpenGL ES
1.0 and 1.1 can be found at `http://people.csail.mit.edu/kapu/siggraph_course`. This
formed the basis for the subsequent book, *Mobile 3D Graphics: with OpenGL ES and
M3G*, by Kari Pulli, Tomi Aarnio, Ville Miettinen, Kimmo Roimela, and Jani Vaarala
(Morgan Kaufmann, 2007).

Another good textbook on OpenGL ES is *OpenGL ES Game Development*, by Dave
Astle and David Durnil (Course Technology PTR, 2004).

The future is OpenGL ES 2.0, which is currently only discussed in *OpenGL ES 2.0
Programming Guide*, by Aaftab Munshi, Dan Ginsburg, and Dave Shreiner (Addison-
Wesley, 2008).

A good strategy for learning OpenGL ES is to study OpenGL first. There's a large
overlap between the two, which will become larger over time. There's a wide range of
tutorial material on OpenGL, much of which is applicable to OpenGL ES. The place to
start is the OpenGL Architecture Review Board web site, at `www.opengl.org`.

OpenGL ES and Java

The 3D APIs for Java are busily multiplying. Table 12-1 lists the four main ones.

Table 12-1. *Java APIs for 3D Graphics*

	Java SE	**Java ME**
Scene graph	Java 3D	M3G (JSR 184)
Lower-level	JOGL: a Java binding for OpenGL (JSR 231)	JSR 239: a Java binding for OpenGL ES

Desktop Java (the Java SE column in Table 12-1) supports two main 3D graphics APIs:
Java 3D (`https://java3d.dev.java.net`) is based around constructing a 3D scene with a
scene graph data structure, and JOGL is a thin Java layer over OpenGL
(`https://jogl.dev.java.net`). There are various implementations of Java 3D, including
ones on top of OpenGL and JOGL.

The situation for mobile devices (the Java ME column in Table 12-1) is strikingly similar—
M3G (`http://jcp.org/en/jsr/detail?id=184`) is a scene graph API that's a subset of Java
3D with some additions, and JSR 239 is a thin layer of Java over OpenGL ES. M3G was
designed to be implemented on top of OpenGL ES, with a code size of around 150KB.

Information on programming with Java 3D, JOGL, and M3G can be found at my web
sites, `http://fivedots.coe.psu.ac.th/~ad/jg` and
`http://fivedots.coe.psu.ac.th/~ad/jg2`.

A good article on the connections between OpenGL ES and M3G is "Designing Graphics Programming Interfaces for Mobile Devices," by Kari Pulli, Tomi Aarnio, Kimmo Roimela, and Jani Vaarala, available at `http://ieeexplore.ieee.org/xpls/abs_all.jsp?isnumber=32639&arnumber=1528436& count=14&index=10`. There's some overlap between the article, the SIGGRAPH presentations, and the book mentioned in the preceding "More Information on OpenGL ES" section, since many of the same authors were involved.

There's not much online information specifically about JSR 239, aside from its JSR page at `http://jcp.org/en/jsr/detail?id=239`.

The BlackBerry Java Application Development v5.0 beta 5 download (`http://na.blackberry.com/eng/developers/devbetasoftware/devbeta.jsp`) includes JSR 239 classes, but no example. `OpenGLTest.java`, which renders a multicolored triangle (see Figure 12-2), is available at `http://docs.blackberry.com/en/developers/deliverables/11942/CS_OpenGLTest_95294 1_11.jsp`.

Figure 12-2. *OpenGLTest example*

The textbook *Mobile 3D Graphics: Learning 3D Graphics with the Java Micro Edition*, by Claus Höfele (Thomson Course Technology PTR, 2007), includes a JSR 239 example in Appendix C (but most of the book is about M3G). The compiled code, in the form of a JAR, can be downloaded from `www.claushoefele.com/m3g/examples.html`. The example is a rotating textured cube, with the cube implemented in a similar way to the TexCube class in this chapter.

The BoxTrix Example

Figure 12-3 shows class diagrams for the BoxTrix application; only public methods are shown.

BoxTrix is a standard top-level UIApplication, which starts BoxTrixScreen. BoxTrixScreen is a threaded MainScreen subclass that executes the JSR 239 animation loop; HelpScreen is a pop-up screen that displays information on how to control the camera.

The floor is created and drawn by a Floor object, the two rotating cubes are instances of TexCube, the two billboards are Billboard objects, and the information shown at the top left of the screen in Figure 12-1 is managed by the Overlay class.

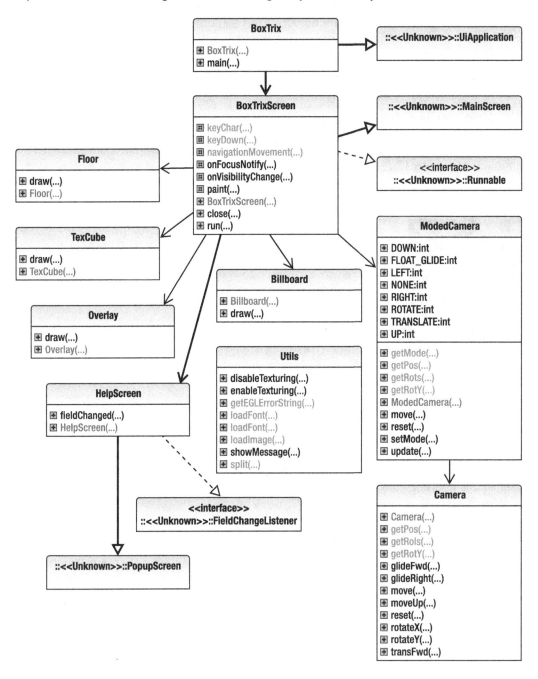

Figure 12-3. *Class diagrams for BoxTrix*

The Camera class implements the moveable camera. ModedCamera is an adapter that converts user key presses, trackball movements, and menu item selections into calls to Camera's public translation and rotation methods.

Animating the Scene

The BoxTrixScreen thread is started when the screen first appears, via a call to onVisibilityChange():

```
// globals
private boolean isRunning = false;
private boolean isPaused = false;

protected void onVisibilityChange(boolean isVisible)
{
  if (isVisible) {    // visible means resumption or start
    if (isRunning)
      resumeRendering();
    else {    // start the render thread and loop
      isRunning = true;
      new Thread(this).start();
    }
  }
  else    // not visible means pause
    isPaused = true;
}  // end of onVisibilityChange()


private void resumeRendering()
{
  isPaused = false;
  synchronized (this) {
    notifyAll();
  }
}  // end of resumeRendering()
```

onVisibilityChange() is also called when the screen is hidden, which should make the animation pause, and when the screen becomes visible again, which should resume the animation. These situation are controlled by global isPaused and isRunning booleans.

Pausing and resumption also occur when the main screen loses and regains focus, by implementing onFocusNotify():

```
// global
private boolean focusRegained = false;

protected void onFocusNotify(boolean hasFocus)
{
  if (!hasFocus)
    isPaused = true;
  else
    resumeRendering();
  focusRegained = hasFocus;
}  // end of onFocusNotify()
```

focusRegained is used to reinitialize the offscreen buffer, as described later. run() can be summarized with the following pseudocode:

```
public void run()
{
  // initialize the 3D graphics engine;
  // initialize the 3D scene;
  while (isRunning) {
   if (isPaused)
     pause rendering;
   // update the application and graphics state;
   // draw the 3D scene to an offscreen buffer
   // perhaps sleep a while to maintain the frame rate;
  }
  // shut down the 3D graphics engine;
}
```

The run() method in BoxTrixScreen is

```
// globals
private float angle;        // rotation angle of the cubes


public void run()
{
  if (!initGraphics())
    return;    // give up if there's an error
               // during OpenGL ES initialization
  initScene();

  long startTime;
  while (isRunning) {
    if (isPaused)
      pauseRendering();
    startTime = System.currentTimeMillis();

    angle = (angle + ROT_INCR) % 360.0f;  // update
    checkBackBuffer();
    drawScene();                      // draw
    maybeSleep(startTime);            // sleep
  }

  shutdown();
}  // end of run()
```

pauseRendering() works in tandem with resumeRendering() (shown previously) to suspend execution while isPaused is true.

```
private void pauseRendering()
{
  synchronized (this) {      // idle if we are in the background
    try {
      wait();
    }
    catch (InterruptedException x) {}
  }
```

```
}  // end of pauseRendering()
```

The only state update carried out inside the animation loop is a change to the angle variable; drawScene() uses it to rotate the cubes.

maybeSleep() allows the execution to temporarily sleep so that the animation frame rate is maintained.

```
// globals
private static final int PERIOD = 200;      // frame rate (in ms)
private long frameDuration;   // in ms
        // how long one iteration of the animation loop takes


private void maybeSleep(long startTime)
{
  frameDuration = System.currentTimeMillis() - startTime;
  try {     // sleep a bit maybe, so one iteration takes PERIOD ms
    if (frameDuration < PERIOD)
      Thread.sleep(PERIOD - (int)frameDuration);
  }
  catch (InterruptedException e){}
}  // end of maybeSleep()
```

The frame rate period (PERIOD) is set to be 200 milliseconds, a value arrived at by noting the frame duration displayed by the application at runtime (it's the black number shown at the bottom of the overlay in Figure 12-1). The chosen period gives the thread a little sleeping time between iterations so that other threads (perhaps at the operating system level) have a chance to execute. The sleep duration is adjusted at runtime by comparing the frame duration with the required period.

Initializing the Graphics Engines

Most of initGraphics() is taken up with the initialization of the 3D graphics engine. There are several stages:

- Initialize OpenGL ES.

- Set up a display connection, which involves choosing a rendering configuration.

- Initialize the OpenGL ES context (the internal state of the graphics engine).

- A drawing surface is specified. This is usually the device's screen, but can also be an offscreen data structure.

- The display, context, and drawing surface are linked to the application thread.

The basic connections between these elements are shown in Figure 12-4.

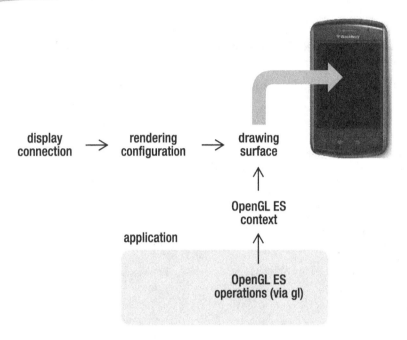

Figure 12-4. *Initializing OpenGL ES*

initGraphics() is complicated, with lots of error checking, but mostly remains unchanged across different applications:

```
// globals
private EGL11 egl;       // OpenGL ES link from Java
private GL10 gl;         // for calling OpenGL ES commands
private EGLDisplay eglDisplay;
private EGLContext eglContext;   // OpenGL ES state
private EGLSurface eglSurface;   // for rendering


private boolean initGraphics()
{
  if (!GLUtils.isSupported()) {
    Utils.showMessage("Graphics Error", "No OpenGL ES");
    return false;
  }

  // initialize OpenGL ES
  egl = (EGL11) EGLContext.getEGL();
  if (egl == null) {
    Utils.showMessage("Init Error", "No OpenGL ES");
    return false;
  }

  // initialize the OpenGL ES connection to the display
  eglDisplay = egl.eglGetDisplay(EGL11.EGL_DEFAULT_DISPLAY);
  if (eglDisplay == null) {
    Utils.showMessage("Init Error", "No display connection");
```

```java
    return false;
}

int[] majorMinor = new int[2];
if (!egl.eglInitialize(eglDisplay, majorMinor)) {
  Utils.showMessage("Init Error", "No OpenGL ES display");
  return false;
}
System.out.println("EGL version: " + majorMinor[0] + "." +
                                     majorMinor[1]);

// determine the number of available configurations
int[] numConfigs = new int[1];
egl.eglGetConfigs(eglDisplay, null, 0, numConfigs);
if (numConfigs[0] < 1) {
  Utils.showMessage("Init Error", "No config found");
  return false;
}

// specify a 5/6/5 RGB configuration
int configAttributes[] = {
  EGL11.EGL_RED_SIZE, 5, EGL11.EGL_GREEN_SIZE, 6,
                         EGL11.EGL_BLUE_SIZE, 5,   // RGB
  EGL11.EGL_ALPHA_SIZE, 0,         // no alpha necessary
  EGL11.EGL_DEPTH_SIZE, 16,        // use a 16-bit z-buffer
  EGL11.EGL_SURFACE_TYPE, EGL11.EGL_WINDOW_BIT,  //use window buf
  EGL11.EGL_NONE
};

// use the first matching configuration
EGLConfig eglConfigs[] = new EGLConfig[numConfigs[0]];
if (!egl.eglChooseConfig(eglDisplay, configAttributes, eglConfigs,
                                    eglConfigs.length, numConfigs)) {
  Utils.showMessage("Init Error", "No suitable config");
  return false;
}
EGLConfig eglConfig = eglConfigs[0];

/* initialize the OpenGL ES rendering state (the context)
   with the display and configuration */
eglContext = egl.eglCreateContext(eglDisplay, eglConfig,
                                   EGL11.EGL_NO_CONTEXT, null);
if (eglContext == null) {
  Utils.showMessage("Init Error", "No rendering state");
  return false;
}

// initialize 3D graphics: the API is called through gl
gl = (GL10) eglContext.getGL();
if (gl == null) {
  Utils.showMessage("Init Error", "No 3D context");
  return false;
}

// set drawing surface to be a window
```

```
    eglSurface = egl.eglCreateWindowSurface(eglDisplay, eglConfig, this, null);
    if (eglSurface == null) {
      Utils.showMessage("Init Error", "No drawing surface");
      return false;
    }

    // bind display, drawing surface, and context to this thread
    if (!egl.eglMakeCurrent(eglDisplay, eglSurface,  eglSurface, eglContext)){
      Utils.showMessage("Init Error", "No current context");
      return false;
    }

    return true;    // everything worked!
  } // end of initGraphics()
```

The error messages are reported in dialog boxes created by Utils.showMessage(),
which was introduced in Chapter 11.

A side effect of calling EGL10.eglInitialize() is that the OpenGL ES version
information is produced (in a two-element integer array). The method also returns a
boolean that is tested to see if the operation actually succeeded. If the method returns
false, then EGL10.eglGetError() can be called to return an integer constant denoting
the reason. Many JSR 239 configuration methods work this way, but I've not bothered
examining the EGL10.eglGetError() value—initGraphics() is long enough already.

The number of available display configurations is retrieved with EGL10.eglGetConfigs().
Then my list of required attributes is used by EGL10.eglChooseConfig() to whittle down
the configurations to only those that match (or surpass) my needs.

My desired attributes include the bit sizes for the RGB and alpha components of the
display, and also the size of the depth buffer. Most attributes have sensible defaults, listed
in the documentation for EGL10.eglChooseConfig(). For instance, the default alpha size is
0, so that attribute could be left out of my configAttributes[] array in initGraphics().
The list of attributes in the array must be terminated with EGL10.EGL_NONE.

The OpenGL ES state (its context) can be initialized once a display and configuration are
available. Once there's a context, a GL10 object, gl, can be instantiated; it will be the
entry point for calling JSR 239 operations.

The drawing surface (the device's window) is set with EGL10.eglCreateWindowSurface().
The surface can also be an offscreen pbuffer (a pixel buffer managed by OpenGL ES) or
a pixmap (managed by the OS).

Once I have a display, drawing surface, and context, they can then be bound to the
application thread with EGL10.eglMakeCurrent(). From here on, the *current* thread can
make JSR 239 calls via the gl object, and their results will be displayed onscreen.

Initializing the 3D Scene

Various aspects of the 3D scene can be initialized before the animation loop starts,
including the viewing volume, camera, lighting, overlay, and scenery. However, all

rendering and object transformations (e.g., rotating a cube) is left to drawScene(), which is called from inside the animation loop.

```
// globals
private static final String FONT_NAME = "Sceptre";    // used in the overlay

private GL10 gl;                    // for calling JSR 239 operations
private ModedCamera modedCamera;
private Overlay statsHud = null;    // 2D panel at front of screen


private void initScene()
{
  setView(60.0f, 0.1f, 50.0f);
  modedCamera = new ModedCamera();

  gl.glClearColor(0.17f, 0.65f, 0.92f, 1.0f);   // sky blue back

  // z-depth testing turned on for hidden surface removal
  gl.glEnable(GL10.GL_DEPTH_TEST);

  gl.glHint(GL10.GL_PERSPECTIVE_CORRECTION_HINT, GL10.GL_NICEST);
  gl.glShadeModel(GL10.GL_SMOOTH);    // use smooth shading

  gl.glEnable(GL10.GL_CULL_FACE);
              // cull backfaces (a useful speed optimization)

  gl.glEnable(GL10.GL_COLOR_MATERIAL); //use default material props

  // vertically flip texturing
  gl.glMatrixMode(GL10.GL_TEXTURE);
  gl.glLoadIdentity();
  gl.glScalef(1.0f, -1.0f, 1.0f);

  addLight();
  createScenery();

  Font msgFont = Utils.loadFont("SceptreRegular.ttf", FONT_NAME,Font.PLAIN,26);
  statsHud = new Overlay(gl, msgFont, 200.0f);
}  // end of initScene()
```

Depth testing is essential if the scene has multiple 3D objects. Although it's enabled in initScene(), it will only work correctly if the display configuration (set up in initGraphics()) has a depth size (which it does).

Backface culling is a simple way of improving the application's running time. Having said that, enabling culling appears to have no effect on the simulator's frame-rendering speed, which is about 150 milliseconds on average. The drawback of culling is that the insides of the cubes and the underside of the floor aren't rendered.

The default material properties (which are described in the documentation for the GL10.glMaterialf() method) cause 3D shapes to respond to ambient and diffuse light, which is sufficient for my needs.

The texture scaling changes positive y-axis values to negative for all texturing done in this application. This "flips" loaded texture images along their vertical axis since OpenGL ES's coordinate system assumes that (0,0) is the lower-left corner of the image, but Java stores them so that (0,0) is at the top left.

The `Utils` class contains two methods to facilitate the loading of fonts: a three-argument `loadFont()` for using a nonstandard font, which must be less than 60KB in size, and be stored in TrueType Unicode format (`ttf`). There's also a two-argument version that employs a specified system font. For example:

```
Font msgFont = Utils.loadFont("BBCasual", Font.BOLD, 20);
```

`setView()` creates a perspective view into the scene. Its arguments are the field-of-view angle along the y-axis, and the near and far clipping planes.

```
private void setView(float fovy, float near, float far)
{
  gl.glViewport(0, 0, getWidth(), getHeight());
                    // set size of drawing area to be the screen size
  // set the projection matrix
  gl.glMatrixMode(GL10.GL_PROJECTION);
  gl.glLoadIdentity();
  GLUtils.gluPerspective(gl, fovy,
                    (float)getWidth()/(float)getHeight(), near, far);
} // end of setView()
```

The hard work is done by `GLUtils.gluPerspective()`, which creates a view frustum for the camera, as shown in Figure 12-5.

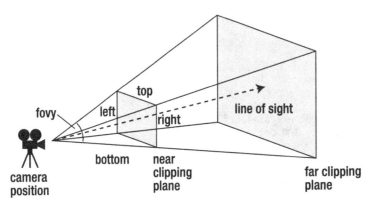

Figure 12-5. *The view frustum*

The frustum (a truncated pyramid) extends from the near clipping plane to the far one, centered along the line of sight from the camera location.

The width and height of the near clipping plane are taken to be the width and height of the device's screen, and used to calculate an aspect ratio. Internally, `gluPerspective()` combines the ratio with the field-of-view angle (fovy) to calculate the coordinates (top, bottom, left, and right) of the near clipping plane.

The width and height are obtained from MainScreen via calls to getWidth() and getHeight(), which let setView() be called when the BlackBerry has been turned on its side, to recalculate the view frustum.

Implementing setView() without GLUtils.gluPerspective() is a bit tricky, but it's easy to find OpenGL examples that explain the necessary techniques. For example, the NeHe site (http://nehe.gamedev.net) contains an article on gluPerspective(), written by James Heggie (http://nehe.gamedev.net/data/articles/article.asp?article=11).

The NeHe site is one of the best places for finding information on OpenGL programming, and Pepijn Van Eeckhoudt has ported all of the NeHe OpenGL tutorials to JOGL (http://pepijn.fab4.be/software/nehe-java-ports). This illustrates one of the great advantages of JSR 239 (and JOGL): the availability of lots of online help for OpenGL. Although most of the examples and tutorials are in C++ or C, translating them to Java is usually trivial because of the direct mapping of the OpenGL functions into Java methods.

Adding Lights

The lighting capabilities of OpenGL ES are almost unchanged from OpenGL: ten light sources can be defined, each with its own ambient, diffuse, specular, shininess, and emissive parameters. A light can have a position or be directional, and positional lights attenuate (weaken) with distance. Light source 0 (GL10.GL_LIGHT_0) comes with useful default values for these parameters, which reduce the coding required for basic scene lighting.

The following addLight() method illustrates (or perhaps that should be *illuminates*) several of these ideas:

```
private void addLight()
{
  gl.glEnable(GL10.GL_LIGHTING);
  gl.glEnable(GL10.GL_LIGHT0);
  gl.glEnable(GL10.GL_NORMALIZE);

  float[] ambientLight = { 0.125f, 0.125f, 0.125f, 1.0f };    // weak gray ambient
  gl.glLightfv(GL10.GL_LIGHT0, GL10.GL_AMBIENT, ambientLight, 0);

  float[] diffuseLight = { 0.9f, 0.9f, 0.9f, 1.0f };   // white diffuse
  gl.glLightfv(GL10.GL_LIGHT0, GL10.GL_DIFFUSE, diffuseLight, 0);
} // end of addLight()
```

Light source 0 is enabled, and its ambient and diffuse parameters are set. Positional information for the light is missing from addLight(); it's defined in the drawScene() method for reasons I'll explain later in the "Drawing the Scene" section.

Making the Scenery

The BoxTrix scenery consists of a floor, two rotating cubes, and two billboards. Scenery is manipulated in three stages: it's created at initialization time, and then it's updated and drawn repeatedly inside the animation loop. createScenery() carries out the initialization stage, using the Floor, TexCube, and Billboard classes to create the necessary objects:

```
// globals
private Floor floor;
private TexCube texCube1, texCube2;    // two textured cubes
private Billboard treeBoard, bozoBoard;
    // a billboard is an image that always faces the camera


private void createScenery()
{
  floor = new Floor(gl, "grass.png", 9.5f);

  texCube1 = new TexCube(gl, "matrix.png", 0, 0.4f, 0, 0.8f);   // (x,y,z), scale
  texCube2 = new TexCube(gl, "metal.png", -2.0f, 2.1f, -1.3f, 0.5f);

  treeBoard = new Billboard(gl, 1.6f, 1.5f, 2f, "tree.png");   // (x,z), size
  bozoBoard = new Billboard(gl, -1.8f, -0.5f, 1.4f, "bozo.png");
} // end of createScenery()
```

The file names passed to the Floor, TexCube, and Billboard constructors are for the shapes' textures. A texture image should be in PNG format, and be square with dimensions that are a power of two (e.g., 32×32, 64×64). It's advisable not to use too large an image; 256×256 is probably the largest size that will be supported by devices when they appear.

The final argument of the Floor constructor is the length of the floor's sides when drawn in the scene.

The third, fourth, and fifth arguments of the TexCube constructor collectively specify the (x,y,z) position of the cube's center, and the final argument is the scale factor applied to the cube at render time. By default, a cube has sides of length 1.

The second, third, and fourth arguments of the Billboard constructor specify the floor position for the board (an [x,z] coordinate) and a size for the board square.

Figure 12-1 shows the scene with the grass.png texture applied to the floor, and matrix.png and metal.png on the cubes. Figure 12-6 shows the floor covered in a grid-like texture, and the cubes decorated with brick and rock images.

Figure 12-6. *Alternative textures for the floor and cubes*

Using a Back Buffer

The animation loop draws the scene into a bitmap acting as an offscreen buffer (also called a *back buffer*), which is drawn to the screen by BoxTrixScreen's paint() method.

checkBackBuffer() decides whether the buffer needs to be regenerated, which can occur in several situations—when the device's orientation has been changed, at startup time when the buffer is null, and also (somewhat surprisingly) when the screen regains focus. If this last situation isn't included, then sometimes the screen goes blank, at least in the 5.0 beta 5 simulator.

```
//globals
private Bitmap offScrBitmap;   // back buffer
private Graphics offGraphics;  // graphics context for the buffer


private void checkBackBuffer()
{
  boolean needsUpdating = false;
  if (offScrBitmap == null)
    needsUpdating = true;
  else if ((offScrBitmap.getWidth() != getWidth()) ||
           (offScrBitmap.getHeight() != getHeight()))
    needsUpdating = true;
  else if (focusRegained)
    needsUpdating = true;

  if (needsUpdating) {
    offScrBitmap = new Bitmap(getWidth(), getHeight());
    offGraphics = Graphics.create(offScrBitmap);
    setView(60.0f, 0.1f, 50.0f);
  }
} // end of checkBackBuffer()
```

A graphics context (offGraphics) is paired with the back buffer bitmap, which I later use as the rendering target for the EGL drawing surface. This means that the large arrow in Figure 12-4 linking the drawing surface to the BlackBerry can be more accurately represented as Figure 12-7.

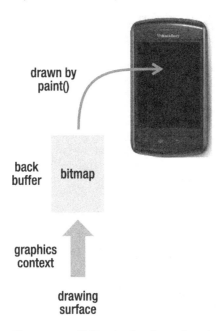

Figure 12-7. *Linking the drawing surface, back buffer, and BlackBerry*

setView() is also called when the buffer is regenerated, since the viewport will need to be recalculated if the screen's width and height have changed. Figure 12-8 shows the simulator turned on its side, with BoxTrix still rendering correctly.

Figure 12-8. *BoxTrix in landscape mode*

The paint() method in BoxTrixScreen only has to draw the back buffer bitmap:

```
protected void paint(Graphics g)
{
```

```
  if (offScrBitmap != null)
    g.drawBitmap(0, 0, offScrBitmap.getWidth(),
                  offScrBitmap.getHeight(), offScrBitmap, 0, 0);
}
```

Drawing the Scene

drawScene() draws the camera, light source, floor, billboards, rotating cubes, and overlay onto the EGL drawing surface:

```
// globals
private static final float[] LIGHT_DIR = { 1.0f, 1.0f, 1.0f, 0.0f };
                                    // right, top, front directional light

private Graphics offGraphics;   // graphics context for the buffer
private EGL11 egl;
private GL10 gl;                 // for calling OpenGL ES

// scene related
private TexCube texCube1, texCube2;
private float angle;            // rotation angle of the cubes
private Floor floor;
private ModedCamera modedCamera = null;
private Overlay statsHud = null;
private Billboard treeBoard, bozoBoard;


private void drawScene()
{
  // wait until OpenGL ES is available before starting to draw
  egl.eglWaitNative(EGL10.EGL_CORE_NATIVE_ENGINE, offGraphics);

  // clear color and depth buffers
  gl.glClear(GL10.GL_COLOR_BUFFER_BIT | GL10.GL_DEPTH_BUFFER_BIT);

  // set modeling and viewing transformations
  gl.glMatrixMode(GL10.GL_MODELVIEW);
  gl.glLoadIdentity();

  modedCamera.move(gl);    // move the camera

  // set light direction
  gl.glLightfv(GL10.GL_LIGHT0, GL10.GL_POSITION, LIGHT_DIR, 0);

  floor.draw(gl);   // floor

  float rotY = (float) modedCamera.getRotY();    // billboards
  treeBoard.draw(gl, rotY);
  bozoBoard.draw(gl, rotY);

  gl.glPushMatrix();
    gl.glRotatef(angle, 0, 1.0f, 0);    // rotate cubes around y-axis
    texCube1.draw(gl);
    texCube2.draw(gl);
```

```
    gl.glPopMatrix();

    statsHud.draw(gl, getWidth(), getHeight(),
                      modedCamera, frameDuration);   // overlay

    // wait until all Open GL ES tasks are finished
    egl.eglWaitGL();

    // pass the EGL drawing surface to the native 'window'
    egl.eglSwapBuffers(eglDisplay, eglSurface);

    String swapRes = Utils.getEGLErrorString( egl.eglGetError() );
    if (!swapRes.equals("EGL_SUCCESS")) // report any problem
      Utils.showMessage("Swap Buffer Error", swapRes);
  }  // end of drawScene()
```

The 3D-rendering code must be preceded by a call to `EGL10.eglWaitNative()`, which delays execution until the device is ready to process OpenGL ES calls and the rendering target (`offGraphics`) is specified.

The rendering code must be followed by a call to `EGL10.eglWaitGL()` to stop the application's execution until all the Open GL ES calls have completed. The `EGL10.eglSwapBuffers()` call passes the contents of the EGL drawing surface to the native "window" (in my case, the back buffer). It corresponds to the thick arrow in Figure 12-7.

The color and depth buffers are reset, and the matrix mode is set to `GL10.GL_MODELVIEW`, which is required before any modeling or viewing transformations are carried out.

The camera should be positioned before anything else in the scene. The reason is that OpenGL ES (and OpenGL) doesn't possess a moveable camera. When the camera is translated or rotated, it's really the scene that's moved. For example, when the camera is translated 2 units along the negative z-axis (i.e., moved into the scene), it's actually the scene that's shifted 2 units along the positive z-axis (i.e., toward the viewer).

Camera movement is really scene movement, and so must be carried out first when the scene is being rendered. Then any subsequent drawing commands (e.g., of the floor and cubes) will be correctly positioned relative to the camera's translations and rotations of the scene.

The light source is "positioned" using the array `{1.0f, 1.0f, 1.0f, 0.0f}`. I put the word *positioned* in quotes because the final 0.0f value converts the (1.0f,1.0f,1.0f) coordinate into a *direction* vector aimed toward the origin. A directional light source can be thought of as being located a great distance from the scene (like the sun relative to the earth), so it casts parallel beams down onto everything in the scene. All the objects are illuminated from the same direction; in this case, on their right, top, and front sides.

If the final value of the array is 1.0f (e.g., `{1.0f, 1.0f, 1.0f, 1.0f}`), then (1.0f,1.0f,1.0f) is really a position. The light source behaves more like a lightbulb at that particular spot, and will be affected by attenuation settings. This means that the source's effect on objects depends on their position relative to the source and their distance from it.

The purpose of the `GL10.glLightfv()` call with the `GL10.GL_POSITION` attribute in `drawSceneGL()` is to position the light source in the scene. Even when the position is really a direction, that direction is in terms of a scene coordinate. Since the attribute relates to positioning, the method call must be performed in drawSceneGL(), after the OpenGL ES matrix mode has been set to GL10.GL_MODELVIEW. Also, the GL10.glLightfv() call must be carried out *after* the camera has been positioned. This is because the light is located in the scene, and this location has to be determined after the scene has been moved by the camera. As a consequence, the light stays in the same place in the scene even when the camera is moved.

The GL10.glPushMatrix() and GL10.glPopMatrix() pair around the call to GL10.glRotatef() isolates the rotation of the cubes from any subsequent object transformations in the scene.

Shutting Down the 3D Graphics

shutdown() is called at the end of run() to disconnect the application thread from the display, drawing surface, and context. It also destroys the context and drawing surface, and breaks the connection between OpenGL ES and the device screen.

```
// global
private static final String FONT_NAME = "Sceptre";
                         // used in the overlay

private void shutdown()
{
  if ((egl == null) || (eglDisplay == null))
    return;

  /* disconnect the display, drawing surface, and context
     from this thread   */
  egl.eglMakeCurrent(eglDisplay, EGL11.EGL_NO_SURFACE,
                      EGL11.EGL_NO_SURFACE, EGL11.EGL_NO_CONTEXT);

  // delete the context
  if (eglContext != null)
    egl.eglDestroyContext(eglDisplay, eglContext);

  // delete the drawing surface
  if (eglSurface != null)
    egl.eglDestroySurface(eglDisplay, eglSurface);

  // break the OpenGL ES connection to the screen
  egl.eglTerminate(eglDisplay);

  FontManager.getInstance().unload(FONT_NAME);

  System.exit(0);
}  // end of shutdown()
```

shutdown() could benefit from more error checking: EGL10.eglMakeCurrent(), EGL10.eglDestroyContext(), EGL10.eglDestroySurface(), and EGL10.eglTerminate() all return booleans indicating their success or failure, which could be tested and reported.

One non–OpenGL ES activity in shutdown() is the unloading of the Sceptre application font, which frees up space on the device.

The Floor

The floor is initialized in createScenery():

```
// globals
private GL10 gl;          // for calling OpenGL ES
private Floor floor;

// in createScenery()
floor = new Floor(gl, "bigGrid.png", 8);    // 8 by 8 size
```

The Floor() constructor takes three arguments: a gl object for executing OpenGL ES commands, the name of the file holding the floor image, and the size of the floor inside the scene. The floor will be drawn so it's centered at the origin and lying flat on the XZ plane.

bigGrid.png is a large, green grid (256×256 pixels; 22.1KB), as shown in Figure 12-9.

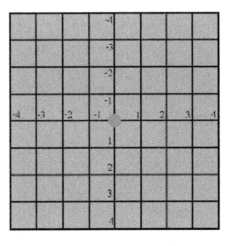

Figure 12-9. *The bigGrid.png image*

When the image is drawn with sides of 8 units, the gridlines coincide with the scene's coordinate spacing on the XZ plane. This allows me to check the positioning of objects.

For example, Figure 12-10 shows the two cubes' original positions in the scene with the animation code commented out; the camera has been moved up off the floor, sent forward, and rotated to face downward.

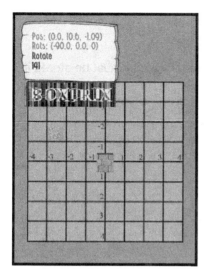

Figure 12-10. *The cubes' initial positions*

createScenery() centers the brick cube at (0,0.4,0) and the rock cube at (−2,2.1,1.3):

```
texCube1 = new TexCube(gl, "brick2.png", 0, 0.4f, 0, 0.8f);
texCube2 = new TexCube(gl, "rock.png", -2.0f, 2.1f, -1.3f, 0.5f);
```

These coordinates can be confirmed by moving the camera around the scene. In Figure 12-10, the floating rock cube is displaced due to perspective effects from looking down on it from a distance.

grass.png contains a 64×64 grass texture, shown as the floor in Figure 12-1. The figure illustrates a drawback of the Floor class—that it stretches (and pixelates) the texture to cover the required area (9.5×9.5 units in the grass's case).

The Floor class has two main jobs. Firstly, when its constructor is invoked, it creates the data buffers necessary for representing the texture-wrapped floor. Its second task is to render the floor when its draw() method is called.

Creating the Floor

The Floor() constructor builds the floor's geometry and loads the texture:

```
//globals
private Bitmap texIm = null;
private int texNames[];    // for the texture name


public Floor(GL10 gl, String floorFnm, float size)
{
  createFloor(size);

  texIm = Utils.loadImage(floorFnm);
```

```
    texNames = new int[1];    // generate a texture name
    gl.glGenTextures(1, texNames, 0);
}  // end of Floor()
```

Texture rendering requires a texture *name* (actually an integer ID) that must be stored in an array (texNames[]).

The floor's geometry is a square resting on the XZ plane, centered at the origin. If the constructor receives a size value for the length of the floor's sides, then the floor's coordinates will be as shown in Figure 12-11 when viewed from above.

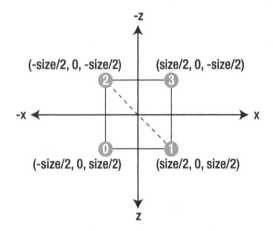

Figure 12-11. *The floor's coordinates*

The coordinates are ordered to define the floor's shape in terms of triangles (OpenGL ES doesn't support quads). I chose to use a triangle strip with the coordinates ordered as shown by the numbers in the circles in Figure 12-11. The initial counterclockwise order for the first three points (0, 1, and 2), means that the "front" face of the floor is pointing upward along the y-axis.

The floor also requires texture coordinates, which are shown in Figure 12-12.

Two-dimensional texture coordinates are specified in terms of s and t values, which can range between 0 and 1. For example, (0,0) denotes the bottom left of a texture, and (1,1) the top right. In Figure 12-12, the four coordinates match the four corners of the image, so the entire image will be utilized for texturing.

The ordering of the coordinates in Figure 12-12 (the numbers in the circles) is the same as the ordering of the vertices in Figure 12-11. This ensures that when the vertices and texture coordinates are matched up at render time, the floor is correctly covered with the image. For instance, the bottom-left texture coordinate is mapped to the front-left vertex of the floor, and the top-right coordinate to the back-right vertex.

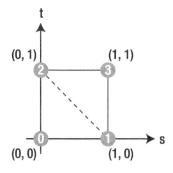

Figure 12-12. *The floor's texture coordinates*

The vertices and texture coordinates are stored in two buffers by createFloor():

```
// globals
private FloatBuffer vertsBuf;    // floor vertices
private ByteBuffer tcsBuf;       // tex coords


private void createFloor(float size)
// create vertices and tex coords buffers for floor of size-by-size
{
    // create vertices buffer  (a triangle strip defining a square)
    float[] verts = { -size/2,0,size/2,   size/2,0,size/2,
                      -size/2,0,-size/2,  size/2,0,-size/2 };
    vertsBuf = ByteBuffer.allocateDirect(verts.length*4).asFloatBuffer();
    vertsBuf.put(verts).rewind();

    // create texture coordinates buffer
    byte[] tcs = {0,0,  1,0,  0,1,  1,1};
    tcsBuf = ByteBuffer.allocateDirect(tcs.length);
    tcsBuf.put(tcs).rewind();
} // end of createFloor()
```

The vertices are stored in a float buffer so that it can accommodate sizes that aren't integers, but the texture can utilize a byte buffer.

Drawing the Floor

The draw() method separates into two tasks: texturing and rendering of the buffer data.

```
public void draw(GL10 gl)
{
    Utils.enableTexturing(gl, texNames, texIm, false);   // no alphas
    drawFloor(gl);
    gl.glDisable(GL10.GL_TEXTURE_2D);   // switch off texturing
}  // end of draw()
```

The Utils.enableTexturing() method turns on texturing using the specified texture, which may contain an alpha channel so that parts of the texture image will be invisible.

```
// in Utils.java
```

```
public static void enableTexturing(GL10 gl, int texNames[],
                                   Bitmap texIm, boolean hasAlpha)
{
  if (hasAlpha) {     // do not draw transparent parts of the texture
    gl.glEnable(GL10.GL_BLEND);
    gl.glBlendFunc(GL10.GL_SRC_ALPHA, GL10.GL_ONE_MINUS_SRC_ALPHA);
             // don't show source alpha parts in the destination

    // determine which areas of the polygon are to be rendered
    gl.glEnable(GL10.GL_ALPHA_TEST);
    gl.glAlphaFunc(GL10.GL_GREATER, 0);  // only render if alpha > 0
  }

  gl.glEnable(GL10.GL_TEXTURE_2D);    // use texturing

  gl.glBindTexture(GL10.GL_TEXTURE_2D, texNames[0]); // use tex name

  // specify the texture for the currently bound tex name
  int format = (hasAlpha) ? GL10.GL_RGBA : GL10.GL_RGB;
  GLUtils.glTexImage2D(gl,0,format,GL10.GL_UNSIGNED_BYTE,texIm, null);
                 // level, format,   type,        bitmap, region

  // set the minification/magnification techniques
  gl.glTexParameterx(GL10.GL_TEXTURE_2D,
                     GL10.GL_TEXTURE_MIN_FILTER, GL10.GL_LINEAR);
  gl.glTexParameterx(GL10.GL_TEXTURE_2D,
                     GL10.GL_TEXTURE_MAG_FILTER, GL10.GL_LINEAR);
} // end of enableTexturing()
```

The floor's texture name is registered with the OpenGL ES state, and the texture buffer is connected to that name with GLUtils.glTexImage2D(). glTexImage2D() specifies the mipmap level (0 is a basic value), the image's format (RGB with no alpha channel for the floor), the image type (unsigned bytes), the bitmap, and the amount of the bitmap to use (null means use everything).

The calls to GL10.glTexParameterx() switches on linear filtering to improve the quality of the image when it's shrunk or enlarged (which occurs when the camera is far away from the floor or close to it).

If the texture employs an alpha channel (as it does in the billboards and the overlay), then enableTexturing() will be called with hasAlpha == true. In that case, the nondrawing of the transparent parts of the image involves the use of blending, alpha testing, and the replacement of the buffer's colors.

At the heart of Floor.drawFloor() is GL10.glDrawArrays(), which can utilize buffers holding vertices, vertex colors, normals, and texture coordinates. The buffers for a particular shape are specified before the GL10.glDrawArrays() call by invoking GL10.glVertexPointer(), GL10.glColorPointer(), GL10.glNormalPointer(), and GL10.glTexCoordPointer().

Several variations of this approach are possible. For example, if a shape doesn't employ colors or texture coordinates, then there's no need to call the pointer methods for that data. If GL10.glDrawArrays() is being used to draw a shape with a single normal (such as the surface of a floor), then there's no need to define a normal for every vertex. Instead, a normal for the entire shape can be set with `GL10.glNormal3f()`.

The floor only uses vertices and texture coordinates, and only requires a single normal (up the y-axis). Here is the resulting `drawFloor()` method:

```
// globals
private GL10 gl;
private ByteBuffer vertsBuf;   // floor vertices
private ByteBuffer tcsBuf;     // tex coords


private void drawFloor(GL10 gl)
{
  // enable the use of vertex and tex coord arrays when rendering
  gl.glEnableClientState(GL10.GL_VERTEX_ARRAY);
  gl.glEnableClientState(GL10.GL_TEXTURE_COORD_ARRAY);

  gl.glVertexPointer(3, GL10.GL_FLOAT, 0, vertsBuf); // floor verts
  gl.glTexCoordPointer(2, GL10.GL_BYTE, 0, tcsBuf);  // tex coords

  gl.glNormal3f( 0, 1.0f, 0);    // facing up
  gl.glDrawArrays(GL10.GL_TRIANGLE_STRIP, 0, 4);

  // disable the arrays at the end of rendering
  gl.glDisableClientState(GL10.GL_VERTEX_ARRAY);
  gl.glDisableClientState(GL10.GL_TEXTURE_COORD_ARRAY);
}  // end of drawFloor()
```

The two calls to `GL10.glEnableClientState()` mean that vertex and texture coordinate buffers are utilized at render time. They're disabled once the drawing is completed so they aren't inadvertently used in the drawing operations for other shapes.

The call to `GL10.glDrawArrays()` includes the geometry scheme used by the buffers (a triangle strip) and how many coordinates are in the strip (four).

A Textured Cube

The TexCube class has a very similar structure to the Floor class—its constructor initializes the data buffers for a cube, and its `draw()` method renders the cube using those buffers.

The constructor stores the cube's (x,y,z) position and scale factor, and then calls `createCube()` to build the buffers for its vertices and texture coordinates.

```
// globals
private Bitmap texIm = null;
private int texNames[];    // for the texture name
private float xPos, yPos, zPos;  // position of cube's center
private float scale;


public TexCube(GL10 gl, String texFnm, float x, float y, float z, float sc)
// (x,y,z) is the cube's position, and sc the scaling factor
```

```
{
    xPos = x; yPos = y; zPos = z;
    scale = sc;

    createCube();
    texIm = Utils.loadImage(texFnm);
    texNames = new int[1];    // generate a texture name
    gl.glGenTextures(1, texNames, 0);
} // end of TexCube()
```

As in Floor(), TexCube() must generate a texture name.

Creating a Cube

By default, the cube is centered at the origin, and has sides that are 1 unit in length. The coordinates for its eight corners are shown in Figure 12-13.

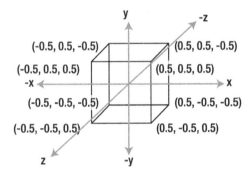

Figure 12-13. *The cube's coordinates*

To make the cube easy to render with GL10.glDrawArrays(), the shape is encoded as six separate faces, with each face represented by a triangle strip of four points. For example, the front face consists of points ordered as in Figure 12-14.

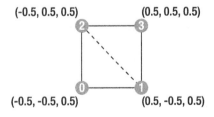

Figure 12-14. *The coordinates for the cube's front face*

The coordinates for all six faces are stored in the verts[] array:

```
float verts[] = {          // organized into 6 faces
        -0.5f, -0.5f, 0.5f,   0.5f, -0.5f, 0.5f,
        -0.5f, 0.5f, 0.5f,    0.5f, 0.5f, 0.5f,       // front
        0.5f, -0.5f, -0.5f, -0.5f, -0.5f, -0.5f,
```

```
    0.5f, 0.5f, -0.5f,  -0.5f, 0.5f, -0.5f,    // back
    0.5f, -0.5f, 0.5f,   0.5f, -0.5f, -0.5f,
    0.5f, 0.5f, 0.5f,    0.5f, 0.5f, -0.5f,    // right
   -0.5f, -0.5f, -0.5f, -0.5f, -0.5f, 0.5f,
   -0.5f, 0.5f,-0.5f,   -0.5f, 0.5f, 0.5f,     // left
   -0.5f, 0.5f, 0.5f,    0.5f, 0.5f, 0.5f,
   -0.5f, 0.5f, -0.5f,   0.5f, 0.5f, -0.5f,    // top
   -0.5f, -0.5f, -0.5f,  0.5f, -0.5f, -0.5f,
   -0.5f, -0.5f, 0.5f,   0.5f, -0.5f, 0.5f     // bottom
};
```

The data is conveniently arranged for GL10.glDrawArrays(), but the downside is the size of the array—24 coordinates representing 8 corners of a cube.

The cube's texture is replicated on each face, requiring each face's texture coordinates to span all of the image. The texCoords[] array holds the coordinates:

```
byte texCoords[] = {  // 4 tex coords for each face
   0,0, 1,0, 0,1, 1,1,   0,0, 1,0, 0,1, 1,1,   0,0, 1,0, 0,1, 1,1,
   0,0, 1,0, 0,1, 1,1,   0,0, 1,0, 0,1, 1,1,   0,0, 1,0, 0,1, 1,1
};
```

The coordinates in texCoords[] are organized in groups of four—a group for each face. The six faces are stored in the same order as the faces in verts[] (front, back, right, left, top, and bottom). For instance, the first group in texCoords[] is for the front face, as shown in Figure 12-15.

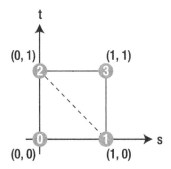

Figure 12-15. *Texture coordinates for the front face*

The order of the texture coordinates in Figure 12-15 is the same as the vertices order in Figure 12-14.

The normals for the cube can be specified in two ways. One approach is to draw the faces of the cube with six separate GL10.glDrawArrays() calls. Each call can employ GL10.glNormal3f() to specify the normal for that face. The code would be something like this:

```
// DOES **NOT** WORK
for (int i = 0; i < 6; i++) {  // draw each cube face
  gl.glNormal3f( normals[i*3 + 0],
                 normals[i*3 + 1],
                 normals[i*3 + 2] );   // normal for the face
```

```
gl.glDrawArrays(GL10.GL_TRIANGLE_STRIP, 4*i, 4);
        // vertices and tex coords for the face
}
```

This only requires six normals: one for each cube face. However, when I tried this approach, the BlackBerry simulator would only render the first face, seemingly discarding the other five calls to GL10.glDrawArrays(). This bug has been reported by other developers (e.g., see http://supportforums.blackberry.com/t5/Java-Development/5-0-Simulator-supporting-OpenGL-ES/m-p/388300).

I turned to the second approach, which involves the specification of a complete set of normal coordinates—one for each vertex in the verts[] array.

```
float normals[] = {    // each normal repeated 4 times, for each face
    0, 0, 1.0f,     0, 0, 1.0f,     0, 0, 1.0f,     0, 0, 1.0f,   // front
    0, 0, -1.0f,    0, 0, -1.0f,    0, 0, -1.0f,    0, 0, -1.0f,  // back
    1.0f, 0, 0,     1.0f, 0, 0,     1.0f, 0, 0,     1.0f, 0, 0,   // right
    -1.0f, 0, 0,    -1.0f, 0, 0,    -1.0f, 0, 0,    -1.0f, 0, 0,  // left
    0, 1.0f, 0,     0, 1.0f, 0,     0, 1.0f, 0,     0, 1.0f, 0,   // top
    0, -1.0f, 0,    0, -1.0f, 0,    0, -1.0f, 0,    0, -1.0f, 0   // bottom
};
```

normals[] employs the same face ordering as the vertices and texture coordinates data (i.e., front, back, right, left, top, and bottom), with each normal repeated four times per face. For example, the first four triplets in normals[] are (0, 0, 1) for the four vertices of the front face. (0, 0, 1) is a vector pointing along the positive z-axis.

createCube() stores the verts[], texCoords[], and normals[] arrays in buffers:

```
// globals
private ByteBuffer vertsBuf;    // vertices
private ByteBuffer tcsBuf;      // tex coords
private FloatBuffer normsBuf;   // normals


private void createCube()
// create the vertices and tex coords buffers for the cube
{
  // create vertices buffer for cube
  float verts[] = { . . . };  // given above
  vertsBuf = ByteBuffer.allocateDirect(verts.length*4).asFloatBuffer();
  vertsBuf.put(verts).rewind();

  // 2D tex coords buffer for cube
  byte texCoords[] = { . . . };  // given above
  tcsBuf = ByteBuffer.allocateDirect(texCoords.length);
  tcsBuf.put(texCoords).rewind();

  float normals[] = { . . . };  // given above
  normsBuf = ByteBuffer.allocateDirect(normals.length*4).asFloatBuffer();
  normsBuf.put(normals).rewind();
} // end of createCube()
```

Drawing a Cube

The TexCube.draw() method separates texture enabling from rendering in the same way as the Floor class:

```
public void draw(GL10 gl)
{
  Utils.enableTexturing(gl, texNames, texIm, false);   // no alphas
  drawCube(gl);
  gl.glDisable(GL10.GL_TEXTURE_2D);   // switch off texturing
} // end of draw()
```

Due to my use of a normals buffer, the cube can be rendered by a single call to GL10.glDrawArrays() in drawCube(). However, the coordinate system must first be translated and scaled to reposition and resize the cube.

```
// globals
private FloatBuffer vertsBuf;  // vertices
private ByteBuffer tcsBuf;     // tex coords
private FloatBuffer normsBuf;  // normals

private float xPos, yPos, zPos;  // position of cube's center
private float scale;


private void drawCube(GL10 gl)
{
  // enable the use of vertex and tex coord arrays when rendering
  gl.glEnableClientState(GL10.GL_VERTEX_ARRAY);
  gl.glEnableClientState(GL10.GL_NORMAL_ARRAY);
  gl.glEnableClientState(GL10.GL_TEXTURE_COORD_ARRAY);

  gl.glVertexPointer(3, GL10.GL_FLOAT, 0, vertsBuf);  // cube verts
  gl.glNormalPointer(GL10.GL_FLOAT, 0, normsBuf);     // normals
  gl.glTexCoordPointer(2, GL10.GL_BYTE, 0, tcsBuf);  // tex coords

  gl.glPushMatrix();
    gl.glTranslatef(xPos, yPos, zPos);   // move to the (x,y,z) pos
    if (scale != 1.0f)
      gl.glScalef(scale, scale, scale);  // uniform scaling
    gl.glDrawArrays(GL10.GL_TRIANGLE_STRIP, 0, 24);
          // works, since only one glDrawArrays() call
  gl.glPopMatrix();

  // disable the arrays at the end of rendering
  gl.glDisableClientState(GL10.GL_VERTEX_ARRAY);
  gl.glDisableClientState(GL10.GL_NORMAL_ARRAY);
  gl.glDisableClientState(GL10.GL_TEXTURE_COORD_ARRAY);
} // end of drawCube()
```

The GL10.glPushMatrix() and GL10.glPopMatrix() pair ensure that the translation and scaling of the cube don't affect any subsequent renderings of other shapes.

The single GL10.glDrawArrays() works correctly, drawing all the faces of the cube.

A Billboard

Billboard wraps an image over a quad (a quadrilateral, implemented using a triangle strip), without drawing its transparent background, and rotates the quad to always face the current camera position. When a billboard is created, the programmer specifies an (x,z) coordinate for it on the floor, and a size for the quad's dimensions.

The Billboard class has a very similar structure to the TexCube and Floor classes—its constructor initializes the necessary data buffers, and its draw() method renders a billboard using those buffers.

The constructor stores the billboard's (x,z) position and size, and then calls createBoard() to build the buffers for its vertices and texture coordinates.

```
// globals
private FloatBuffer vertsBuf;     // billboard vertices
private ByteBuffer tcsBuf;        // tex coords
private Bitmap texIm = null;
private int texNames[];           // for the texture name

private float xPos, zPos;         // position of board's base center


public Billboard(GL10 gl, float xc, float zc, float size, String texFnm)
{
  xPos = xc;
  zPos = zc;
  createBoard(size);

  texIm = Utils.loadImage(texFnm);
  texNames = new int[1];    // generate a texture name
  gl.glGenTextures(1, texNames, 0);
} // end of Billboard()


private void createBoard(float size)
// create vertices and tex coords buffers for overlay
// with dimensions of size-by-size
{
  // create vertices buffer
  float[] verts = { -size/2, 0,  0,     size/2, 0, 0,
                    -size/2, size, 0,    size/2, size, 0
                  };  // billboard coords
  vertsBuf = ByteBuffer.allocateDirect(verts.length*4).asFloatBuffer();
  vertsBuf.put(verts).rewind();

  // create texture coordinates buffer
  byte[] tcs = {0,0,  1,0,  0,1,  1,1};
  tcsBuf = ByteBuffer.allocateDirect(tcs.length);
  tcsBuf.put(tcs).rewind();
} // end of createBoard()
```

The board's geometry is a square standing on the XZ plane, centered at the origin. The size value for the length of the board's sides means that its coordinates will be as in Figure 12-16, when viewed from the front.

The numbered circles in Figure 12-16 indicate the order that the quad's vertices are specified as a triangle strip. The order is used when mapping the texture onto the quad.

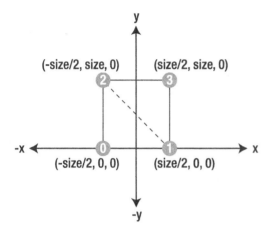

Figure 12-16. *The billboard's coordinates*

Drawing a Billboard

The `Billboard.draw()` method separates texture enabling from rendering in the same way as earlier classes:

```
public void draw(GL10 gl, float rotY)
{
  gl.glDisable(GL10.GL_LIGHTING);
  Utils.enableTexturing(gl, texNames, texIm, true);    // uses alphas

  drawBoard(gl, rotY);

  Utils.disableTexturing(gl, true);
  gl.glEnable(GL10.GL_LIGHTING);
}  // end of draw()
```

This time `Utils.enableTexturing()` is called with its `hasAlphas` argument set to `true`, and also lighting is disabled, since it adversely affects the appearance of the board image as it rotates.

After the drawing has been completed, texturing is disabled using `Utils.disableTexturing()`, which changes back to normal modulation of shape colors and textures, and switches off alpha blending.

```
// in Utils.java
public static void disableTexturing(GL10 gl, boolean hasAlpha)
{
  gl.glDisable(GL10.GL_TEXTURE_2D);    // switch off texturing
```

```
      if (hasAlpha) { //switch back to modulation of quad cols and textures
        gl.glTexEnvx(GL10.GL_TEXTURE_ENV, GL10.GL_TEXTURE_ENV_MODE, GL10.GL_MODULATE);
        gl.glDisable(GL10.GL_ALPHA);  // switch off transparency
        gl.glDisable(GL10.GL_BLEND);
      }
    } // end of disableTexturing()
```

The billboard keeps facing the camera, which amounts to having it replicate the camera's y-axis rotation. The rotation is obtained from the camera in BoxTrixScreen and passed as an argument to Billboard.draw(), and then to drawBoard().

drawBoard() utilizes the vertices and texture coordinate buffers in the usual manner. Also, the coordinates system must be adjusted to place the board at its required (x,z) location, with the specified y-axis rotation.

```
// globals
private FloatBuffer vertsBuf;    // billboard vertices
private ByteBuffer tcsBuf;       // tex coords

private float xPos, zPos;        // position of board's base center


private void drawBoard(GL10 gl, float rotY)
{
  // enable the use of vertex and tex coord arrays when rendering
  gl.glEnableClientState(GL10.GL_VERTEX_ARRAY);
  gl.glEnableClientState(GL10.GL_TEXTURE_COORD_ARRAY);

  gl.glVertexPointer(3, GL10.GL_FLOAT, 0, vertsBuf); // verts
  gl.glTexCoordPointer(2, GL10.GL_BYTE, 0, tcsBuf);  // tex coords
  gl.glNormal3f( 0, 0, -1.0f);    // facing out

  gl.glPushMatrix();
    gl.glTranslatef(xPos, 0, zPos);    // move to (x,y,z) pos
    gl.glRotatef(rotY, 0, 1, 0);       // rotate toward camera
    gl.glDrawArrays(GL10.GL_TRIANGLE_STRIP, 0, 4);
  gl.glPopMatrix();

  // disable the arrays at the end of rendering
  gl.glDisableClientState(GL10.GL_VERTEX_ARRAY);
  gl.glDisableClientState(GL10.GL_TEXTURE_COORD_ARRAY);
}  // end of drawBoard()
```

The Overlay

An overlay draws a 2D image in front of the 3D scene, which always stays at the front without changing its size, as the camera moves around the scene. The most common example is a heads-up display (HUD) showing player information during the course of a game. In BoxTrix, an overlay is used to show camera position, rotation, and mode details, and the current frame rate.

My overlay implementation utilizes OpenGL ES by switching to an *orthographic projection,* which is commonly seen in engineering diagrams where 2D pictures represent a 3D object from the top, front, and side. Orthographic projections don't perform perspective correction, so objects close to or far from the camera appear the same size. This is ideal since the overlay image must not change its size depending on its distance from the camera. Once the overlay has been drawn, the projection mechanism is switched back to a normal 3D volume.

An alternative implementation approach is to perform the 2D operations outside OpenGL ES, in the `BoxTrixScreen` `paint()` method. If you recall, `paint()` currently only draws the offscreen buffer:

```
// in BoxTrixScreen class
private Bitmap offScrBitmap;
          // back buffer used for offscreen rendering

protected void paint(Graphics g)
{ if (offScrBitmap != null)
    g.drawBitmap(0, 0, offScrBitmap.getWidth(),
                      offScrBitmap.getHeight(), offScrBitmap, 0, 0);
}
```

Unfortunately, when I tried extending `paint()` with extra 2D operations in the v5.0 beta simulator, I couldn't get the 2D and 3D elements to update at the same rate in a reliable way. So I stuck with the first approach, using orthographic projection inside JSR 239.

The Coordinates of the Overlay

The `Overlay()` constructor is supplied with a size for the overlay, which is a transparent textured square quad. I also pass in the font used for writing on the overlay.

```
// globals
private final static String TEX_FNM = "noticeBd.png";
private Bitmap texIm = null;
private int texNames[];    // for the texture name
private Font msgFont;


public Overlay(GL10 gl, Font font, float size)
{
  msgFont = font;
  createOverlay(size);

  texIm = Utils.loadImage(TEX_FNM);
  texNames = new int[1];    // generate a texture name
  gl.glGenTextures(1, texNames, 0);
}  // end of Overlay()
```

The texture image is loaded from `noticeBd.png`, which is shown in Figure 12-17.

The image must have a dimension that's a power of 2 (in this case 256×256 pixels), but any part of it can be transparent.

Figure 12-17. *The overlay texture image*

The drawing area should be simple to wipe clean when new information needs to be shown on the image. The notice board is a single color (0x00ffdca8 in hexadecimal), which makes it easy to delete any old data by drawing a filled rectangle of that color over the text.

The task of building the shape involves creating vertices and texture coordinate buffers in createOverlay(), but the vertices are ordered differently from all of my earlier quads, as shown in Figure 12-18.

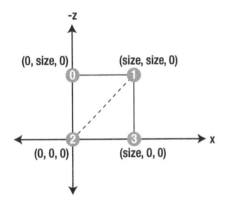

Figure 12-18. *Top-down ordering for the overlay quad*

The shape is ordered so that its vertices run top-down rather than bottom-up. The reason for this will become clear when I explain the details of the orthographic projection that follows.

```
// globals
private FloatBuffer vertsBuf;    // overlay vertices
private ByteBuffer tcsBuf;       // tex coords


private void createOverlay(float size)
// create vertices and tex coords buffers
// for overlay with dimensions of size-by-size
{
  // create vertices buffer (a triangle strip defining a square)
  float[] verts = {0,size,0,  size,size,0,   0,0,0,  size,0,0};
      /* the vertex ordering is top-down,
          to match the orthographic projection */
  vertsBuf = ByteBuffer.allocateDirect(verts.length*4).asFloatBuffer();
```

```
vertsBuf.put(verts).rewind();

    // create texture coordinates buffer
    byte[] tcs = {0,0,  1,0,  0,1,  1,1};
    tcsBuf = ByteBuffer.allocateDirect(tcs.length);
    tcsBuf.put(tcs).rewind();
} // end of createOverlay()
```

Drawing the Overlay

Overlay.draw() is called from BoxTrixScreen in drawScene(), which passes it the current screen dimensions, the frame duration, and a reference to the camera. The latter two are needed for the information that's written onto the board.

```
// BoxTrixScreen globals
private Overlay statsHud;
private ModedCamera modedCamera;
private long frameDuration;  // in ms
    // how long one iteration of the animation loop takes

// in BoxTrixScreen.drawScene()
statsHud.draw(gl, getWidth(),getHeight(), modedCamera,frameDuration);
```

In Overlay.draw(), 2D viewing is turned on while the overlay is being drawn (with the begin2D() method), and is then switched back to 3D (with end2D()). I borrowed this technique from an example posted by ozak at www.javagaming.org/index.php/topic,8110.0.html.

```
public void draw(GL10 gl, int width, int height,
                        ModedCamera modedCamera, long frameDuration)
{
  begin2D(gl, width, height);  // switch to 2D viewing
  gl.glDisable(GL10.GL_LIGHTING);
  Utils.enableTexturing(gl, texNames, texIm, true);    // uses alphas

  redrawTexture(modedCamera, frameDuration);
  drawOverlay(gl);

  Utils.disableTexturing(gl, true);
  gl.glEnable(GL10.GL_LIGHTING);
  end2D(gl);  // switch back to 3D viewing
} // end of draw()
```

begin2D() switches the view to an orthographic projection with GLUtils.gluOrtho2D():

```
private void begin2D(GL10 gl, int width, int height)
// switch to 2D viewing (an orthographic projection)
{
  gl.glMatrixMode(GL10.GL_PROJECTION);
  gl.glPushMatrix();    // save projection settings
  gl.glLoadIdentity();

  GLUtils.gluOrtho2D(gl, 0.0f, width, height, 0.0f);
                    // left, right, bottom, top
```

```
/* The y-axis of the orthographic projection is reversed to be
   top-down, by switching top and bottom values in gluOrtho2D()
*/
gl.glMatrixMode(GL10.GL_MODELVIEW);
gl.glPushMatrix();    // save model view settings
gl.glLoadIdentity();
gl.glDisable(GL10.GL_DEPTH_TEST);
} // end of begin2D()
```

The 3D projection and model view settings must be saved so they can be restored at the end of draw(). They're pushed onto their respective matrix stacks with GL10.glPushMatrix() calls, and retrieved with GL10.glPopMatrix() in end2D().

GLUtils.gluOrtho2D() defines a viewing volume for the projection—a rectangular box within which things are drawn. The x-axis of the volume is defined by the second and third arguments (the box's left and right edges), and the y-axis is defined by the fourth and fifth arguments (bottom and top). The z-axis values (i.e., the front and back of the box) are assumed to be –1 and 1. A standard projection would be defined by

```
GLUtils.gluOrtho2D(gl, 0.0f, width, 0.0f, height);
```

The x-axis runs left to right from 0 to width while the y-axis runs bottom-up from 0 to height. For my purposes, it's more useful to have the y-axis run top-down from height to 0. This is done with

```
GLUtils.gluOrtho2D(gl, 0.0f, width, height, 0.0f);
```

This causes the 2D overlay to be rendered starting from the top left of the screen, but flipped along its y-axis. However, the flipping can be negated by also flipping the vertices of the overlay in createOverlay().

end2D() pops the stored projection and model view matrices from their stacks, and restores them:

```
private void end2D(GL10 gl)
{
  gl.glEnable(GL10.GL_DEPTH_TEST);
  gl.glMatrixMode(GL10.GL_PROJECTION);
  gl.glPopMatrix();      // restore previous projection settings
  gl.glMatrixMode(GL10.GL_MODELVIEW);
  gl.glPopMatrix();      // restore previous model view settings
} // end of end2D()
```

The texture that's wrapped over the quad must be updated each time Overlay.draw() is called, to show the current camera and frame rate information.

The expense and complexity of this redrawing can be greatly reduced by a careful design of the notice board image, as mentioned. redrawTexture() changes the information shown in the texture image by first filling the writing area with the texture's background color, and then drawing new text on top of it.

```
// globals
private Bitmap texIm;
private Font msgFont;
```

```
private void redrawTexture(ModedCamera modedCamera, long frameDuration)
{
  Graphics g = Graphics.create(texIm);
  g.setColor(BG_COLOR);
  g.fillRect(25, 25, 215, 115);     // wipe the text area clean

  if (modedCamera != null) { // show camera's posn, rot, and mode
    g.setColor(0xff0000);    // red
    g.setFont(msgFont);
    g.drawText( modedCamera.getPos(), 30, 25, DrawStyle.TOP|DrawStyle.LEFT);
    g.drawText( modedCamera.getRots(), 30, 48, DrawStyle.TOP|DrawStyle.LEFT);
    g.setColor(0x0000ff);    // blue
    g.drawText( modedCamera.getMode(), 30, 73, DrawStyle.TOP|DrawStyle.LEFT);
  }
  // show the current frame duration
  g.setColor(0x000000);    // black
  g.drawText( "" + frameDuration, 30, 98, DrawStyle.TOP|DrawStyle.LEFT);
}  // end of redrawTexture()
```

The code assumes the writing area is the rectangle defined by the Graphics.fillRect() call, but makes no attempt to check that the strings in the subsequent Graphics.drawText() calls stay within that region. If the texture is modified outside that area, then the changes will stay visible until the application exits.

After redrawTexture() has finished, the texture image changes and the overlay is drawn using drawOverlay():

```
private void drawOverlay(GL10 gl)
{
  // enable the use of vertex and tex coord arrays when rendering
  gl.glEnableClientState(GL10.GL_VERTEX_ARRAY);
  gl.glEnableClientState(GL10.GL_TEXTURE_COORD_ARRAY);

  gl.glVertexPointer(3, GL10.GL_FLOAT, 0, vertsBuf); // verts
  gl.glTexCoordPointer(2, GL10.GL_BYTE, 0, tcsBuf);  // tex coords

  gl.glTranslatef(10, 10, 0);    // move overlay left and down

  gl.glNormal3f( 0, 0, -1.0f);    // facing out
  gl.glDrawArrays(GL10.GL_TRIANGLE_STRIP, 0, 4);

  // disable the arrays at the end of rendering
  gl.glDisableClientState(GL10.GL_VERTEX_ARRAY);
  gl.glDisableClientState(GL10.GL_TEXTURE_COORD_ARRAY);
}  // end of drawOverlay()
```

After a bit of experimentation, I felt that the overlay looked better onscreen if moved down and to the right a little bit (e.g., see Figure 12-1). I did this by calling GL10.glTranslate() in drawOverlay() before rendering the overlay. Note that the positive y-value means a shift downward because of y-axis flipping in GLUtils.glOrtho2D().

The Camera

Most OpenGL programs use the `GLU.gluLookAt()` function to position the camera. OpenGL ES doesn't include the GLU library, but BlackBerry offers `gluLookAt()` in its `GLUtils` class. Surprisingly though, the tricky part of camera navigation isn't positioning the camera, which even without `gluLookAt()` is just a couple of rotations and a translation (see my `Camera.move()` method later). The hard part is converting user input into 3D coordinates, and maintaining and modifying those coordinates during the lifetime of the application.

My `Camera` class offers several translation and rotation operations that move the camera forward, backward, left, right, up, and down, and rotate it around the x- and y-axes. There's a glide-forward operation that moves the camera forward or backward without any change in its y-axis position, which is useful when the camera is pointing up or down. The `Camera.reset()` method returns the camera to its starting position and orientation. Rotation around the z-axis isn't supported since it complicates the implementation.

Faced with a somewhat tricky coding exercise, I deployed my "reuse existing code" strategy. My `Camera` class is based on an OpenGL example coded in C++ by Philipp Crocoll (at `www.codecolony.de/opengl.htm#camera`). His web site also includes a more advanced camera example that can rotate around all three axes. The treasure trove of OpenGL examples out on the Web (and in textbooks) is one of the best reasons for using OpenGL (or OpenGL ES).

The camera object moves with the help of two data structures, a camera position, and a forward direction vector, which are shown diagrammatically in Figure 12-19.

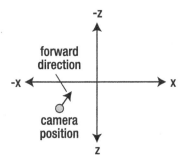

Figure 12-19. *The camera's position and direction (viewed from above)*

When the user rotates the camera, its forward direction is affected (i.e., the arrow in Figure 12-19 moves left or right, or up or down). When the camera is translated, it uses the forward direction to calculate its step forward, back, left, or right.

The starting position is passed to the `Camera` object when it's created.

```
// globals
private double xStart, yStart, zStart;        // starting position

public Camera(double x, double y, double z)
```

```
{ xStart = x; yStart = y; zStart = z;
  reset();
} // end of Camera()
```

reset() initializes the camera position and forward direction, placing the camera at the starting position, and aiming it along the negative z-axis.

```
// globals
private double xCamPos, yCamPos, zCamPos;      // camera position
private double xFwdDir, yFwdDir, zFwdDir;      // forward direction
private double rotX, rotY;
       // rotation in degrees around x- and y-axes


public void reset()
{
  xCamPos = xStart; yCamPos = yStart; zCamPos = zStart;
  xFwdDir = 0; yFwdDir = 0; zFwdDir = -1.0;
     // forward direction is along -z-axis

  rotX = 0;    // no rotations initially
  rotY = 0;
}  // end of reset()
```

The position and direction are stored as their component x-, y-, and z-axis values. The current rotations of the camera around the x- and y-axes are held in the rotX and rotY variables.

Rotating the Camera

rotateX() and rotateY() modify the rotX and rotY variables:

```
public void rotateX(double angle)
{
  rotX = (rotX + angle) % 360;
  updateFwdDir();  // since the rotation has changed
} // end of rotateX()


public void rotateY(double angle)
{
  rotY = (rotY + angle) % 360;
  updateFwdDir();  // since the rotation has changed
}  // end of rotateY()
```

When a rotation changes, the forward direction vector needs to be recalculated by updateFwdDir():

```
private void updateFwdDir()
{
  /* Calculate x- and z- dir components when fwd dir is rotated
     around the y-axis. The angle is measured from the + x-axis. */
  double yRotRad = Math.toRadians(rotY + 90);
  double xDir = Math.cos(yRotRad);
  double zDir = -Math.sin(yRotRad);
```

```
/* Calculate XZ plane component when fwd dir is
   rotated around the x-axis */
double xRotRad = Math.toRadians(rotX);
double xzProj = Math.cos(xRotRad);

// combine the components to get the forward direction
xFwdDir = xDir * xzProj;
yFwdDir = Math.sin(xRotRad);
zFwdDir = zDir * xzProj;
}  // end of updateFwdDir()
```

The forward direction is a unit vector rotated around the x- and y-axes. The task of updateFwdDir() is to convert the two rotation angles (in rotY and rotX) into (x,y,z) values for xFwdDir, yFwdDir, and zFwdDir.

The conversion is done in two steps. First, the y-axis rotation around the XZ plane is translated into x- and z-components, as shown in Figure 12-20.

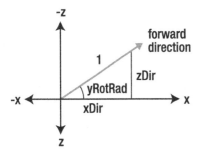

Figure 12-20. *Converting the y-axis rotation (viewed from above)*

The angle is assumed to be relative to the positive x-axis, so 90 degrees must be added to the rotY value, which records the angle relative to the negative z-axis.

xDir and zDir are *not* the forward directions along the x- and z-axes, since there's also an XZ component supplied by the rotation around the x-axis. It's obtained from the rotX value, and is labeled as xzProj in Figure 12-21.

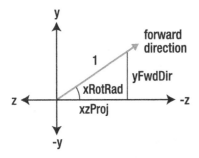

Figure 12-21. *Converting the x-axis rotation (viewed from the right)*

The xzProj value is multiplied to the xDir and zDir values to get the forward direction components along the x- and z-axes. However, the y-axis component of the direction (yFwdDir) can be extracted directly from the x-axis rotation.

Translating the Camera

The forward direction vector is enough to calculate a step forward from the current camera position. The distance that should be moved is multiplied by the components of the unit vector, and then added to the position. This is carried out by the transFwd() method:

```
public void transFwd(double dist)
{
  xCamPos += (xFwdDir * dist);
  yCamPos += (yFwdDir * dist);
  zCamPos += (zFwdDir * dist);
} // end of transFwd()
```

If the dist value is negative, then the camera will move backward.

The forward direction vector can also be used to move the camera right and left. Figure 12-22 shows how the x- and z-components of the forward vector can be converted into a translation to the right.

This is implemented by the glideRight() method:

```
public void glideRight(double dist)
// move right in the x- and z-dirs, without any y-axis move
{
  xCamPos += (-zFwdDir * dist);
  // no change to yCamPos
  zCamPos += (xFwdDir * dist);
} // end of glideRight()
```

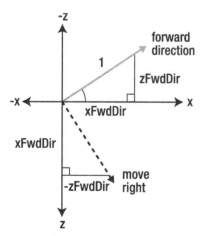

Figure 12-22. *Moving to the right (viewed from above)*

The distance to move is supplied by the dist value. glideRight() doesn't include a change to the y-axis component of the camera, which would be

```
yCamPos += (yFwdDir * dist);
```

This line is missing since it seems more natural for a translation to the right not to affect the camera's height.

A movement to the left is possible by supplying a negative dist value to glideRight().

There's also a glide-forward method, which moves the camera forward without adjusting its height, and an up/down translator:

```
public void glideFwd(double dist)
// move forward in the x- and z-dirs, without any y-axis move
{
  xCamPos += (xFwdDir * dist);
  // no change to yCamPos
  zCamPos += (zFwdDir * dist);
}  // end of glideFwd()


public void moveUp(double dist)
{  yCamPos += dist;  }
```

Moving the Camera

The rotation and translation methods just given change the values stored in rotX, rotY, xCamPos, yCamPos, and zCamPos. The camera position is only updated onscreen when Camera.move() (shown following) is called from the animation loop in BoxTrixScreen:

```
public void move(GL10 gl)
{
  gl.glRotatef((float)-rotX, 1.0f, 0, 0);    // x-axis rotation
  gl.glRotatef((float)-rotY, 0, 1.0f, 0);    // y-axis rotation
  gl.glTranslatef((float)-xCamPos, (float)-yCamPos, (float)-zCamPos);
} // end of move()
```

As mentioned earlier, OpenGL ES (and OpenGL) doesn't support a moveable camera. The scene is moved instead, in the opposite direction from the rotation and translation values for the camera.

Using Camera Modes and Direction Constants

It's useful to separate the camera's user interface from the processing required to translate and rotate the camera. The processing is located in the Camera class, while the user interface elements (modes and direction constants) are managed by ModedCamera.

BoxTrixScreen listens for key presses and trackball movements by overriding keyChar() and navigationMovement().

```
// in the BoxTrixScreen class
```

```java
// global
private ModedCamera modedCamera;


protected boolean keyChar(char key, int status, int time)
// camera movement, and game terminate with <ESC>
{
  if (key == Characters.ESCAPE) {
    isRunning = false;
    return false;
  }

  if (modedCamera == null)
    return false;

  /* The left character (e.g. 's') corresponds to a QWERTY keyboard,
     the second (e.g. 'd') is for models with just a number pad. */
  if((key == 's') || (key == 'd'))
    modedCamera.update(ModedCamera.LEFT);
  else if((key == 'f') || (key == 'j'))
    modedCamera.update(ModedCamera.RIGHT);
  else if((key == 'e') || (key == 't'))
    modedCamera.update(ModedCamera.UP);
  else if((key == 'x') || (key == 'b'))
    modedCamera.update(ModedCamera.DOWN);
  else  // key not relevant
    return false;

  return true;
}  // end of keyChar()


protected boolean navigationMovement(int dx, int dy, int status, int time)
// pass trackball movement info to the camera
{
  if (modedCamera == null)
    return false;

  if (dx < 0)
    modedCamera.update(ModedCamera.LEFT);
  else if (dx > 0)
    modedCamera.update(ModedCamera.RIGHT);
  if (dy < 0)
    modedCamera.update(ModedCamera.DOWN);
  else if (dy > 0)
    modedCamera.update(ModedCamera.UP);
  return true;
}  // end of navigationMovement()
```

keyChar() is a good place to translate the (rather arbitrary) choices of keys into direction constants: ModedCamera.LEFT, ModedCamera.RIGHT, ModedCamera.UP, and ModedCamera.DOWN.

Another user interface design issue is how to divide the large number of possible translations and rotations into categories that a user can understand. I went for three modes: translation, rotation, and floating/gliding. The direction constants' meanings vary depending on the current camera mode.

A simple way of letting the user change between camera modes is via menu items, as shown in Figure 12-23.

Figure 12-23. *The menu items for BoxTrixScreen*

These are implemented inside the BoxTrixScreen constructor, and call the ModedCamera.setMode() method to change to the selected mode.

```
public BoxTrixScreen()
{
  super(FullScreen.DEFAULT_MENU | FullScreen.DEFAULT_CLOSE);

  // set up menu items for the three camera modes, reset, and help
  MenuItem transCamera = new MenuItem("Translate", 10, 10) {
    public void run()
    { if (modedCamera != null)
        modedCamera.setMode(ModedCamera.TRANSLATE);
    }
  };
  addMenuItem(transCamera);

  MenuItem rotCamera = new MenuItem("Rotate", 20, 10) {
    public void run()
    { if (modedCamera != null)
        modedCamera.setMode(ModedCamera.ROTATE);
    }
  };
  addMenuItem(rotCamera);

  MenuItem glideCamera = new MenuItem("Float/Glide", 30, 10) {
    public void run()
    { if (modedCamera != null)
        modedCamera.setMode(ModedCamera.FLOAT_GLIDE);
    }
  };
  addMenuItem(glideCamera);
```

```
MenuItem resetCamera = new MenuItem("Reset", 40, 10) {
  public void run()
  { if (modedCamera != null)
      modedCamera.reset();   // reset camera posn/orientation
  }
};
addMenuItem(resetCamera);

MenuItem help = new MenuItem("Help", 50, 10) {
  public void run()
  { UiApplication.getUiApplication().pushScreen(
                                  new HelpScreen());  }
};
addMenuItem(help);
}  // end of BoxTrixScreen()
```

The three modes are represented by the public constants ModedCamera.TRANSLATE,
ModedCamera.ROTATE, and ModedCamera.FLOAT_GLIDE.

Creating the Camera

The ModedCamera class constructor creates a Camera instance and places it at a
predetermined starting position, in the translation mode.

```
// globals
// key modes -- public so they can be used in BoxTrixScreen
public static final int TRANSLATE = 0;
public static final int ROTATE = 1;
public static final int FLOAT_GLIDE = 2;

// initial camera position
private static final double X_POS = 0.0;
private static final double Y_POS = 1.0;
private static final double Z_POS = 6.1;

// navigation related
private Camera camera;
private int keyMode;


public ModedCamera()
{ keyMode = TRANSLATE;   // default mode
  camera = new Camera(X_POS, Y_POS, Z_POS);
}
```

Processing Menu Items

The menu items set the mode by calling ModedCamera.setMode(), and reset the camera
to its original position and orientation by calling ModedCamera.reset():

```
public void setMode(int mode)
{ if ((mode == TRANSLATE) || (mode == ROTATE) || (mode == FLOAT_GLIDE))
```

```
      keyMode = mode;
}


public void reset()
{ keyMode = TRANSLATE;
  camera.reset();
}
```

Updating the Camera

Updating means changing the camera's current direction constant, which can be LEFT, RIGHT, UP, or DOWN. This is done via calls to ModedCamera.update() in BoxTrixScreen's keyChar() and navigationMovement().

updateCamera() examines the direction constant and the current mode to decide which translation or rotation method to call in the Camera object.

```
// translation and rotation increment globals
private static final double MOVE_INCR = 0.1;
private static final double ANGLE_INCR = 5.0;    // in degrees


public void update(int dir)
{
  if (keyMode == TRANSLATE) {
    if (dir == UP)
      camera.transFwd(MOVE_INCR);      // translate forward
    if (dir == DOWN)
      camera.transFwd(-MOVE_INCR);     // translate backward
    if (dir == LEFT)
      camera.glideRight(-MOVE_INCR);   // move left parallel to XZ plane
    if (dir == RIGHT)
      camera.glideRight(MOVE_INCR);    // move right parallel to XZ
  }
  else if (keyMode == ROTATE) {
    if (dir == UP)
      camera.rotateX(ANGLE_INCR);      // rotate camera up around x-axis
    if (dir == DOWN)
      camera.rotateX(-ANGLE_INCR);     // rotate camera down
    if (dir == LEFT)
      camera.rotateY(ANGLE_INCR);      // rotate camera left around y-axis
    if (dir == RIGHT)
      camera.rotateY(-ANGLE_INCR);     // rotate camera right
  }
  else if (keyMode == FLOAT_GLIDE) {
    if (dir == UP)
      camera.moveUp(MOVE_INCR);        // move camera up
    if (dir == DOWN)
      camera.moveUp(-MOVE_INCR);       // move camera down
    if (dir == LEFT)
      camera.glideFwd(MOVE_INCR);      // move forward parallel to XZ
    if (dir == RIGHT)
      camera.glideFwd(-MOVE_INCR);     // move backward parallel to XZ
```

```
  }
  else  // should not happen
    System.out.println("Unknown key mode");
} // end of update()
```

The values for MOVE_INCR and ANGLE_INCR were chosen through experimentation.

Moving the Camera

All the ModedCamera methods described update the camera's state, but its position and orientation are actually rendered when BoxTrixScreen calls ModedCamera.move() inside the animation loop. ModedCamera passes the call onto the Camera object.

```
public void move(GL10 gl)
{ camera.move(gl);  }
```

Summary

In this chapter, I looked at how to build a 3D scene with JSR 239. In the process, I explained an animation technique based around updates, rendering, and sleeping using an offscreen buffer. The contents of the 3D scene include a textured floor, rotating cubes, billboards, a 2D overlay, and a moveable camera that can translate, rotate, and even glide.

Index

O